THE CAMERAWORK ESSAYS

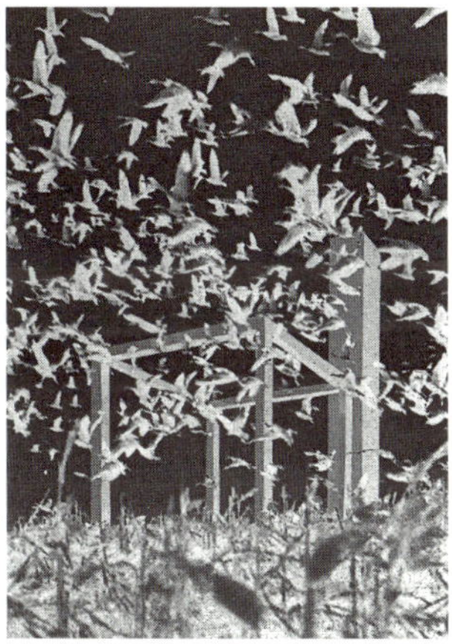

# The Camerawork Essays

## Context and Meaning in Photography

Edited by Jessica Evans

Picture Research by Sandy Weiland

Preface by Barbara Hunt,
Director of Camerawork



Rivers Oram Press / London

First published in 1997 by
**Rivers Oram Press**
144 Hemingford Road
London N1 1DE

Published in the USA by
**New York University Press**
Elmer Holmes Bobst Library
70 Washington Square South
New York
NY 1002-1091



Designed by John Gibbs
Set in Helvetica by N-J Typographics, Romsey
Printed in Great Britain by Butler and Tanner Ltd, Frome

Front cover illustration from *16 Situations* by Derek Boshier



British Library Cataloguing in Publication Data
A catalogue record for this book is available from
the British Library

ISBN 1 85489 080 8
ISBN 1 85489 081 6 (pbk)

# Contents

# Acknowledgements

I would like to thank Sandy Weiland for her intellectual support and enthusiastic help with the book as a whole. Paul Antick deserves a special mention for his incisive and constructive criticism and his patience during a project that engulfed me for a lengthy period.

For their editorial and technical contributions the following have been invaluable: Janina Struk for some useful discussions, editorial advice and help with locating authors and photographers, Alan Slingsby for his assistance with scanning old copies of *Camerawork*, Jane Evans for undertaking rapid typing and for advice on textual style, Mary Doherty at the University of Westminster for typing, Michael Evans for advice on textual style, Terry Dennett for giving time for an 'interview' and providing access to and copies of Jo Spence's work, and Martin Faulkner at the University of Westminster for undertaking library searches. I would also like to thank Hatice Abdullah, Geoff Cox, Stefan Follows, Virginia Nimarkoh, Sarah Parkinson and Dave Than at Camerawork Gallery and Darkroom.

For their help and generosity in providing photographic prints and assistance with picture research, I am very grateful to the following organisations and individuals: Derek Boshier, Bob Carlos-Clarke, Philip Dunn at the National Museum of Labour History, Karen Knorr, *New Statesman and Society*, Jean Mohr, David Morris and Rebecca Morris at the Bolton Museum and Art Gallery, Clair O'Leary, Struan Robertson, Jo Spence Memorial Archive, Paul Wombell, Chris Wright at the Royal Anthropological Institute, and the Mass Observation Archive at Sussex University.

The following need to be acknowledged for kindly providing illustrative material and granting copyright: The Advertising Archive, Anthony D'Offay Gallery, Associated Press Picture Library, Bolton Museum and Art Gallery, Samuel Bourdin, The British Library, C.D.P. Advertising, Canon, *Daily Mirror*/Syndication International, French Vogue, George Eastman House, Hamiltons Photographers Ltd., Hulton Deutsch Collection, Jo Spence Memorial Archive, Konica UK Ltd, the Labour Party, McCann-Erickson Advertising, the Photography Yearbook 1977 (Fountain Press), Psychology Today, Royal Anthropological Institute, Seagram Distillers Ltd, Slix, Staatlichen Galerie Moritzburg, Deborah Turbeville/Studio Inc.

**Jessica Evans**

# Preface

Camerawork was founded in 1975 as the first combined photography gallery and darkroom resource in Britain and was organised on principles of equality of access. It aimed to facilitate 'the production and consumption of photography' and to show work 'which examines social issues or is itself of a radical and socialist nature'.

Since then, Camerawork has become renowned for its adventurous programme of exhibitions, publications and seminars on issues contentious within Western society. In the 1970s and 1980s, the organisation developed a reputation for its pioneering work in documentary photography, being the first arts organisation to programme what were, then, radical exhibitions on political, social and economic concerns, such as Troops Out of Northern Ireland and Nicaragua, at a time when these issues were not discussed in the mainstream press.

The *Camerawork* magazine was published in A3 format from 1975 to 1985 and was central to debates about the use of the visual image within popular culture, initiating a critical reading of photography and a new consideration of issues of representation in the media. It combined theoretical discourse with articles which proposed a role for photography within the community and practical 'how to' features, for example, on pinhole cameras, portable darkrooms and touring exhibitions. This approach mirrored Camerawork's philosophies for education and empowerment—realised through an active combination of darkroom practice, visual theory and the presentation of exhibitions, all integrated in one building in the East End of London.

Bearing in mind the critical stance of the magazine to the use and commodification of visual imagery within western capitalism, it is ironic to consider that a perfect copy of issue 1 (and in fact any complete set of originals) has become a collector's item valued at around £500 when its original mail order price was 25 pence.

The magazine now appears dated, its stencilled black and white logo fondly remembered by many who are active in cultural theory and the media industries. The magazine folded in 1985, the mid-point of the Thatcher years, due to increased pressures on resources and the widespread loss of faith in a socialist approach.

Whilst Camerawork's identifying logo and frontage have since changed, its core aims have not altered in principle in the twenty years since it was founded, namely to provide an accessible, creative and supportive site for the production, exhibition and discussion of contemporary photography and image technologies.

The conditions and the language of the arts sector within which we operate have evolved to include a broader conception of lens-based practice and 'new' technologies, and Camerawork continues to provoke thought and debate through a diverse programme of activity. The concept of the 'gallery' has developed through the exhibition of work which challenges traditional presentation practices: work using projected imagery, mixed media, film, video, sound or digital technologies; time-based work; site-specific work, and projects on the Internet.

The *Camerawork Essays* presents fourteen articles from the original magazine which continue to bear relevance to contemporary debate and which we hope will be of use within media education. It also includes a new essay on Jo Spence who was of course instrumental to the very existence of Camerawork and whose work and energy were so vital to the map of radical photography as it emerged in Britain in the 1970s. I would like to thank Jessica Evans, Editor, and Sandy Weiland, Picture Researcher, for their detective work in tracking down authors and photographers now dispersed across the globe in professions ranging from art criticism to lecturing and academic research, and to the commercial sector and the entertainment industry. Thanks must also go to the original authors for their enthusiastic support on this project.

**Barbara Hunt**
Director of Camerawork

# Introduction

## Jessica Evans

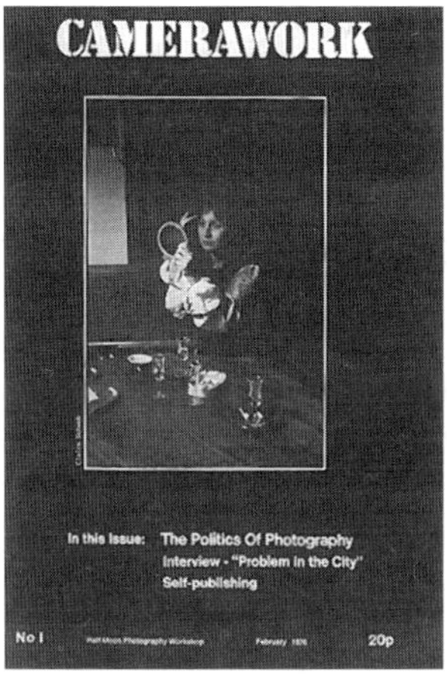


The *Camerawork Essays* form an anthology originallly printed in *Camerawork* magazine, which published from 1976 until 1985. There is one additional essay on the work of Jo Spence, who was a major originator of the *Camerawork* project and is widely credited for her pioneering work on class, self-identity and therapeutic representation. However, as she only wrote one major essay for the magazine which has in any case been subsequently published elsewhere,[1] this new essay appears as a tribute to her interventions into photography and identity.

*Camerawork* was the first and only UK magazine devoted to a critical and contextual study of photography, and was well established by the beginning of the 1980s as an authoritative source for challenging hallowed ideas about photography and photography education. Many of its contributors and editors are now highly regarded internationally as pioneering photography practitioners, artists, theorists and teachers; most of them are represented here. In particular, the orthodoxies which *Camerawork* aimed to dismantle were those which claimed for photography the status of art with its ideological baggage of expressive individualism. *Camerawork* largely operated outside the assumption that the primary aim of its readers as photographers and cultural producers was to become established as 'artists'.[2] As John Tagg has reminded us, in the 1970s people gravitated toward photography because it was not bound by a specific institutional canon; its 'aesthetic' was excessive for the paradigm of art, its practices too diverse *and* formulaic.[3] *Camerawork*'s metamorphosis was part of a whole shift in ways of thinking about cultural processes and cultural artifacts, one in which the disciplines of sociology and semiotics were to play a decisive role.

Photographic theory has lacked prominence and visibility in the last few years. The demise of *Ten.8* is pertinent here, as it was the only high-profile publication seriously addressing specific aspects of photographic production and consumption. On the one hand, in the world of photographic magazines for example, photography has been displaced into the category of fine art and criticism. Thus *Portfolio* and *Creative Camera* have consolidated a primarily 'fine art photography' constituency. On the other hand, photographs have become something to which cultural and media studies make regular reference, but in this case the specificity of the *practices, genres and environments* of the medium has diluted into a concern with generalised systems of representation; photography appears as a fragmentary moment, a metaphor for a larger story such as the domination of culture by the visual. Whilst I concur with the argument, made since the early 1980s by John Tagg and others, that it is not possible to study photography as a discrete and inherently coherent discipline, it seems that the study of *both* the discursive and the social organisation of photographic production, consumption and distribution are being neglected. Some of the essays in this book may be read as addressing precisely this underdeveloped area.

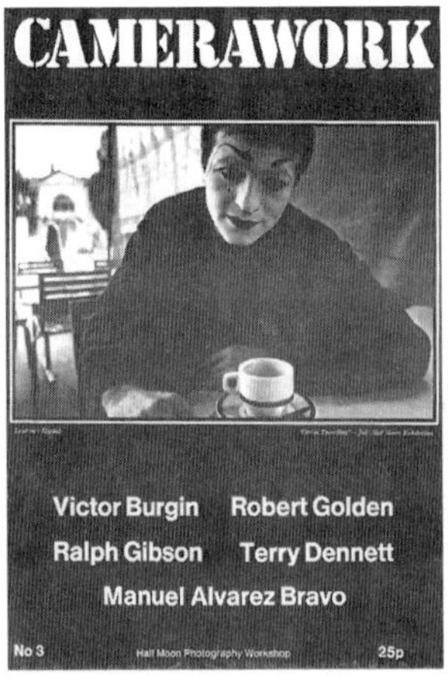


Each essay is presented here with a new introduction, in almost all cases by the authors themselves, which puts their original essay in historical context and reflects upon developments related to the project of the essay in the intervening years. I have compiled a new 'further reading' section at the end of each piece, so that readers may pursue some recent thinking on the subject at hand. The essays selected represent the significant achievement of *Camerawork* in laying the foundations for the development of a critical photographic theory as opposed to journalism or criticism. They also reflect the wide range of photographic genres that *Camerawork* covered throughout the period, for example, documentary, fashion, amateur photography, and this is also intended as an acknowledgement of the functional multiplicity of photographs. The essays are organised into three thematic areas which cover the the relationship between context, form and meaning; the relationship between photography and history; and the contributions in the last section consider particular institutional domains of photography and their ideological practices. Taken together they represent the following range of approaches, which should not be interpreted as necessarily mutually exclusive: *methodological* issues in the analysis of photography, from the problems of historical interpretation to those of the analysis of the production of textual meaning; *substantive* analyses of the ideological implications of particular photographic 'styles' and institutions; and *theoretical* presentations of a preferred and argued for stance on photography. In so doing my intention is that contrasts and comparisons can be made between the essays for it is important that differences are not elided and that the entity called 'photography theory and history' is seen to be constituted by healthily diverse sets of interests and approaches. In particular, the selection for this book acknowledges the importance of respecting the two separate moments of analysis that were identified by Simon Watney in *Photography/Politics Two*. Watney said, 'we still need to distinguish between those institutions which facilitate the production of photography in all its forms, and those bodies of beliefs/values/associations which inform and organise the 'look' of photographs and their meanings'.[4] While these two systems 'interpenetrate with one another in all circumstances of use' it is not logically helpful to apply the same term, 'institution', both to limited measurable entities such as advertising companies or newspapers *and* to the larger ideological and psychic forces which are continually reconstituted across the entire domain of photo-practices.[5] For an example of the latter, one might think of the family and familial discourse which is constituted across a whole range of photographic practices, from amateur photography to women's magazines, by a regime of idealising images. Watney's distinction is, then, between institution and ideologies: ideally, the challenge is to account for their points of intersection, rather than polarise one over the other. However, this must be regarded as the challenge for future photographic theory and history since many of the essays in this book are weighted to one side or the other of this equation, and others are in any case more speculative. What I suggest readers might do is to see how some of the areas under discussion could be re-read in the light of Watney's programme for photographic studies.



John Berger in 'Ways of Remembering' offers a methodology for a photographic practice based on the reconstruction of photographic meaning. This is derived from a critique of the public photograph in its detachment from the experience of any one person in particular. John A. Walker in 'Context as a Determinant of Photographic Meaning' argues that the meaning of the photograph is dependent upon context, and thus his is a challenge to the assumption that images have a pure core of stable meaning. John Tagg's 'The World of Photography or Photography of the World?' discusses the humanist premise which enables a quite diverse range of photographic imagery to be united in the homogenising rubric of the *Photographer's Yearbook*. In Victor Burgin's 'Art, Common Sense and Photography', a semiotic and rhetorical analysis of the photograph is proposed as an antidote to the habitualising effects of capitalist ideology. He considers the photograph as a set of signs, organised into formal rhetorical devices, which can be made to produce certain ideological 'contents'. However, the formal devices used by advertisers are in themselves neutral and can therefore be appropriated by the oppositional practitioner.

Don Slater's 'The Object of Photography' prefigures the debate on postmodernism; he explores the historical career of the use of realism, which is interpreted chiefly as the positivist orientation of modernity. Towards the end, he considers the implication of his proposition that, under the conditions of our twentieth-century capitalist culture of consumption, in the way we perceive and consume images, we have lost a sense of the real in everyday life. In 'On Foucault: Disciplinary Power and Photography' David Green presents an overview of the work of Michel Foucault and suggests how it can be employed as a framework for thinking about the realist discourses which encirculate photography, in particular how the processes of individuation and categorisation are linked to the power/knowledge nexus. Both David Mellor's and Don Macpherson's essays are concerned with the Mass Observation documentation movement of 1930s Britain, but while Mellor is concerned to trace the paradoxes and vicissitudes of its historical emergence, Macpherson defines the rhetoric of documentary as a nationalist aesthetic which seeks to invent a spurious 'national past'. Terry Smith in 'Pictured History—Matchgirls' Strike 1988' considers some of the problems of methodology when using photographs for labour history. In his analysis of a range of pictorial representations of the Matchgirls' Strike, he argues that historians who fear photographs are denying themselves a key resource, for photographs can be used as evidence rather than as illustration if we are prepared to employ visual as well as textual methodologies for interpreting the historical.

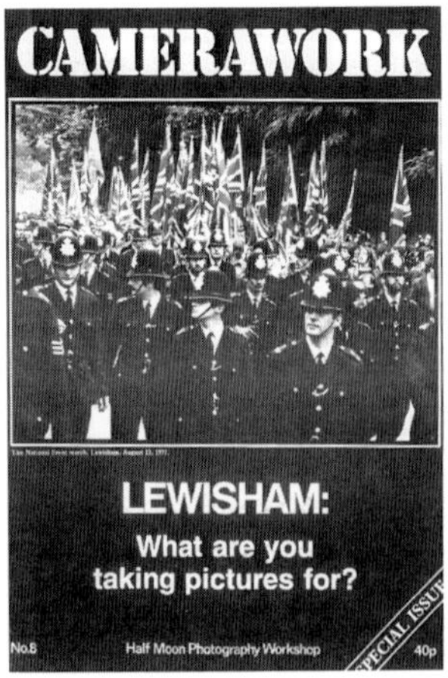


Don Slater's 'Marketing the Medium' explains the structuring of the different priorities in the marketing of snapshooter and serious amateur photography and indicates how this impinges upon the kinds of pictures that get taken by amateur photographers. He has said to me recently that the article's sociological orientation aimed:

> to counter semiotic arguments which assumed that analyses of texts were sufficient for understanding popular photography (indeed for understanding social life in general). In fact, analysing texts is no substitute for trying to understand the social structures and conditions in which people act, and to analyse the forms of practice they devise for operating in these conditions. (private conversation)

In 'Towards a Feminist Erotica', Kathy Myers's analysis of how sexuality is sold to women subverts the old assumption, shared by many feminists of the time and by male-dominated society, that women are innocent when it comes to sexuality and that male sexuality is the sole agency of desire. She considers the discursive elements that allow us to recognise the difference between the institutions of pornography and advertising in their treatment of women's bodies and argues that any critique of representation in the area of sexual difference and sexuality must start from the fact that women derive pleasure from looking at images of women. Rosetta Brooks's 'Double-Page Spread' is similar in its deliberate disturbance of the 1970s' stasis in thinking sexual politics. She explores the 1970s' fashion photography of Newton, Bourdin and Turbeville and argues against the grain of much feminist thinking of the 1970s that in their emphasis upon the alien and artificial qualities of the picture a straightforward accusation of sexism on the part of these photographers is problematic. 'Left in Sight', an interview with Stuart Hall, and Kathy Myers's 'Loves Labour Lost' have to be situated in the context of the aftermath of the 1983 general election, lost disastrously by Labour. The election was the first in which the Labour Party had used a professional advertising agency. But it appeared that their use of black and white 'documentary montage' for their poster campaign and their emphasis on the people as victims had failed to learn from what they felt was represented by the imaginative and seductive pleasures embodied by the commercial sectors. Hall and Myers were both concerned that the electorate had left the Labour Party behind, in the sense that the language of labourism was not able to meet what had to be faced as the concrete aspirations of the people in the context of new social and economic conditions. Finally, my essay 'An Affront to Taste? The Disturbances of Jo Spence' both situates the development of Spence's photographic interventions and considers her self-representation work in relation to power, the body, taste, and psychoanalysis. I trace the logic of Spence's 'shocking' work.

Over the last decade the *Camerawork* magazines have become lost to history and lost with them is the possibility of encountering an authoritative set of ideas on critical photographic theory and practice. Moreover, the kinds of debates and political disputes that went on behind and 'through' the essays have largely been forgotten. Thus, the task of the latter part of this introduction is, in part, to begin to provide an understanding of the context of development for *Camerawork* magazine and its wider importance during the 1970s and 1980s. It is not always easy retrospectively to unravel the lines of development of an emerging theoretical discourse, in this case 'photographic theory', and so part of the aim of this publication as a whole is to recover an historical understanding of *Camerawork's* motivation for encouraging a democratising practice of photography. Words such as 'empower','representation', 'positive/negative image', 'politics of representation' and 'cultural production' are now the habitual parlance of the critical photographer. But it is often forgotten that these ideas gained currency precisely because of the initiative of institutions such as

Camerawork in stimulating debates on the power of visual culture and in creating the conditions for photographic literacy. I must say at the outset that as an introduction my account of *Camerawork* is necessarily biased toward the specificity of the shifts and debates within the magazine, and does not do justice to the wider social and political context of British culture during the period of the magazine. I have tried above all to present an accessible but critical introduction to the twists and turns of the debates in recent British radical photography. I hope it will prove to be of some help to those who will be researching this period in greater detail or wish to be reminded of the main lines of development.

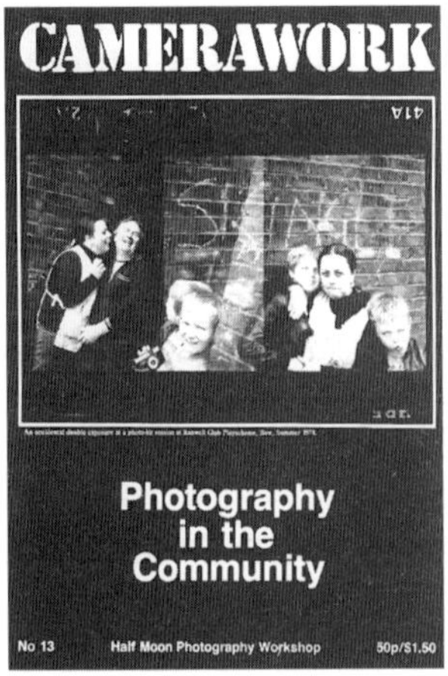


### *Camerawork* 1976-85: Narratives of Power and Representation

Photography has often been condemned for its part in creating a flickering world of superficial appearance; it has been dismissed as an irredeemable aspect of mass commodity culture: ephemeral, banal, insubstantial. For those who adhere to a Frankfurt School 'culture industry' analysis, photography typifies a world in which experience is converted into the pseudo-reality of an image, thus jeopardising face to face interaction—a view expressed in Susan Sontag's *On Photography*. Her conservationist remedy was that we should ration the amount of images produced and circulated. The *Camerawork* of the 1970s in its championing of community photography, as we will see, formulated a similar analysis but proposed a different solution—to find compensation for alienation in the integrative values of local life. Susan Sontag sums up the Marxian approach to the capitalist commodity culture of images, one which dominated much of *Camerawork* in the 1980s and still characterises much critical work on photography:

> A capitalist society requires a culture based on images, it needs to furnish vast amounts of entertainment in order to stimulate buying and anaesthetise the injuries of class, race and sex....The camera's twin capacities, to subjectivise reality and to objectify it, ideally serves these needs and strengthens them. Cameras define reality in the two ways essential to the workings of an advanced industrial society: as a spectacle (for masses) and as an object of surveillance (for rulers). The production of images also furnishes a ruling ideology. Social change is replaced by a change in images. The freedom to consume a plurality of images and goods is equated with freedom itself.[6]

Reading through back issues of *Camerawork* I was first of all struck by its 'culturalism'—its emphasis on the authenticating power of lived experience. Of course, the very study and practice of photography was legitimated in the early work of Raymond Williams whose democratic humanism led him to develop the idea of culture 'as ordinary', to be studied as 'a set of relationships between elements in a whole way of life'. But the culturalist emphasis came under some strain, as we will see, when it was later realised that it was not enough just to have access to *making* photographs, for the multifarious and institutionalised practices of photography have embedded themselves into the cultural everyday in a way which most of the time lies beyond our threshold of consciousness. For this reason, as the magazine followed the trajectory of a 1970s Marxist analysis that had initially regarded cultural production in direct terms as an agency of class consciousness, but then added a structuralist emphasis on the relative autonomy of the structures of meaning of meaning, the concept of ideology became central as a way of thinking of representation in the mass media.[7] The point here is that photography is central to the twentieth-century's symbolic landscape and firmly integrated into the ways we all manage our identities and have them managed for us. There can be few of us who have not attempted to control the image of ourselves by posing purposefully for a photograph or tearing up the one that makes us feel uncomfortable. Additionally, the very categories with which we readily identify ourselves as photographers, be they amateur photographer or snapshooter, fine-art photographer or photo-journalist, actually constitute the *conditions* of our practice.[8] It is these conditions which both create and delimit our sense of what is 'appropriate': what to take pictures of, with what technical and formal means, and for whom. Spence's critique of the family album, and Don Slater's essay reprinted here, 'Marketing the Medium', were undertaken in order to address this problem. What if the images we actually take for our family albums merely mimic the idealistic and sentimentalised rhetoric of the family that is prefigured in other family albums, in the marketing strategies of the camera manufacturers and the technologies of processing and developing companies?

In November 1975 the Photography Workshop, an educational group comprised of two core members, Terry Dennett and Jo Spence, merged with the Half Moon Gallery, an educational charity. Out of this was born the Half Moon Photography Workshop (HMPW), a collective based in the foyer of an old synagogue in the East End of London, under whose auspices *Camerawork* magazine was produced. The magazine was, however, quite separate in its organisational structure from the HMPW and had a collective of its own.

*Camerawork* had its precursor in three issues of a stencilled newsletter produced by the Photography Workshop, based on the alternative local newspaper movement of the 1970s. Spence and Dennett were involved for seven issues until August 1977, when the Half Moon Gallery, which had remained a limited company throughout the unofficial merger with Photography Workshop and thus had rights as a legal holding company, sacked Spence from the magazine where she was the paid administrator. *Camerawork* had a wide readership, and brought radical and pathbreaking socialist arguments to bear on photography in a way which has not been achieved in a magazine since. We have to imagine the moment of 1976 as one in which the optimism of the 1960s has not receded, where the Left and the trades union movement is relatively strong, and there is an abundance of community and grassroots organisations outside the Left establishment, including a national explosion in local alternative newspapers.[9] It is important to remember that the Photographer's Gallery was the only national space for photographic exhibition. Terry Dennett has stressed to me in conversation that in the early days of *Camerawork* and the HMPW the ethos was one of improvisation; money was raised though jumble sales and auctions.[10] In the 1970s Spence and Dennett set up a series of workshops called 'Kids and Photography', working with children's playschemes in adventure playgrounds making pinhole cameras and other DIY photo-kits (see Dennett's influential 'We also use film to take pictures'). The culture was largely unprofessional—people printing in their bathrooms and learning about photography outside the formal structures of education. Terry Dennett pointed out that in the early days of *Camerawork* much of so-called 'community photography' was independent of benevolent structures such as arts boards. The notion of the community as an organising concept for photographic practice was of central importance to *Camerawork*. But, as we will see, it was fairly unproblematic—the 'community' was a more or less homogeneous, more or less knowable, self-generated entity.[11]

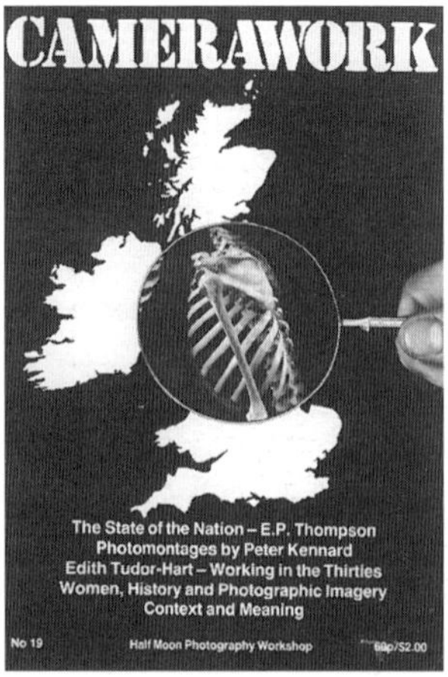


Spence and Dennett's attitude toward the political use of photography has to be contextualised with the important debates about the people's history movement taking place at Ruskin College and in the pages of the *History Workshop Journal*, established in the same year as *Camerawork* (1976). The emergent 'people's history', favouring mainly autobiographical accounts, was based upon the assumption that for working people to speak for themselves, about their own history, is a political act in itself. Stephen Yeo listed the characteristics of community practice and local history as follows.[12] The process of showing writing is through person-to-person contacts, or through quite distinct

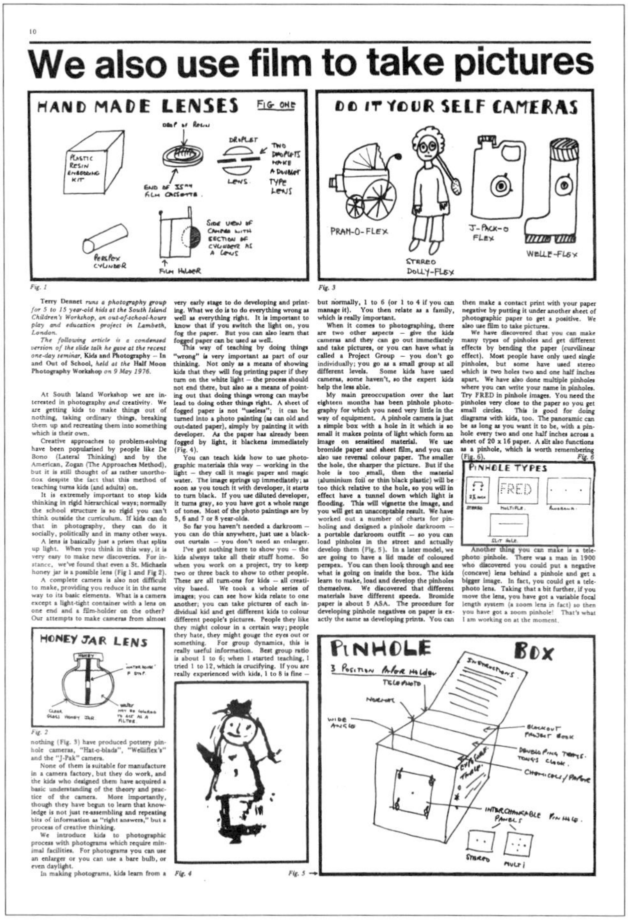
10

# We also use film to take pictures

HAND MADE LENSES  FIG ONE

Fig. 1

DO IT YOUR SELF CAMERAS

PRAM-O-FLEX
STEREO DOLLY-FLEX
J-PACK-O FLEX
WELLE-FLEX

Fig. 3

*Terry Dennet runs a photography group for 5 to 15 year-old kids at the South Island Children's Workshop, an out-of-school-hours play and education project in Lambeth, London.*

*The following article is a condensed version of the slide talk he gave at the recent one-day seminar,* Kids and Photography – In and Out of School, *held at the* Half Moon Photography Workshop *on 9 May 1976.*

At South Island Workshop we are interested in photography *and* creativity. We are getting kids to make things out of nothing, taking ordinary things, breaking them up and recreating them into something which is their own.

Creative approaches to problem-solving have been popularised by people like De Bono (Lateral Thinking) and by the American, Zogan (The Approaches Method), but it is still thought of as rather unorthodox despite the fact that this method of teaching turns kids (and adults) on.

It is extremely important to stop kids thinking in rigid hierarchical ways; normally the school structure is so rigid you can't think outside the curriculum. If kids can do that in photography, they can do it socially, politically and in many other ways.

A lens is basically just a prism that splits up light. When you think in this way, it is very easy to make new discoveries. For instance, we've found that even a St. Michaels honey jar is a possible lens (Fig 1 and Fig 2).

A complete camera is also not difficult to make, providing you reduce it in the same way to its basic elements. What is a camera except a light-tight container with a lens on one end and a film-holder on the other? Our attempts to make cameras from almost

HONEY JAR LENS

Fig. 2

nothing (Fig. 3) have produced pottery pinhole cameras, "Hat-o-blads", "Welliflex's" and the "J-Pak" camera.

None of them is suitable for manufacture in a camera factory, but they do work, and the kids who designed them have acquired a basic understanding of the theory and practice of the camera. More importantly, though they have begun to learn that knowledge is not just re-assembling and repeating bits of information as "right answers," but a process of creative thinking.

We introduce kids to photographic process with photograms which require minimal facilities. For photograms you can use an enlarger or you can use a bare bulb, or even daylight.

In making photograms, kids learn from a very early stage to do developing and printing. What we do is to do everything wrong as well as everything right. It is important to know that if you switch the light on, you fog the paper. But you can also learn that fogged paper can be used as well.

This way of teaching by doing things "wrong" is very important as part of our thinking. Not only as a means of showing kids that they will fog printing paper if they turn on the white light – the process should not end there, but also as a means of pointing out that doing things wrong can maybe lead to doing other things right. A sheet of fogged paper is not "useless"; it can be turned into a photo painting (as can old and out-dated paper), simply by painting it with developer. As the paper has already been fogged by light, it blackens immediately (Fig. 4).

You can teach kids how to use photographic materials this way – working in the light – they call it magic paper and magic water. The image springs up immediately; as soon as you touch it with developer, it starts to turn black. If you use diluted developer, it turns gray, so you have got a whole range of tones. Most of the photo paintings are by 5, 6 and 7 or 8 year-olds.

So far you haven't needed a darkroom – you can do this anywhere, just use a blackout curtain – you don't need an enlarger.

I've got nothing here to show you – the kids always take all their stuff home. So when you work on a project, try to keep two or three back to show to other people. These are all turn-ons for kids – all creativity based. We took a whole series of images; you can see how kids relate to one another; you can take pictures of each individual kid and get different kids to colour different people's pictures. People they like they might colour in a certain way; people they hate, they might gouge the eyes out or something. For group dynamics, this is really useful information. Best group ratio is about 1 to 6; when I started teaching, I tried 1 to 12, which is crucifying. If you are really experienced with kids, 1 to 8 is fine – but normally, 1 to 6 (or 1 to 4 if you can manage it). You then relate as a family, which is really important.

Fig. 4

When it comes to photographing, there are two other aspects – give the kids cameras and they can go out immediately and take pictures, or you can have what is called a Project Group – you don't go individually; you go as a small group at all different levels. Some kids have used cameras, some haven't, so the expert kids help the less able.

My main preoccupation over the last eighteen months has been pinhole photography for which you need very little in the way of equipment. A pinhole camera is just a simple box with a hole in it which is so small it makes points of light which form an image on sensitised material. We use bromide paper and sheet film, and you can also use reversal colour paper. The smaller the hole, the sharper the picture. But if the hole is too small, then the material (aluminium foil or thin black plastic) will be too thick relative to the hole, so you will in effect have a tunnel down which light is flooding. This will vignette the image, and you will get an unacceptable result. We have worked out a number of charts for pinholing and designed a pinhole darkroom – a portable darkroom outfit – so you can load pinholes in the street and actually develop them (Fig. 5). In a later model, we are going to have a lid made of coloured perspex. You can then look through and see what is going on inside the box. The kids learn to make, load and develop the pinholes themselves. We discovered that different materials have different speeds. Bromide paper is about 5 ASA. The procedure for developing pinhole negatives on paper is exactly the same as developing prints. You can then make a contact print with your paper negative by putting it under another sheet of photographic paper to get a positive. We also use film to take pictures.

We have discovered that you can make many types of pinholes and get different effects by bending the paper (curvilinear effect). Most people have only used single pinholes, but some have used stereo which is two holes two and one half inches apart. We have also done multiple pinholes where you can write your name in pinholes. Try FRED in pinhole images. You need the pinholes very close to the paper so you get small circles. This is good for doing diagrams with kids, too. The panoramic can be as long as you want it to be, with a pinhole every two and one half inches across a sheet of 20 x 16 paper. A slit also functions as a pinhole, which is worth remembering (Fig. 6).

Fig. 6

PINHOLE TYPES

FRED

SLIT HOLE

Another thing you can make is a telephoto pinhole. There was a man in 1900 who discovered you could put a negative (concave) lens behind a pinhole and get a bigger image. In fact, you could get a telephoto lens. Taking that a bit further, if you move the lens, you have got a variable focal length system (a zoom lens in fact) so then you have got a zoom pinhole! That's what I am working on at the moment.

PINHOLE BOX

Fig. 5 →

1 We also use film to take pictures. Terry Dennett. Reprinted from *Camerawork* no. 3, July 1976

places; there is a close relationship to personal narrative, since much work was on the public/private borderline. Work arises through emulation rather than competition, by using others as resources. Community history was thus against the commodity form, involving a collective approach based on a critique of bourgeois individualism:

> The function of the work is to return experience to the places where it has already been nurtured so that it and other experiences can be transformed and developed in those places, rather than being transported for manufacture into finished goods miles away.[13]

The vision of the authorship of all readers meant an attack on divisions between writing and reading, consumption and production, teaching and learning, the 'cultured' and 'the masses'. What was perhaps of most significance to community photography was the emphasis on the demystification of production processes so that the emphasis was on labour itself. This did not mean a self-conscious reference to the materials used, as in modernist formalism. Rather, following Walter Benjamin, it meant inserting 'the message' into new and democratic social relations of production which paid attention to the ways in which the message was disseminated.[14]

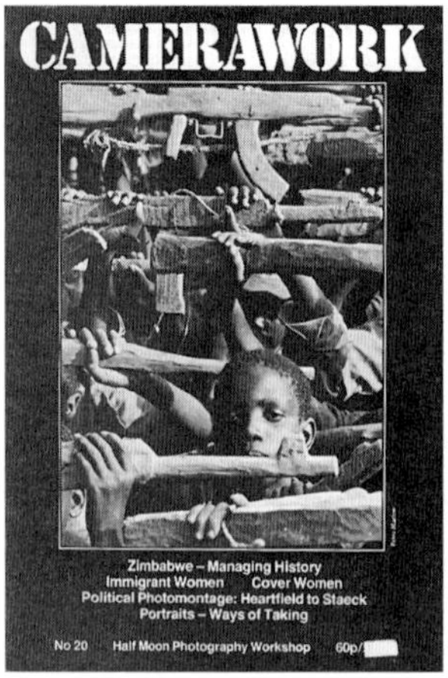


**'Our central concern in photography is not "Is it art?" but "Who is it for?"'**

With this statement of aims on its back cover in February 1976, the first issue of *Camerawork* was born. The statement continues with the following, the section that is reproduced in all the issues up to no.19:

> By exploring the application, scope and content of photography, we intend to demystify the process. We see this as part of the struggle to learn, to describe and to share experiences and so contribute to the process by which we grow in capacity and power to control our own lives.

The HMPW collective brought together a gallery area, publishing projects, educational workshops and information and advice on photography. Its demystification of the process of photography would take place in the field of 'play, literacy and schooling'; it would constitute 'practical help for community activists and people working with children outside the state school system in setting up their own facilities, mobile darkrooms'. It 'would enable specific documentary projects to be set up as requested by community groups', 'would promote the photographic recording of contemporary local history by people themselves, with or without the help of professional photographers'. It would 'promote the collection of existing local photo history from all sources, including public and private institutional archives, old personal photographs, local newspaper files and with special emphasis on the family album as a valuable social document'. It would give 'practical help to encourage fine printmaking, archival processing' and 'systematise the investigation of alternate photo technology so as to develop a basic independence from monopoly companies'. Finally in the development of a local photography project in Spitalfields it would 'evolve a programme of work designed to help local people learn about themselves and their relationship to people and institutions around them, and encourage them to become actively involved in the management and future of the community'. Issue no.1 is representative of these concerns; it contains an essay by Jo Spence, 'The Politics of Photography' in which community photography is suggested as an alternative both to the mass culture industry and to the victim industry of documentary photography; an essay by Terry Dennett on 'alternative technology'; an interview with community photographers Ron McCormack, Nick Hedges and Larry Herman; and an article on self-publishing by Paul Trevor.

There was, however, an intriguing problem of editorial coherency right from the magazine's inception and this lay in an inability to tie together its liberal humanism and its structuralist-Marxism. Hence the function of the documentary form for the magazine, which appeared to unify (the photographs of a Richard Greenhill or a Bill Brandt could appear superficially similar to those of a Robert Golden or a spread from Exit photography group) a set of conflicting ideals. Perhaps these contradictions indicate that *Camerawork* was more pluralist and politically liberal than people often remember. The tone of *Camerawork*, even within the same issue, oscillated between hardline Marxism, humanist individualism, and the rhetoric of the 1960s' counterculture—often with blissful unawareness. We have to look to *Camerawork* magazine's history for the reasons for this, for 'the viewpoint of *Camerawork* [had] always revolved around the fact that the collective grew out of two separate groups'. Those who ousted Spence and other members of the Photography Workshop clearly felt (according to documents of the time) that their ideas for the direction of the magazine were 'too political' and they were accused of bringing to bear feminist and Marxist theories to photographic culture which were, it was felt, alien to it.[15] Quite frequently there were items which presented, for a quite uncomplicated adulation, the work of 'great' photographers with little or no contextualisation other than biographical or career details, sometimes in the form of a respectful interview. Photographs were often taken-for-granted as inherently 'good' or meaningful with little attempt at explanation or extrapolation. At other times propagandist photo-spreads, on Nicaragua, the People's March for Jobs, El Salvador, Lewisham Riots were heavily captioned with political information so that the images acted as evidence or illustration for the text. There were also, less often, pieces on montage by John Heartfield, Peter Kennard and others; the implication here being that these forms could be used to challenge the social realist hegemony of Left photography. But as the late 1970s work of Spence, the Hackney Flashers and Victor Burgin shows, montage was firmly entrenched in the juxtaposition of opposites, showing media fiction counterposed to fact or challenging a photograph's meaning through the assemblage of ironic or disturbing texts.[16] This was a time in which the correctionist 'positive image' was widely spoken of—as if the distinction between false and true could be simply disaggregated and

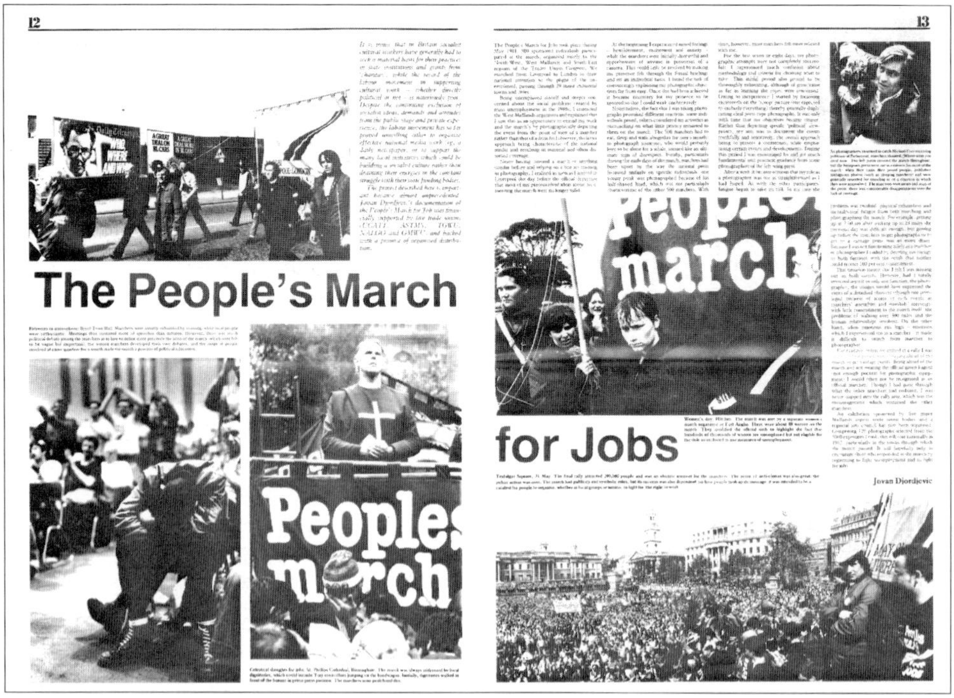

12

13

The People's March for Jobs

Jovan Djordjevic

2 *Camerawork* no. 24, March 1982

mapped on to 'the image' and something more foundational lying outside it called 'reality'.

The hegemony of documentary photography was such that its critics only went so far as to acknowledge that it could be abused—as if this was to distort an otherwise neutral project. This was, after all, a pre-Foucauldian critique of realism, and documentary was still felt to have a privileged relationship to showing 'things as they really are'. Issue no. 20 of December 1980 is a typical moment of confusion where an interest in the implications of the term 'politics of representation' have been suspended. On page four there is a spread of documentary portraits of the daily conditions of immigrant women in Holland. This is juxtaposed with an essay on page five, 'Cover Women', which makes a semiotic and sociological analysis of the construction of particular social categories of woman on the cover pages of various women's magazines. Taken as a whole the pages point to a contradiction. The photographs of the immigrant women are treated as fundamentally transparent. By contrast we are asked to think about the magazine cover photographs as fabrications, the product of particular commercial markets which construct myriad categories of woman. *Camerawork* seems to be implying here that when the primary task is to represent political and social relations one is freed from

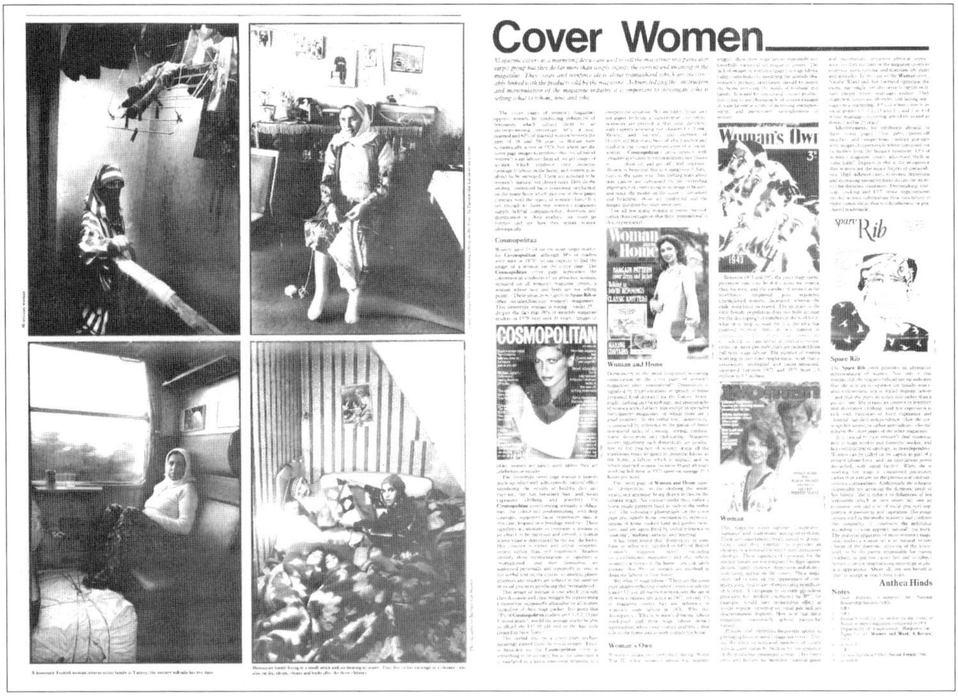

# Cover Women

Anthea Hinds

3 *Camerawork* no. 20, December 1980

the question of the politics of representation; but when images are obviously 'commercial' their ideological mechanisms can be laid bare, their truths shown to be partial. It seems that a particular kind of realist dogma was so powerful that the issues of ideology, power and fantasy could not be brought to bear on the study of documentary photography—they were seen as mutually exclusive categories. It was Jo Spence who first made an intervention in this area, after she was sacked from the Half Moon Photography Workshop collective that ran *Camerawork*. In March 1978 a black-and-white documentary style (natural lighting, no signs of 'artifice' such as cosmetics) portrait of Spence appeared on the front cover of *Spare Rib* in direct reference to the conventionalised glamour of the women's magazines cover-girls (see p.74). Which woman is the more 'real'? The mental comparison one makes between the *Spare Rib* cover and the others invites us to wonder whether we really can refer to a world outside the field of representation for a final answer to whether the Spence image portrays a 'more real' woman. In fact their difference lies at the basic pictorial level of what signifiers (from their various paradigmatic sets of hairstyle, lighting, expression etc.) have been selected to manufacture the photograph, and thus the image and identity of particular types of 'woman'. My analysis may go further than Spence herself intended; it would seem that for Spence the cover was designed to show the 'reality' of women against the fiction of mass media woman. Nonetheless Spence's projects demonstrate a daring experimental concern with the relationships between factual and fictional discourses which was, at this time, ahead of *Camerawork's* programme for photographic practice.

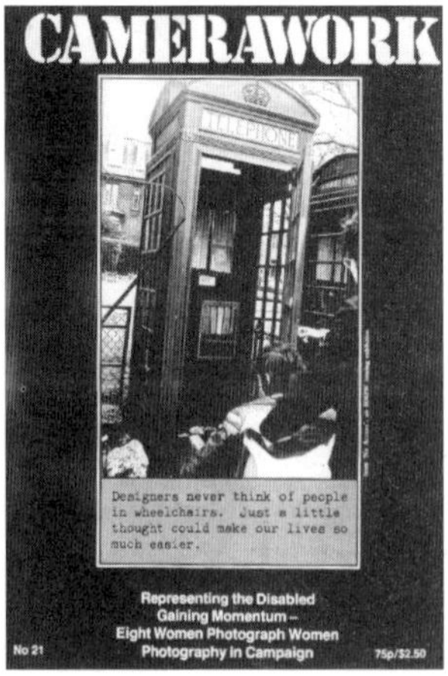


However, it is necessary to point out that from the beginning there were numerous essays, and other contributions in the form of a debating series of letters insisting on the fundamental importance of the politics of representation for photography. The work of Victor Burgin, John A. Walker, Terry Smith, Don Macpherson, Rosetta Brooks, Don Slater and Kathy Myers are those represented here. For example, Victor Burgin's early essay 'Art, Common Sense and Photography' (1979) set out the terms for thinking the photograph as representation. His was an influential argument for the photograph as sign; he showed concisely how the power of semiotics lies in its analytical approach to that which appeared self-evident, i.e. the relationship between the photograph and the world it depicts. It is precisely in the formal devices of photographic construction that the workings of ideology reside and Burgin pointed out that the activist who believes in the autonomy of content is just the inversion of the aesthete who believes in the autonomy of form. The whole project of Saussurean linguistics, so important to communications theory, aimed to blow apart the assumption embedded in both 'reflection' and 'expression' theories that you can have 'content' without 'form' and vice versa, as if the image were just a means of gaining access by proxy to the external objective world of 'reality' or the subjective internal world of the 'artist'. The project of semiotics was precisely to draw attention to the materiality of the photograph-as-text. The photograph actually *works* its constituent elements; it produces meaning by routinely ordering the relationships (i.e. by placing them in a code) between material forms (signifiers) and concepts/meanings (signifieds). Although the relationship between signifier and signified is in itself arbitrary it appears to be natural and inevitable. Thus, just when the photograph seems to be a denotative fact, a passive description of reality, it is uncovered by the semiotician as highly *connotative*—as structuring a particular, preferred point of view, yet one which masquerades as a universal truth.

Nonetheless, in spite of interventions such as Burgin's, it would in general be fair to say that *Camerawork* was dominated by an assumption, popular throughout the traditional Left, that when photographs can be demonstrated to be the agents of a class- and gender-divided society they are 'false', but when they are the products of 'our' correct moral and political approach they are unproblematically truthful. The idea of much Left campaign photography and community photography was that the community has self-transparent access to its 'real needs', and this, buttressed by a belief in photographic veracity, gives automatic rise to political agency. Thus the 'dominant ideology' of capitalist society—assumed by *Camerawork* during much of the 1970s to be unified and homogeneous—could be exposed as a false consciousness by the socialist with the 'correct' class consciousness, and reality seen for what it really is. In the terms of much documentary campaign photography of this time, a purist Marxism assumed that a critical position on capitalist society could only arise from the exclusive structural position of the working classes. This 'experience' was, however, confined to an arid routine of aligned left photographs of demonstrations and meetings, mugshots of significant left personalities, pictures of doomed hospitals, and so forth. Philip Wolmuth complained about this in in *Camerawork* no.18, in a reference to the photographic agency Report:



> Photographs used in this way do not explain or relate events and situations to the lived experience of the bulk of the population....They are simply used to confirm the existence of whatever is being described in the written text. They are waste photographs—superfluous to argument ('Photography in Opposition').

Images of this kind can only perform a gratifying 'preaching to the converted'—they provided 'evidence' for their viewers that their view was correct. John Berger was an early critic:

> You can use photography in all kinds of agitprop ways, you can make propaganda with photographs—you can make anti-capitalist progaganda, anti-imperialist propaganda. I wouldn't deny the usefulness of this, but at the same time I think the answer is incomplete. It's like taking a cannon and turning it round and firing it in the opposite direction. You haven't actually changed the practice, you've simply changed the aim. (see 'Ways of Remembering', p.38)

He advocated that photographs need to be put back 'into the context of experience, social experience, social memory'—they need to express the conflicted areas of people's lives in the concrete conditions in which they actually are. Berger's argument is in some ways comparable to the culturalism of Raymond Williams—his call for a 'radial' practice is grounded in a notion of the authenticity of 'lived experience'. But Berger's work was a departure from naturalist documentary practice. In his collaborative work with Jean Mohr, he was approaching a more psychodynamic model in which the totality of 'experience' as thought, fantasy and feeling is considered to be conflicted at an unconscious level.[17]

What happened to the tradition of social realism to which *Camerawork* had adhered for much of its life, whether in the form of community or campaign photography? As we have seen, documentary photography whether in its 'community' or reportage forms was the sacrosanct area of practice for *Camerawork*, for the first twenty issues at least. Although there was a nod here and there to other kinds of practice such as photo-montage, these are more often seen as 'documentary' forms of culture in Raymond Williams's sense—that is, as recorded texts and practices of the culture to be studied for their conventions and meanings but not to be practised. It was not until the last issues of *Camerawork* that the idea of making interventions in the mass media was entertained. Thus there had always been a tension in the magazine between an advocation of a localised high-access community photography and the political analysis of highly dispersed sophisticated mass media forms. The former was seen as an antidote to the latter but there had been little attempt for the first two thirds of *Camerawork*'s life to think coherently about the relationship between the two discourses nor their suppositions about issues of agency and determination, be it in the form of photography activism or that of the 'consumption' of images.

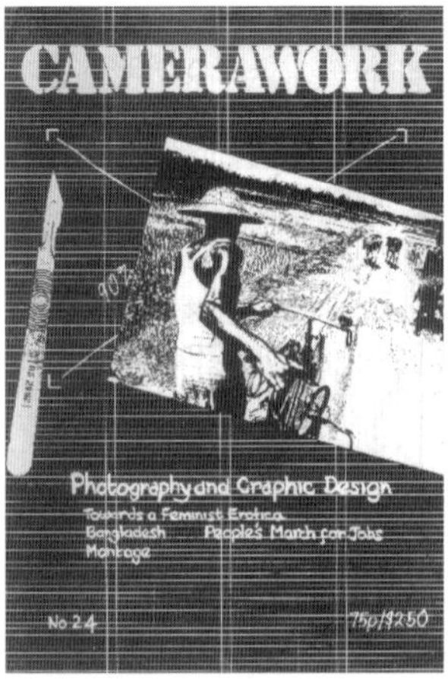


Of signal importance for the demise of community photography was the realisation that 'the community', previously imagined as stable and self-evident was as much the object of the photographer's imagination as it was a reflection of any community photographed. Furthermore, it emerged that in many, if not most, community photography projects the photographer came from outside the community. The critique of the inequality and the power differential between researcher and researched, photographer and photographed cast a deep scepticism over these projects. There have since the early 1980s been various solutions to this: withdrawing from representation altogether (not taking pictures), giving up on the naturalist representation of the 'other' (a solution which Jo Spence temporarily used when she and the Polysnappers resorted to using dolls);[18] or displacing the visual with text so as to undermine the apparently evidential status of the photograph. A similar debate about the power in/of representation had been going on since the 1970s in North America. In ethnography, James Clifford was pointing out the powers and presuppositions hidden away in the participant–observer's innocent 'I was there'. Perhaps Foucault's project of demonstrating the integral relationship between power and the acquisition of knowledge was the most important; for Foucauldian commentators on photography in the 1980s, documentary realism, in its effacement of the often middle-class position of the photographer and viewer, voyeuristically offered up the working-class or disabled body as a spectacle of passivity and unselfconsciousness. A whole regime of representation, typified by the *naturalism* of the black and white, grainy, and naturally lit photograph, was reserved for those lower down in the social and class hierarchy. Encapsulated by the rhetoric of liberal humanism, documentary subjects appeared as creatures patiently awaiting 'our' benificence rather than as self-consciously demanding their rights and needs be met. Obsessed with appearances and never able to point to the underlying structures which cause inequality, it was argued that documentary could only reinforce a view of the world as it is.[19] More generally, across many disciplines which have contributed to contemporary cultural theory—semiotics, art history, postmodern anthropology and feminist philosophies of science—the idea that the *visual* has a privileged relation to truth has come under attack. Voices, for example, are now valued over seeing in the new postmodern anthropology, and much of the impetus for this move in cultural theory over the past fifteen years is from French anti-ocular thought, as has been described by Martin Jay.[20] James Clifford in the introduction to his influential book *Writing Cultures* says,

> cultures are no longer prefigured visually—as objects, theatres, texts—it becomes possible to think of a cultural poetics that is an interplay of voices, of positioned utterances. In a discursive rather than a visual paradigm, the dominant metaphors for ethnography shift away from the observing eye and toward expressive speech (and gesture). The writer's 'voice' pervades and situates the analysis, and objective, distancing rhetoric is denounced.[21]

There are, however, two problems with postmodern ethnography. First, the model of the voice does not guarantee protection from exploitation any more than that of vision. The second is that if ethnographic research becomes, as indicated above, only an 'interplay of voices' then presumably there can be no more ethnographic research. *Who* does the research, *into* what? It seems to me that we have to maintain the sense of a difference between the person carrying out the research and the researched (object). The danger is that the new-found passion for dialogical methods can act as a denial of this difference (of power and privilege), which in the end cannot be wished away by altering research methodology. Moreover, it can also obscure the ways in which this difference *can be valuable* for the production of useful social knowledge.[22] The critique of community photography and documentary form was absolutely necessary, but it is a category mistake to go on to use this as a way of undermining the whole project of producing knowledge about something outside of the knower.

To return to *Camerawork* itself, a fascinating and unforeseen admixture of radical French social theory and Thatcherite ideology saw to the final destruction of community photography. In terms of the effects on the study of photography the 1970s and 1980s critiques of the realist mode of representation, central to the film theory of the journal *Screen*, are of very great significance. The *impression* of reality, argued Stephen Heath, Colin MacCabe and others representing *Screen* in the 1970s, is produced by a self-effacing signifying practice. This production of 'obviousness' needed to be countered in avant-garde film by the Brechtian devices of 'distanciation' which would take the form of destroying the pleasure of the text, a prevention of the processes of identification with characters, and the subversion of conventional 'Hollywood' narrative.[23] In the UK radical photography sector, the rejection of realism led those working with photography into the area of 'constructed images'—a development which I explore in more detail in my chapter on Jo Spence. Those making 'constructed images' used the studio or 'artificial' environments, props and models to make an image which is clearly fabricated in order to *tell* a story, or persuade someone of something, rather than to pretend that *showing* is enough, as documentary photography would have it. Formal devices from the world of advertising were plundered and deliberately referred to in order to point to the arbitrariness of the signifier–signified relationship and as an acknowledgement that these are not the exclusive property of adverts and therefore can be 'filled up' with 'oppositional' signifieds.[24] The ideology of the commercial world and its commodification of, for example, women's bodies, could be unpicked in order to show that culture is manufactured by and for particular social groups rather than an inevitable or natural process which we have to take for granted.[25] Where one might want to take issue with this argument is in its assumption that once one can demonstrate that the object of analysis is *culturally* produced, *ergo* it have to be changed. Nature is always assumed to be on the side of stasis; culture on the side of mutability. It seems to me that the burden of proof is upon social constructionists, as they are sometimes called in the social sciences, to prove this. We now need to do more than show the rule-governed, conventional aspect of social life; at times social constructionists talk as if in conversation with an imaginary interlocutor who believes that society is composed of relationships with pre- or non-social individuals.

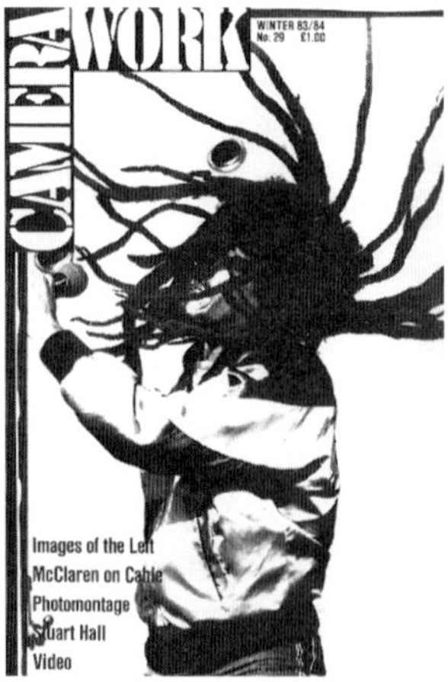


In addition to the trenchant critique of realism, the influence of post-Althusserian theories had ensured that the category of experience was sapped of any power. There are two aspects to the sense of 'experience' here; it has a minimal neutral sense of a subjective response to the external world, but also a more loaded meaning, as a lesson that those who live through history learn from it—in other words, accumulated and irreversible knowledge. Both of these were problematised together. Ideology could not be combated by experience, according to this critique of humanism, since what could be the homeland of ideology if not what we believe to be commonsense, everday experience?[26] But how might these shifts in thinking experience have challenged the very terms of community photography, particularly in the context of the left's shock and disarray after losing the second general election of 1983? To give a hypothetical example: a working-class family has bought its own council flat and worries that the squatters next door will affect the value of property prices—how could this be taken account of in the discourse of community photography? The discourse of the community was often based on the assumption that identities are just there, ready-formed and waiting to be found, rather than having to be actively struggled in and for, or articulated, as Stuart Hall has put it.[27] They always assumed that as the community was on the margins there was therefore unity in oppression; what about conflict in oppression? As Iris Marion Young has recently said, 'The ideal of community...privileges unity over difference, immediacy over mediation, sympathy over recognition of the limits of one's understanding of others from their point of view'.[28]

The last serious article in *Camerawork* to be written on the subject of community photography was by Don Slater, in issue no.20 (1980). He was concerned that in its fetishisation of access and accessibility, community photography had neglected to engage with the rhetoric and power of the dominant media. However, the political importance of community photography for Slater was its refusal to reduce the photograph to being a merely commercial object. Community photography was the outcome of a specific form of production and consumption which overruled the laws of the market-place by 'keeping the least possible distance between those who produce and those who consume images....This breaks through many ideas of what photography is and what photographs do...' Making your own images is in exemplary form a way of

> feeling for yourself...the visual options available within the medium....The 'I know how s/he took that picture' reaction to the news photo is vital: breaking down the distance between what I can do with a camera and what they do is what demystification is all about.

When the 'transparent' processes of commercial photography are made visible this is a 'giant step in distancing oneself from the advert's intentions'.[29] Slater's call for retaining the idea of access to the making of pictures, as at least a minimal condition for a critique of the mass media, is important. He has recently continued this argument for visual literacy by placing it in the context of digital culture.[30] Snapshooting, he points out, was at least based in self-representation, however conventionalised, but a culture modelled on the computer creates only the possibility of consumption, ruled by the ideology of choice, thus threatening the very possibility of representation at all: 'digital culture involves tapping into flows of images which originate outside the private sphere', such as the pre-programmed 'decision pathways' of the new cameras.[31]

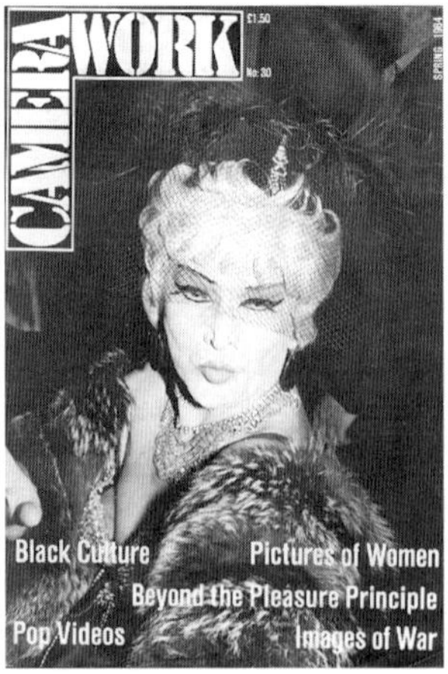


Kathy Myers points to the shift that took place over the last few years of *Camerawork*'s life:

> The debate was not so much about how one could create a safe alternative so much as the creation of opposition and intervention—recognising that the medium of documentary was not necessarily on the side of the people but had to be articulated as such, in specific contexts.[32]

By 1983, the alternative community sector had all but been abandoned by 'the people' who voted in the general election for the right wing popularism of Thatcherism, with its repudiation of the language of class and victimhood and its culture of individualist aspiration and self-improvement. With issue no.29 of Winter 1983, the shibboleths of left photography were finally dismantled in the magazine itself—two pieces, by Stuart Hall and Kathy Myers were concerned with the poverty of Left propaganda and socialist realism, in the context of the disastrous 1983 election campaign of the Labour Party. Kathy Myers in particular felt that Thatcher's success in denigrating Labour for its associations with a whole host of class-ridden preoccupations (high taxation and public spending, restrictive union practices, strikes, and so on) proved that Labour needed urgently to shed its old 'loves' in order to meet the new loves and aspirations of the electorate.

*Camerawork* issue no.20 announced a new manifesto:

> *Camerawork* is a journal for the politics of photography. It is designed as a forum for analysis, critique, theory and information in order to provide the basis for using photography within socialist and feminist practices and to develop and encourage socialist strategies within the politics of representation.

'Representation' is now the central political category and from this point onwards *Camerawork* paid attention in a more focused way to mainstream media culture, with essays by Kathy Myers (a long-term member of the editorial group and editor for issues 29 and 30) and Don Slater, 'The Object of Photography', reproduced in this volume. But it was only in the last four or five issues that the stand-off between the politics of representation and the representation of politics was broken down. In issue no.24 *Camerawork* indicated its abandonment of showcasing alternative community or photo-journalistic work with a renewed emphasis on the politics of representation. Photography, as Kathy Myers has pointed out in her commentary on *Camerawork*, became for the magazine 'an ideological weapon'; the emphasis is now on 'how images create and sustain meanings in ideology'. So issue no.29 saw the definition of photograph expanded to include other media—film, TV, video, graphics. And in issue no. 31, its editors say: '*Camerawork* provides a forum for debates about photographic practices and broader questions of representation'. The widening out of its agenda, its concern with 'representation' in general, and the lack of specificity as to its audience is a notable departure from the 1970s magazine. The demise at the beginning of the 1980s of community photography, in part linked to the withdrawal of local government and arts bodies' public funding schemes, was no doubt a factor here, although I suspect that if we take a longer view the internal critiques of community photography were more significant. But in order to understand the rise to prominence of the politics of representation in the 1980s, we have to consider a far wider social context—the main lines of which I can here do no more than indicate. Throughout the 1980s, *Camerawork* had become progressively closer to the academic worlds of cultural theory and media studies; a consideration of the names heading the editorial groups of the last ten issues shows that there were at least as many academic writers as photographers. Photo-journalists and documentary photographers were no longer represented; instead the mainstay of both the production and the audience for the magazine were becoming polytechnic lecturers and students, and practitioners whose work was aimed at a gallery audience. *Camerawork* thus became more specialised. We have to remember that the main mass forum for documentary, the colour supplements, were rapidly transmuting in the early 1980s into 'advertorial' lifestyle sections, aimed at attracting increased advertising revenue. In the 1980s, photographer-intellectuals, 'independent-sector' photographers and media commentators were increasingly likely to be professionalised, and this can be understood as part of a rapid expansion of media culture itself. The 1980s explosion in marketing and promotion in almost all areas of cultural life had its spin-off in the increasing numbers of people—academics, photographer-intellectuals—who were hired to comment in and on the media in both words and pictures. What I am suggesting here is that there was an emerging rapprochement between the culture of critique and the culture that constituted the object of that critique. 'Intertextuality' was not just an intellectual exercise in pointing out the latest rhetorical device of a postmodern media, but can be read as actually describing the particular texture of experience of those who live by the (media) image.[33]

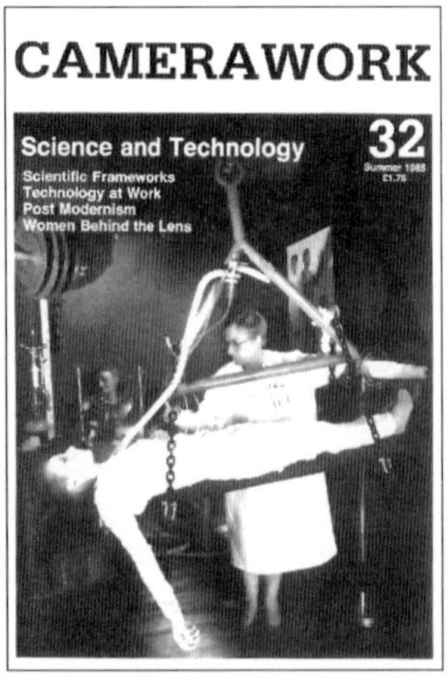


For too long now photography has been seen by the cultural Left as part of a popular culture which is colonised by the beast of 'dominant ideology'—and of course the analyst who can point out a case of dominant ideology is always exempt from its effects! Could we shift our starting point for debate to one which does not assume such a determinatory fit between 'image' and 'effects', subjectivity and 'representation'? This, I will end by proposing, should be the task of future photographic theory. *Camerawork's* strength and innovation was its continuation of Walter Benjamin's project of thinking of photography and the photograph as a social practice involving a network of relations between the intentions and ideologies of the producer, the inherent qualities and constraints of the medium, the forms of distribution and presentation, and the particular audiences and viewers on whom 'meaning' also depends. But this was never pushed so far as to think of the audience or users of photography as having a life outside the text, a possibility which was however a feature of Jo Spence's reading of her own family album. Much British academic writing on photography has been confined largely to a study of the isolated photograph as a coded text which is presumed to have particular 'effects' on viewers, whose subjectivity is all too often conceptualised as being the by-product of the text. This predicament is the effect of the domination of a Saussurean model of language, which prefers to study language as an abstract system of signs (*langue*) rather than a concrete utterance. Could we begin to think of photographs as akin in this way to the act of speech, rather than to that of writing and representation? It is to be hoped that the work developed in media studies by David Morley, Janice Radway and others on the ethnography of audiences, and that of Bourdieu on the habitus of audiences will be taken up in future work on photography.[34] For we urgently need to incorporate a sense of the capacity for human agency into our analyses of photography and its uses.

## Reference Notes


**1** See Spence's 'The Politics of Photography', *Camerawork*, no.1, reproduced in Jo Spence and Jo Stanley, eds, *Cultural Sniping*, Routledge, London, 1995.

**2** See Victor Burgin, 'Something about Photography Theory', in A.L.Rees and F. Borzello, eds, *The New Art History*, Camden Press, London, 1986, and his 'Introduction' to Burgin, ed., *Thinking Photography*, Macmillan, Basingstoke, 1982.

**3** John Tagg, 'Practising Theories: An Interview with Joanne Lukitsh', in *Grounds of Dispute: Art History, Cultural Politics and the Discursive Field*, Macmillan, Basingstoke, 1992, p.76.

**4** Simon Watney, 'On the Institutions of Photography', in P. Holland, J. Spence and S. Watney, eds, *Photography/Politics Two*, Photography Workshop/Comedia, London, 1986, p.189.

**5** Watney, 'On the Institutions of Photography', pp.189-90. And see Watney's later critique of Barbara Rosenblum's important if limited sociology of photographic style, pp.191-3.

**6** Susan Sontag, *On Photography*, Penguin, Harmondsworth, 1978, pp.178-9.

**7** See Stuart Hall, 'Cultural Studies: Two Paradigms', in R. Collins, J. Curran, N. Garnham, P. Scannell, P. Schlesinger and C. Sparks, eds, *Media, Culture, Society Reader*, Sage, London, 1986. For the tension inherent in the attempt to bring together Marxism and semiotics see Simon Watney, 'On the Institutions of Photography', p.187.

**8** See Simon Watney, 'Photography—Education—Theory', in *Screen*, vol.25, no.1, Jan-Feb., 1984; Jan Zita Grover, 'The Subject of Photography in the American Academy', *Screen*, vol. 27, no.5, Sept.-Oct., 1986.

**9** See *Here is the Other News: Challenges to the Local Commercial Press*, Minority Press Group, London, 1980.

**10** Interview with Terry Dennett, London, October 1995.

**11** For more information on Photography Workshop see J. Spence and T. Dennett, 'Ten Years of Photography Workshop' in S. Bezencenet and P. Corrigan, eds, *Photographic Practices: Towards a Different Image*, Comedia, London, 1986.

**12** S. Yeo, 'The Politics of Community Publications' in R. Samuel, ed., *People's History and Socialist Theory*, Routledge & Kegan Paul, London, 1981.

**13** Ibid., p.44.

**14** See W. Benjamin, 'The Author as Producer' in V. Burgin, ed., *Thinking Photography*, Macmillan, Basingstoke, 1981.

**15** Jo Spence, Terry Dennett and Liz Heron's 14 October 1977 Press Release 'A Statement on the Question of *Camerawork*', Photography Workshop Archive, c/o Terry Dennett.

**16** See Burgin's *UK 76*, in his *Between*, Basil Blackwell, Oxford and ICA, London, 1986; The Hackney Flashers, *Who's Holding the Baby?*, in J. Spence, *Putting Myself in the Picture*, Camden Press, London, 1986.

**17** See my introduction to J. Berger, 'Ways of Remembering' in this volume. For a sympathetic and complex analysis of Berger's ideas on photography and experience see Bruce Robbins, 'Feeling Global: John Berger and Experience', in J. Arac, ed., *Postmodernism and Politics*, Manchester University Press, Manchester, 1986.

**18** This was a point made to me by Don Slater. See the Polysnappers' exhibition, *Family, Fantasy, Photography*, in J. Spence, *Putting Myself in the Picture*, pp.134-41. For more on this point see my 'An Affront to Taste? The Disturbances of Jo Spence' in this volume.

**19** For two opposing views of 1930s documentary see David Mellor, 'Mass Observation: The Intellectual Climate', and Don Macpherson, 'Nation, Mandate, Memory' in this volume. For Foucault, see David Green, 'On Foucault: Disciplinary Power and Photography' in this volume. See also M. Foucault, 'Truth and Power', in C. Gordon, ed., *Power/Knowledge*, Harvester, Brighton, 1980. For the 1980s Foucauldian readings of photography, see John Tagg, *The Burden of Representation*, Macmillan, Basingstoke, 1988; Jessica Evans, 'The Iron Cage of Visibility', *Ten.8*, no.29, 1988; Steven Edwards, 'Disastrous Documents' (on *Picture Post* magazine and its representation of the northern working class), in *Ten.8*, no.15, 1984.

**20** See M. Jay, 'In the Empire of the Gaze' in David Couzens Hoy, ed., *Foucault: A Critical Reader*, Basil Blackwell, Oxford, 1986.

**21** J. Clifford, 'Introduction: Partial Truths', in J. Clifford and G. E. Marcus, eds, *Writing Culture: The Poetics and Politics of Ethnography*, University of California Press, Berkeley, p.12.

**22** For an important argument to this effect see 'The Work of Knowledge and the Knowledge of Women's Work' by Miriam Glucksmann in Mary Maynard and June Purvis, eds, *Researching Women's Lives from a Feminist Perspective*, Taylor and Francis, London, 1994. For an opposing argument see the interview with Michel Foucault, 'Truth and Power', in P. Rabinow, ed., *A Foucault Reader*, Penguin, Harmondsworth, 1984.

**23** For a book-length critique of narrative, realism, and by implication, documentary, see Stephen Heath, *Questions of Cinema*, Indiana University Press, Bloomington, 1982. See also his 'Lessons from Brecht', *Screen*, vol.15, no.2, 1974. For a lively and more accessible account of these issues by a writer sympathetic to a contingent and situated realism, see Bill Nichols, 'The Fact of Realism and the Fiction of Objectivity', in his *Representing Reality*, Indiana University Press, Bloomington, 1991.

**24** See Victor Burgin, 'Art, Common Sense and Photography' in this volume for a seminal statement on this as a practice of political intervention. My points here are indebted to the many conversations I have had over the years with Andy Golding at the University of Westminster (formerly Polytechnic of Central London), which as an institution was largely responsible for the development of this practice. See Jessica Evans, 'The Iron Cage of Visibility', op.cit., for an argument for the social constructionist view.

**25** See Roland Barthes for the classic statement of this position in terms of myth, which for him has the function of turning history into nature: *Mythologies*, Paladin, London, 1972. For a more detailed application of semiotic ideas to advertising see Judith Williamson, *Decoding Adverts*, Marion Boyars, London, 1981.
**26** Terry Eagleton, *Criticism and Ideology: A Study in Marxist Literary Theory*, New Left Books, London, 1976, p.15.
**27** See S. Hall, 'The Rediscovery of Ideology: The Return of the Repressed in Media Studies', in V. Beechey and J. Donald, eds, *Subjectivity and Social Relations*, Open University Press, Milton Keynes, 1985.
**28** 'The Ideal of Community and the Politics of Difference', in Linda J. Nicholson, ed., *Feminism/Postmodernism*, Routledge, London, 1990.
**29** Don Slater, 'The Politics of Community Photography', *Camerawork*, no.20, December 1980, p.8.
**30** Don Slater, 'Domestic Photography and Digital Culture', in Martin Lister, ed., *The Photographic Image in Digital Culture*, Routledge, London, 1995.
**31** Ibid., p.137; p.141.
**32** Kathy Myers, 'Camerawork', in *Photographic Practices*, op.cit., p.90.
**33** See P. Bourdieu, 'How Can "Free-Floating Intellectuals" Be Set Free?' in his *Sociology in Question*, Sage, London, 1993. And N. Garnham and R. Williams, 'Bourdieu and the Sociology of Culture....An Introduction', in *Media, Culture, Society: A Critical Reader*, op.cit.
**34** For an excellent overview of this area see David Morley, *Television Audiences and Cultural Studies*, Routledge, London, 1992; for Pierre Bourdieu, see his *Distinction*, Routledge & Kegan Paul, 1984.

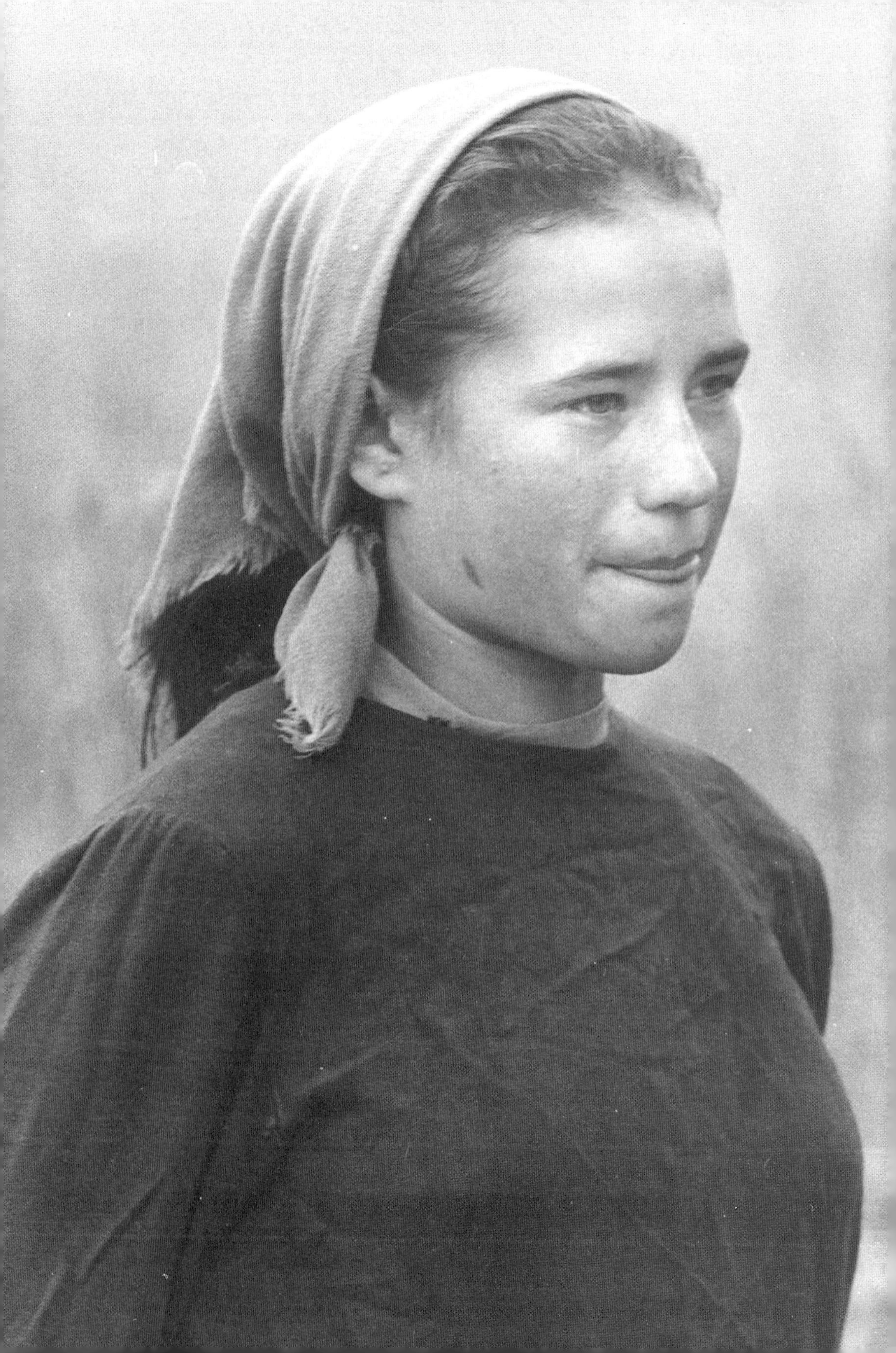

# 1

# The Photograph: Contexts of/for Meaning

# 1 Ways of Remembering

## John Berger

Introduction by
**Jessica Evans**

In *Ways of Remembering* and in various books written with the photographer Jean Mohr during the 1970s and early 1980s, John Berger developed a photographic practice which aimed to counter what he saw as the brutalising effects of modernisation.[1] Understood as a process which had split asunder the spheres of the public and private, it had engendered a partial, ruptured form of experience. In particular the form of mechanical reproduction had effected practices of distribution of images which meant that image was separated from its origin, instantaneously inhabiting a plurality of spaces. Berger saw in the uses of and projections of meaning on to the photograph within the *private sphere* an ideal-type of emancipated viewing experience. In this way he reinterprets the critical edge of the romantic anti-capitalist tradition, one which emerges with the moment of the romantic poets and is intertwined with the Frankfurt School tradition of critical theory. I want to think in particular about Berger's work as an encounter with Walter Benjamin's writings and also broaden our conception of his work via the British sociologist Anthony Giddens's recent work on modernity.

What I wish to emphasise is the trajectory of Berger's desire for a radical photography practice to overcome the fissures of modernity. That is, the need to make the alienated public experience of the photograph conform to the spatially close and affective experience of personal life. It is worth remembering that during the 1970s socialist feminist theorists aimed their fire at the ideological and political division between public and private which they saw as maintaining patriarchal structures. In these circumstances, what remains provocative about Berger's work is his respect for the emotional qualities and intersubjective experiences of the private sphere; its intimacy and bonds of connectedness are considered to be fundamentally reparative.

In his book *Another Way of Telling*, Berger interprets the photograph as an instance of modernity's 'shock of discontinuity'; he spoke, as did Roland Barthes in *Camera Lucida*, of the abyss between the moment of the recording of the picture and that of its viewing.[2] This abyss can be understood in Berger's work as a metaphor for the dislocating processes of capitalist modernity and in particular the historical process during which time and space become increasingly separated and independent of one another. Anthony Giddens has recently drawn our attention to this dynamic character of modern social life. In two recent books, *The Consequences of Modernity* and *Modernity and Self-Identity,* he points out that in pre-modern settings, time and space are connected through the reliable boundedness of place, and an affiliation of place with kinship relations.[3] But modernity is characterised by a process he calls 'disembedding': the 'lifting out of social relations from local contexts' and their 'recombination' across infinite tracts of time/space.[4] Modern social organisation is thus 'the precise coordination of the actions of many human beings physically absent from each other—not constrained by the mediation of place'.[5] The importance of photography as a constituent part of this process, in its inherent divorcing of meaning from an originary context, the way it makes all meaning subject to the mediating processes of *transmission*, cannot be underestimated. John Berger pursued this way of thinking about photography in his *Ways of Seeing:* an argument strongly marked by the work of Walter Benjamin.[6]

Walter Benjamin is well known for his prognosis that the very quality of mechanical reproduction, outlined above, would spawn new democratic modes of perception, themselves intimately connected to what he rather ambiguously refers to as the 'mass movements'.[7] Through the substitution of a plurality of copies for a 'unique existence' and the discursive recasting of the reproduced object into situations and contexts chosen by producers, distributors and viewers, the techniques of reproduction detach the reproduced object from its traditional domain. The production of meaning can then become understood as contingent and intersocial, in accordance with Baudelaire's original definition of modernity as creating an arbitrary, fleeting, and unstable experience.

However, there was an interesting tension in Benjamin's writings between a negative and positive response to the loss of aura in the work of art. In 'On Some Motifs in Baudelaire' he identified the decline of the aura as paradigmatic of a cultural decline in the quality of experience, particularly given the rapid loss of the intersubjective face-to-face experience.

Following the earlier work of Georg Simmel, Benjamin says that 'the privatised experience is a consequence of the fact that he [the viewer/reader] is unable to assimilate the data of the world around him by way of experience'. For example the intention of the press, through such means as the lack of connection between individual news items, is to prevent 'the reader assimilating the information it supplies as part of his own experience' in order to 'isolate what happens from the realm in which it could affect the experience of the reader'. He goes on: 'The historical forms of communication actually constitute experience so that the replacement of the older narration by information, of information by sensation reflects the increasing atrophy of experience'.[8] For Benjamin, it is the very capacity for storytelling that is at risk: 'It is not the object of a story to convey a happening per se, which is the purpose of information; rather, it embeds it in the life of the storyteller in order to pass it on as experience to those listening'.[9] In 'Ways of Remembering' and other works during this period, Berger, prompted by Benjamin's concerns, asks whether the ambiguity of the photograph could lead to 'another way of telling'.

Berger argues that in 'real life' (the routines of everyday experience) meaning is discovered in what connects, for it cannot exist without development. To interpret a picture, he says, is to lend it a past and a future, to insert it, in other words, into a narrative. In his chapter 'Appearances' John Berger noted how in modernity 'the timeless has been abolished, and history itself has become ephemerality'.[10] Foreshadowing the concerns of later postmodernist critics, themselves reworking Georg Simmel's work on the popular culture of fashion, Berger is concerned with the rapidity with which the present becomes the historical, and the historical is recycled as the present. Consequently, 'the common experience of those moments which defy time is now denied by everything which surrounds them' and the inevitable but unsatisfactory solution is that 'experiences which prompt the term *for ever* have now to be assumed [assimilated] alone and privately.' Images are used to refer to that which historical time has no right to destroy—such as the bedside pictures of the one you love.[11]

The narrative form which photography can employ is memory, a field in which different times coexist because memory, as an aspect of unconscious life, does not conform to a linear conception of time in which, for example, the modern suspense story is constructed.[12] This form is not connected with events understood positivistically as temporally dissociated facts. Rather, Berger's 'radial' method is concerned with their rehabilitation into areas of desire, contradiction and self-reflexivity within a person's day-to-day life; to the extent that we can say the photo-narrative has a continuity, this lies in the way it re-assembles the variable contexts of its subject's experience. Thus, the photo-story by Jean Mohr, reproduced as part of 'Ways of Remembering' and originally part of Berger and Mohr's book *A Seventh Man*, intends to speak about a migrant worker's sexual deprivation. Experience, as Benjamin put it, is 'indeed a matter of tradition, in collective experience as well as private life. It is less the product of facts firmly anchored in memory than of a convergence in memory of accumulated and frequently unconscious data.'[13]

## Ways of Remembering

*They are coming to offer their labour. Their labour power is ready made. The industrialised country, whose production is going to benefit from it, has not borne any of the cost of creating it; any more that it will bear the cost of supporting a seriously sick migrant worker, or one who has grown too old to work. So far as the economy of the metropolitan country is concerned, migrant workers are immortal: immortal because brought up: they do not age: they do not get tired: they do not die. They have a single function—to work. All other functions of their lives are the responsibility of the country they come from.*

*Migrant workers, already living in the metropolis, have the habit of visiting the main railway station. To talk in groups there, to watch the trains come in, to receive first-hand news from their country, to anticipate the day when they will begin the return journey.*

*In his imagination every migrant worker is in transit. He remembers the past; he anticipates the future; his aims and his recollections make his thoughts a train between the two.*

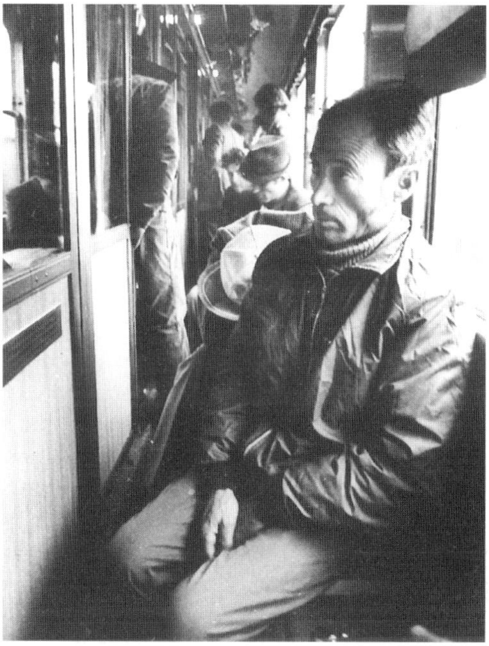

1.1

*In the winter the main railway station is warm, and it is one of the few places where events occur and they can remain spectators, and at the same time outnumber the citizens. The constituents of leisure: the right to watch, and the capacity to be at ease with those of your own choosing.*

*He is listening to the noise of the train in the throat of the journey. The noise is as regular as the lines. Over this, irregularly, rising to crescendos and falling away, are the noises of what the train is passing: the fields murmur, brick walls pound fists on metal, a station throws gravel against the windows. When the terminus first arrives, it does so in silence.*

Text and illustrations from *A Seventh Man* by John Berger and Jean Mohr

*How in practice can we use photographs so that, even though we are using them publicly, they are replaced in a context which is comparable to that of private photographs. This is what Jean Mohr, Sven Blomberg and myself have tried to do in our books. What we have achieved is only a tentative beginning, others later will make us look like primitives.*

**John Berger** is an author and art critic living in France. He co-produced and wrote the influential BBC television series and book *Ways of Seeing* (1972). He wrote three books in collaboration with Jean Mohr as photographer: *The Seventh Man* (1975); *A Fortunate Man* (1967); *Another Way of Telling* (1982) and the books of essays *About Looking* (1980); *The Sense of Sight* (1985). Recent fiction includes the trilogy entitled *Into Their Labours* and in 1994 he published the novel *To the Wedding.*

A book by Susan Sontag was recently published in the United States. Called *On Photography*, it will soon be published here.[14] I think that it's perhaps the most important book on photography ever written. In what I'm going to say I am borrowing a great deal from her insights.

One can begin by asking—before the invention of photography what served in its place? What was there before photography? The obvious answer would be engravings, drawings, paintings, graphic works of one kind or another. Yet, if one doesn't look at it from a purely technical point of view, what served the function that photography now serves is none of those things, given the vastness of today's global system of photography. What served that function before photography was the faculty of memory. If that sounds paradoxical I hope it will become clear in a minute.

A photo's relation to the object or event depicted is different from that of a painting or engraving, because the latter is a reconstitution of the event, whereas a photograph is, as it were, a trace of that event. A photograph is similar to a footprint or a deathmask. It is a trace of a set of instant appearances. The camera, like the eye, records appearances through the mediation of light. But the camera, unlike the eye, fixes the set of appearances which it records. It preserves those appearances from the supersession of other appearances. If I look at you and then I look around, the appearances recorded by my eye are continually changing. What the camera does is to fix a set of appearances and, in so far as it does that, it is like memory. Memory preserves an event from being covered and therefore hidden by the events that come after it. It holds a single event. So does the camera.

When one really begins to think about it, the practice of photography is unprecedented, there was no equivalent before it. In a sense if I compare photography with memory I am comparing two completely incomparable things. It is an unsatisfactory comparison, but we are forced to make it. When photography was first invented and used, there were considerable debates about whether it was a form of art or a science. What I'm suggesting is that our systematic use of photography is almost a metaphysical process.

Photography was discovered in 1839 by Fox Talbot. One of the things that immediately strikes one is how quickly the possible uses of this new discovery were taken up and applied by the industrialised countries at that time. Within thirty years it was being used for nearly all the purposes to which we are accustomed. It was being used to make postcards of places, it was being used for police records, war reporting, military reconnaissance, pornography, family albums, anthropological records (often, as with the Indians in the US, accompanied by genocide), sentimental moralising, news reporting and formal portraiture. Capitalism needed photography.

Nevertheless it was not until the period between the two world wars that the photograph became the dominant and most 'natural' way of referring to appearances. It was then that it replaced the word as immediate testimony. It was the period when photography was thought of as being most transparent, offering direct access to the real—the period of the great witnessing masters of the medium like Paul Strand and Walker Evans. It was, in the capitalist countries, the freest moment of photography: it had been liberated from the limitations of fine art, it had become a public medium and so could be used democratically, and had not yet become the febrile production of consuming dreams—or nightmares.

Yet the moment was brief. The very 'truthfulness' of the medium dialectically encouraged its deliberate use as a means of propaganda. The Nazis were among the first to use systematic photographic propaganda. At the same time, less perceptibly, photography was beginning to become, everywhere in the industrially developed world, an ideological component. In the first period of its existence, photography had offered a new technical opportunity, it had been an implement. Now, instead of offering a new choice, its usage and its 'reading' were becoming habitual, an unexamined part of modern perception itself. Many developments contributed to this transformation: the new film industry; the invention of the lightweight camera, so that the taking of a photograph ceased to be a ritual and became a 'reflex'; the discovery of photojournalism, whereby the text follows the picture instead of vice versa; the emergence of advertising as a crucial economic force.

The first really large circulation picture magazine was started in the US in 1936. At least two things were prophetic about the launching of *Life*, the prophecies to be fully realised in the postwar television age. The magazine was financed not by its sales, but by the advertising it carried. One-third of its pages and images were devoted to publicity. The second prophecy lay in its title. *Time* magazine had been started ten years earlier as a *digest* of the news, on the assumption that a mass audience could not have the time to read the full news reports. *Life* intended to fill the space thus emptied with pictures. Its title is ambiguous. It can mean that these pictures are about life, yet it seems to promise more: that these pictures *are* life. The first photograph in the first issue played on this ambiguity. It showed a newborn baby. The caption underneath read: 'Life begins . . .'

Why has photography lent itself so easily to usages which are relatively independent of the photographers' intentions? I think the reason is fairly simple. The photograph offers a set of appearances prised away from their context and therefore from their meaning, because meaning is always a question of process—meaning lies in narrative, meaning is born out of development and process. If you stop that process, and take a set of images out of their context, they are prised away from their meaning. Something of the violence of that prising away of appearances from the continuum in which they once existed is suggested by the following thought. Imagine that the life of a photograph is only ten years, and most photographs last longer, the ratio between that life and the instant it represents will be something like 200,000 million to one. This perhaps gives one some idea of the violence of the fission that occurs when a set of appearances is prised away from its context. The violence destroys meaning. And the set of appearances is then available to any meaning being put upon it.

Now there are two distinct uses of photography: the private and the public. The private, that is to say the photographs one has of the people one loves, one's friends, the class one was in at school, etc.; in private use a photograph is read in a context which is still continuous with that from which it was taken. Take a photograph of your Mother. There's still that prising away of an instant. But there remains a continuity between you and your experience and your Mother. The private context creates a continuity which is parallel to the continuity from which the photograph was originally taken.

Private photographs are nearly always of something which you have known. By contrast public photographs are usually images of the unknown or, at best, they are images of things which are known only through other photographs. The public photograph has been severed from life when it was taken, and it remains, as an isolated image, separate from your experience. The public photograph is like the memory of a total stranger, a total stranger who has shouted 'Look' at the event recorded.

There is something about every photograph which is intimate. It's bound to be so because it goes in, it isolates and it frames. You are always in a situation of intimacy towards what has been photographed. That is another reason why I talk about memory. At the same time because the public photograph is divorced from all first-hand experience, it represents the memory of a total stranger.

Who is this stranger? One could answer that it is all the photographers. Yet the photographers are only the agents of this memory. They do not construct the system.

There is a cartoon that Daumier made of Nadar in a balloon over Paris. His hat is blowing off in the wind, and he has this very large clumsy camera with which he is photographing the whole of Paris below. This cartoon offers us a clue. Perhaps the eye of the total stranger is the eye of God, but the eye of a totally secularised, totally estranged God. A God of nothingness.

The faculty of memory allows us to preserve certain events from oblivion. Because of their experience of this faculty, women and men in nearly all cultures have assumed that there was somewhere an all-seeing eye. They accredited this eye to spirits, ancestors, Gods or a single God. Such an all-seeing eye recorded all events, and the idea of this eye was connected with the idea of justice, to be remembered was to be redeemed; to be forgotten was to be condemned. The all-seeing eye saw in order to judge. The all-seeing eye recorded all events and in that recording was implicit a kind of judgement.

Nineteenth-century capitalism elided the judgement of God into the judgement of history. Today we live in a culture which denies history, which cuts itself off from history, a culture of pure opportunism. So we have the systematic use of photographs, used as an all-seeing eye, recording events. But this all-seeing eye judges nothing: it uses neither the judgement of history, nor the judgement of God, it is totally without judgement. *It is an eye which records in order to forget.*

Is an alternative use of photography conceivable? Is it possible to use photography addressing such a use to the hope of an alternative future?

The immediate answer to that is yes. You can use photography in all kinds of agitprop ways, you can make propaganda with photographs—you can make anti-capitalist propaganda, anti-imperialist propaganda. I wouldn't deny the usefulness of this, but at the same time I think the answer is incomplete. It's like taking a cannon and turning it round and firing it in the opposite direction. You haven't actually changed the practice, you've simply changed the aim.

How is it possible to use photography so that it doesn't function like the eye of a totally estranged God? We have to go back to the distinction I made between the private and public uses of photography. In the private use of photography, the photograph does not lend itself to any use, it does not become a completely value-free object because the use reconstitutes the continuity from which it was taken. Maybe one has to consider how the private use of photography could be extended, could be enlarged so that it might cease to be private and become public.

One of the most important and most popular photographic exhibitions ever put on was called *The Family of Man*. It was organised by Steichen in 1955. Steichen, I think, had a starting point not far from what I'm saying. The exhibition was arranged like a family album. The overall notion was that the world is like a family with birth, death, marriage, unhappiness, hopes, fears, dreams, etc., everywhere. Such a notion was a sentimental short cut because it is not possible to treat the existing world as if it were without contradictions, without murderous struggles, as if it were a family. The unity of the world has not yet been achieved. And so the exhibition as a whole was evasive and sentimental although many of the images in it were not. Yet Steichen's intuition was not wrong. If the camera is not to be used as if it were the eye of a totally estranged God, we can say that photography awaits a world historical consciousness which has yet to be achieved. It awaits a social memory which will transcend the distinction between public and private.

How in practice can we use photographs, so that, even though we are using them publicly, they are replaced in a context which is comparable to that of private photographs? This is what Jean Mohr, Sven Blomberg and myself have tried to do in our books. What we have achieved is only a tentative beginning, others later will make us look like primitives.

The problem is to construct a context for a photograph, to construct it with words, to construct it with other photographs, to construct it by its place in an ongoing text of photographs and images. How? Normally photographs are used in a very unilinear way—they are used to illustrate an argument, or to demonstrate a thought which goes like this:

Very frequently also they are used tautologically so that the photograph merely repeats what is being said in words. Memory is not unilinear at all. Memory works radially, that is to say with an enormous number of associations all leading to the same event. The diagram is like this:

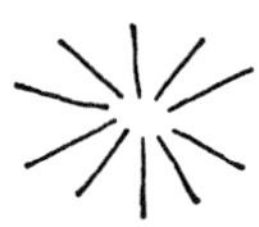

If we want to put a photograph back into the context of experience, social experience, social memory, we have to respect the laws of memory. We have to situate the printed photograph so that it acquires something of the surprising conclusiveness of that which was and is.

What Brecht wrote about acting in one of his poems is applicable to such a practice. For *instant* one can read photography, for *acting* the re-creating of context:

So you should simply make the instant
Stand out, without in the process hiding
What you are making it stand out from.
    Give your acting
That progression of one-thing-after-another,
    that attitude of
Working up what you have taken on. In
    this way
You will show the flow of events and also
    the course
Of your work, permitting the spectator
To experience this Now on many levels,
    coming from Previously and
Merging into Afterwards, also having
    much else Now
Alongside it. He is sitting not only
In your theatre but also
In the world.[15]

There are a few great photographs which practically achieve this by themselves. Any photograph may become such a 'Now' if an adequate context is created for it. In general the better the photograph, the fuller the context which can be created.

Such a context replaces the photograph in time—not its own original time for that is impossible—but in narrated time. Narrated time becomes historic time when it is assumed by social memory and social action. The constructed narrated time needs to respect the process of memory which it hopes to stimulate.

There is never a single approach to something remembered. The remembered is not like a terminus at the end of a line. Numerous approaches or stimuli converge upon it and lead to it. Words, comparisons, signs need to create a context for a printed photograph in a comparable way; that is to say, they must mark and leave open diverse approaches. A radial system has to be constructed around the photograph so that it may be seen in terms which are simultaneously personal, political, economic, dramatic, everyday and historic.

The original version of this article was presented to the British Sociological Association Conference at the University of Sussex in April 1978. It was revised for *Camerawork* issue no.10 by John Berger.

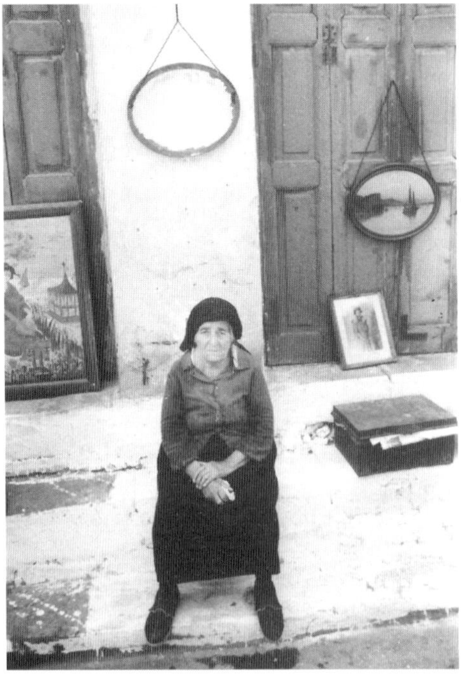

1.2

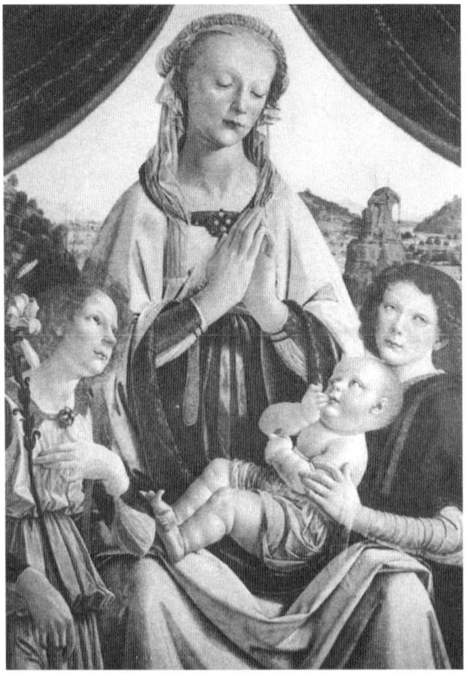

1.3

*In* A Seventh Man *there is a photograph which is in a wooden barracks where Portuguese and Yugoslavs live. They work in a tunnel, they live in a wooden barracks, they have bunks two above the other. Around the bunks, on the roof of the bunk above, all the way round are pictures, sexy pictures, which they did not of course bring with them. They bought them in Germany or Switzerland or somewhere. The room is absolutely plastered with these. We wanted to use that picture because it was important, first of all because it was like that, second because it is, in a sense, an indirect index of the sexual deprivation suffered by these men. How to do it? Because you put that picture on a page and what does it say? How is that image going to work?*

*It first, maybe, approves of the virulent sexism of the images stuck up. It's going to confirm the superstition that these men are all sex maniacs and it's probably also going to give a vicarious thrill to some. You see, it's not going to work and it was a problem which we actually worked on for about a week. How could we use this in order to escape this automatic and false meaning? We tried juxtaposing that picture with pictures of the men's faces, it doesn't work because it doesn't really mean anything—it really only adds the personalities of these people. We tried putting in a photograph of something in the street, some sex shop in the street where the bourgeois of the city go. But again that says it is okay the petty bourgeois go to the sex shop the same as the migrant workers. It doesn't help. I'm not saying that the solution we found is the ideal one, but finally we found a photograph of an old peasant woman in her village who could have been the mother of any of those workers—in fact she wasn't—but she could have been. It was a picture of a mother, quite influenced in some respects by Catholic iconography with the Madonna, and so on. The kind of picture that one of those workers might have carried around with him. It had a kind of icon value, it was*

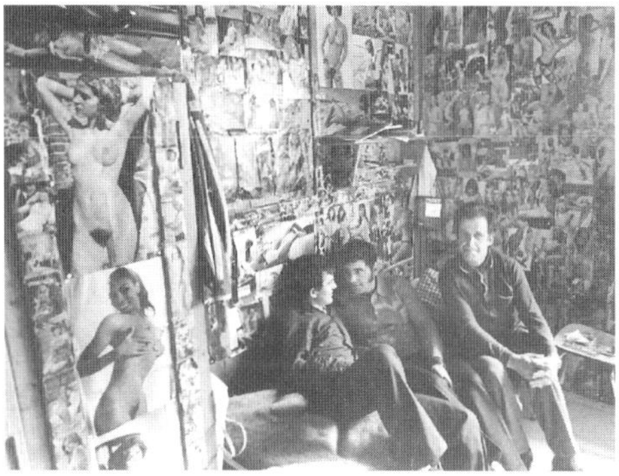

1.4

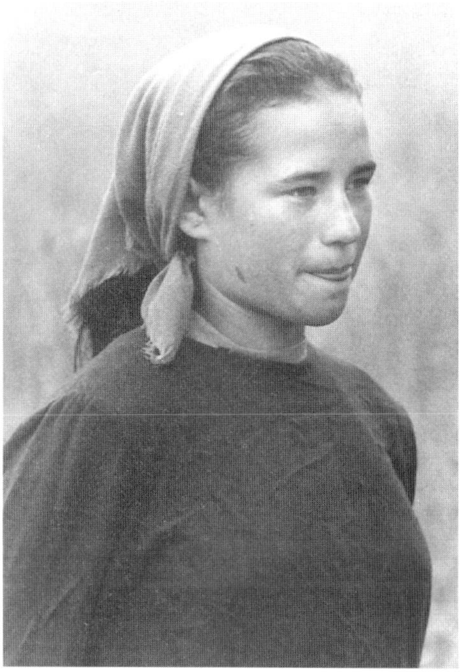

1.5

*sacred. We then put next to it, not a photograph at all, but a reproduction of a Madonna, a painting by Perugino. There begins to be a juxtaposition between idealised maternity and real maternity—that's to say a woman of 45 looking like 65 and probably with eight children. Then we turned the page and in that context we put the picture of the barracks with the sexy pictures all round. Beginning to relate, to talk about a life story, beginning to talk about women in more than one dimension, beginning to talk about the experience of those men. And then finally we chose to put opposite that barracks picture an extraordinary photograph that Jean took of a young Polish peasant girl—at that time totally uninfluenced and untouched by sexist consumerist glamour, who at the same time has a very beautiful face, young and questioning, the exact opposite in fact of the women in the barracks picture but corresponding very likely to one of the girls in the village. Now with those four pictures we perhaps began to put back the first one—that is to say the barracks one—in a context.*

Text from a discussion at the BSA Conference, April 1978.

1.2 Old Woman in Market, Greece. Jean Mohr

1.3 Madonna by Perugino. Jean Mohr

1.4 Wall above Bed in Barracks, Switzerland. Jean Mohr

1.5 Peasant Girl Working in Field. Jean Mohr

**Reference Notes**

**1** John Berger and Jean Mohr, *Another Way of Telling*, Writers and Readers, London, 1982; J. Berger and J. Mohr, *A Fortunate Man,* Writers and Readers, London, 1968, and J. Berger and J. Mohr, *A Seventh Man*, Penguin, Harmondsworth, 1975.

**2** Berger and Mohr, *Another Way of Telling*, pp.83-90

**3** A. Giddens, *Modernity and Self-Identity*, Polity, Oxford, 1990, p.147. See also Peter Berger, et al., 'The Pluralisation of Lifeworlds' in his *The Homeless Mind*, Penguin, Harmondsworth, 1974, p.63.

**4** Giddens, *Modernity and Self-Identity*, p.18.

**5** Ibid., p.17.

**6** John Berger, *Ways of Seeing*, BBC Books, 1972; see ch.1.

**7** See Walter Benjamin, 'The Work of Art in the Age of Mechanical Reproduction', in Benjamin, *Illuminations*, ed. H. Arendt, Schocken, New York, 1968, p.239.

**8** Walter Benjamin, 'On Some Motifs in Baudelaire' in *Illuminations*, pp.158-9. See also G. Simmel, 'The Metropolis and Mental Life', in D. Levine, ed., *Georg Simmel on Sociability and Social Forms* (trans. E. Shils), Chicago/London, 1971; and A. Giddens, *Modernity and Self-Identity.*

**9** Benjamin, 'On Some Motifs in Baudelaire', p.159.

**10** In Berger and Mohr, *Another Way of Telling*, p.107.

**11** Ibid., p.108. See also G. Simmel's essay, 'Fashion' in D. Levine, ed., *Georg Simmel on Sociability and Social Forms.*

**12** Berger in 'Stories', in *Another Way of Telling*, p.279.

**13** Benjamin, 'Some Motifs in Baudelaire', in *Illuminations*, p.157.

**14** Susan Sontag, *On Photography*, Allen Lane, Harmondsworth, 1978.

**15** From 'Portrayal of Past and Present In One' by Bertolt Brecht: trans. John Willett, in *Bertolt Brecht, Poems 1913-1956*, ed. John Willett and Ralph Manheim, Eyre Methuen Ltd, London, 1976.

**Further Reading**

• W. Benjamin, 'The Work of Art in the Age of Mechanical Reproduction', and 'Some Motifs in Baudelaire', in *Illuminations*, H. Arendt, ed., Schocken, New York, 1968.

• John Berger and Jean Mohr, *A Fortunate Man*, Allen Lane, The Penguin Press, Harmondsworth, 1968.

• John Berger, 'Photography and Memory', *New Society*, vol.45, 17 August, 1978.

• John Berger and Jean Mohr, 'Stories' and 'Appearances', in Berger and Mohr, *Another Way of Telling*, Writers and Readers, London, 1982.

• Peter Berger, *The Homeless Mind*, Penguin, Harmondsworth, 1974 (see ch.3 'The Pluralisation of the Lifeworld').

• Anthony Giddens, *The Consequences of Modernity*, Polity, Oxford, 1990.

• Anthony Giddens, *Modernity and Self-Identity*, Polity, Oxford, 1991.

• John Roberts, 'John Berger and Jean Mohr: The Return to Communality' in his *The Art of Interruption: Realism, Photography and the Everyday*, Manchester University Press, Manchester, 1997.

• Georg Simmel, 'The Metropolis and Mental Life', in D. Levine, ed., *Georg Simmel on Sociability and Social Forms* (trans. E. Shils), Chicago/London, 1971.
• Georg Simmel, *The Philosophy of Money* (trans, T. Bottomore and D. Frisby), Routledge, London/New York, 1990 (second edition).
• John Tagg, 'Totalled Machines: Criticism, Photography and Technological Change', in his *Grounds of Dispute Art History, Cultural Politics and the Discursive Field*, Macmillan, 1992.

2

# Context as a Determinant of Photographic Meaning

John A. Walker

Introduction by
**John A. Walker**

My interest in photographs is part of a general fascination with pictures of all kinds. The 1980 article was prompted by a desire to clarify in my own mind the role that context plays in modulating the meanings of photographs. Shortly before, I had written two articles about photographs: first, a structuralist-type analysis of a 1930s' documentary photo by Margaret Bourke-White; second, an iconographic analysis and ideological critique of a photo used as part of an advertising campaign for Benson and Hedges cigarettes.[1] The 1980 article thus marked a logical extension in my thinking from the internal, form and content of photos to their external, social and physical contexts.

During the 1970s and 1980s I was employed as a part-time lecturer in two art colleges; therefore one could say that my article was literally a contribution to the 'Contextual Studies' art and design students were expected to take. I found it disturbing that so many students subscribed to the ideology of individualism—cited in the article—that prompted views of this kind: 'Individuals are unique therefore everyone is different, therefore everyone interprets images differently, therefore one cannot speak about *the* meaning of an image; there are as many meanings as there are human beings'. Taken to an extreme, this argument seemed to imply that every photo had, potentially, billions of meanings. But if an image had so many meanings, did this not render it meaningless? The argument denied the fact that consensuses are reached regarding the denotation and implied/intended meanings of images, that humans are social beings who are, in many respects, similar to one another and who share many experiences. It also undermined the educational process by making the lecturer's efforts to discuss photography and meaning vacuous.

Naturally I was reluctant to agree with the students but they did have a point: photographs do prompt a variety of interpretations, different people do respond differently to the same stimulus. Clearly, the theoretical problem was, on the one hand, to acknowledge the range of responses photos generate and, on the other hand, to find logical explanations for those variations.

If one considers simple drawings found in psychology of perception textbooks—the duck/rabbit figure, for example—it is clear that some images are ambiguous (in this case the same signifier has two signifieds: duck and rabbit. The viewer oscillates back and forth between the two. Recognition depends, of course, on the viewer already being familiar with the two animals). Most photographs are more complex than the duck/rabbit figure; consequently they lend themselves to multiple interpretations but, it seems to me, the number of meanings derived will not be enormous.

Ambiguity and complexity of the image itself was one reason for variations of interpretation. Another was the variety of contexts in which photographs are encountered. One of those contexts I described as 'mental'. (In effect I was trying to take into account the variability of viewers.) After the article was published, I became aware of an expanding branch of criticism and history-writing called 'reception aesthetics/history/theory' specifically concerned with 'mental context', with the impact works of art make upon views, and with the way texts, images and objects are differentially 'read', interpreted, evaluated, used and 'consumed'.[2] Hence this kind of analysis marked a shift of emphasis away from cultural production to cultural consumption, from 'authors' to 'readers'. (Roland Barthes's influential 1968 essay 'The Death of the Author' had appeared in an English translation in 1977. The author's 'death' supposedly heralded 'the birth of the reader'.) Reception *theory* tends to concern itself with the ideal reader implied by a text or work of art, while reception *history* tends to be concerned with actual readers and readings that have taken place over time.

We cannot directly share the mental experiences of others; therefore gaining insight into their responses to images is a problem. Only through discussion with others can we learn about their thoughts and feelings regarding pictures. The analyst does have privileged, intimate access to at least one response—his or her own. Readers of this book will no doubt recall a famous example of a major theorist who reflected in print upon the emotional impact of a family photograph: Barthes writing about a photo of his mother (recently deceased) as a child, which, paradoxically, was not reproduced in Barthes's book.[3] While Barthes's response to the family photo was a personal one, we have surely all experienced similar reactions to photos of loved ones.

In the light of the above I would now categorise part of my 'context' article as a contribution to reception studies. Re-reading it today, I feel that its arguments and conclusions are still sound. The photographs used to illustrate the article may require a word of explanation. Faced by the difficulty of finding photos showing the same image in a range of contexts, I decided to use some photographs by the British painter Derek Boshier, photos selected from an artist's book that showed the same sculpture in sixteen, very different, settings.

Since 1980 there has been a greater awareness of context in various quarters. For example, architects now speak of 'contextual architecture', that is, new architecture that seeks to take the existing urban environment into account. Fine artists and theorists have also become more conscious of the display context: witness the symposium 'Space Invaders? Issues of Presentation, Context and Meaning in Contemporary Art' held at the University of Southampton in October 1992.[4] In terms of subsequent writings on photography itself, those by Allan Sekula in particular have shown an acute awareness of the ways the meanings of photographs are governed by the contexts of encounter and the social class of the viewers.[5]

When the editor of this anthology invited me to write this introduction to my article, she was in effect asking me to re-contextualise it. In reflecting on the changes that have taken place between then and now, I note with regret the demise of *Camerawork* magazine itself and the death of that vibrant being Jo Spence, whose memorable photographs I discussed in 1980.

---

## Context as a Determinant of Photographic Meaning

**John A. Walker** (b. Grimsby, 1938) was trained as a painter in the late 1950s and has worked as an art critic and art history lecturer in several art schools and is now a Reader in Art and Design History at Middlesex University. He has published many articles and books on contemporary art, design and mass culture. He is the author of: *John Latham—the Incidental Person—His Art and Ideas* (1995) and *Introduction to Visual Culture Studies* (forthcoming).

Consider a wedding photograph, and then the variety of contexts in which such an image could be encountered: in a family album; framed on the mantelpiece of a living room; in the window of a local commercial photographer's shop; in a local newspaper; in a national newspaper; in a fashion magazine; in a women's journal; in an advertisement on a street hoarding; in an art gallery; in a social history museum; in a television series on photography; inside another photograph... With each shift of location the photograph is *recontextualised* and as the context changes so does the meaning. For example, in the family album the wedding photograph is a treasured memento of a particular social ritual, whereas in the local photographer's shop window the 'same' picture is the token of a type, that is, one which represents the whole genre of wedding photographs which the commercial photographer is capable of producing. In the shop window the formal and technical

2.1

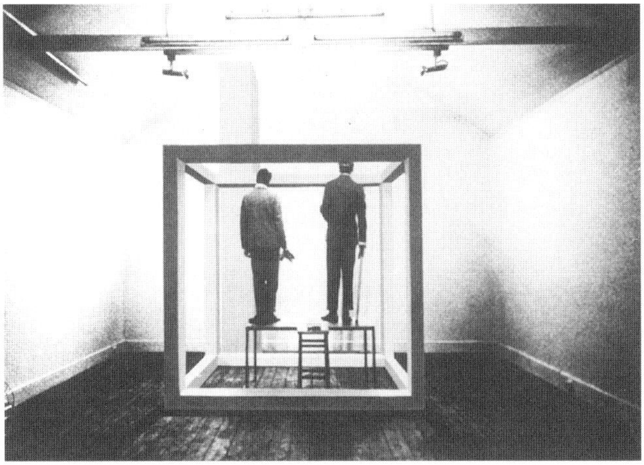

2.2

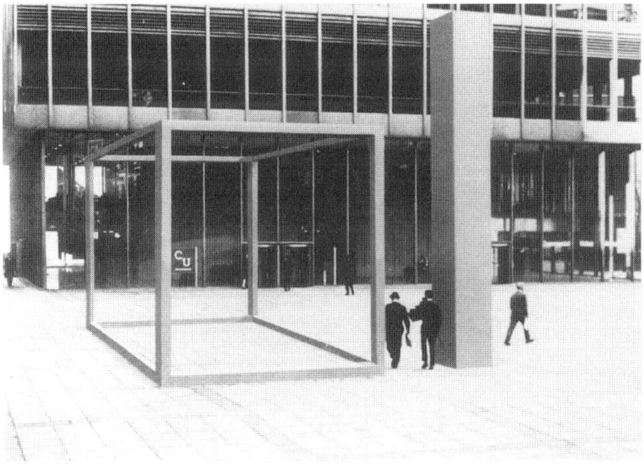

2.3

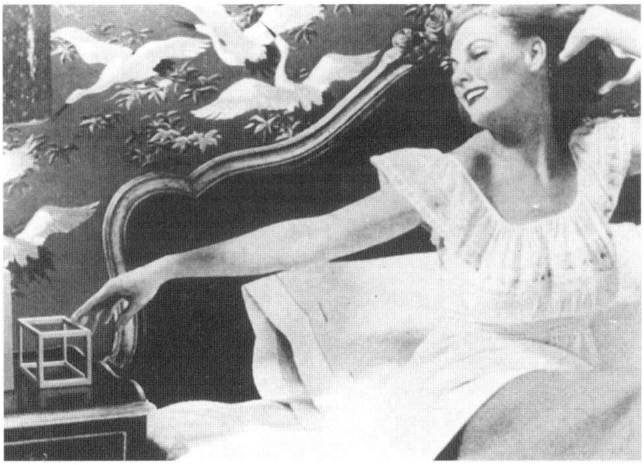

Photographs from Derek Boshier's artist-book *16 Situations* (London, Idea Books, 1971). A contructivist-type sculpture is placed in various situations

qualities of the photograph are foregrounded in a way they are not in the family album because their purpose is to serve as exemplars of the photographer's aesthetic sensibility and technical competence.

Most critical analyses of photographs concentrate on their *immanent* structure, that is, their internal relations (part to part, parts to whole within the framing edge). The frame of the photograph encloses a space, a world, which we can enter (in our imaginations). This space appears self-contained and therefore it is natural for us mentally to place in brackets the context in which the photograph is viewed, even though that context is one important determinant of photographic meaning. Context continues to influence our perception because, although our attention is primarily directed towards the image, we always retain a subsidiary awareness of its/our environment. No figure can be perceived except in relation to a ground.

When the word 'context' is used, it should really be qualified in order to make it clear which of the several different types of possible context is being referred to. For instance, contexts can be architectural, media, mental, socio-historical, etc. Recontextualisation does not generally produce a radical transformation of the photographic denotation (its depicted content): a car in a photograph does not become a monkey's head simply because the photograph is moved from a private house to a public gallery. (However, if the shift involved a photo-montage transposition such an alteration of meaning could be brought about.) In the majority of cases, the result of a context shift is a change of emphasis in the photograph's depicted content: different parts or characteristics of the image appear important in different display contexts. Alternatively, its whole meaning is given a new significance, is enhanced or modified. Indeed when a photograph—considered as a single unit of meaning—enters into a montage relationship with either a caption, text, another picture, or a particularly potent display context, then a 'third-effect' meaning can be generated from that juxtaposition which was not inherent in either of the terms seen in isolation. For example, if a photograph of commuters crowding into an underground station entrance is placed next to a photograph of sheep crowding into a fold, the third-effect implication is plain: 'these commuters are sheep-like in their behaviour.' And this pictorial insult to commuters would gain in intensity if it were to be displayed inside a tube station.

In the distant past, paintings and sculptures were generally produced for specific locations and were designed as integral parts of architectural structures. As panel paintings in oils supplanted mural paintings in fresco and tempera, and as the capitalist market/gallery system replaced the old patron/artist relationship, the mobility of artworks increased until they lost all connection with specific places. Their geographic dispersal and mobility was extended by the development of various kinds of reproductive processes, culminating in the invention of photography. The mechanical reproducibility of photographs means that the same image can appear in thousands of settings simultaneously and in a variety of sizes and media. News photographs can now be transmitted by wire with extreme rapidity from country to country, that is, from one cultural context to another. The effect of this phenomenal mobility of the image has been, no doubt, to lessen the importance of architectural or physical display context. Photographs reproduced in a magazine can be studied at home, in a library, on a train, in an aircraft, etc. In this instance, the media context (newspapers, books, magazines) tends to replace architectural setting as a determinant of meaning.[6]

To illustrate the influence media context can have upon the way a photograph is read, consider the difference between encountering a photograph surrounded by text on the front page of a newspaper and encountering that same photograph in the form of a glossy print surrounded by a wide border of white paper in the pages of a 'serious' art photography journal. In the first case we are encouraged to accept the photograph as documentary evidence contributing to a news story; in the second case we are encouraged to regard the photograph as a precious object to be admired for its aesthetic and technical qualities.

### Circulation/Currency

As we all know, a photograph captures the visual appearance of a particular place at a specific moment. Apparently, therefore, its meaning is determined by its spatio-temporal point of origin. Subsequently the photograph is viewed in other places at other times, that is, in different socio-historical conjunctures. Consideration of a photograph's meaning generally involves a 'blacking-out' of the contemporary situation (as in a lecture) in order to focus attention on the image and to recover (by means of historical research) the original social circumstances in which the photograph was taken. Unfortunately, as a result, a photograph's meaning tends to be regarded as eternally fixed. Obviously, meaning is crucially influenced by moment of production, but it is also subject to changes as the photograph enters into relationships with new circumstances and publics. In other words, there is a need to examine the *life* of an image as well as its birth, to consider its *circulation*, its *currency*, as it moves through time and space from context to context, as it is used by various individuals and groups for different purposes until eventually it is destroyed or lies forgotten in an archive. The terms 'circulation' and 'currency' are borrowed from John Tagg who derived them via an analogy with money.[7] By 'circulation' is meant the distribution/transmission of an image through the communication networks of the world and its movement through various social strata and institutions. While an image circulates it is current—it has a meaning, a use, a value for a particular community. Even after it has been 'withdrawn from circulation' it may enjoy an 'after-life' by being re-used from time to time in, say, exhibitions and history books.

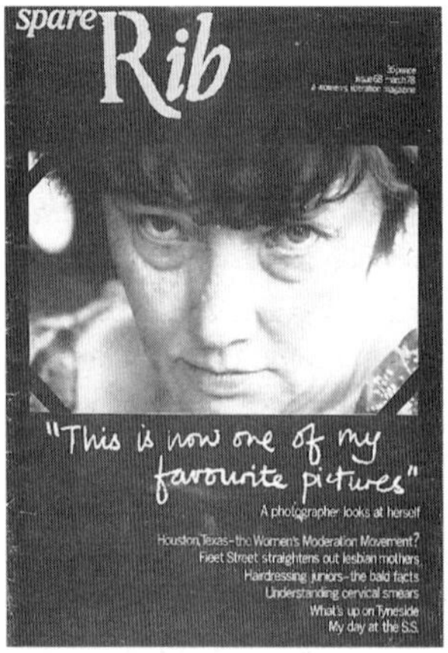


2.4 *Spare Rib* cover, March 1978. Photograph: Terry Dennett

**Jo Spence**

*Beyond the Family Album, Private Images, Public Conventions*, a series of photographs of Jo Spence by Terry Dennett and others from the age of eight-and-a-half months to her forties, was displayed recently in the Feminism and Photography section of the *Three Perspectives On Photography* exhibition at the Hayward Gallery (1979). I had previously encountered some of these images in two different contexts: the entrance hall of a public library in Finsbury and as a cover/feature article in *Spare Rib* which I purchased from a high street newsagent's shop. Spence's photographs explicitly challenge context conventions by transposing images which are normally found only in family albums (the private realm) into the public sphere. As her title makes clear, the images may be private and personal but the conventions at work are public and social. The frankness of the exposure, combined with the feminist polemic and the transition from private to public, endows the series with considerable stimmung or shock value. Especially striking was the conjunction of the black-and-white *Spare Rib* cover photograph—Spence at her plainest and with a dour expression—with all the other women's magazines in the newsagent's racks with their glamorous, smiling, full-colour, synthetic model girls or optimistic housewives. In this context the feminist aspect of the critique really told, it seemed to me (figure 2.4).

Perhaps the most striking images of the series were two showing Spence reclining nude as a baby and as a mature woman (figure 2.5). This juxtaposition was extracted from the set as a whole by the art press (they were reproduced on the art page of a London evening newspaper and in *Art & Artists*). Wrenched from their context the images acquired a sensationalist, voyeuristic and prurient gloss.

By including conventionally unflattering photographs of herself in the family album, Spence undermined the norms of perception induced by such albums. 'Putting these photographs in my album', Spence remarks, 'has forced my family to see me in a new way'.[8]

In the Hayward Gallery Spence displayed her private images in conjunction with a series of public images (advertisements) featuring secretaries (Spence earned her living as a secretary) which were addressed to specific audiences (e.g. employers, typists as consumers). This device enabled her to make visible the stereotyping of women taking place within various genres of photography, and in particular the way in which the public/private division results in representations of women according to a work/leisure division. She also featured examples of private images used by advertisers when addressing defined, limited, audiences of professionals—for example, photographs of tired, ill, and anxious people appearing in drug adverts addressed to doctors.[9]

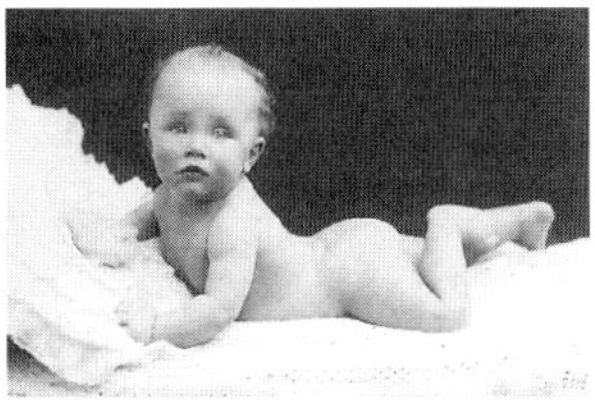

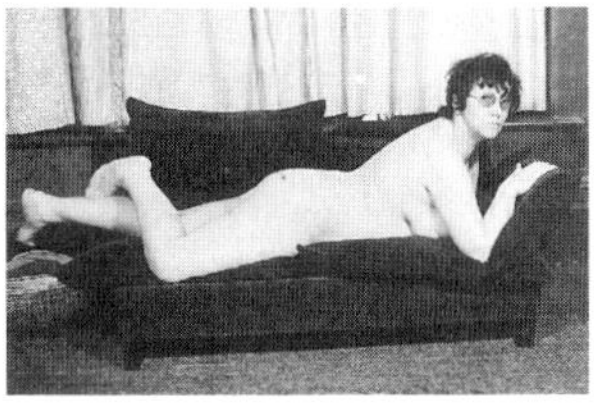

2.5 Jo Spence, 'The Family Album 1939 to 1979', from *Beyond the Family Album* exhibition, Hayward Gallery, 1979. Top picture: High Street photographer, Woodford; bottom picture: Terry Dennett

Each of the three contexts in which I encountered the images of Spence produced a different emphasis in their reading: in the magazine it was the feminist dimension which was highlighted; in the public library it was the private/public, personal/social contrast; in the Hayward, amongst other socialist and feminist photographic displays, the critical work upon photography itself was foregrounded. It is somewhat difficult to isolate the precise influence of display context because the context is, of course, only one factor amongst many. Furthermore, the difficulty is compounded in Spence's case because her work is self-reflexive; it is specifically about, and involves manipulations of, changes of context.

It is clear from the above that Spence's exhibit had a didactic aim; the Hayward Gallery became a learning centre. But before we can judge the efficacy of Spence's exhibit we need to know more about the motivations of those who visit art galleries. Do people go to be educated or entertained? Are they receptive to this kind of exposition or would they prefer it in book form? Also, we need to undertake research to discover whether in fact they learn anything from such shows.[10]

If display context can influence the meaning of a photograph, the photograph can influence the meaning of the context. This reasoning lay behind John X. Berger's comment at a Hayward Gallery evening discussion that socialist and feminist photography 'had radicalised the gallery space'. But the influence is two-way: it could also be argued that the gallery—a High Art cultural institution serving the interests of the bourgeoisie—had de-radicalised radical photography! This issue cannot be settled in the abstract: a survey of visitors would help to establish a typology of responses. With reference to the Agit-Prop photo-montage panels by the Hackney Flashers, it is fairly evident that displaying this work in the Hayward was comparable to exhibiting a piece of engineering equipment in the Science Museum: it is displayed as an example, as a working model, of what happens outside the museum.

## Mental Context or Set

So far I have focused principally upon the display and media contexts in which photographs appear, but photographs only exist as meaningful representations *for* someone; the artefact is only *part* of the work of art, hence we must also take into account what Ernst Gombrich calls 'the beholder's share'.[11] A viewer approaches an image not with a blank mind but with a mind already primed with memories, knowledge, prejudices; there is a *mental* set or context to be taken into account. For example, in John Berger and Jean Mohr's book *A Seventh Man*, a photograph of a young boy is carried by a migrant worker far from home to remind him of his family. Berger remarks: 'Seen in the darkroom when making the print, or seen in this book when reading it, the image conjures up the vivid presence of an unknown boy. To his father it would define the boy's absence'.[12] That is, people have different relations to the same image according to the different places they occupy in society, determined by such factors as gender, race, nationality, class, age, education, kinship, etc.

Another example: the reaction to Peter Marlow's photograph of a National Front steward (see *Camerawork*, no.8, p.2) is likely to be very different according to whether the viewer is a member of the Front or a member of the Anti-Nazi League; and different again if the viewer is an immigrant who has been abused or assaulted by racists. It has often been pointed out that the Front are photogenic, as were the German Nazis before them. Their facial expressions, body language and clothing connote a set of values: toughness, masculine virility, aggression, latent power—which are perceived by the Left as negative values but which may appear positive to Front members. It may, therefore, be politically more valuable for the Left photographer to stress the weak and pathetic aspects of the racists rather than to celebrate their toughness.

Analysis of people's experiences of images is, of course, much more difficult than analysing photographs (the analyst is in fact reflecting upon his or her own experience of the image); after all, what does go on inside other people's heads? There is a danger here of lapsing into an ideology of individualism: 'everyone is different, a unique individual, therefore every person's response to an image is different and exclusive to them'. Such a conclusion overlooks what millions of individuals have in common (e.g. a language), how much experience is shared, especially the fact that individuals belong to social groupings—above all social classes—within a particular social formation and therefore it is possible to describe responses to images which are similar for large numbers of the populace. The mass media would simply find communication impossible if there were not common desires, experiences and values to appeal to and to work upon. Pictorial stereotypes do not merely exist externally in the world of the mass media, they inhabit us.

It is, however, problematic to judge the impact of a single image when we are exposed to a veritable floodtide of visual imagery daily, in addition to all the other kinds of experience which form us ideologically. To many people it seems that imagery is having no effect at all. But it does serve to affirm and reinforce the existing dominant conceptions of human society so that they appear 'natural'. Only when the social context changes dramatically (as in a revolution) is the oppressive character of pictorial and sculptural representations, serving the ruling elite, revealed; in such moments the icons of power are smashed by the people. For example, in Paris during the 1871 Commune, the Vendôme column, symbol of Napoleonic imperialism, was destroyed by the Communards. To cite a contemporary example: ever since the advent of the women's movement we have seen a guerrilla campaign of defacements, slogans and stickers waged against sexist advertising. This example reminds us that although our freedom to decode or read images is highly restricted—the structure of the 'text' structures the way we experience it—we can still make an oppositional response (this has been called 'aberrant decoding' or 'oppositional consumption').[13] In 1933 a statue commemorating Poland's fallen war heroes was unveiled in Warsaw; it represented a gladiator struck to death in the arena raising himself on his elbow to draw his last breath. The populace of Warsaw understood its *official* meaning perfectly well but they proposed an *unofficial* meaning by declaring that it represented the Polish people expiring under the burden of taxation!

Context is a troublesome determinant of meaning for artists because so often it lies outside their control. Left-wing theatre, film and community photography groups are usually keen to exercise control in this area in order to ensure the most favourable and appropriate conditions for the reception of their work. They are also concerned with mental context in the sense that their work is generally produced with the needs of specific audiences in mind or is adapted to suit local circumstances. Recent film theory has addressed itself to problems of the subject's relationship to the film text and also the more general relationship between film and audience.[14] This appears to be one area in which practice is further advanced than theory.

## Reference Notes

**1** The articles in question were: 'Reflections on a Photograph by Margaret Bourke-White' in *Creative Camera*, no.167, May 1978, pp.148-9, and 'All that Glitters...' in *Camerawork*, no.15, Sept 1979, pp.4-5. In the first article I did pay some attention to journalistic layout context by commenting on the publication of Bourke-White's photo in a *Life* magazine article and by reproducing the double-page spread in which the photo appeared.

**2** Reception studies have been particularly associated with German literary criticism since the mid-1960s, that is, the work of scholars such as Hans Jauss and Wolfgang Iser. See P. Hohendahl, 'Introduction to Reception Aesthetics in New Germany', *Critique*, no.10, Winter 1977, pp.29-63; H. Jauss, *Toward an Aesthetic of Reception*, University of Minnesota Press, Minneapolis, 1982; R. Holub, *Reception Theory: A Critical Introduction*, Methuen, London, 1984. There are, however, equivalent studies in the field of visual culture. See, for example, my article: 'Pop Art: Differential Responses and Changing Perceptions', in *AND: Journal of Art and Art Education*, no.26, 1991, pp.9-16, and *Over Here*, vol.11, no.2, Winter 1991, pp.49-62.

**3** Roland Barthes, *Camera Lucida*, Jonathan Cape, London, 1982.

**4** A publication based on the symposium was issued later: Nicholas de Ville and Stephen Foster, eds, *Space Invaders: Issues of Presentation, Context and Meaning in Contemporary Art,* John Hansard Gallery, Southampton, 1993.

**5** Allan Sekula's *Photography Against the Grain*, Press of the Nova Scotia College of Art and Design, Halifax, Nova Scotia, 1984. In his article 'Reading an Archive: Photography between Labour and Capital', in *Photography Politics: Two*, eds, P. Holland, J. Spence and S. Watney, Comedia, London, 1986, pp.153-61, Sekula remarks: 'it is clear that photographic meaning depends largely on context'.

**6** Andy Warhol's silk-screen paintings are exemplary in the way they insist upon the reproducibility of images in the age of mechanical reproduction.

**7** See John Tagg, 'The Currency of the Photograph', in *Screen Education*, no.28, Autumn 1978, pp.45-67.

**8** Jo Spence, 'Facing up to Myself', in *Spare Rib*, no.68, March 1978, pp.6-9, plus front cover.

**9** See *Three Perspectives on Photography: Recent British Photography*, Hayward Gallery/Arts Council Catalogue, 1979, pp.60-3.

**10** Many exhibitions are mounted with an educational aim in mind; for example, the mammoth *Dada & Surrealism Reviewed* show at the Hayward Gallery in 1978 was organised on this basis. However, a sociological study of this exhibition—by Christopher Wilson, *Dada & Surrealism Reviewed: Audience to Audience*, Arts Council, London, 1978—revealed that despite the fact that most people attended the show to learn about Dada and Surrealism they learnt very little.

**11** E.H. Gombrich, 'Part Three: The Beholder's Share', in *Art and Illusion: A Study in the Psychology of Pictorial Representation*, Phaidon Press,

London, 1960, pp.181-287.

**12** John Berger and Jean Mohr, *A Seventh Man*, Penguin Books, Harmondsworth, 1975, p.17.

**13** See Stuart Hall, 'Encoding/Decoding' in *Culture, Media Language*, ed., S.Hall, D. Hobson, P. Willis, Hutchinson, London, 1980.

**14** For a summary of this area see Ros Coward and John Ellis, *Language and Materialism: Developments in Semiology and the Theory of the Subject*, Routledge & Kegan Paul, 1977. See also M. McLoone, 'Report of BFI Summer School 1978', *Screen Education*, no.28, Autumn 1979, pp.86-8.



**Further Reading**


- Richard Bolton, 'In the American East: Avedon Incorporated', in R. Bolton, ed., *The Contest of Meaning*, MIT Press, Cambridge MA, 1989.
- Pierre Bourdieu, 'The Production of Belief: Contribution to an Economy of Symbolic Goods', *Media, Culture, Society*, vol.2, no.3. Reprinted in R. Collins, J. Curran, N. Garnham et al., eds, *Media, Culture Society: A Critical Reader*, Sage, London, 1986.
- Stuart Hall, 'Encoding/Decoding', in *Culture, Media, Language: Working Papers in Cultural Studies 1972-79*, eds, S. Hall, D. Hobson, A. Lowe, P. Willis, Hutchinson, London, 1980.
- Roger Hull, 'Emplacement, Displacement, and the Fate of Photographs', in *Multiple Views: Logan Grant Essays on Photography, 1983-89*, Daniel P. Younger, ed., University of New Mexico Press, Albuquerque, 1991.
- Rosalind Krauss, 'Photography's Discursive Spaces', in R. Bolton, ed., *The Contest of Meaning*, op.cit.
- Martha Rosler, 'In, Around, and Afterthoughts (on Documentary Photography)', in R. Bolton, ed., *The Contest of Meaning*, op.cit.
- Allan Sekula, 'The Instrumental Image; Steichen At War', in his *Photography Against the Grain: Essays and Photoworks 1973-1983*, Novia Scotia Press, Halifax, 1984.
- Allan Sekula, 'Reading An Archive: Photography Between Capital and Labour', in *Photography/Politics: Two*, eds P. Holland, J. Spence, S. Watney, Comedia, London, 1986.
- Susan R. Suleiman, 'Introduction: Varieties of Audience-Orientated Criticism', in *The Reader in the Text*, eds Susan Suleiman and D. Crosman, Princeton University Press, New Haven, 1980.

3

# The World of Photography or Photography of the World?

## John Tagg

Introduction by
**John Tagg**

It is almost twenty years since I have seen this essay, in thrall as it is to Benjamin and Barthes; twenty years, and that was in another country. Even this much-reduced and poorly legible Xerox, sent by the editor, is, however, enough to remind me of the feel of the big pages of the original and the stiff, shiny paper with its very black ink. What it is harder to recover is the feel of the arguments and antagonisms that animated its prose and, indeed, the sense of the community of discourse to which it once belonged in the mid-1970s in London. It is easy to assume the continuity of one's life and therefore the continuity of one's project. But if—as, in deference to Althusser, I was wont to tell my students at the time the essay was written—'You are no more than a flickering across the face of a field of institutions', then it is questionable that my project has been a unity and that it has been my own. And if this essay is not mine, then I may not be the best one to introduce it.

The essay was written, originally, as a book review for a fortnightly paper of comment published by the Communist Party of Great Britain. Since it was treated with the editorial respect democratic centralism always accorded individual comrades, I then offered it to Jo Spence, for it was the time when *Camerawork* was her new and energetic project. This much alone ought to be enough to conjure up the remoteness of its moment: a time before the appalling watershed of 1979; a time, if you can recall it, when *Ten.8* was also to begin publishing in a tabloid newspaper format, but as an avowed defender of fine art photography against the onslaught of Jo and Terry's sinister, black-covered magazine.

I had met Jo Spence after a talk she gave at the Polytechnic of Central London, some years before she became a student there, but in that period when, under Victor Burgin's influence, PCL was doing something decidedly different in photographic education. I had an office in a shop-front, round the corner from Riding House Street, and the Arts Council were paying me—ah, yes, indeed an alien time—to watch the passing pedestrians through the Venetian blind and mull over the arguments that became 'The Currency of the Photograph' and 'Power and Photography'. Later—in 1978 and 1980—these essays were to be published in

*Screen Education*, whose editorial base was only ten minutes walk away across Soho. But in 1976, *Screen Education* was still playing second fiddle to the high theory power-house of *Screen*, though not for long. It was a time, then, when new theoretical resources made possible a rethinking of the relations of power and representation that transformed conceptions of 'cultural politics'. It was a time when, in some special places, the hierarchical distinction of critics and practitioners began to break down. It was a time when photography as a 'space of intervention' seemed to offer room for manoeuvre denied to those cultural practices more deeply mired in the graveyard of the canon.

I say all this not for nostalgia, not to wander off into maudlin memoirs of a time when we were all Marxists in our youth, and certainly not because, by comparison, I now find myself 'demoralised', as one crude recent commentary has claimed to know. It is not a matter of the drift of memory in flight from the present. It is a matter of recalling that if we were 'a community of discourse' and if we were able to think at all, outside the smug and shop-soiled clichés of the southern English art world, then it was because a network of relationships, institutions, collectives, agencies, spaces of practice, conversations and routeways of communication was coming into existence—and certainly not only in London—that was to transform the discursive field of British photography. The emergence of this complex network of discursive spaces was the emergence of theory. And—for those who think that 'theory' is something that goes on in books or in your head—what, I might ask, could be more 'material' than that?

What we need, then, is not more forgetting, but more of the awkward work of counter-memory. Not as the fodder for more promotional shows and publications, for 'bigger pictures' that prepare the career tracks and the stars, the new British this and the new British that. Not as the material of textbooks that have turned the counter-courses of the 1970s into the examination syllabi of the 1990s. But as a refusal of forgetting: as a work of intransigence, with all the urgency and disrespect and bloody-mindedness that come from the need to find a space to speak that cannot be ruled out. Why else bother about all this out-dated stuff?

# The World of Photography or Photography of the World?

**John Tagg** is Professor of Art History at Binghamton University, New York. He is the author of *The Burden of Representation: Essays on Photographies and Histories* (1988) and the editor of *The Cultural Politics of 'Postmodernism'* (1989). He is working on a book entitled *The Disciplinary Frame: Picturing, Power, History and Art.*

The *Photography Yearbook* continues to be like all the magazines you ever found in dentists' waiting rooms.[1] Turning its pages is like flicking through a colour supplement denuded of text: advertisement merges with feature photo, documentary image with fashion pic. The captions at the back of the book read like the hackwork of the ill-named popular press: 'Excuse me, this is where I get off', as a cyclist falls headlong into a river; 'It's not all make-believe in Hollywood', as two Los Angeles policemen from the Special Weapons and Tactics Section charge from a doorway, in battle-dress, wearing gas masks and clenching automatic weapons.

Image follows image so that their individual sense is lost. What you see is a medley: the whole book is a cinematic montage. A protector on a National Abortion Campaign rally follows a nude captioned 'Love' from an 'Essay on Women'. A blown-up Saracen in an Irish country lane, lying on its side like a dead beast, fades into a grainy, mood-filled vision of the 'timeless' Spanish landscape. German Chancellor Schmidt faces a Maka Indian from Paraguay. Prince Philip finds it thirsty work at the National Carriage Driving Championships and Cuban workers sweat in the fields of a sugar cane plantation. The famous rub shoulders with the unknown in the democracy of the page. Each plate has equal standing. Meaning cancels out meaning.

Yet, as part of the very same process, a further meaning arises which embraces all the images. It is the editor's belief that, merely by avoiding the pairing of images by different photographers, one can escape the suggestion of meanings different from or additional to those intended by the individual photographers concerned. Such a view, however, is not just naive. It conceals the fact that what happens to the images is more significant than their individual distortion. The equal weighting given to them, despite great differences in subject matter, purpose and method, suggests that while, on the one hand, each image possesses a singular value which cannot be compared, on the other hand, taken together, the images are in some way equivalent. The exact nature of this equivalence is important to specify for it is through it that the individual photographs become vehicles for more general and extensive themes.

It is the concealed ability to make the particular stand for the general which gives photography its special ideological power. Such power is exercised as well in single images as in combinations of them—though here we are dealing mainly with the latter—and it trades on photography's widely accepted authority as a recorder of the concrete and the real. Through it a dialectical process which binds a class and its members is usurped by an unmediated conjunction of individual and universal. In the representation of people, for example, photography has the potential to picture specific individuals, in all their particularity, as both composing and representing the social class or classes within which their individuality is realised. Yet, portrait photography has almost invariably given us unique, even if anonymous, individuals who by intention or by the unprompted effect of image on image, come to stand for universal categories: the thinker, the toiler, the mother, the lover, the mourner, the clown, the sufferer. The camera lens has given us God's eye-view of the human condition. Woman is woman eternal. Man is born, learns, works, plays, laughs and cries, and dies. Everywhere the same; all over the world.

'The toil of life from youth with its eagerness to the tranquility of old age never ceases to intrigue,' writes Eric Cookson, a magistrate, property developer and Lloyds underwriter, who has included photographs of a shepherd boy in Egypt and a young scholar from the independent school Eric owns in England. The processes of life—most remarkably those of labour—are thus bereaved of their reality, divorced from the conditions in which they occur, and abstracted to the point where they hardly retain any meaning. Even a portfolio of photographs from Turkey, which are an intense and unsentimentalised image of ritual circumcision 'at an age when the boy will never forget it', comes to seem no more than a rendering of the ancient myth of the 'Seven Ages of Man'.

Woman does not seem to undergo this evolution. She inhabits a pre-cultural plane. Pictured with a rose, a leafing tree, a ploughed field, or even the man-made props of modern life, she offers her nakedness as evidence of an unaffected, unchanging nature. How soon in the history of photography women are placed in this passive and subservient relation to the camera. Men may employ the full rhetoric of costume, dressing up for the camera in a celebration of their differences. Women at least, until the age when they can be pictured with babies—are stripped and become all the same. The thin veils of artifice and so-called creative camerawork hide nothing.

This *Yearbook* contains the usual quota of sexist images, in inverse proportion to the quota of women photographers. Towards the end of the book is a single photograph which pictures this very relation of women to the camera with pathetic, unconscious clarity. It is depressing to note that it comes from Poland. A naked woman crouches on the ground—out in the country, somewhere

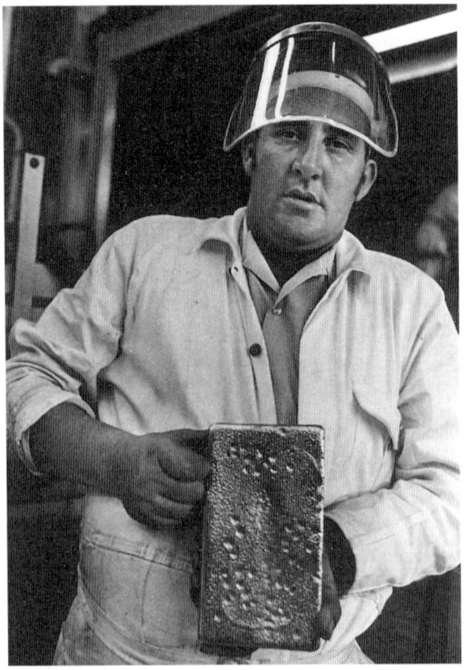

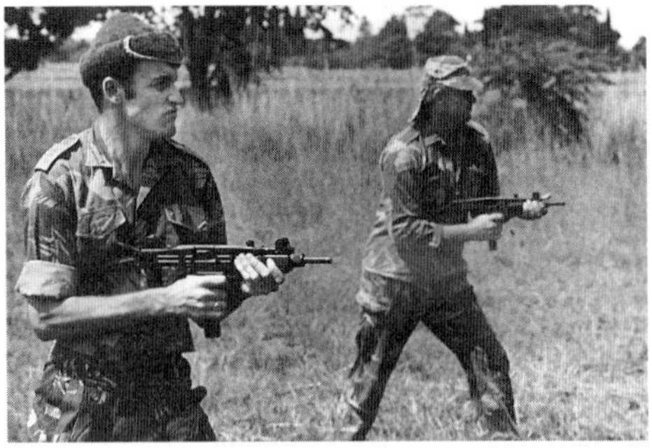

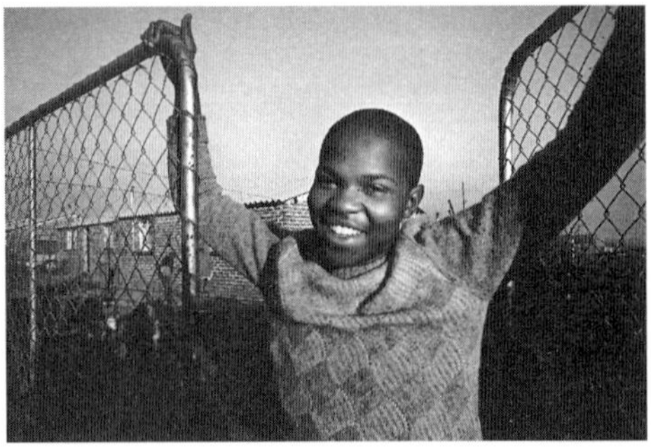

3.1-3.3
*Figures 135 to 137.* Struan Robertson (South Africa). Originally reproduced in the *Photography Yearbook 1977* as a double-page spread

on the edge of a forest. We see her from behind as she goes on all fours; beyond her buttocks and upraised head, another five male photographers are eagerly taking her. She is submissive and vulnerable; enticing and seemingly willing; animal-like, one might say, if the copulating giant tortoises in the photograph by Heather Angel did not show so much more dignity in their sexual fulfilment than these protagonists. She falls before the camera but nothing passes between them. The exposure is filled with the emptiness of a faked climax.

Here, a translation of the concrete into the universal is not achieved: the situation reveals too much of the moment to take on the appearance of a timeless confrontation. That such a translation be accomplished is, however, essential to the success of a photograph in realising its ideological purpose. I shall return to this point but let us, for the moment, pursue the theme into a complementary area: the way the *Photography Yearbook* presents the contributing photographers themselves.

The main section of the *Photography Yearbook* is called 'International Photograph'. Here, the works of photographers from twenty-six nations appear entirely intermixed, with only the names to identify them. The general method of presentation is familiar from the earliest editions of the *Yearbook* and the specific format has remained unchanged for nine years. Details of nationalities, subjects and the very different purposes for which the photographs were produced—advertising, newspapers, competitions, freelance commissions, industrial uses, private or sponsored research, leisure—appear separately, in small print at the back of the book.

The categories of photographic production endorsed by the *Photography Yearbook* also remain fairly constant from year to year: sports photography, natural history photography, portraits, ethnography, exotica, erotica, landscape, fashion, photojournalism and the various modes of 'art photography', especially Surrealism. They take on the appearance of given categories through which the photographer, of whatever nation, class or creed, must seek expression. There is only one transcendent criterion and that is technique, which is raised by the *Yearbook* to the level of a fetish.

The implications of this way of presenting the work are that the problems confronting photographers are the same the world over but achieve their solution in the individual photographer's personality. Just as the subject appears to take on a significance that is, at once, universal and particular—just as the sitter can present, at one and the same time, the face of humanity and the face of a unique individual—so the great family of international photographers, whose kinship is based on expertise, is made up of unique individuals.

Attempts by community photographers to wrest the camera from these experts and not only put it at the service of ordinary people, but actually place it in their hands, are misconceived, editor John Sanders writes:

> There is an aphorism that when everybody is somebody, nobody is anybody, and this may be the fatal flaw in a philosophy that places such emphasis on the promotion of egalitarianism that it forgets the uniqueness of individuals....Memorable photographs by talented photographers usually happen because the person who made them is fully aware of his or her own individuality. (Editor's Introduction, p.3)

As we observed earlier in relation to subject-matter, anything intervening between the unique and the universal is excluded. Class, nationality, tradition do not matter. And now, the knotted cords of ideology are given one more twist. The editor continues:

> The fact that such photographs are still being taken in parts of the world where individuality is not exactly encouraged, is a heartening reminder that artists usually manage to have the last laugh over their patrons, if not always in their own lifetimes. (Editor's Introduction, p.3)

People are people, the world over. Photographers are photographers, the world over. It may not be given to anyone to take a good photograph: to do so requires talent. But talent is talent, across the world.

It is no accident that these are familiar claims. It is absolutely necessary for bourgeois democracy to seek to establish them as indelible truths. On the one side, we are all unique personalities. Our consciousness is our own—the product of our personality. We are free and equal as individuals. On the other side, we are in some deep way all the same: equal and united in our submission to certain universal truths.

Though it may never be able to achieve a synthesis of these two strands of argument, bourgeois ideology must, if it is to be successful, contain them and hold them together. This is imperative if the illusion of personal freedom within common purpose is to be achieved; if the existence of rifts, radical inequalities and conflicts within society is to be denied; if, in short, the bourgeois social order is to defend itself against the consequences of deepening class consciousness and class struggle. The category which, above all others, must be denied is that of class.

We have seen how this central contradiction which arises from the attempt to contain the unique and the universal informs two areas—the picturing of people and the image of photographers. It is also at work in a further feature of the *Photography Yearbook*: in the conflicting demands of photography as a form of human communication which needs no translators, since the pictures speak for themselves, regardless of who took them or whence they came, and photography as personal expression; in the duality of the commercial exploitation of photography as a means of mechanically reproducing imagery and of photography as the production of limited editions of original prints; in the contradictory but coexisting identifications of photography as a truthful, natural, evident and impartial record and of photography as art.

It is where it has been able to contain these contradictory tendencies that photography has been most effective as an instrument of ideology. The photograph has appropriated certain elements of the ideology of art, while preserving certain advantages not given to the processes of Fine Art. If this appropriation goes too far, however—as it does in all the featured contributions from the Royal College of Art, with the exception of the photographs of the paraplegic Olympics—then these advantages will be lost and the photograph's special ideological effectiveness will be threatened. The most explicitly 'artistic' photographers may receive critical acclaim, exhibitions and government grants, but they do so at the price of quitting the mainland of ideological production. They

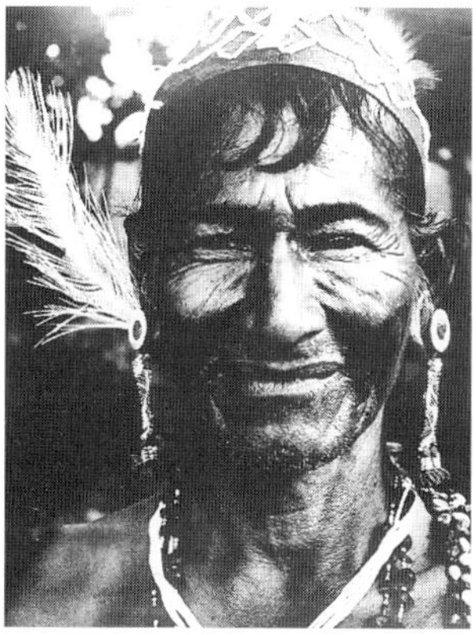

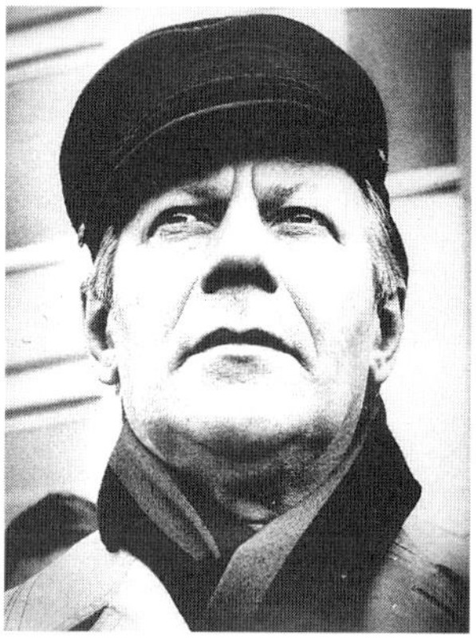

Left: 3.4 *Figure 214*. Erwin Kneidinger (Austria)

Right: 3.5 *Figure 215*. Gerhard Ludwig (Germany)

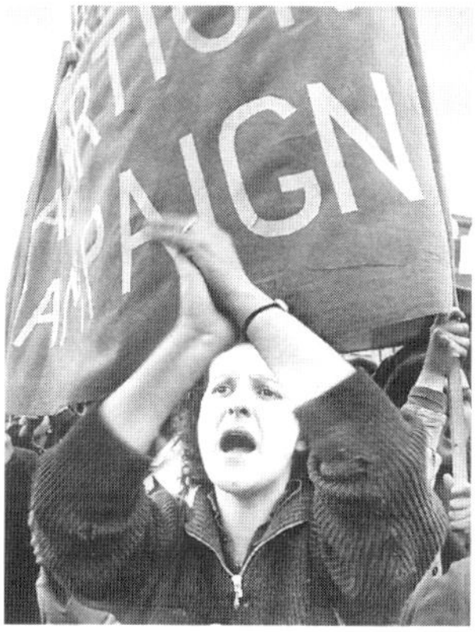


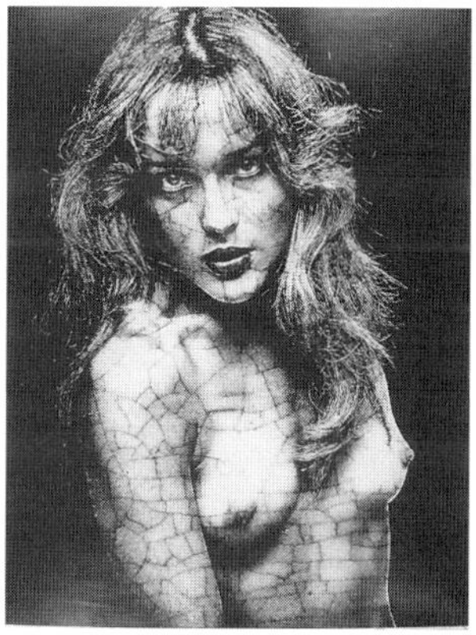

Left: 3.6 *Figure 19*. Erika Sulzer-Kleinmeier (Germany)

Right: 3.7 *Figure 105*. Bob Carlos-Clarke (UK)

join that crew of 'Fine Artists' whom capitalist economies have been prepared to support only to a limited and temporary extent. They are, as they have recently been described: 'people rowing out to join a sinking ship'.

What we see here is a process which has been characteristic of photography throughout its history. From its beginnings in the eccentric experiments of isolated inventor scientists in the early decades of the nineteenth century, photography underwent an extremely rapid development. In this, it followed the pattern of many other scientific and technological differences—in the fields of printing, transport, engineering and chemistry, for example—which provided the impetus for, and received their unbridled exploitation in, the hectic growth of early capitalism.

The market both for photographs and for photographic equipment did not cease to expand in the nineteenth century, encompassing, by stages, more and more sectors of society. However, this expansion brought photography into direct competition with existing means of manufacturing images. In particular, it engendered early conflict with the great numbers of portrait painters and miniaturists, of all kinds and levels, who tried, in vain, to protect their trade from the advances of the photographic salons. It is in the context of this economic struggle within early capitalism that the idea of spirit and soul in art first emerges. The very economic processes which, particularly after the invention of glass negatives enabling multiple reproduction, led to the ever-accelerating development and exploitation of photography, also produced and sustained an ideological recoil which seemed to contradict the workings of the economic laws yet which, here as elsewhere, served to limit control of the means of production.

Photographic technology did not stand still and soon the same contradiction was generated within the new medium itself. The first claims to artistic quality in photography come at a time when the first photographers, who concentrated on the production of limited numbers of large-scale, high-quality prints, were themselves threatened by the commercial operators, led in France by Disderi, who industrialised the process, increasing their production and making their products available to a wider and wider clientele. For their part, the mass producers of 'visiting card' portraits endeavoured to make their mechanical output acceptable to the taste, as well as to the pocket, of the bourgeoisie. Whilst for theirs, the art photographers sought to consolidate their superior rank by disdainfully rejecting commercial necessity and by exploring, as in the fashionable photography of today, every technical device such as blurring, tinting or gum printing, and every form of manipulation of the subject which might recapture that very 'aura' of art which the invention of photography had so emphatically abolished.

What united both categories of photographer was that they operated in the capitalist art market, either by selling their wares and services on the high street, or by proffering their independent products in the vast and prestigious salons of art. The latter were as much a consequence of the development of photography under capitalism as the former. It is only with the predominance of the free market and the consequent withering away of the old patron-artist relations that the idea of the free artist emerges.

These are the conflicts which make up the history of photography. On one side, the manufacturers of photographic equipment and materials have argued, since the marketing of the first Kodak camera in 1888, that anyone can take a photograph: you just point the camera and press the button; they do the rest. On the other, mass participation and the collective recording of the world have been denigrated in favour of the individual artist-photographer's subjective interpretation of what he sees. Between the two— feeding on the conventions of the one and transmitting them to the other—are the ranks of the mostly anonymous producers of photographic images for mass consumption: the 'power workers of bourgeois ideology'—the photojournalists, feature photographers, advertising image-makers, illustrators and shop photographers.

There is a certain degree of mobility in these classes: a small minority of commercial photographers do emerge as 'personalities' in their own right and thereby win title to greater artistic 'freedom' in their work; certain amateurs, not always of private means, do win photographic competitions or have photographs published in yearbooks such as this. Such social mobility is no greater here, however, than it is in society at large, though the institutional and ideological channels which reproduce the hierarchical order, procuring both dominance and consent, do not operate in a crude and exposed way. One such channel is *The Photography Yearbook*. It may repay further analysis.

---

**Reference Note**

**1** John Sanders, ed., *Photography Year Book 1977*, Fountain Press, 1977.

**Further Reading**


- Pierre Bourdieu, et al., *Photography: A Middle-Brow Art*, Polity Press, Oxford, 1990. (First published in French in 1965 as *Un Art Moyen*.)
- Paul Hill, Angela Kelly and John Tagg, *Three Perspectives on Photography*, Arts Council of Great Britain, London, 1979.
- Dick Hebdige, 'The Bottom Line on Planet One: Squaring Up to *The Face*', in his *Hiding in the Light*, Comedia, London, 1988.
- John Tagg, *The Burden of Representation: Essays on Photographies and Histories*, Macmillan, London, 1988.
- John Tagg, *Grounds of Dispute: Art History, Cultural Politics and the Discursive Field*, Macmillan, London, 1992.
- John Tagg, 'The Pencil of History', in Patrice Petro, ed., *Fugitive Images: From Photography to Video*, Bloomington and Indianapolis, Indiana University Press, 1995, pp.285-303.
- John Tagg, 'A Discourse (With Shape of Reason Missing)', in Stephen Melville and Bill Readings, eds, *Vision and Textuality*, Macmillan, London, 1995, pp.90-114.

# 4 Art, Common Sense and Photography

Victor Burgin

Introduction by **Victor Burgin**

I wrote 'Art, Common Sense and Photography' at the request of Jo Spence. She had read my longer and technically more detailed essay 'Photographic Practice and Art Theory' in *Studio International*.[1] She asked me if I could explain the core ideas of that piece in a shorter and more accessible article for issue number three of *Camerawork*.

My essay, and Jo Spence's request, were responses to the glacial situation of politically interested photography practice and theory in the mid-1970s. At that time, such practice was exclusively 'documentary'—it was known as 'concerned photography'. This kind of photography had become frozen in a self-servingly pious sentimentality. The (middle-class) photographer's narcissistic display of concern for the poor and oppressed took the place of any real analysis. The 'theory' we wished to bring to bear on this, and other photographic practices (especially advertising), took place in the gulf between the then prevailing aestheticist and sociologistic attitudes. For aestheticism, the photograph was an occasion for 'purely visual' pleasures, to which considerations of content were largely irrelevant. For sociologism, the photograph was a window on the world, a transparent means of access to the truth of an experience, to which formal considerations were entirely secondary.

In the silent space between aestheticism and sociologism it became necessary to speak of the political dimensions of visual pleasures (and of the often perverse pleasures of politics). It became necessary to speak of the formally complex *construction* of experienced 'truth'. 'Art, Common Sense and Photography' (essentially an introduction to the rhetoric of word and image) made a modest contribution towards thinking about the latter question. Laura Mulvey's article 'Visual Pleasure and Narrative Cinema' would open the former question to interrogation by means of a radical use of psychoanalytic theory. My own short piece for *Camerawork* differs from my longer essay in that it makes no mention at all of psychoanalysis. However, the emphasis it places on the role of rhetorical structures in the production of meanings is fundamental to Freudian and Lacanian theory. (My own subsequent work on the analysis of images developed as a psychoanalytic semiotics.)

With hindsight, it is clear that the threat which psychoanalytic theory poses to narcissistic self-certainty has guaranteed an undying hostility to its use in the analysis of politics and photography. Today's generation of students, with no memory of the intense and detailed debates of the 1970s, confronts a generation of teachers who themselves often prefer to forget the difficulty of theory as a daily practice of intellectual work. Some of these have adopted a lazy partisanship for one methodology, and a facile hostility towards another. I prefer to think of methods of theoretical analysis much as we might think of the contents of a tool kit. The question is not 'is this tool better than that tool?' The question is rather 'what tool is best suited for this particular job?' I urge skepticism towards the teachings of those who insist that we use a wrench to change a fuse.

---

## Art, Common Sense and Photography

**Victor Burgin** is an artist and writer. He teaches semiotic and psychoanalytic theory of images in the History of Consciousness program at the University of California, Santa Cruz. His books include: *The End of Art Theory: Criticism and Postmodernity* (1986) and the edited collection *Thinking Photography* (1982); his catalogues include *Between* (1986) and *Passages* (1991). His latest book is *In/Different Spaces: Place and Memory in Visual Culture* (1996).

The main thrust of photographic criticism these days is towards the consideration of photography as Art. *Camerawork*, on the other hand, has raised the issue of photography as an instrument of ideology. Many people believe that these two approaches are incompatible. Art is thought to have nothing to do with politics, 'political' art is thought to be irretrievably compromised as Art. But the two may not be quite as mutually exclusive as these people like to think.

Work with an obvious ideological slant is often condemned as 'manipulative'; that is to say, first, that the photographer manipulates what comes over in the image; second, that as a result his or her audience's beliefs about the world are manipulated. Not much is known about how the media influence opinions, although we can be fairly sure that people aren't simply led by the nose by photographs. Whatever the case, both charges can be similarly answered: manipulation is of the essence of photography; *photography would not exist without it.*

In photography, certain physical materials are technically handled so that meanings are produced. Photographers are people who manipulate the physical means of production of photography; cameras, film, lighting, objects, people. Using the productive capabilities of photography to reproduce the world as an object of aesthetic contemplation, and nothing else, is no less 'manipulative' than is any other use of photography: to turn away is an act, to turn away from situations of immediate social relevance is a political act, and to perform such acts in every working moment adds up to a political policy.

The only imaginable non-political being is a totally self-sufficient hermit. The photographer who has chosen to live in a society and enjoy its benefits, even though he also chooses to put on blinkers when he squints into a viewfinder, is willy-nilly an actor in a political situation. So how is it that so many people can genuinely believe that they lead a-political lives and that it is others—'militants' and 'extremists'—who 'have' ideology, not themselves? We must first say what we mean by 'ideology'.

When we look at the day-to-day life of a distant culture— behaviour, customs, dress, diet—we are immediately struck by its strangeness: why do they do that? Why do they eat those? What does it all mean? Few such questions trouble us as we pursue our own lives in our own culture, and if they were asked, they would probably get short shrift. Why does a man generally let a female stranger precede him when he is going into a shop, but not when he is boarding a bus? Why do men hang ties around their necks when they wear a shirt, but not when they wear a roll-neck jumper? The questions appear silly, the answers obvious....This is ideology as 'world-view', a common-sense understanding of 'the way things are' which is unquestioningly 'taken for granted'.

What we do ourselves seems so natural to us that we even cease to notice what we do. 'Habitualisation', said the critic Viktor Shklovsky 'devours work, clothes, furniture, one's wife and the fear of war'. Through habitualisation, working men and women accept lives of tedium, or even misery, as their natural lot, while others accept the social cost of their own greed as being just as unavoidable. The media by which we are informed characteristically reinforce such attitudes: 'Unemployment is expected to rise next month....More rain is expected in the south-west'—both facts appear equally to belong to the natural order of things, acts of God against which there can be no insurance.

The sort of habitualisation which leads millions to collude in their own repression, and which allows the rich and privileged to continue to act selfishly 'in all good faith' Marx called 'false consciousness'. For example, in order that the institutions of the state should continue to serve the interests of a ruling oligopoly, it is necessary that most people should continue to believe that such institutions serve everyone equally. Or again, the belief common to both those who own the means of production and those who do productive work that labour may fairly be bought for wages is a mystification which conceals the fact that, as the value of a commodity depends on the labour invested in it, the owner is appropriating as profit what belongs by right to the labourer: profits are unpaid wages. The idea of false-consciousness is another important aspect of the meaning of the term 'ideology'.

The politically 'Left' photographer wants to help correct society's false picture of its actual conditions of existence, to raise such questions as: why this practice? What does it mean? What interests does it serve? Such a photographer wants to help people become conscious of the forces which shape their day-to-day lives; to realise that the social order is not a natural order and thus beyond all change, but is made by people and can be changed by them. The political dissident photographer however is involved in an apparent paradox, that of seeking to penetrate appearances with an instrument designed specifically to record appearances and appearances alone.

Bertolt Brecht found the camera a politically deficient instrument: a photograph of a factory, he pointed out, tells us nothing of the economic forces governing the lives of those who work in it. Roland Barthes made a similar point when he reviewed *The Family of Man* exhibition: of course babies are born and nursed by their mothers all around the world, but photographs of them tell us nothing of the child's life expectancy or of the likelihood that its mother might have died giving birth.[2]

Such writers, notably including Walter Benjamin, have concluded that as language itself is the instrument best adapted to making a politically specific statement, then the photograph can only serve the text. But, although the premise here is correct, the conclusion does not necessarily follow from it. In his essay on 'The Family of Man', Barthes condemns the failure of photography to make a political statement, yet in this same essay he condemns the exhibition precisely for making such a (mystificatory) political statement.

A photograph of a baby at the breast of a woman in a private nursing home in Switzerland may be placed alongside a photograph of a similarly composed mother and child group in a village in rural India. Assuming that there are no obvious signs of deprivation on the one hand, or of privilege on the other, the two images together will pronounce: 'Mothers and their babies are the same everywhere'. Such a smugly reassuring message was indeed communicated by *The Family of Man* exhibition. The caption, the title of the exhibition, served mainly to underline what had already been said. In this case, the texts served the photographs.

Here, an ideological content is produced by a formal device. The message: 'The condition of motherhood is the same all over the world' would not have been conveyed so readily by either of the photographs alone. Only the juxtaposition of the two creates such a content, in such clarity, and with all the immediacy of an observed natural truth. (The message is ideological not simply because it is wrong in what it says—simply to be mistaken is not necessarily to be in a state of false-consciousness—it is ideological because it misrepresents the actual material condition of the world *in the service of specific vested interests.*)

Because we have separate words for 'form' and 'content', we are easily misled into believing that they stand for totally distinct areas of experience. But there is no content without a form, and no form which which does not shape a content. In that they have both been misled by a picture of the world given to us by language, 'artists' and 'activists' alike tend to inhabit the same aesthetic ideology. Artists believe that they can present a totally content-free world of pure forms. Activists believe in the autonomous power of 'the truth' which will impose itself regardless of formal considerations. It will pay us, if we are concerned with what photographers 'say', to examine the devices which enable photography to say things, devices so familiar to us they may pass unnoticed.

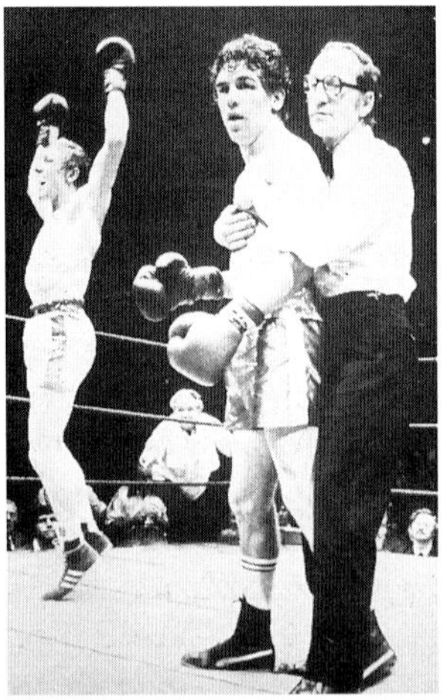

4.1 Victory and defeat

Popular photography magazines periodically carry articles advising their readers to look for 'contrast'. Such articles generally begin with a directive to look for contrasts of light and dark tones, rough and smooth textures...and then move from form-orientated to content-orientated oppositions such as young/old, happy/sad, etc. Such contrasts are indeed part of the stock-in-trade of the professional—take, for example, the picture of victory and defeat in figure 4.1.

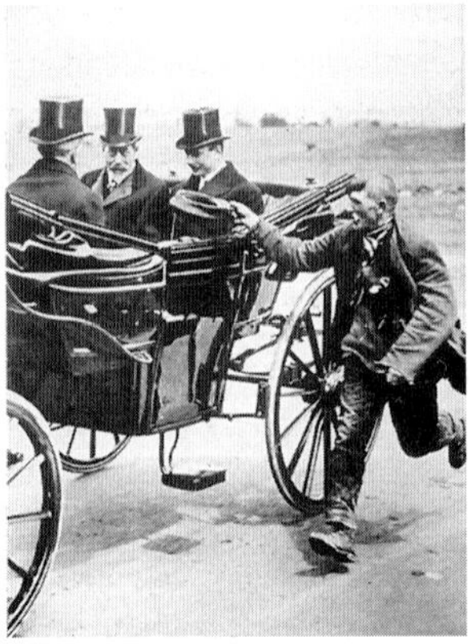

4.2 George V on Derby Day

Most active photographers are aware of the phenomenon of the 'third effect': two images side by side tend to generate meanings not produced by either image on its own. This effect may be produced by bringing together two physically-distinct prints (from two separate negatives), or by juxtaposing two distinct elements within a single frame. In the latter case, the juxtaposition may be brought about by chance (happy coincidence) or by design; if by design, then either 'natural' means (casting, posing, etc.) or 'technical' means (darkroom manipulation, collage, etc.) may be used.

For example, take the picture of George V on Derby Day in figure 4.2: in this image, we believe that the contrast of rich and poor is made on the basis of a coincidence—the photographer just happened to be there when—but it is equally possible, although perhaps less likely, that the two main elements of the image were assembled in the darkroom from separate negatives. Or, again, it is not beyond possibility that the situation depicted was 'set up' for the camera—for example, the photographer could have directed a suitably-cast and dressed person to run up to the coach at a predetermined spot. Further to all this, the contradiction of rich and poor could have been communicated by juxtaposing two separate photographs, taken at different times and places from one another.

Of the above possibilities, we would probably conclude that the picture we have here is in actuality the most effective. The photojournalistic 'snap' has an authority which other forms of picture-making lack; it presents itself as factual evidence of an actual state of affairs. In photojournalism, a particular moment may somehow come to signify a general truth. This 'somehow' is generally considered to be unaccountable except in terms of such things as 'luck', 'talent' or a combination of the two. Certainly the photographer of George V was lucky, and he may very well have been 'talented' (whatever that means), but while the picture before us may have depended on luck for its existence, it does not depend upon luck or talent for its meaning—its meaning is something we can account for.

All communication takes place on the basis of signs, most predominantly on the basis of visible and audible signs. To say that one person has communicated with another is to say that each of them has understood how to use and interpret the signs which made up the message between them. If you speak to me in Greek, I have no problem hearing the noises you are making, but if I do not 'know Greek' in common with you, then I cannot understand what you are saying.

The photograph is a sign, or more correctly speaking, a complex of signs, used to communicate a message. If you show me a photograph of a pile of stones then, at an immediate level, my eye receives visual noise just as my ear received verbal noise when you spoke to me in Greek. We can suppose that I have seen photographs since I was a child and so have no problem interpreting these irregular patches of light and dark tones as representing stones. (When African bushmen were first shown photographs, they had to be taught to read them.) But what beyond this? If I go on to remark that the photograph depicts a temple, that the temple is ruined, and that it is Greek, then I am relying upon knowledge that is no longer 'natural', 'purely visual'; I am relying upon knowledge that is cultural, verbally transmitted, and in the final analysis, ideological (I might think 'cradle of civilisation' or 'damned Greeks' according to when and where I happened to be born).

Most photographers are aware of using some sort of system of effects in their work, but such systematisation as may be achieved is generally believed to concern only the purely formal—the 'visual'. Content, it is believed, is just there in the world, and therefore in the picture, whether lined up with the frame or composed on the diagonal. But once we reject the idea of photography as a purely visual language, understood equally by everybody everywhere, then we may begin to consider the possibility that content too, may be produced as deliberately as one may plan the formal composition of the photograph.

To return, then, to contrast. All contrasts are juxtapositions, but not all juxtapositions are contrasts. The *'Derby Day'* and *'Boxing'* pictures are based upon a contrast; that is to say, a dissimilarity of contents (rich/poor, victory/defeat). The well-known Diane Arbus

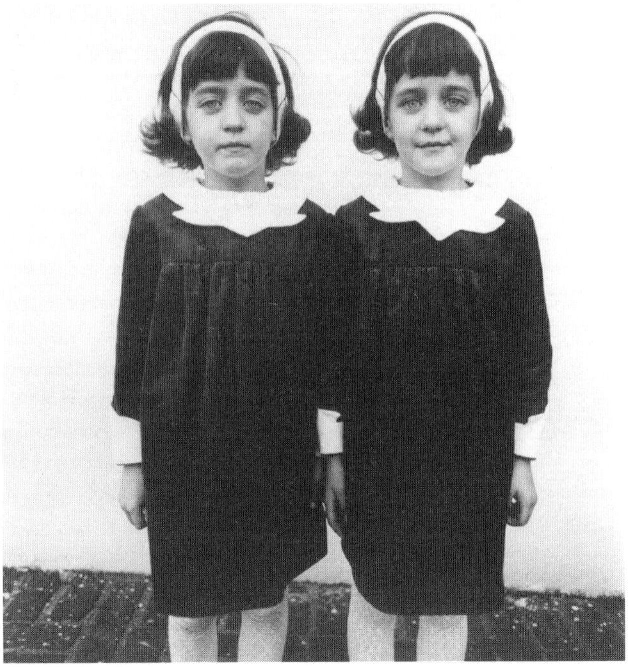



4.3 Identical Twins, Roselle, New Jersey, 1966. Diane Arbus

picture of identical twins, on the other hand (figure 4.3) is based upon a similarity of both form and content. The fashion picture (figure 4.4) is based upon a juxtaposition of similar forms which have dissimilar contents (e.g., animate/inanimate).

Looked at more closely, the photographer's stock in trade of 'contrast' may be seen to consist of a number of distinct communicative devices, devices which nevertheless seem to evolve upon the common basis of the various relationships into which two or more visual elements may enter. The nub of such a system is formed by relationships of similarity and dissimilarity of form and of content, with additional manipulations in the form of substitutions and permutations of elements. The working out of such a system in its entirety is one of the tasks which might be undertaken within a 'semiotic' study of photography.

Semiotics, or semiology, is the science which studies signs. We recognise that some photographers are more successful communicators than others. The semiotician is interested in the reasons for their success or failure—not, of course, in terms of the photographer's personal history, but in terms of the photographic sign itself. The semiotician works from the assumption that wherever we recognise 'mastery' of an art, we also implicitly acknowledge the existence of some system which has been mastered—whether the 'master' is consciously aware of the system or not.

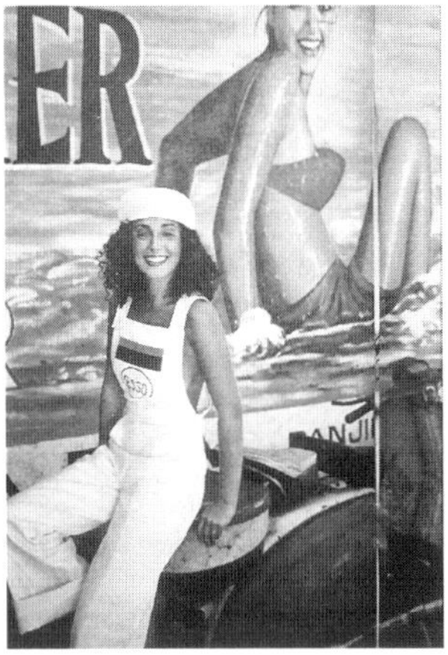

4.4

In the early days of 'structuralist' semiology (Roland Barthes's *Elements of Semiology* first appeared in France in 1964) exclusive attention was paid to the analogy between 'natural' language (the phenomenon of speech and writing) and visual 'language'. It had long been common for people to speak loosely of 'the language of...' this or that activity, including, of course, 'the language of photography', but it was not until the 1960s that any systematic investigation of forms of communication outside of natural language was conducted from the standpoint of linguistic science.

There were two main reasons for approaching visual communication through linguistics: first, language is the most elaborate and comprehensive form of communication ever evolved, and it seemed at least a reasonable working hypothesis to assume that other forms of human communication might have evolved along basically similar limes; second, modern structural linguistics was itself a sufficiently established science to provide the necessary ready-made theoretical models of communication to start the new science of semiology on its way.

One aspect of natural language use which was found to have a particular bearing on the topic of visual communicative devices is rhetoric. Simply speaking, rhetoric is the artful use of language in order to persuade. In rhetoric, language draws attention to itself in order to attract and retain the attention of the listener or reader—form is manipulated to engage interest in the contents.

Rhetoric first evolved in the Classical period, and one of the difficulties in studying rhetoric today is that the ancient terms are still in use to label its 'figures': terms such as *antanaclasis*, *chiasmus*, *synechdoche*, etc. However, the meaning of most of these terms becomes clear once examples are provided: In *antanaclasis*, a single word is repeated with different senses, e.g., 'Learn a craft in your youth so that in your old age you can earn your living without craft'; in *chiasmus*, words are repeated but inverted in their order in the course of a single sentence, e.g., 'You should eat to live, not live to eat'; in *synechdoche*, a word is used in a sense of which its usual sense is only a part, e.g., 'Give me your heart' (when the entire body is being sought).

Advertising is the most obvious place we might expect to find rhetorical figures (of which there are literally hundreds). In the first place, there is no doubt that someone is setting out deliberately to persuade; in the second place, there is little doubt that everything in the advertisement has been most carefully placed for maximum effect. Commercial publicity, obviously, endorses and perpetuates the commodity values central to our capitalist ideology. On the Left, the prevailing view of advertising tends to be simply one of disapproval. From one point of view in 'classic' semiology, however, the structure of advertising may be disengaged from its contents: the rhetorical structures of advertising are 'indifferent' to the emotional and ideological value of the contents they handle; much as, for example, an arithmetical structure like 2 plus 2 equals 4 'doesn't care' whether we are adding up taxicabs or tomatoes. In this view, therefore, there is no reason why, once the devices of advertising have been isolated by semiotic analysis, they may not be 're-cycled' in counter-ideological message-making. Another opinion to be derived from semiotics argues against this, but there is insufficient space here to discuss the apparent contradiction.

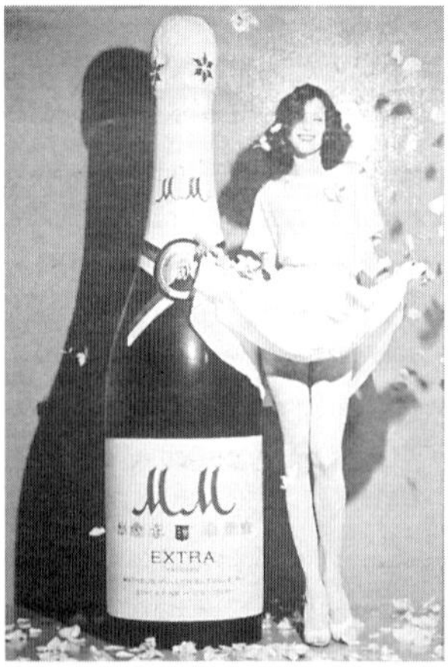


4.5

The rhetorical analysis of advertising may be conducted along three main 'planes': the image plane; the plane of the text (headline, caption, body-copy); and the plane of the text/image bond. For example, an image which showed a bottle of milk as big as a house would present a figure of *hyperbole* (overstatement). If we then added the headline 'Pour Some More, Mum', the text would be based in rhyme, and we would have established a figure of *litotes* (understatement) in the relationship of the text to the image. Let's take some further, actual examples: figure 4.5 is a visual *hyperbole* much like our hypothetical example except that in this case the exaggeration is doubly charged through sexual allusion; figure 4.6 is an example of *chiasmus* in the plane of the text; figure 4.7 presents a paradox in the text/image plane...and may be worth considering in some more detail. The image in this example draws upon the iconography of poverty—the bath in a zinc tub, the squalid 'back yard', the washing on a line (as opposed to in a spin-dryer). These remarks suffice to show that this is 'poverty' in the definition of a particular culture at a particular historical juncture—the same assembly of signs might connote relative affluence in a 'third world' context. The striped T-shirt is associated in the British mind with the iconography of France and the sea, its connotation of 'St Tropez-ness' establishes a figure of *irony* within the image.

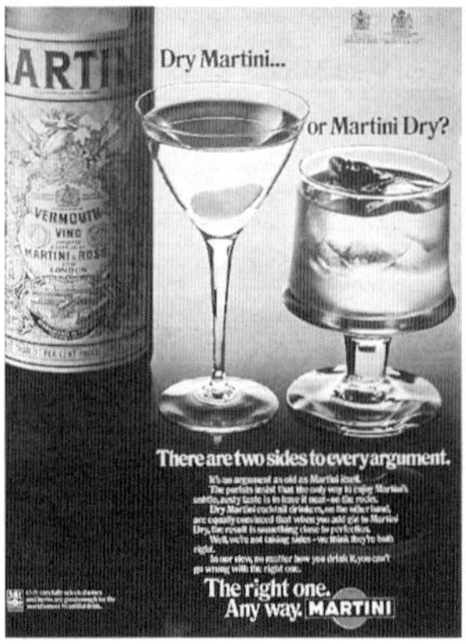


4.6

It is likely that the people in the photograph will have been chosen for their—in Barthes's expression—'canonic generality'; that is to say, each individual represents his or her own 'type', each individual stands for a class of individuals. In rhetoric the figure of *antonamasia* is the one in which the particular stands for the general. Nearly all advertising images contain this figure. Thus, the woman in our example represents all economically-disadvantaged mothers (there is no evidence in the picture which proves she is the mother of these children, but the very wide use of images of the family dictates that she represent one). The scene depicted here should cause no offence to either the poor or the comfortably-off: there are no torn clothes or matted hair, the children are being washed and (imminently) fed; this is a 'poor but honest' milieu.

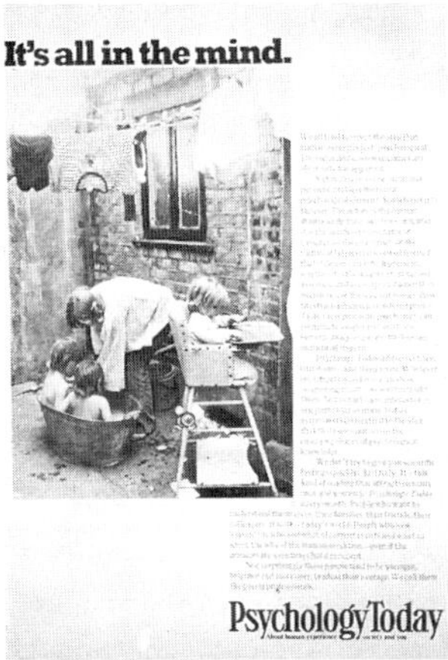


4.7

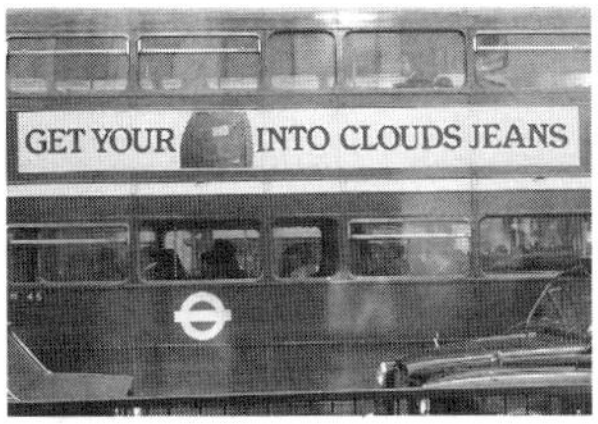


4.8

The remarks I have made so far concern what is actually to be observed in the image; more observations could be added along these lines. Beyond what is to be seen in the image, however, there are many stories to be *construed* from what is seen. This photograph could serve equally well to illustrate a variety of stories. For example: 'one-parent families'; 'health in the home'; 'domestic life in industrial towns', and so on. The photographic image can carry a large number of different meanings. It is 'polysemic'. Generally, the polysemy of the image is controlled by its juxtaposition with a verbal text.

Roland Barthes has identified two different functions which the verbal message can adopt in relation to the image, these he calls *anchorage* and *relay*.[3] The text adopts a function of anchorage when, from a multiplicity of connotations offered by the image, it selects some and thereby implicitly rejects the others. Thus, in a cigarette advertisement, the contradictory connotations 'cigarettes give pleasure' and 'cigarettes give cancer' are selectively handled in such a caption as *cool as a mountain stream*, a simile which endorses the suggestion of pleasure while rejecting that of unwholesomeness.

In relay, the image and the linguistic text are in a relationship of complementarity: the linguistic message explains, develops, expands the significance of the image. (figure 4.8 is a particularly clear and simple example of relay.) In our previous example, the caption is in a relationship of relay to the image. 'It's all in the mind' is not amongst the connotations we might expect to be summoned by the image alone. It is not therefore 'anchored' from amongst the connotations already available. The rhetorical structure of the text/image relation in this case is that of *paradox*. The dominating connotation of the image may be labelled (but not contained) by the linguistic term 'poverty'. Substituting this term for the image gives us the statement: 'Poverty. It's all in the mind.' However, we know the poverty depicted in the image to be a material poverty, hence the paradox, and hence the effect gained by the juxtaposition of such a caption with such an image.

The semiotician Jacques Durand made these remarks in the course of his 1970 study of rhetoric in advertising:

> The myth of 'inspiration', of 'the idea', reigns supreme in the creation of advertising at the present time. In reality, however, the most original ideas, the most audacious advertisements, appear as transpositions of rhetorical figures which have been indexed over the course of numerous centuries. This is explained in that rhetoric is in sum a repertory of the various ways in which we can be 'original'. It is probable then that the creative process could be enriched and made easier if the creators would take account consciously of a system which they use intuitively.

Typical of the nineteenth-century Romantic aesthetic attitudes which prevail in present-day writings on photography is the notion that there are unique essences within things and people which are ordinarily concealed from us but which artistic genius can reveal. This is an idea which photographers had handed down to them from the 'Fine Art' they originally sought to emulate (and often still wish to emulate, albeit they are in the position of people rowing out to join a sinking ship). Largely, this idea is a projection of the market relations which characterise our commodity society—the concept of 'genius' guarantees the investment: value of the product; the concept of transcendental 'essences' protects the product against practical interrogation.

Brecht took the view that what essences there are behind appearances are to be reached through investigation rather than through intuition. Photography has tended to treat us to an interminable rhetoric of 'humanity—its joys, its sorrows'. The material forces which cause such emotions and, further, shape our entire lives, may be described. It remains to be seen whether photography will become effective in showing them. What is certain is that if it is to do so, we need to treat the photographic image as an occasion for skepticism and questioning—not as a source of hypnosis.

---

**Reference Notes**


**1** 'Photographic Practice and Art Theory', *Studio International*, vol.190, no.976, 1975. Reprinted in Victor Burgin, *The End of Art Theory*, Macmillan, Basingstoke, 1986.

**2** 'The Great Family of Man', in R. Barthes, *Mythologies*, Paladin, London, 1973.

**3** See 'The Rhetoric of the Image', in *Image-Music-Text*, Hill and Wang, New York, 1977.

## Further Reading


• Roland Barthes, *Elements of Semiology*, Jonathan Cape, London, 1967.
• Roland Barthes, 'The Great Family of Man', *Mythologies*, Paladin, London, 1973.
• Roland Barthes, 'Rhetoric of the Image', in his *Image-Music-Text*, op.cit.
• Walter Benjamin, 'The Author As Producer', in V. Burgin, ed., *Thinking Photography*, Macmillan, Basingstoke, 1982.
• Tony Bennett, *Formalism and Marxism*, Methuen, London, 1979.
• Victor Burgin, 'Looking at Photographs' and 'Photography, Phantasy, Function', in Burgin, ed., *Thinking Photography*, Macmillan, Basingstoke, 1982.
• Victor Burgin, *The End of Art Theory*, Macmillan, Basingstoke, 1986.
• Jaques Durand, 'Rhétorique et Image Publicitaire', *Communication*, no.15, 1970.
• Terry Eagleton, *Literary Theory*, Basil Blackwell, Oxford, 1983.
• John Fiske, *Introduction to Communication Studies*, Methuen, London, 1990.
• Terence Hawkes, *Structuralism and Semiotics*, Methuen, London, 1977.
• Dick Leith and George Myerson, *The Power of Address: Explorations in Rhetoric*, Routledge, London, 1989.
• Viktor Shklovsky, 'Art as a Technique', in *Russian Formalist Criticism*, University of Nebraska Press, Lincoln.
• Tony Thwaites, Lloyd David, Warwick Mules, *Tools for Cultural Studies, An Introduction*, Macmillan, Melbourne, 1994.

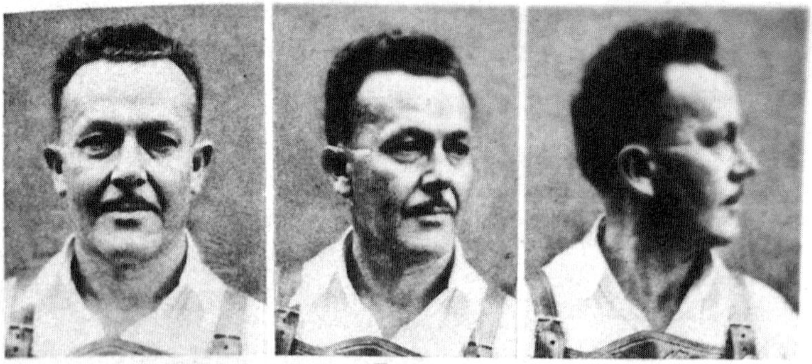

FIG. 1

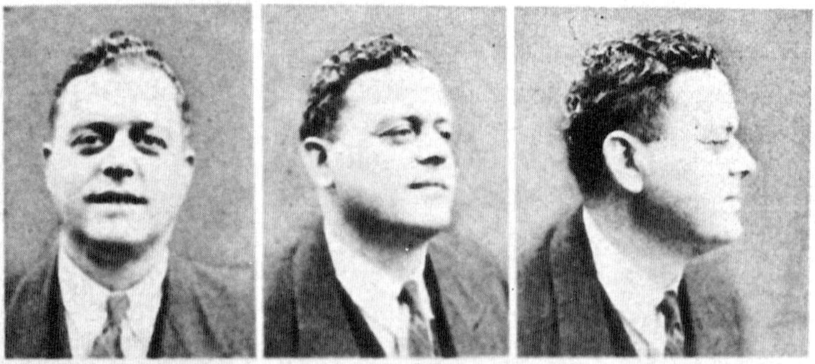

FIG. 2

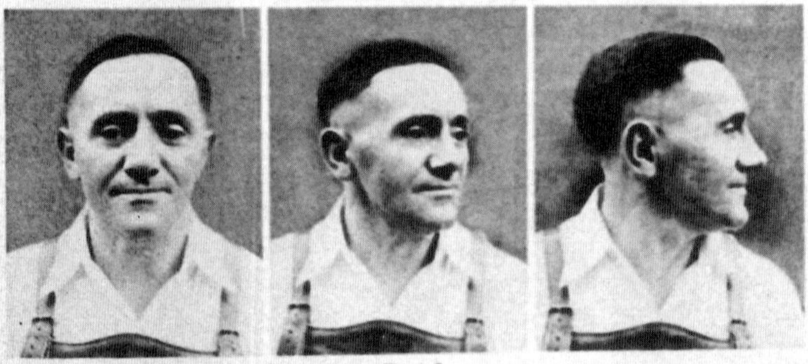

FIG. 3

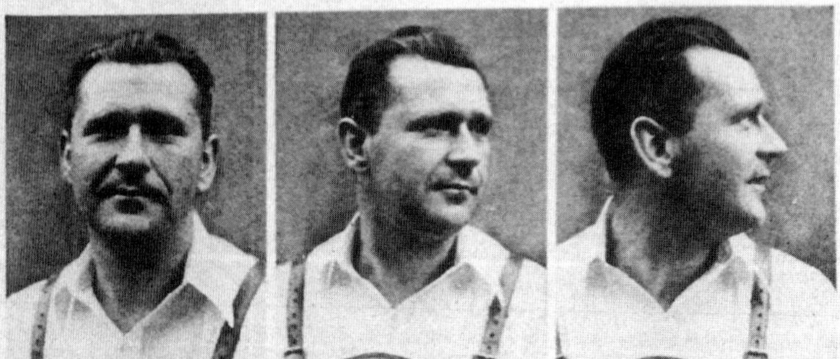

FIG. 4

# 2

# Photographs of History, or Photographs as History?

# 5 The Object of Photography

## Don Slater

Introduction by **Don Slater**

'The Object of Photography' represents for me a very productive and confused period at *Camerawork*. Towards the end of my time as editor I put together a small editorial group (Yve Lomax, Kathy Myers, Mike Hughes, myself). We saw ourselves as breaking with *Camerawork's* past, particularly fighting our way out of the increasingly untenable contradictions between its representations of politics and its politics of representation. The former—exemplified in special issues on Northern Ireland and exhibitions on El Salvador—was rooted in 'realisms' of all sorts: a belief that images can 'represent' a 'truth', that one can distinguish appearance and 'essence', that images should serve social struggles (rather than being a/the medium in which struggles are constituted).

The politics of representation, on the other hand, under the impact of semiotics and poststructuralism ('postmodernism' was not yet an available concept), meant that an image was not a representation *of* something, but merely a fact, a social object, in its own right and reality, a thing which circulated in the world: a phrase from Godard was important at the time—there is no such thing as 'l'image juste, mais juste une image'. But if our politics of representation was founded on the 'loss of the real' then both our politics and our representations of politics could no longer be defended against the implications—as we felt they had been for too long. How could we continue an allegiance to the documentary traditions of photography when they depended on notions of truthful representation (as well as humanist versions of the honest political 'bearer of witness')? And underlying that photography were equally problematic notions of true politics based on 'objective' interests (of objective classes, genders, 'races'). Another crucial dilemma: political and representational realism entailed an obligation or responsibility to a truth or reality beyond subjectivity; it was founded therefore on notions like guilt, duty, sacrifice, liberation. This felt uncomfortable in a world that seemed increasingly constituted by a quite different politics/representation: notions of pleasure and desire, empowerment and self-creation which were evident equally in advertising and in the new political groupings of identity politics and later, postmodernism.

The atmosphere was excited and optimistic, a feeling of breaking out of a brittle old shell. Yve, for example, stressed that we should not 'lament' the loss of depth in our images but should embrace what were indeed new openings; Kathy and Mike stressed that we must have the courage of our pleasures and desires, that we could have fun and that politics/representation *had to be* fun. We wanted to get rid of the 'policemen in our head', in our images, in our politics, in our writing.

At the same time, I found it very hard to leave behind many of the commitments which underlay the earlier politics/representation: to Marxism, to modernity, to the possibility of rational social knowledge, and so on; over a decade later, I still feel poised on the brink. The problem—which structured this article—is having to choose between two completely contradictory impulses within what later came to be known as postmodernism: on the one hand, there is the poststructuralist impulse which argues that 'the real', that which a representation 'represents', is always a mystification produced by the image itself (as in Barthes's notion that denotation is merely the final connotation); if we have lost the real in everyday life, in the way we perceive and consume images, this can only be a liberation from the oppressive myths of modernity. There is indeed nothing to lament. On the other hand, there is a socio-historical argument in postmodernism (usually told now as the narrative of post-Fordism, of consumerisation, of the collapse of modern identities). This story can be happy or sad, a tale of liberation or loss, but its form is that of good old-fashioned rational modernist social explanation: there is a real world out there in which x caused y; we can reconstruct these relations in the form of representations which we deem to be 'knowledge', knowledge of society. This kind of postmodernist argument requires recourse to forms of reason which, it argues, have progressively departed the social world. In this context, the 'loss of the real' is something to be explained as a part of a social history of photography and culture, but it is also something from which this social history must be distanced and insulated.

*The Object of Photography* fell into the latter camp: it makes empirical claims rather than poststructuralist deconstructions. It argues that there has been a shift in the way the photograph is experienced in everyday life, in the role it plays, in the relation to reality we expect it to have. This shift, crudely, corresponds to a shift from productivist nineteenth-century capitalism to consumerist twentieth-century capitalism. Sociologically there has been a transformation in beliefs about vision and truth, representation and reality, and the article gives a fairly deterministic account of it. That account draws mainly on the Hegelian-Marxist critique of reification (Frankfurt School theory, especially *Dialectic of Enlightenment*;[1] Lukacs, Lefebvre, Situationism), a tradition which focused on the invasion of everyday life, consciousness and culture by the logic of commodification. This entire tradition is concerned with demonstrating that modern modes of appearance and representation made the social processes which are enacted by human subjects appear to be natural objects or things. Positivist notions of science and language are exemplary of this process: the world (including the social world) is reduced to discrete things with observable and usable properties, to pure objects. In everyday life, photography appears to exemplify this kind of vision, the world reduced to its visible surface. The critique of reification gives a compelling account both of how the world is so reduced, and of why it produces *wrong* (undialectical) knowledge and oppressive social power: representations simply and slavishly mirror the appearance of the world created by capitalism, depict that world as a natural object rather than social product to which there are alternatives and internal contradictions. Photography is a form of this 'identity thinking' (Adorno), of a false and forced reconciliation of subject and object, representation and reality, culture and society.

At the same time, this tradition also explored the ways in which all this 'objective' and objectifying vision has come to permeate everyday life, producing not only power but also alienation, boredom, passivity, nihilism, rebellion. If this sounds postmodern (a word none of us had heard at the time of this article) it is largely because Baudrillard rather shamelessly appropriated much of this tradition, largely by rewriting the Situationists' work (and through them, Lukacs and Lefebvre) in the language of semiotics.[2] What is at stake in all this work are notions of the spectacle and the spectacular: once modern vision reduces the world to things and their appearances and has produced technologies for depicting those appearances realistically, it is capable of producing not only 'knowledge' (however mystified) but also astonishing and engaging spectacles—modernity as a kind of magic show of scientific and technical wonders, consumer culture as a spectacular of desire and fetishism. Representation is transformed from a channel of knowledge to an engine of desire.

The weakest aspect of the article is its most specifically postmodernist feature: its crude periodisation, its association of photographic realism and the photograph-as-knowledge with nineteenth-century modernism and competitive capitalism; its association of spectacular representation and consumerism with the twentieth century. This turns the complex dialectic developed by the critique of reification (not only in Marx but also, we later learned, in Weber and Simmel) into a mechanical empiricism which delineates historical 'stages' or 'phases'. The article itself points out that the idea of vision as magic attends the very birth of photography, as much as did the notion of photography as scientific knowledge. Rather than try to split them up schematically into two different periods (neatly aligned with production and consumption respectively) it is rather more interesting to see how they are internally connected to each other. Photography and all other modern realisms partake of the same 'dialectic of enlightenment' by which modernity both reduces the real to visible appearances and is then able to use its consequent control over both objects and images to produce entirely new realities. To the extent that modernity asks us to believe in appearances (and appearances which are produced and controlled by modern knowledges and institutions), we can also be deceived, astounded and entertained, confused and pleasurably disoriented by appearances. Science and magic, visual technologies of 'truth' and of 'deception' go together from the earliest days and photography was born of that dialectic.[3] It is true, as the article insists, that photographic realism's ability to compel belief in non-existent ('simulated') realities has a privileged relationship to commercialisation and consumer culture. However, that is only another argument for tracing consumer culture further back into early modernity, rather than treating it as a twentieth-century or even postmodern phenomenon.[4]

---

## The Object of Photography

**Don Slater** is a Lecturer in Sociology at Goldsmith's College, University of London. His research focuses on theories of consumer culture, economic sociology and photography. Publications include *Consumer Culture and Modernity*.

Today, we do not read photographs, we consume them: they—and the systems of commodities, media, politics, cultures, within which photographs circulate—whirl about in a vast and meaningless game of meaning. We do not ask these images, or these systems, for knowledge, or for a purchase on reality; we expect nothing of the image but the continuation of that limitlessly productive game. Whether we think this through in terms of style and trends, the loss of authenticity, the spectacle or the Code, we are dealing with the same problem: an explosion of signs without escape, without a means of exit. There is nothing solid behind these signs. Behind the photograph there is no real object, only another image (even if this 'image' happens to be in the form of a commodity, or an unemployment figure, or a Falklands war). We consume photographs of photographs of photographs....

Yet, representation and the visible have taken on many different forms: there is a history of meaning. The present article contrasts two periods of this history: the nineteenth and twentieth century. Each of these centuries was pre-occupied with different tasks in Western Europe and America: the first was the age of production, the age of heroic capitalism, which brought about a new domination of nature and humanity through new technology in the production process and the rise to dominance of the commodity form; the second is the age of consumption, of commercial capitalism, in which the organisation of consumption through economic and cultural means is pursued to secure the swift and predictable absorption of goods.

Each of these had both entailed and been constructed by a different model of representation. In the nineteenth century representation (and photography in particular) was taken to be a form of knowledge, of knowing the object. It fitted within a specific idea of knowledge—positivism—which aimed at the control and appropriation of nature.

In the twentieth century objects are not merely commodities, but are ideological motivators of a mass consumption system. Representation is now not a way of knowing about objects in the world, but a play of signs which ceaselessly creates, recreates and renews 'objects'. Representation now aims never to allow the object to settle into the possession of fixed properties which can satisfy the drive to consumption. Under the regime of consumption there is no object of representation, there are only signs within the signs and therefore a potentially infinite flexibility of meaning which no 'real world' can anchor or halt.

## Part 1: The Production of Knowledge

Bertolt Brecht offers us a seminal statement on the relationship between photography, power and knowledge:

> Less than ever does the mere reflection of reality reveal anything about reality. A photograph of the Krupp works or the A.E.G. tells us next to nothing about these institutions. Actual reality has slipped into the functional. The reification of human relations—the factory, say—means that they are no longer explicit.[5]

For Brecht, the 'reality' of Krupps is its history and structure, the forces and relations of its production, its financial and political power, the function of its products. This reality is not immediately visible, we cannot see it in the bricks and mortar of the factory itself: thus, however 'realistic' a photograph of the factory might be, it will not offer up any knowledge of this truth. We cannot photograph history or social structures, and so the real power of Krupps hides itself in its visible appearance: the visible, which photography so intimately captures, contains no knowledge, and obscures power.

Brecht is working here with the most subversive philosophical tenet of Marxism: that appearance and reality are quite distinct things. Appearances (the visible) are partial, incomplete, abstractions: they only show the superficial constellation of objects and events in the world. They are not unreal, but they do not tell their own story. The determinations—forces, relations, history—which have formed and sustained an object are not visible in its immediate appearance, yet it is only by assembling the totality of these determinations that we can have an image of the Real. Only knowledge of this totality is the Truth.

In this, Brecht (and Marx) were opposing a central project of Western bourgeois thought which for several centuries sought to establish that only the Visible actually existed. The Visible, the observable, was called the 'positive', 'that-which-is': it was held that knowledge of the Visible was the *only* valid knowledge, that to claim to find Truth outside the Visible appearance of objects was metaphysical and unscientific.

Brecht's central concern (shared by many cultural forms at this time) was to break the link between the Visible and the True. Over the past two decades, photographic theorists, largely within the semiotic tradition, have worked on a similar question, but given it a rather different inflection. Through semiotics, we have looked at Krupps saying: this photograph does not contain 'the Truth' because there is no objective Truth.

With each change of angle, lens, perspective, caption, context and audience we construct a quite different universe of meanings. The particular universe we might label 'realistic' is so-called only because it conforms to certain conventions which denote 'realism' in representation. But photographs are constructions: the 'knowledge' they contain is a system of meanings within representation, not the truth offered up by the object.

Yet Brecht says 'the mere reflection of reality'—as if he believes that the photograph does 'reflect' reality. The semiotician cringes at this gaffe, but Brecht is making a crucial point: what is powerful in Brecht's comment is a distinction between two concepts of 'realism'. First, there is a 'trivial realism' of the photograph: yes, we can recognise a photograph as depicting—'realistically'—the Krupps factory in that it corresponds to certain codes of acceptable representation and does so according to rigorous optical rules. More fundamentally, we accept that photograph as a record of an encounter between a scientific apparatus and a real object in the world, which encounter must actually, physically, have taken place in order for that photograph to be taken.

But, says Brecht, that is not very interesting, for trivial realism does not tell us much more. There is a higher, second, realism (implicitly Marxist theory) which realistically reflects, not the visible, but the inner structure, the 'truth' of what we see. The individual photograph is incapable of capturing this truth because it is trapped within the appearance of objects.

Brecht accepts the trivial realism of the photograph and in doing so shows that he stands on the other side of a great divide from the present age. Semioticians do not see photography as a problem of knowledge, but of ideological effect, of the production of the Imaginary, of the construction of subjectivity. For Brecht, on the other hand (and the century preceding him) cultural production was about truth-values, about correct or incorrect knowledge of the world. Brecht does not dispute that a representation can claim knowledge; he merely holds that trivial realism produces partial and mystifying knowledge, produces a 'truth' which is based on a bourgeois model of knowledge. Brecht is interrogating trivial realism not in order to trivially explode it, but to ascertain what notion of the Visible, hence of the Real and of Truth, has been holding power. What concept of knowledge could make us believe that in looking at a photograph of Krupps we now have knowledge of anything other than the appearance of a factory? Why, under the bourgeois order, is the Visible so valued as to be the limit of Truth?

This question leads us far beyond the photograph to the Real which the nineteenth-century bourgeoisie constructed, and the forms of knowledge of that reality which it constructed in the same movement. There is another quotation, as famous, yet closer to the original terms and premises of the problems of photography and Truth. The poet Baudelaire, addressing photography in 1859, puts the following words into the mouths of the 'idolatrous mob' who have 'rushed, Narcissus to a man, to gaze at its trivial image on a scrap of metal':

> I believe in Nature, and I believe only in Nature....I believe that Art is, and cannot be other than, the exact reproduction of Nature....Thus an industry that could give us a result identical to Nature would be the absolute of Art.[6]

Baudelaire himself wants an absolute divorce between Science and Art (the divine, the imagination, the beautiful), which have been collapsed together, threatening the imminent destruction of the latter. Photography has a functional role where 'absolute factual exactitude' is required, in the laboratory and in recording that

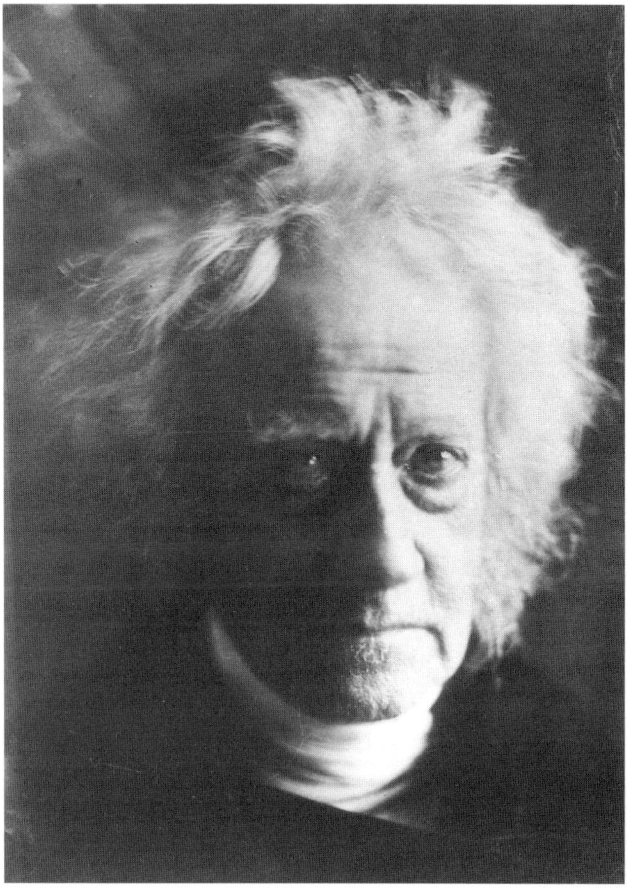

5.1 Sir John Herschel, 1867. Julia Margaret Cameron

'which time is devouring'. But photography must be restricted to Science and Industry not only because it is not art, but because it will *destroy* art:

Each day art further diminishes its self-respect by bowing down before external reality; each day the painter becomes more and more given to painting not what he dreams but what he sees. Nevertheless it is a happiness to dream, and it used to be a glory to express what one dreamt....Are we to suppose that a people whose eyes are growing used to considering the results of a material science as though they were the products of the beautiful, will not in the course of time have singularly diminished its faculties of judging and of feeling what are among the most ethereal and immaterial aspects of creation?[7]

'Industry' and 'material science' are Baudelaire's enemies. What do they mean to him? He is writing during the period of triumphant entrepreneurial capitalism. The gods of Industry, Science and Progress, have victoriously instituted a new mode of production and new social relations. Before Marxism, 'materialism' was the proud banner of the bourgeoisie: the material was the only Real; the task was control over the material world for profit and progress; control through material science, technology, economic rationality, institutions. The opposition was 'idealist': romantics, mystics, metaphysicians, priests and even the workers with their Utopian socialisms and millenarian movements. 'Materialism' was the opposition's taunt: the bourgeoisie could not see beyond its materialistic obsession with money and capital and the production of commodities. Moreover, the material world was now the bourgeois world, denuded of all values or knowledge save those—economic, moral, disciplinary, technical—appropriate to living in its material world.

For Baudelaire as for Brecht, then, the limitation of the Real to the 'appearance of things' is dangerous not merely because of its superficiality, but because the 'appearance of things' is being captured, controlled and constructed by the bourgeois order. To Baudelaire the trivial realism of the photograph is the final imperialism of the bourgeoisie: the world of the mind, like that of nature, and the truth of beauty will now be colonised by the fact and become a district of the material world from which there will then be no escape. The slavish realism of the camera is the conqueror's new weapon and the idolatrous mob is fairly bursting to surrender their last sphere of freedom and truth to it—their art and their poetry, and the truths *they* contain.

The bourgeois order, by limiting knowledge and the Real to knowledge of its own appearance, of the world *it* made, posits itself as universal: knowledge of it is the only valid knowledge. Yet it is only by declaring truths independent of the positive, of that which is, that those under the domination of the bourgeoisie can imagine and work for their liberation from this order, that they can dream of rights and possibilities, of that which is not *yet*. And their capacity to do *that* is their only real freedom.

What was the model of knowledge and the real which lay beneath the materialism of the nineteenth-century bourgeoisie, and which credited photography's trivial realism with such purchase on knowledge through its power over appearance? Most of its concepts can be grouped under the term 'positivism'.

The word 'positivism' was introduced by Auguste Comte in 1830 to name his philosophy of science and knowledge. Comte was working within a general framework which long preceded him and continues to exert enormous control over science today. Within this framework, science—as opposed to religion or metaphysics—is knowledge of the positive, of that which is, of the real world, and is thus the highest form of knowledge. The core of positivism is precisely its definition of this 'real world': according to it, nothing exists but what can be perceived through the senses. There are no ideal types or metaphysical substances, no invisible 'real' world which stands behind the one we see. According to positivism, all that exists are individual objects which are made up of physical properties (colour, weight, mass). Unless we can observe (and measure) the properties of the thing we are talking about, we are merely dealing with a figment of our imagination.

Moreover, we cannot *perceive* laws of nature, we cannot *see* the manner in which this mass of discrete objects/sense impressions is organised to produce the moving picture of our world. We can only observe how these objects act and react on each other and *infer* from the regularity of these observations the *probability* of their recurrence. In Hume's famous example, our expectation that the sun will rise again tomorrow morning is based solely on our having observed it consistently rising in the past. But however many times we make this observation, the rising of the sun is forever an hypothesis deduced from observation: no invisible force of necessity guarantees it.

Knowledge of the world then cannot be achieved through abstract reason or divine revelation, but only through the accumulation of observed appearances: the world is a collection of individual bits of data—*facts*—to be unearthed, assembled and organised. This observation must be impartial and objective (knowledge must be independent of the social status or political beliefs of the knower) and uncontaminated by theory, which is not knowledge but hypothesis (positivism long believed in the possibility of a neutral observation language, of a language which is a pure reflection of the world, object by object).

This limitation of the real to the observable altered the fundamental question knowledge is meant to answer: knowledge is no longer about 'What is the nature or meaning of the universe, its sense?' but 'What is there in the universe and how does it work?' Positivism is a philosophy of *practical* knowledge, of knowing what objects *do*, and through experimentation and technology, of manipulating them to control and alter their actions to ends of man's own making.

Positivism does not posit a system in the classical sense (in which, by virtue of rationalist induction from *a priori* truths, knowledge is always already present in the very first step). With the death of both rationalism and metaphysics, knowledge becomes a shop-floor activity: guided by the imperatives of the economic system, and unhindered by any values which might stand behind the empirical, usable properties of the object, the world of nature is to be exhaustively strip-mined, dug-over, and turned into objects of instrumental technical control. Knowledge is reduced to knowledge of the Visible, because only the practical qualities of the object are usable. Moreover, those qualities, in the form of individual facts, are quantifiable, measurable. Knowledge becomes a matter of accumulating facts in order to appropriate and use objects. Positivism is the form of knowledge for a world of production and the ownership of objects.

Positivism was initially the banner of a 'progressive' (indeed, revolutionary) project; what has been called the project of 'disenchantment': gods, spirits, the supernatural and the arrogance of pure reason were to be erased from the book of the world. The natural world was no longer to be explained by divine will, humours and monads, sin or invisible metaphysical substances which stood behind the visible and sensible. Positivism led the march out of superstition into knowledge which had the power to control nature.

Of course, this was hardly a disinterested pursuit of the truth (which is why it was literally revolutionary): 'disenchantment' meant in practical terms the dispossession of certain classes and groups of their claim to knowledge, hence social power. The bourgeoisie limited truth to that appropriate to their own form of domination over both nature and society.

In establishing a productive technology and such social relations as free competition and continued reinvestment, the emergent bourgeoisie was challenging two allied powers: the hegemony of religion and its institutions, which were based on knowledge as revealed and sacerdotally consecrated; and the monarchy, supported by the aristocratic classes, for whom truth, knowledge and power were based on tradition and authority, which was given by divine right. Against these the bourgeoisie raised the democracy of the fact: knowledge was now to be judged by its technical efficacy, its potential for practical control and appropriation rather than its adherence to the codes of a moral and political order, or the status of the knower.

On the other hand, the practical and theoretical knowledges of folk culture—especially the knowledges possessed by women—stood outside the formal institutions and formal systems of bourgeois science. Positivism, therefore, concentrated the very possibility of knowledge in a method (the scientific method) and in the person of the scientist—trained to be impartial, the conduit of nature's truth. Folk culture and women's knowledge—medical, social, psychological, agricultural—along with the entire realm of lived experience, was trivialised, declared technically inefficacious, and associated with superstition and the arcane knowledges of clerics and mystics.

Finally, positivism posited itself as *universal* knowledge. What was not accessible to its Vision did not exist. What it could see, it could control: the world was its canvas to map and explore, to exploit and manipulate. This is the parallel voyage of the *Beagle* and the slaving ships.

In photography, this society of production and ownership obtained both a pure exemplar of its form of knowledge, and a symbol of its relation to the world. It is no wonder that photography epitomised the new truth: trivial realism glories in the materiality and surface properties of objects, capturing form, texture, light, etc. as if they were the sole properties of the world and utterly solid in their reality. The photograph intends no higher meaning than the object itself, a monumental re-presentation of the object to be idolised.

In its limitation to the assertion of materiality, photography can roam the world, collecting objects and appearances, inexhaustably accumulating *facts*. Transcending the great classificatory systems of eighteenth- and nineteenth-century science—biology, philology, medical psychology, zoology—photography promised an infinite map: its topography was of the total Visible.

The photograph, as understood by the nineteenth century, was the epitome of the neutral observation language. We must take Fox Talbot's notion of the 'pencil of nature' seriously: Nature inscribed itself on the sensitive emulsion, wrote in man's book. The camera presumed not a human interpreter, but a rigorously scientific optics: an idealised monocular perspective—a mathematical point in space which produced replicable vision. Like the impartiality of science, the camera offered Vision which was not dependent on the viewer. The photograph simply fixed the world: except in its carnival life as illusionism, photography slavishly held to the positive, posited nothing beyond what was presented to it, was the idolator of that-which-is. Moreover it did so not because of human restraint, but because it was guaranteed by its non-humanness, or because the social nature of its vision was inscribed so deeply within its technology as to be invisible.

As a cultural artifact, the photograph appeared as atheoretical in the positivist sense: uncontaminated sense impression. 'Is photography art?' asked the nineteenth century. John Berger is quite correct in locating the problem of photography as art in the photograph's lack of a worked-over surface—for unlike the painting, sketch or sculpture, the mark of the conscious human hand is not visible.[8] In Barthes's words, it is a message without a code: seam-

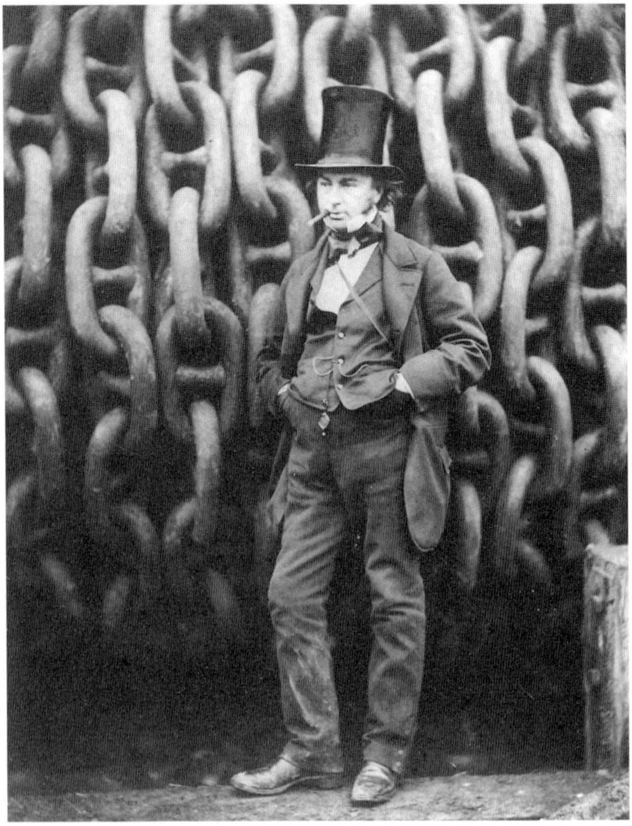

5.2 Isambard Kingdom Brunel, 1857. Robert Howlett

less, made by neither god nor man. It bears no mark of intentionality and therefore eludes art.[9] Art, over the nineteenth-century, is increasingly defined as an act of intentionality, a subsumption of natural and social chaos within human, later individual-subjective, order. Expression and subjectivity, the two new values of high culture, recently enshrined by the romantic movement, were still taking Europe by storm in the 1840s (through Baudelaire not least). Yet neither could be seen as inscribed in the photograph: precisely by becoming a perfect mirror, the photograph lost all value as expression, becoming perfect as representation. Photography passed out of art at the moment of its birth, resigning one power as it monopolised another.

The history of photography is filled with attempts to insert the mark of the artist's hand—the mark of interpretation and re-ordering—into the field of re-presentation, of duplication, from the preference for the textured, crafted feel of the callotype over the metallic daguerrotype, through hand colouring of portraits to the manipulations of the Pictorialists. These artists were not kitschmongers but would-be signmakers spitting in the wind of science: what they did not understand was that the photograph was simply not about expression or self-declaration, but about knowledge and the appropriation of the world through knowledge and the Visible.

On the other hand, the reception given photography by the Classicists is equally illuminating: Ingres is quoted as saying, 'Look at this gentleman! Which of you would be capable of such fidelity, such firmness of line, such delicacy of modelling?' The Salon establishment was heard to give a similar, envious welcome: the public art of commemoration, the memorialisation of the event and the person could find a use for photography that the new art of subjective expression could not. Its symbologies of state and power and civil stability depended on the meticulous assertion of the presence of the object.

Semiotics, from the time of Peirce and Saussure, divided the sign into three parts: the signifier—the material substance of the sign, the sound of the word, the mark on the page; the signified—the psychological meanings of the sign as understood by its reader; and the referent—the actual physical object or action in the world to which the sign refers, for which it stands. The twentieth century has been extremely embarrassed by this third element, by this assumption that signs reflect the world in so simple a way, that the word tree should ultimately point to a real tree. Eventually it denied the referent not only for itself but for all centuries, universalising its embarrassment. Yet, the nineteenth century was decidedly not embarrassed by the referent—the entire culture was devoted to the cognitive and economic grasping of the object itself, in the form of the physical material and the natural fact. The nineteenth-century photograph is seriously and in good faith *solely about its referent*: the presentation of the full materiality and presence of the object.

Marxist art historians have described that tradition of realism in which the painting is a memorial to the man and his possessed objects, but this takes a broader significance when it is connected with positivism as a general form of knowledge. Photography's obsession with the referent is valued because the referent is all that is left, positivism having done away with the ineffable, the revealed, the immaterial. The object can refer to nothing but itself, can lead one no further, nothing stands behind it—and it has become so in order that we may manipulate it efficiently, without distractions, exercise a progressively more perfect technical and economic control over it.

In the photograph this new order achieved a symbolic apotheosis.

The positivist logic of disenchantment installed a new mystique: power, against whose erasure from the Visible Brecht warns, reappears in new forms and symbologies. Photography is itself a statement of the bourgeoisie's power over the material world. Photography in and of itself is an ultimate, gratuitous, symbolic, luxurious appropriation of the Real and denial of the non-Visible. The medium itself, whatever it depicts, proclaims the bourgeoisie's latent ownership of everything.

Let us finish this section with two distinctions which might crystallise some of the above and link it to the very different world we shall describe in Part II.

First, stated baldly, the nineteenth-century photograph was concerned with Being; the twentieth century photograph is concerned with Time. The pre-1900 photograph pointed to its lens as the decisive structuring element; post-1900 to the shutter speed, to the camera's entrance into a flow of events.

Photographs of the last century were nouns: they were about space, solidity, permanence, factness, about the continuity of a valued object achieved through its memorialisation. We think of the statue-like portraits of the Victorians, for example, Cameron's face of Herschel, moulded like two-dimensional sculpture; the posed bodies in an eerie stasis which is not merely the product of antiqueness but of the photographs' aim of giving the object an immutable individuality. Even the blur of subjects which moved during the long exposures seem to show up not the actuality of an event but the hardness of the object beneath the blur. The early uses of photography employed this monumentalist quality, this ability of the photograph to give its subject the solemn dignity of bodies out of time: not only in portraits but in the crucial use of the camera to portray architecture and monuments, both at home and abroad.

The photograph today is a verb, it is about events, action, movement, about the transportation of insubstantial realities across time. We look to the photograph not for *knowledge* of an object, nor even the magical presence of an object, but for the outlines of a story, for some chain of events outside the frame which could give some sense to the arbitrary collection of things, meaningless in themselves, assembled on paper. Even the advertising packshot seems to imply a narrative.

Certainly technical factors entered into the making of this distinction: slow films above all. But we need only look at the concentration of resources on lens-making in the last century to see that decisions were made about priorities, and we could also interpret the search for faster film in terms of wanting a sharper *object*, wanting to capture the more transitory *object*, rather than a desire for an involvement in time *per se*.

Second, we must distinguish between two different conceptions of people's relations to objects within the social relations of consumption: the nineteenth-century bourgeoisie owned objects (which incidentally they also used); today, we *consume* things (which incidentally we also possess). Owning, the acquisition of objects, is measured by Being, by the duration of the object itself, as object. Consumption, the devouring of an object through use, is measured by Time and turn-over. The bourgeois object, and its celebration in the image, must be understood in terms of owning a materiality. Owning meant control over the object, power over a resource, capital—an investment whose value is calculated over generations, a purchased permanence and legacy. The image must capture this, and at the same time, sustain itself as permanent and unique. Present-day consumption is a steady flow of substitutable objects across our space rather than the projection of unique objects through time, and it is hard to imagine backwards to when the photograph did not reflect this devalued turn-over rather than the glorification of the referent itself.



### Part II: The Consumption of Signs

In Part I, I described positivism as an ideology for the bourgeoisie as owners and appropriators, an ethos of control and manipulation, an ideology symbolic of and commensurate with the operation of a new organisation of production. The present section focuses on a major shift of orientation within capitalism and its consequences for the meaning of representation. For, by the second decade of the present century, the essential structure of the capitalist mode of *production* was basically in place: the value-form of the commodity was dominant and generalised to a world market; the labour force was organised and disciplined into wage labour and the factory system; the institutions of capital accumulation and investment were established; the invention of new production methods was routinised; the basic infrastructure of communications and transportation constructed. The technical problems of commodity production were either solved or soluble by extending existing institutions and procedures. A system and material basis for the production of commodities on an expanding scale was available.

On the other hand, from the 1880s onwards, capitalism was more and more consciously preoccupied with solving the technical problems of consumption: how to reorganise the relations of consumption into forms appropriate to the scale and form of the exponentially expanding productive forces. A problem of absorption:

how to effect a shift from private consumption based on the public model of thrift and accumulation to consumption adequate to realise the investment thus accumulated. A problem of management: how to make the worker as profitable and productive in his or her leisure time as at work. A problem of control: how to systematise consumption so that it becomes as predictable and crisis free as the production line. A problem of expansion: how to create spaces within already exhaustively exploited product categories so that the field of competition may be broadened, the rate of expansion of production increased, so that more can be produced.

The new focus on consumption involved such things as the reorganisation of retailing in line with emerging national mass-markets, with unified pricing and standardisation of products under brand names; the development of the ability to market new categories of products; the combating of traditional notions of consumption which were based on saving, durability, heritage, functional utility, and the avoidance of debt; the extension of the notion of work to include the citizens' duty to consume. The capitalism of consumption was concerned with an economy of rapid turn-over and replaceability, newness and perpetual revolution in taste and technology, a shift from acquisition as a mode of private accumulation to buying as a form of high-velocity waste, a way of making room for the next onslaught of goods.

The relation of *consumption*, properly so-called, as opposed to that of owning or possessing, has been sketched out in Part I. It is an act which leaves the object and its instrumental qualities far behind in a fluid game of meaning. For this new game of consumption, the old structure of reference—of signs that point to tangible objects-in-the-world and enhance their sturdiness, factness, intractability—is too fixed and firm. Through its assertion of power through tangible presence the calling up of the referent inflames greed but deflates fantasy. According to Marx, to the capitalist worker greed is the emptiest of fantasies, for it represents a hopeless desire to accumulate like a capitalist, to turn wages into capital, to treat purchase as if it were investment, when all a worker is structurally capable of doing is to consume, literally to *use* up, use-values in order to maintain oneself as labour. Labour is a furnace which must consume in order to produce. The capitalist worker's object is by its nature transient, fluid, repeated, illusory, ungraspable except in the form of a flow, an intravenous drip.

However, as Marx wrote in the *Grundrisse*, there is a contradiction here: to the capitalist, his own workers appear to him as mere labour, whose consumption must be kept to a minimum level of mere subsistence.[10] However, everyone else's workers appear to the capitalist as consumers, purchasers of his commodities, and must represent the largest possible effective demand. The capitalist therefore works upon the transitory object of the worker, the worker's model of consumption as opposed to accumulation, speeding it up and channelling it beyond the realm of necessity into a way of life, using advertising, retailing, marketing, popular culture, etc. to intervene in the most intimate areas of life—the domain of the private and of the family—and to brand them with the stamp of consumption. An organisation is created: leisure is the time devoted to consumption; wives and women are the decision-makers and motivators of consumption, youth their informants and allies, husbands their *raison d'etre* and inspector of consumption; their home a reflection of the world of goods, a place of symbolic lacks, perpetually ageing and falling behind.

Under the older regime of ownership, the process of consumption was exhausted in the act of purchase: consumption came to an end in the object itself and its properties, in the enjoyment of its use-value. However, under the regime of consumption, this process must never be allowed to end: consumption must be made a constantly renewed and inexhaustible process. The 'real object' as an end point, as a use-value which satisfies, becomes a barrier to the forces of consumption: it is a relationship appropriate to accumulation not consumption. The object must be made transient so that no desires leave the market for long. What is needed is a system which never allows the object to become fixed and stable and thus a finality.

Thus the consumer object—the contemporary form of the workers' object—is hardly an object at all: the object is made to disappear in the very act of its purchase. Owning the object does not confer a fixed, recognised cultural position, or even the enjoyment of usable properties of the object, the stable filling of a need—because what is being sold now is not the 'real object' at all but participation in the game of consumption, a game in which, through representation, the properties of the object (particularly properties of style, image) are kept in a constant state of flux, never allowed to solidify for longer than is required for people to identify and learn to desire them. The object can thus be made to disappear in owning it—because the game has already begun to move on. You may have bought the goods, but you have not captured the sign, which is detachable from the object and always a step ahead: the object alone lies in your hands, meaningless, insignificant.

In terms of culture and meaning, then, from the turn of the century, capitalism became increasingly driven by the need to produce *not* more referents or signifieds (neither objects nor conceptual systems) for consumption, but more and more *signifiers*—visible rallying points for fantasy and 'consumer investment': Youth, Motherhood, Conformity, Modernity, Leisure, Home, Function made manifest in infinite variations. This production of signifiers is not characterised by coalescence around a stable system of solid objects, but flexibility, re-arrangeability, looseness.

The Situationists have described the results of this process with the metaphor of 'the Spectacle': in contemporary culture, the manufactured world of representations and images has utterly detached itself from 'reality', bears no relation to lived experience and constitutes itself as a 'pseudo-world apart', but one upon which our vision is fully concentrated. The signs of the Spectacle do not refer to the world but only to other signs and so the play of signs becomes autonomous and infinitely flexible: the Spectacle can be judged by no standard of meaning but its own constantly changing codes. The production of possible signifiers is unlimited; their meaning (i.e., other shifting signs) to be set at will.

From production to consumption: the Visible no longer presumes to be Truth, nor appearance to be knowledge—for the sign must not refer to a Real at all. The positive, the that-which-is, is no longer the intractable reality of durable, ownable nature: reality is rather the closed system of commodities and their allures. The positive is now made positive not by the limiting of knowledge (the expulsion of metaphysics by disenchantment) but by an explosion of unstoppable signification (the creation of objects as signs). The signifier without referent allows the diminution and substitution of reality itself. In place of reference we have the construction of a manufacturable real, a real which can be perpetually renewed, reconstructed, re-possessed.

I am not putting forward the Situationist fallacy that the world was somehow more authentic or real before the Spectacle. What we are describing are movements within ideology: nineteenth-century positivism desired a stable and eternal nature and worked hard to produce the *fact*. I don't know or care if their signs *really* referred to referents; the point is that their system only makes sense in terms of such reference, whereas ours only make sense when we see how it selectively cut itself off from adherence to fixed entities. Moreover, what is important for us now, and in this essay, are the consequences for the Visible: meaning means something fundamentally different now, being neither knowledge, nor evidence, nor solidity, but flow, play, self-reference, emptiness.

A new object of photography thus emerged: the object as sign, as transitory and fluid and therefore manipulable meaning. Yet what is most crucial is that in encountering and constructing this new object in the consumer world, photography's positivist core—its trivial realism—was simultaneously reduced to absurdity and turned into the basis of photography's new power. The history of photography over the present century is a movement whereby that realism which was once the basis of its claim to knowledge becomes the foundation on which it constructs the Spectacle. At the core of this movement is a demotion of the Visible, of appearance, from the status of Truth, a demotion carried out not by the likes of Brecht or Baudelaire, but by commercial capitalism for its own needs and ends.

There is a tradition even in nineteenth-century photography which runs counter to the pursuit of knowledge: the camera as toy, as carnival or side-show attraction, as marvel, as gimmick. Wedgewood, Niepcé, Fox Talbot and his friends had impeccable credentials as gentleman of science. But Daguerre? He was a showman whose feet were firmly planted in the circus ring and illusionism. His quest for the fixed image began with the construction of panoramas, an illusion of depth and reality to be unveiled before a paying audience. Daguerre and his hawking, quick-buck hangers-on were selling access to a funfair. Yes, they immediately launched into portraiture—the monumentalising and memorialising of the bourgeois in his own image. However these portraits were also a *fad*, a matter of fashion (like the duplicated calling cards which took Paris by storm in the 1850s). The photograph signified a game as well as an acquisition, something frivolous while still recognisably decisive and powerful.

The photographic craze was constantly renewed throughout the century. There was a vast output of trick apparatuses and gimmicks: miniature and detective cameras, an industry in cheap frames and containers for the new talismen, photographic jewellery (as worn by Queen Victoria). Above all, the stereoscope was intermittently resurrected, and with the same duality as marked the portrait: yes, the illusion of the third dimension could be seen as another extension of the bourgeoisie's dominion over 'the object itself', a heightening of its solidity and factness; but it could also be simply a matter of the marketing of illusion as illusion, the stereoscope as a drawing-room object whose primary reference was to magic and magic-shows for children, parlour-games and leisure, to something taken seriously only for fun. As an experience, its meaning (like that of the holograph today) was exhausted in the audience's wonder at the completeness of the illusion.

The photographic craze was also renewed through its articulation with other fads: pre-eminently the marriage of Kodak and the bicycle in the 1890s (later duplicated in the 1920s with the advent of the mass motor car and motor tourism). The bicycle was a

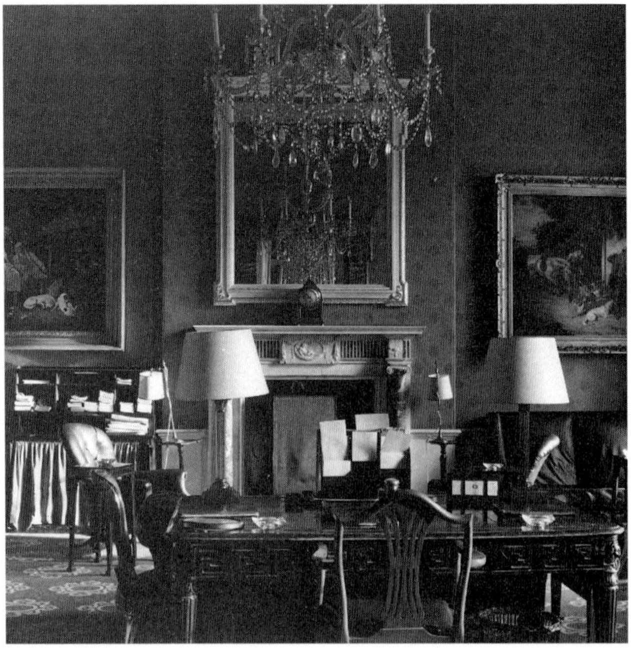

Unwritten laws Bound him
as much as if They had been
Printed
in black and white.
They came down to him
from Old Times.

5.3 and 5.4 *Gentlemen*, 1982.
Karen Knorr

prototype in the development of commercial capitalism. Uniting function and leisure in one relatively cheap commodity and sold as an item of family leisure, it captured a truly mass market. Coupled with the bicycle, the new and more simple camera found its way into its familiar mass-market role of recorder of personal events, tourism and happy days (the family photographer as somewhat irritating figure of ridicule emerged at this time). Especially in France, the camera joined the bicycle in a forward-looking structure of consumption and leisure which involved clubs, publications, regular sporting events, development of restaurants and hotels, a rediscovery of the countryside and a nostalgia for a vanishing peasant life experienced by urbanites through tourism, an institutionalisation in practice and ideology of family-based leisure activity and of the holiday. But above all, camera and bicycle, alone and together, created the figure of mass, capitalised, leisure expenditure.

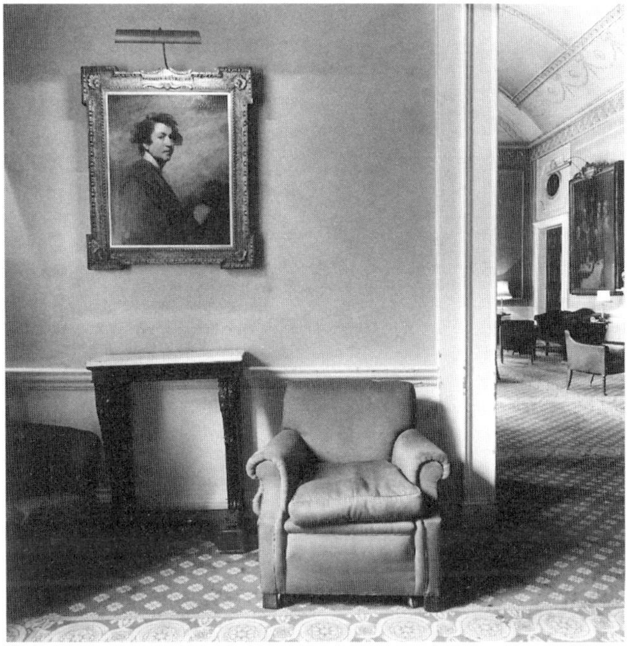

How he longed
desperately
for the halcyon Days
of his Youth
when an Englishman
could satisfy his own Honour.
No questions asked

An important theme can be seen emerging from these early years of mass (amateur, snapshot) photography, a theme that presages a new structure of the Visible, a tear in the photograph as knowledge:

A new and qualitatively different imperative was emerging as the motor of image-making: velocity of turn-over, of proliferation of images, *throughput*. For example, the case of photographic manufacturers: Kodak's profits and growth potential were based on the sale and processing of film. Its marketing was therefore geared to producing the largest possible number of film users consuming as much film as possible. Camera technology and all ancillary services were tailored to the highest degree of simplicity, requiring the least possible knowledge or thought on the part of the amateur. But beyond the specific marketing logic of Kodak, based on film and box cameras, the very idea of mass-production in photography required the creation of a mass usership, the widest possible proliferation of users with a constantly expanding production of images.

But the image became an object of high-velocity consumption in other forms too, heating up consumption to the same degree as the new productive forces: what is important about the 'mechanical reproduction' of images, for example, is not the potentially infinite multiplication of a single image which destroys its artifactual sanctity (as shown by the Surrealist attitude to found objects—which Walter Benjamin himself championed—mass-produced detritus was still collected for its aura, though it was now called 'dialectical image'). Rather, it is the insatiable demand for new images, of short currency and in need of constant renewal and replacement, generated by the commercial apparatus of mass reproduction—the magazine, newspaper, advertisement. Mass reproduction did not simply multiply images, but produced multiplicity. In a sense, this multiplicity was a culmination of the notion of knowledge as accumulation, as collection of facts, enshrined by positivism. But as it came to fruition, its significance reversed itself: it is not multiplicity as discovery of objects in the world, but as creation of the idea of a changing world, a replaceable and disposable world, a world which puts on a new face each morning.

A grave doubt about the meaning of images begins to emerge as positivist accumulation turns to simple turn-over—the spectre of the Arbitrary:

I am not alone in the following experience: beside my enlarger, I face a pile of contact sheets representing 20-odd rolls of film I've just processed, a backlog from several weeks' miscellaneous snapping. They contain a mixture of intense and careless, functional and whimsical, personal and private photography, and they lie beside a very much larger pile of many years' worth of yet more diverse shooting.

I am at a complete loss as to what to do with all of it. Why would I print any one negative rather than any other: any choice seems arbitrary. Indeed, I have some reasonably clear aesthetic fancies; I respond to some inexplicable resonances; I note some personal or political relevances or potential connections with ongoing projects; I sniff out distant memories of why I originally took some of these pictures.

But there is an underlying unease: all these pieces of the world suddenly appear so diverse as to be homogeneous. In their quality of awesome individuality and concreteness they are all identical. They offer up no meaning of themselves.

The new weight of imagery, the triumph of turnover and throughput, the endless duplication of the world through slivers of two-dimensional brute realism—these release some unquiet doubts about the meaning of 'the image'. Why this and not that? In mass photography, the weight of imagery increases our awareness of arbitrariness (we despair of sustaining meaning) while their actual use is progressively stereotyped and constrained (we reduce meaning in order to strengthen it). What can a 'piece of the world' mean?

Enlightenment philosophy accelerated the descent towards the concrete insofar as the concrete was in some ways brought to power with the revolutionary bourgeoisie. From the ruin of Heaven, man fell into the ruins of his own world. What happened? Something like this: ten thousand people are convinced that they have seen a fakir's rope rise into the air, while as many cameras prove that it hasn't moved an inch. Scientific objectivity exposes mystification. Very good, but what does it show us? A coiled rope, of absolutely no interest. I have little inclination to choose between the doubtful pleasure of being mystified and the tedium of contemplating reality which does not concern me. A reality which I have no grasp on, isn't this the old lie reconditioned, the ultimate stage of mystification? (Raoul Vaneigem)[11]

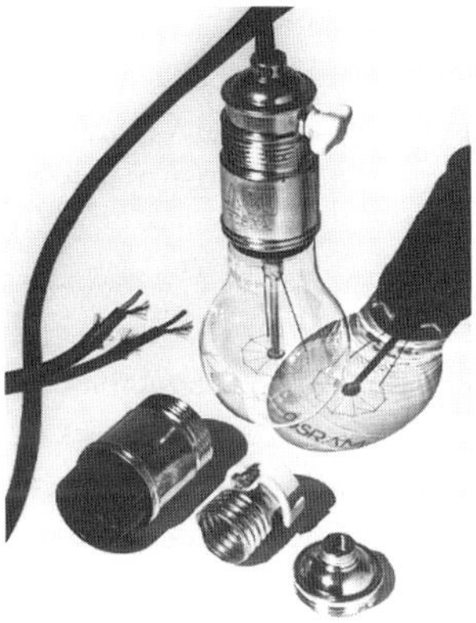

5.5 Incandescent Lamp, 1929. Hans Finsler

Positivism urged disenchantment—the triumph and embodiment of practice-able knowledge. What it accomplished was the flattening or reducing of truth to the trivial, the reduction of the real to the visible, partial, singular, *dead.* For, if nothing stands behind the appearance, the closer we get to the object, the less meaning it can have.

New Objectivity was a decisive moment for photography. It was the apotheosis of that positivism in which detailed, detached observation constituted knowledge of the thing itself. By entering and embracing the photograph's trivial realism as the 'truth of the medium', it tried to turn the photography of record into art (figure 5.5). Carrying futurism to its apogee, it mystically believed that *on the other side* of (positivist) science lay supreme beauty and a truth which transcended science by becoming human once again. Edward Weston and Karl Blossfeldt turned mystical over their discoveries of order, symmetry and anthropomorphism in nature. The world was indeed beautiful. August Sander more naively continued the classificatory quest of nineteenth-century science aimlessly and emptily. The less significance they found, the more mystical meaning the artists inserted. (Tina Modotti, seeing Weston's *Capsicums* for the first time, thought they revealed a terrible illness and wrote him a concerned letter.)

Surrealism is the nightmare truth of positivism and New Objectivity. Lautréamont foreshadowed surrealism by presiding over the marriage of the umbrella and the sewing machine. Those trivially 'realistic' objects placed side by side within the photographic frame (the signifier of intentionality, the promise of readable meaning) mock knowledge and truth. Within that frame *everything means*, and therefore nothing is of dependable significance. The found and random objects of the world, an umbrella and a sewing machine, are mixed within the frame which asks us to make links and connections between an essentially arbitrary assemblage. If the world is a random display generator, then photographic vision is not the power of truth but the mad king's court jester. Its power is simply the power to spin significations, to mystify by convincing us that sense exists where all is lunatic and contingent. Photography power is the power of sophistical play. After the surrealism of photography, how can we ever trust meaning? The marriage of the umbrella and the sewing machine ridicules the notion of the readability of the real: it makes obvious that what we read, what is visible, is accidental, is ironic, is not knowledge.

In fact the fate of New Objectivity was not to be absurdity but advertising. By the 1930s, its fetishisation of the object as fact, its loving representation of the object through scrupulous detail, was no longer the foundation of a science but a style of advertising.[12] (Many commercial concerns financially supported polemicists against pictorialism.) The image now had nothing to do with truth about the object—the detail of observation existed only to make us desire more, to stimulate our drooling. The point was to make a better signifier, by presenting what was once meant to be a more present and tangible referent.

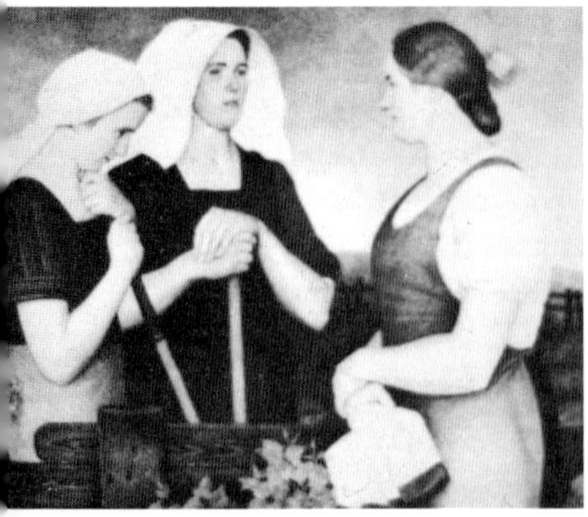

5.6 Young farm women, 1935. Adolf Wissel

The Nazis stated clearly and without embarrassment the new levels of manipulation that could be achieved by detaching image from referent while at the same time increasing emphasis on the trivial realism of the photograph. Nazism rejected aesthetic realism as decadent: realism (besides being sociologically the domain of cultural bolsheviks and Jews) focused on the dirt of the world, evading and degrading art's real duty, which was to substantialise the 'ideal' (pure racial types, the perfect female form, virility and motherhood). Photography could never be an art while it—in the words of a National Socialist aesthetician—'adheres more rigorously than any other medium to the dogma that reality reflects truth'.[13] Thus art photography had to return to pictorialism (while painting, ironically, had to avoid all abstraction and be photographic in its embodiment of the ideal in concrete form, making the universal and the true visible). (figure 5.6.)

And yet—the Nazis relied on the trivial realism of the photograph to confirm the Ideal presented by painting. Berthold Hinz describes books in which juxtaposed paintings depicted ideals of

German superiority with photographs set next to them, and which by mirroring the paintings' form, style, poses, etc., were to show, crudely, that these ideals *really* existed in everyday German life. It took a photograph to do that, to concretise the stereotype.[14]

But another example is more stunning: Hinz describes how, although very few of the Reich's architectural projects were ever actually built, 'it was a continuous stream of publications about these projects, the cleverly photographed models, and the life-sized mock-ups of details that created the still prevailing impression of the quantity and quality of National Socialist architecture.' Hinz describes the method as 'multiplying aesthetic appearances':[15] 'It was therefore not so important that anything was actually created or achieved in the field or art...but that the public was convinced that a project or a promise had been carried out'.[16] (figure 5.7)

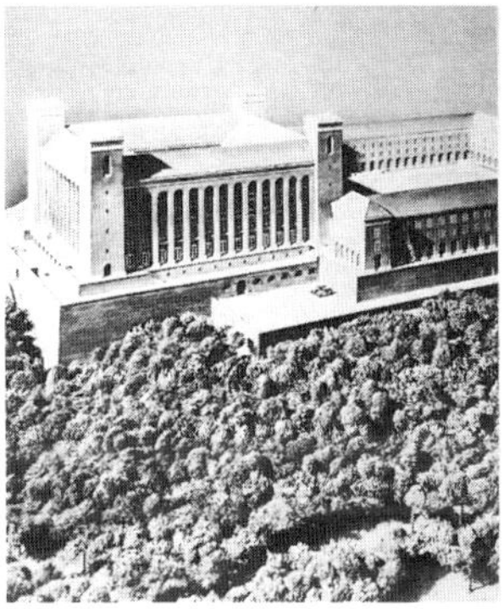

5.7 Model for the Danzig Military Academy, 1938. Hans Hermann Klaje

The impression of a national culture was built upon partial 'objects' which referred to nothing at all. If 'propaganda' means anything it is precisely this instrumental technology of constructing a real of images, whose judge is neither truth nor reason but a certain plausibility of illusionism. But it is a puffery blown up through realism: its building blocks are photographs which are taken to be 'pieces of the world'. The trivial realism of the camera is irrefutable: we are dealing with *laws* of optics and chemistry—*something*, something *real*, stood or swept before the lens and now flows before our eyes, in inhuman precision, coded chemically. A photograph is always 'circumstantial evidence'—no longer sufficient proof in today's court of knowledge but still, always, swaying the minds of we-the-jury.

Today's photography makes use of the same dynamic: use is made of the belief that however bizarre or obviously constructed the photograph might be, it is always 'somewhere-real', a real object takes its place at some level of the image. Erving Goffman used the concept of 'commercial realism' to describe this process in advertising: suppose we are looking at an advertisement which depicts a family. Through certain signs we will easily and immediately recognise and describe the people in the photo as 'a family'. But if we were asked whether the models who posed for the photo were *really*, in real life, a family, the answer could well be, 'Probably not, but what does it matter?': 'the viewer is to engage knowingly in a kind of make-believe, treating the depicted world as if it were real-like [sic] but of course not actually real'.[17]

Something real is there—models congealed through careful stereotyping into a family, real people acting plausibly—but we are well-trained to understand what level of reality to expect and not demand any more. Within commercial realism, images are treated—knowingly, playfully—*as if they were real.* Through the trivial realism of the photograph, the referent—the dependable— real haunts the photograph like an amputee's phantom limb.

Positivism limited the real to the visible; on the basis of the visible could now be constructed a new real, new reals: we can make of the real a most flexible instrument on which any tune can be played by treating the represented *real* as the *represented* real.

What have been the strategies through which photographers have dealt with this new and shifting game? How does one construct oppositional knowledges, truths, realities, when the very notions of knowledge, truth and reality have been turned into a quaint and nostalgic fantasy?

The avant-gardists of the 1920s recognised the banality of trivial realism and renounced the identity of vision and knowledge. Hence Brecht. But in asking if the visible meant anything at all, they also asked, 'How can the visible be *used*? Can we return our arbitrary bits of the visible to their structures in the real (e.g. John Heartfield)? If positive vision does not yield knowledge, can we use vision to destroy the positive: by disrupting illusionism, by straining vision to make it a problematic activity and hence a dynamic, creative, struggling force (e.g. Alexander Rodchenko, Moholy-Nagy)?'

Social documentarists, on the other hand, (whose interests were more vitally vested in the photograph as knowledge of a referent) attempted to escape the subversion of knowledge/ vision by sheer will-power and good intentions. Can we inform our vision with concerned passion and thereby fill it with meaning again (the F.S.A., Gene Smith, etc.)? If we are sufficiently compassionate/ committed/well-informed, perhaps our pictures will tell the truth about power and the world again? Or, latterly, in the socialist photography of the 1970s, if we demystify the process/relinquish control to the represented/nail-down meanings through captions and constructions, perhaps we can *evade* power and allow people to tell their own truth (and with positive images, of course).

But as Marx said *a propos* Proudhon and the Utopian socialists, this is merely the application of morality to economics: for the problem is simply that the visible is no longer about knowledge at all.[18] The semioticians' attack on documentary truth, contending that photography is not truth but system, is in a sense a step behind what everyone else already knew and lived—for we have long since ceased to believe that any photograph, any representation, refers to the real world at all.

Documentary has always been a test case for realism, being that imagery which is defined by its engagement with the real, its loyalty and sense of responsibility to its object, its witness. We look to documentary for a point of exit from the circle of pictures of pictures of pictures of pictures. Yet the documentary photograph has become literally *incredible*—we have to force ourselves to believe in a reality which stands behind it. We bemoan the extent to which we are inured to the impact of photographs of horror and pain, or the extent to which we treat them as a Sunday morning colour supplement thrill. Yet at some level we are neither inured nor unbelieving: we simply know that our response is irrelevant, that we have ceased to believe in the consequences or stability of any meaning, that vision as knowledge is irrelevant, impotent, unusable, whereas vision as spectacle is how we participate in our own culture. For many people, the spectacle was symbolically completed when they watched scenes from Vietnam on TV. The shock and outrage at seeing the war in your own living-room was not revulsion at war itself when presented so immediately. It was revulsion at this sign of a society that could turn anything into a commodified image, could package even the ultimate real of death and drain it of reality (one strained to convince oneself that one was *really* watching people dying), could—without embarrassment—process war through the same mechanism it used for soapsuds, and without missing a step. Vietnam on TV showed people not reality in close-up, but reality irretrievably unhinged. The Spectacle uses the photographic frame not to provide a window on the world, but to present the game of looking out the window on the world. (Even in the 1940s there was the joke: did you see that in life or *Life* magazine?)

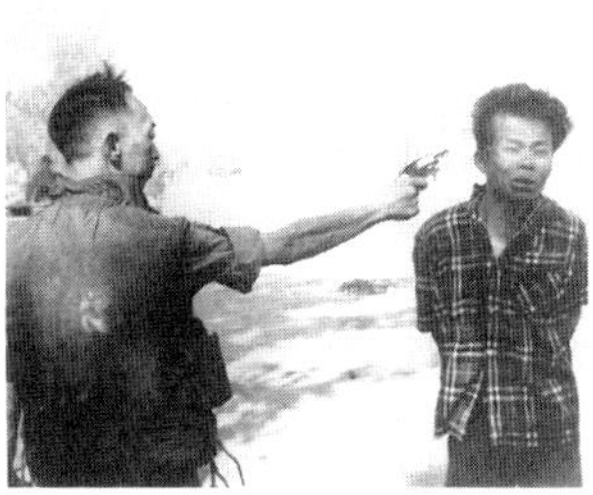

5.8 Execution in Saigon Street, 1968. Eddie Adams

Documentary operates a nineteenth-century ethic: it aims to make visible that which is excluded from vision—sub-cultures and ethnic minorities, positive images, the poor. Exclusion is the mode of operation of positivism. Apartheid is its exemplar: if you can't see it, it isn't there. But the whole point of the Spectacle is that it excludes *nothing*, makes everything visible in order to consume it, incorporate it into the play of signs and use it for new meanings. Documentary merely churns out more images to be co-opted.

But if documentary photography shows us that spectacular photography constructs a staged reality; that it is the triumph of the open signifier, the infinitely fixable sign; that we no longer engage with the image in a search for the referent, in order to feel the reality or truth of that-which-is-represented—if all that has come to pass, the question for photographic practice becomes: Is there anything that the photograph no longer refers us to? Is there a field outside the image with which we have now lost touch? If there is no reference, can there be any engagement? If the photograph no longer points to a reality can it be effective?

We have—some of us—been well-trained over the 1970s never to talk about, never to mention 'reality' without grievous intellectual embarrassment. We can only talk, experience, be constituted *within* ideology and language. We can only produce ideologies, not knowledges of the real, for we can have no separate access to 'reality' and therefore cannot talk of it except in inverted commas, the 'reality we produce in theory and in ideology'.

This perspective was in part a thorough-going attack on positivism, but an attack which very closely parallels the Spectacle so that it seems to arise and draw its image of the world from the Spectacle itself (I would argue that it does): it glories in the self-referring system without point of exit, a system with no referent but only reference to its own imaginings. Against the complete independence of the fact as in positivism, this perspective posits the world's total construction in and by theory: a kind of academic spectacular.

In terms of suggestions for practice, for what photographs to make, this perspective seems to suggest only a masochistic absorption in the play of the Spectacle, of the unhinged signifier, of one's own work as simply another image floating in this stream.

Yet it would seem absurd to be loosened from the referent-as-truth-of-the-photo, from a logic of appropriation, merely in order to collapse into a photography parasitically working over the text of dominant imagery, parodying advertisements, chasing signifiers (of the feminine, of capital) which are always one step ahead of us; or in order to escape into endless self-reflexive comment on the image as representation, as mediation, as media. The photograph as knowledge, even as witness, no longer works; the photograph as self-reference is impotent; the image as irony is self-indulgent and soon boring: we want no documentary, no modernism, no pop art.

When modern theory turns from this negative absorption, from playing *into* the Spectacle, it embraces the play of the signifier as the foundation of a liberation of meaning, of a belief in the nearly utopian potential of limitless signification. As if the Spectacle has shown us now what meaning really is: we can simply construct fields of tension wherein, because final meanings are suspended, we are offering a site for continuous production of meaning.

What is missing here is the recognition that this 'limitless signification' is not limitless at all, except within quite specific parameters. For example, the play of signs within advertising is so constructed as to be infinitely flexible, so that meaning can emerge anywhere, but meaning does not in fact emerge *everywhere*. The meanings, or the range of playable meanings which emerge in the advertisement are chosen according to very precise and specifiable logics, needs, imperatives (of marketing, production, finance, of systems of commodities). As this essay has tried to suggest, the very notion and practice of free signification rest on specific notions and practices of the object, consumption, need, economy. The photograph is not knowledge, but it is also not simply an abstract assemblage of rules, or arbitrary and volatile signs: the photograph is a highly intentional material object, a 'piece of the world' in the different sense of an object in the world, as 'determined' as any other.

That sense of 'objectness' need not lead us into more deconstruction or more indeterminate signification, but into something else: if that 'object' (the photograph) represents determinate economic, political and ideological practices working to produce manufactured and very flexible real, what other practice and real can we counterpose to it? Given that the aim can no longer be to substitute one truth ('our' truth) for another, the aim is to find new sources for a new real, an oppositional real.

Perhaps a new photography of engagement, a new vision of politics, would construct new codes, new fantasy, new and deeper reservoirs of imagery drawn from lived experience and practical understandings. Perhaps it would construct its own field of reference. This new photography would indeed carry out raids on the dominant imagery and play in its openable spaces, but, crucially, it could also be read in its own right, have its own form of consistency and logic. It would aim to be an authentically alternative imagery—a play of signs ordered according to rhythms, structures and desires which are quite independent of the Spectacle.



**Reference Notes**

**1** Max Horkheimer and Theodor Adorno, 'The Culture Industry: Enlightenment as Mass Deception', in *The Dialectic of Enlightenment*, trans. John Cumming, Verso, London, 1979 (first published 1944).

**2** See Sadie Plant, *The Most Radical Gesture: The Situationist International in a Postmodern Age*, Routledge, London, 1992.

**3** I have explored this more recently in D. Slater, 'Photography and modern vision: the spectacle of "natural magic"', in C. Jenks, ed., *Visual Culture*, Routledge, London, 1995.

**4** See also my *Consumer Culture and Modernity*, Polity Press, Oxford,1996.

**5** B. Brecht, cited in Walter Benjamin, 'A Short History of Photography', in W. Benjamin, *One-Way Street and Other Writings*, Verso, London, p.255.

**6** B. Baudelaire, 'Photography' (1859), in B. Newhall, *Photography: Essays and Images*, Secker & Warburg, London, 1980.

**7** B. Baudelaire, 'Photography' (1859), in B. Newhall, *Photography: Essays and Images*, Secker & Warburg, London, 1980.

**8** John Berger, *Ways of Seeing*, BBC Books, 1972, ch.1.
**9** R. Barthes, 'Rhetoric of the Image' in *Image-Music-Text*, Hill and Wang, New York, 1977.
**10** K. Marx, *Grundrisse*, Penguin/New Left Review, Harmondsworth, 1975, p.283.
**11** Raoul E. Vaneigem, *The Revolution of Everyday Life*, Rising Free Collective, London, p.6.
**12** See W. Benjamin's critique of New Objectivity (Neue Saklichkeit), in particular the work of Renger-Patzsch in 'The Author as Producer' in *Thinking Photography*, ed. V. Burgin, Macmillan, 1982. See also 'A Short History of Photography', *Screen*, vol.13, no.1, Spring 1972; extract reproduced in *Germany: The New Photography 1927-33*, ed. David Mellor, ACGB, 1978.
**13** Buldur von Schirach, Reich Youth Leader, 1941, quoted in B. Hinz, *Art in the Third Reich*, Blackwell, Oxford, 1980, p.173.
**14** Hinz, *Art in the Third Reich*.
**15** Ibid., p.182.
**16** Ibid., p.181.
**17** Erving Goffman, *Gender Advertisements*, Macmillan, London, 1976.
**18** K. Marx, *The Poverty of Philosophy*, Progress Publishers, Moscow.

**Further Reading**


• Theodor Adorno and Max Horkheimer, *Dialectic of Enlightenment*, Verso, London, 1979.
• Jean Baudrillard, *For a Critique of The Political Economy of the Sign*, in Telos, 1981.
• Ernst Bloch et al., *Aesthetics and Politics*, Verso, London, 1980.
• Terry Eagleton, 'Capitalism, Modernism and Postmodernism', *New Left Review*, no.146, July 1984.
• Stuart Ewen, *Captains of Consciousness: Advertising and the Social Roots of the Consumer Culture*, McGraw-Hill, New York, 1976.
• Stuart Ewen and Elisabeth Ewen, *Channels of Desire: Mass Images and the Shaping of American Consciousness*, McGraw-Hill, New York, 1982.
• Erving Goffman, *Gender Advertisements*, Macmillan, Basingstoke, 1976.
• Berthold Hinz, *Art in the Third Reich*, Blackwell, Oxford, 1980.
• Fredric Jameson, 'Postmodernism or the Cultural Logic of Late Capitalism', *New Left Review*, no.146, 1984.
• Leszek Kolalcowski, *Positivist Philosophy*, Penguin, Harmondsworth, 1972.
• David Mellor, ed., *Germany: The New Photography 1927-33*, Arts Council of Great Britain, London, 1978.
• Daniel Miller, *Material Culture and Mass Consumption*, Blackwell, Oxford, 1987.
• Mark Poster, ed., *Jean Baudrillard: Selected Writings*, Polity, Oxford, 1988.
• Peter Wollen, 'Photography and Aesthetics', *Screen*, vol.19, no.4, Winter 1978/9.

6

# On Foucault: Disciplinary Power and Photography

David Green

Introduction by
**David Green**

The following essay was written with one objective in mind. This was to produce a short and accessible outline of some of the key issues raised in the work of Michel Foucault which, in the late 1970s and early 1980s, had been highly influential in formulating a critical account of the historical relationships between photography, ideology and forms of social power. Insofar that the writings of Foucault continue to be central to any attempt to conceptualise the mechanisms of power operative in modern societies and offer us valuable insights into how power is inscribed within particular forms of visual representation, I hope that this essay may still prove useful as an introduction to these areas of debate, especially where they contribute to the study of photography.

'On Foucault: Disciplinary Power and Photography' was written shortly after Foucault's death in June 1984 and before the belated appearance of his final two books, *The Use of Pleasure* and *The Care of the Self*, these being the second and third volumes of the projected six-part *The History of Sexuality*. These late works appeared to mark a substantive shift in Foucault's concerns and one that seemed entirely unexpected on the basis of what had gone before. To begin with there was the abandonment of a history of the discourses of sexuality in the modern period (which the author had outlined in the first volume) to be replaced by a series of reflections on sexuality and issues of ethics in classical antiquity. Moreover, whilst there clearly is a continuing concern with a history of subjectivity in which the concept of power remains central, what was novel in *The Use of Pleasure* and *The Care of the Self*, was the extent to which Foucault deployed an idea of an ethics of the self as the basis for a notion of individual agency capable, if not of overturning, at least of resisting the forces of a disciplinary and normalising regime. There was then a measure of self-critique on Foucault's part of a nihilistic emphasis in his earlier work on power and the body which left very little room for the 'struggle against the forms of subjection', that is, against the forms of normalising regulation of our sexual and social identities. If there is a major shortcoming to the following essay it is that it does likewise.

The essay stresses Foucault's formulation of the historical emergence of the body as the nexus of power/knowledge relations which give rise to what he termed a 'politics of the body'. Given the convergence of these issues with Foucault's later interest in themes of sexuality it is surprising that the question of gender (and the politics of gender) is so understated in Foucault's writings. Even more surprising, however, looking back to when this essay was written, was how few feminist appropriations of Foucauldian analysis there had then been. Yet it would seem obvious that Foucault's analysis of the (sexualised) body as the object and vehicle of forms of power/knowledge has a significant bearing upon feminist analyses of patriarchal control over women's bodies, be it in the domains of science, medicine or art; and that his notions of disciplinary power and the regimes and techniques of surveillance lend themselves to feminist critiques of the subjugation of women as the objects of both knowledge and desire. Such things are, of course, never so simple and, as recent studies reveal, the relationship between Foucault and the politics of feminism is far from unproblematic, not least for the fact as previously noted that his earlier studies are at the very least ambivalent as to the prospects of resistance to the operations of power in modern societies. However, my own guess as to why Foucault was not—at least until the later 1980s—as central a figure in feminist academic studies as one might have expected, is that the period in which his work was rapidly gaining attention in Britain and the USA coincided with growing influence of Freudian psychoanalytical theory, rekindled initially through the work of Jacques Lacan. Thus it was that Freudian and post-Freudian models of subjectivity and sexual identity gained ground seemingly at the expense of the types of analysis offered by Foucault and this was certainly the case with regard to much of the critical and theoretical work on visual representation, particularly with regard to photography. One hope for the future would be that Foucault's conception of a history of subjectivity would be able to take its place alongside psychoanalytical theory to produce a more adequate basis for thinking of our selves and thus for ourselves.

# On Foucault: Disciplinary Power and Photography

**David Green** is Senior Lecturer in the History of Art at the University of Brighton. He has published widely on photography and contemporary art in *Ten.8*, *Oxford Art Journal* and *Creative Camera*.

Recently the writings of the French historian and philosopher, Michel Foucault, have been increasingly widely reviewed in this country and if their reception has not always been entirely favourable the consensus has been that they merit careful consideration. Foucault's influence, however, has been largely confined to the realms of academia. Thus one suspects that the potential value of his ideas to cultural practitioners working within an oppositional politics has yet to be fully realised. It is, therefore, with the aim of extending the audience for his ideas that I shall attempt here briefly to recapitulate the principal components of Foucault's work, to trace the trajectory of his arguments and to assess the importance and use of his conclusions for a contemporary cultural politics of photography.

## Power/Knowledge

Foucault's writings are notoriously 'difficult' but the challenge to the reader is not so much at the level of language or terminology but with his general refusal to acknowledge the traditional boundaries of academic disciplines. The main body of Foucault's work can be said to be located within the history of ideas or more specifically within the history of science. Initially, however Foucault's points of departure seem bewilderingly diverse: from his earlier studies of psychology in *Madness and Civilisation* (1961) and the birth of modern medicine in *The Birth of the Clinic* (1963), through the much more apparently eclectic grouping of philology, biology and political economy to be found in *The Order of Things* (1966) to the study of criminology in *Discipline and Punishment* (1975) and finally to the projected six volume analysis in *The History of Sexuality* (1976). Yet behind the investigations of these varied phenomena lie two central interconnecting themes: the development of certain forms of rationality which posit 'man' as both the subject and object of knowledge; second, the complex relations bonding power and knowledge which are implicit to such forms of rationality. The historical focus of Foucault's work has thus been that moment *when man constitutes himself in Western culture as both that which must be conceived of and that which must be known*, that is, the period of the late eighteenth and early nineteenth century. Prior to this, he has argued, there was no specific domain of knowledge proper to 'man' himself. The modern notion of man as a unitary and ultimately knowable subject is the product of an historical process and one that is formulated in the appearance of all that we understand today by the human and social sciences. Foucault's work can then best be viewed as an attempt to understand how the human and social sciences became historically possible, to map out the conditions that enabled their emergence, and to indicate the consequences of their existence.

The fulcrum of these investigations has been the idea that the human and social sciences represent not only the emergence of new forms of knowledge about 'man' but also the development of new forms and modalities of power over man. The reflexive relations of power and knowledge which Foucault has sought to define require a fundamental shift in our usual understanding of these concepts. Thus power cannot be regarded only, as it often has been, as a negative force which makes itself known through the operations of repression, exclusion, limitation or censorship. Power must also be recognised in its positive forms when it enables the production of knowledge:

> the problem is not therefore that of determining how power subjugates knowledge and makes it serve its ends, or how it imprints its mark on knowledge, imposes on it ideological limits. No body of knowledge can be formed without a system of communication, record, accumulation and displacement which is in itself a form of power and which is linked, in its existence and functioning, to the other forms of power. Conversely no power can be exercised without the extraction, appropriation, distribution or retention of knowledge. On this level, there is not knowledge on the one side and society on the other, or science and the state, but only the fundamental forms of power/knowledge.[1]

Foucault's insistence on the recognition of the positive, productive characteristics of modern modalities of power offers an alternative to the ideological critique of science in which power appears only as a corrupt or distortive force. If the knowledges of 'man' provided by the human and social sciences are able to serve the needs of power this is not attributable to the veils of ideological mystification but to their ability to define a certain field of empirical truth, what Foucault has called a 'politics' or 'regime of truth'. Power, therefore, does not stand outside of truth as the potential transgressor of the boundaries of legitimate scientific knowledge; power is itself already truth and the very terrain upon which knowledge is possible:

> The important thing here, I believe, is that truth isn't outside power, or lacking in power: contrary to the myth whose history would repay further study, truth isn't the reward of free spirits, the child of protected solitude, nor the

privilege of those who have succeeded in liberating themselves. Truth is a thing of this world: it is produced only by virtue of multiple forms of constraint. And it induces regular effects of power. Each society has its regime of truth, its 'general politics' of truth: that is, the types of discourse which it accepts and makes function as true; the mechanisms and instances which enable one to distinguish between true and false statements, the means by which each is sanctioned; the techniques and procedures accorded value in the acquisition of truth; the status of those who are charged with saying what counts as true.[2]

Foucault is not necessarily concerned with the 'correctness' or otherwise of the concepts, methods and content of the modern sciences but with the effect of power which is *linked to the institution and functioning of an organised scientific discourse* within society. It is a question of what and who governs scientific statements so as to constitute a set of propositions, a discursive formation, which is accepted as true; *at this level it is not so much a matter of knowing what external power imposes itself on science, as what effects of power circulate among scientific statements.*

### Disciplinary Power

Foucault's most widely read work, *Discipline and Punishment*, first published in 1975, returns to the analysis of a single discourse/institution relation which had provided the structure of his earlier studies of *Madness and Civilisation* and *The Birth of the Clinic*. It charts the origins of the prison and the development of modern penology during the eighteenth and early nineteenth centuries. But in this work especially, the implications of Foucault's analysis reach far beyond his immediate subject matter, and the broader theme of the book is the emergence of an entirely new form of power and means of domination which define, what Foucault has called, a 'disciplinary society'. The emergence of this new form of power is traced through the changes which occur in the concept of punishment from a system of retribution to a system of reform. It involves the gradual replacement of types of punishment which are spectacular, ritualistic and manifestly violent, and in which the body of the offender was the direct and immediate target of retribution, by a more modest, discrete and subtle means of correction and training whose target was no longer the body of the offender but his 'soul', understood in terms of subjectivity, consciousness and personality. It would, says Foucault, be a mistake to see these changes simply as the inevitable triumph of reason over barbarism, the replacement of a tyrannical and brutal regime by a more humane and benevolent system. It was, of course, precisely these things but it was also the implementation of a more pervasive and more calculated form of power at the heart of which lay the exercise of discipline:

> Discipline may be identified neither with an institution nor with an apparatus; it is a type of power, a modality for its exercise, comprising a whole set of instruments, techniques, procedures, levels of application, targets; it is a 'physics' or an anatomy of power, a technology.[3]

Foremost amongst this 'technology' of disciplinary power are the mechanisms of surveillance for which Jeremy Bentham's 'Panopticon' provided the ideal model. As originally envisaged by Bentham, the Panopticon was an architectural construction: a central tower is enclosed by a circular building whose cellular spaces are open on the inside and their occupants exposed to the unremitting gaze the tower affords. In this field of uninterrupted visibility, in which only the observer remains unseen, it becomes possible to compare individuals to each other and to impose a system of formal equality, thereby exercising a normalising judgement. Yet by providing the measure of comparison the mechanisms of surveillance make it possible to gauge differences between individuals. Surveillance is above all an exercise of hierarchical observation. The Panopticon was the perfect manifestation of disciplinary power and the principles of its functioning—if not replication of its architectural form—could be utilised in a variety of contexts other than the penal institutions for which it was intended. In the extension of its mechanisms of surveillance and in the coincidence of the organisation of the prison, the hospital, the school and the factory, the disciplinary technology of 'panopticism' became diffused throughout society. Thus whilst the initial development of the technology of disciplinary power may have been directed towards prohibitive and repressive functions its subsequent proliferation indicates an inherently productive and positive capacity.

*Discipline and Punishment* stakes out more clearly than any other of Foucault's writings the conception of the necessary interdependence of power and knowledge, a conception of power/knowledge relations. Indeed it would be impossible to conceive of the emergence of the forms of disciplinary power without the emergence of an accompanying field of knowledge which permeates and sustains them. The specific techniques of surveillance, documentation and administration of individuals which are constitutive of the forms of disciplinary power are the product of those new 'rationalities', those new kinds of knowledge about 'man', the human and social sciences. The provenance of the human and social sciences cannot be located in some disinterested search for pure knowledge since their origins are bound to the birth of those disciplinary institutions—the prison, the asylum, the hospital, the school, the factory—of what Foucault has called, the 'carceral network'.

> The carceral network, in its compact or disseminated forms, with its systems of insertion, distribution, surveillance, observation, has been the greatest support in modern society of the normalising power. The carceral texture of society assures both the real capture of the body and its perpetual observation; it is, by its very nature, the apparatus of punishment that conforms most completely to the new economy of power and the instrument for the formation of knowledge that this very economy needs. Its panoptic functioning enables it to play this double role. By virtue of its methods of fixing, dividing, recording, it has been one of the simplest, crudest, also most concrete, but perhaps most indispensable conditions for the development of the immense activity of examination that has objectified human behaviour....I am not saying that the human sciences emerged from the prison. But, if they have been able to produce so many profound changes...it is because they have been conveyed by a specific and new modality of power: a certain policy of the body, a certain way of rendering the accumulation of men docile and useful. This policy required the involvement of definite relations of power; it called for a technique of overlapping subjection and objectification; it brought with it new procedures of individualism. The carceral network constituted one of the armatures of this power/knowledge that has made the human sciences historically possible. Knowable man (soul, individuality, consciousness, conduct, whatever it is called) is the object-effect of this analytical investment, of this domination–observation.[4]

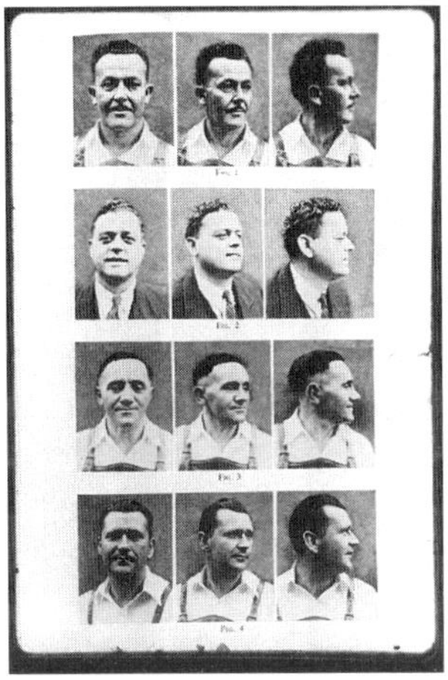

6.1 Source and subject unknown

Foucault's concept of power/knowledge relations as integral to the existence and functioning of the modern human and social sciences takes one beyond the idea that power is always located and emanates from a central nexus of domination whether this is seen as an individual, a ruling class or the state to a conception of multiple forms of domination which permeate the social fabric. Power is not so much possessed as exercised through the myriad institutions and discursive practices that exist at all levels of social life. Clearly this has consequences for the analysis of power hence the concept formulated by Foucault of a 'microphysics of power' which seeks to reveal how the mechanisms of power in a disciplinary society operate routinely at the level of everyday life, localised in the minutiae of social relations, present in the prosaic encounter of criminal and criminologist, patient and doctor, pupil and teacher, child and parent.

### The Politics of the Body

A consistent theme in Foucault's work and, in particular, in his analysis of discipline has been with those forms or tactics of power which have been directed towards, perhaps one could say inscribed upon, the body. These forms or tactics of power are not manifest as physical violence—indeed the body is touched as little as possible. Rather it is the case that this power is realised only by the subjection of the body as the object of knowledge, and the function of this power lies in its ability to extract knowledge, not pain, from the body. It is, I believe, in this analysis of how and why the body becomes, at a certain moment in time, the nexus of power/knowledge relations in a disciplinary society that Foucault's work has been of the most profound importance. His concern with and historical conception of the body, or, more precisely, with those discourses of the body which are always historically situated, has permitted an understanding of the entry of the body into the sphere of politics:

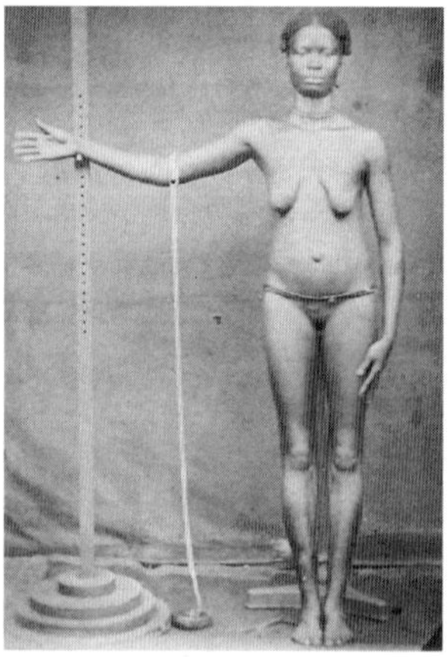

6.2 Taken in Africa, c.1890, photographer unknown

> The body is directly involved in a political field; power relations have an immediate hold upon it: they invest it, mark it, train it, torture it, force it to carry out tasks, to perform ceremonies and to emit signs. The political investment of the body is bound up, in accordance with complex reciprocal relations, with its economic use; it is largely as a force of production that the body is invested with relations of power and domination; but, on the other hand, its constitution as labour power is possible only if it is caught up in a system of subjection...the body becomes a useful force only if it is both a productive body and a subjugated body.[5]

Foucault's earlier historical studies cover the period of the eighteenth and early nineteenth centuries. The developments of those phenomena he is concerned with are therefore contingent to a series of profound demographic, political, social and cultural changes consequent upon the rise of industrial capitalism. The question is whether the emergence of the forms of disciplinary power which Foucault has analysed in terms of quite specific discursive and institutional practices are related to these other levels of the social formation and, if so, in what manner are they related. He is careful to distance himself from a simple causal relation based upon the Marxist principle of economic determination:

> I believe that anything can be deduced from the general principle of the domination of the bourgeois class. What needs to be done is something quite different. One needs to investigate historically, and beginning from the lowest level, how mechanisms of power have been able to function....We need to see how these mechanisms of power, at a given moment, in a precise conjuncture, and by means of a certain number of transformations, have begun to become economically useful.[6]

Foucault goes on to suggest that it is not the exclusion of the criminal and the insane which served the interests of the bourgeoisie but the techniques and procedures themselves of such an exclusion. It was the actual mechanisms of disciplinary power, the apparatuses of surveillance, which become politically useful and lent themselves to economic profit. In the case of the factory or workshop discipline may have been evoked as a moral incentive but the importance of discipline increasingly become one of maximising productivity and thereby the profitability of labour. The physical division of space and the imposed segregation of individuals, the carefully controlled rhythm of activities and the imposition of rigid temporal sequences, became common features of both the prison and the workplace. It is this 'economy' of power which distinguishes discipline and which prompts Foucault to view it as one of the great inventions of bourgeois society and as a fundamental instrument of industrial capitalism and the type of society which is its accompaniment.

The emergence of a disciplinary society corresponds to a particular historical conjuncture: the growth of new modes of production centred upon the factory and the increase of population concentrated within urban communities. The mechanisms of discipline which Foucault describes at length in *Discipline and Punishment*, gave rise to a *political anatomy of the body, a certain way of rendering the accumulation of men docile and useful.* The techniques of disciplinary power enabled the improvement of the efficiency and profitability of labour. In so far that discipline is a power which engages and infiltrates the physical capabilities of individuals caught within its mechanisms we can speak of a politics of the body. But disciplinary power also engaged the body as a 'species' body and it gave rise to a 'politics of population', the focus of which was a series of regulatory controls effective at the level of the 'social'. As the problems caused by the rapid expansion of urban populations became more evident the need for political control and intervention became more necessary. In this context the body took on a new and crucial importance as the bearer of those qualities of fertility, health and sickness, strength and weakness, which were seen as vital to the future of society and the nation as a whole. Hence we can understand the significance and importance of the proliferation of the discourses of sex in the nineteenth century analysed by Foucault in *The History of Sexuality.* Contrary to the popular myth what is involved in this 'incitement to discourse' is not a renunciation of pleasure nor a rejection of the flesh but an intensification of the body through the concern for its health and vitality. The organisation and the articulation of the discourses of sexuality in the nineteenth century produced a new conception of the body which became the focus of discipline not only as a means to render it more productive but also more morally and physically healthy. The effect of this was to subject the body in an ever more detailed way to endless medical and psychological examination and to the mechanisms of surveillance.

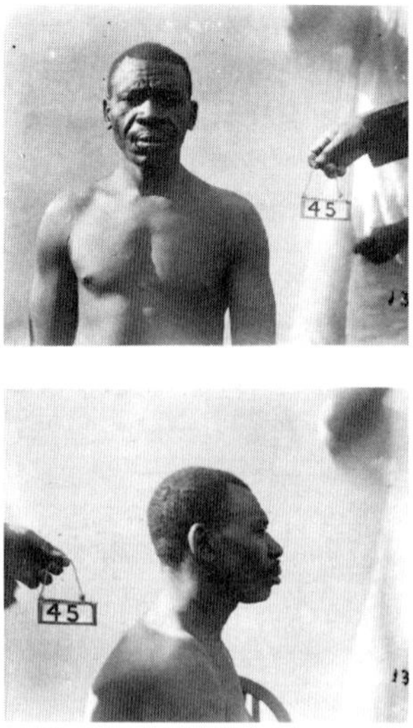


6.3 These images are part of a series of measurement cards and photographs of natives of the Anglo-Egyptian Sudan taken by Professor C.G. Seligman between 1909 and 1922. They are indexed at the Royal Anthropological Institute as follows: *Each photograph bears a number, under which are one to three numbers in parenthesis. The number not in parenthesis corresponds to the number on the measurement card and on the photograph, i.e. a type number. The number or numbers in parenthesis refer to the number given to the negative in the total series of Sudan photographs taken by C.G. Seligman. On some of the cards under eye-colour, will be found CGS, CGS+, or CGS-. These compare with Seligman's eye-colour, a medium brown.* They were presented to the Royal Anthropological Society in July 1935.

### Photography and Power

Photography has been historically important to the formation of the discourses of the body which have been such a vital constituent of disciplinary power. In part this was due to the widespread belief in the objective nature of the photographic process which ensured its privileged position in the procedures of scientific investigation and which meant that the photographic image would be regarded as a form of empirical truth or evidence of the real. But clearly involved here was not the discovery of pre-existent truths which the camera so meticulously revealed but the construction of new kinds of knowledge about the individual in terms of visible physiological features by which it is possible to measure and compare each individual to another. Photography, therefore, was contingent to other methods used in the observation and classification of individuals, forming a part of the mechanisms of surveillance and the exercise of a normalising, disciplinary power.

The compilation of photographic records, often used in conjunction with techniques of physiological measurement and written documentation, became common practice for a variety of scientific disciplines. The employment of photography in the fields of anthropology, medicine and criminology, in particular, draws together a whole series of discursive operations levelled at the body and organised along the axes of race, class or gender. Subject to the gaze of the camera the body became the object of the closest scrutiny, its surface continually examined for the signs of its innate physical, mental and moral inferiority. From this science of corporeal semiotics there emerged new forms of knowledge about the individual and new ways of mapping depravity. These simple, almost banal images cannot reveal the full complexity of the power/knowledge relations which lie behind their surface but, as John Tagg has indicated, they retain the traces of their functioning:

> The body isolated; the narrow space; the subjection to an unreturnable gaze; the scrutiny of gestures, faces and features, the clarity of illumination and sharpness of focus; the names and the number of boards: these are the traces of power, reduplicated in numberless images, repeated countless times, whenever the photographer prepared an exposure, in police cell, prison, consultation room, asylum, home or school.[7]

The historical investigation of photography as a mechanism of surveillance in the exercise of disciplinary power remains an important initiative. The work of John Tagg, myself and others have begun this task through a series of analyses which have concentrated upon the uses of photography in the late nineteenth century within such fields as criminology, medicine, anthropology and eugenics. But an historical perspective is only necessary and defendable as a means of helping us to understand the present and allowing us to create the appropriate and effective means of working strategically within the relations of power and knowledge which currently endure. The force and value of Foucault's ideas are owed to the fact that we continue to live in a society which is characterised, perhaps increasingly so, by the forms of discipline and mechanisms of surveillance which he has identified. However, a major criticism of Foucault's work has been that it creates a picture of society in which the presence of power is so pervasive, so diffuse and polymorphous that it would appear to make implausible any form of resistance. Foucault's response has been to insist that wherever there is power there is the potential for its resistance. But just as the forms of power are localised and specific so should be the forms of resistance. We must engage power at the points of its application and operation; that is, within the particular domains of knowledge and the particular institutions through which it is operative. This means that there cannot be an overall strategy for an oppositional cultural politics of photography; on the contrary it is necessary to develop alternative ways of working with photography, and to develop different photographic forms and devices suitable to the varied contexts in which the photograph is placed and used.



---

**Reference Notes**

**1** Quoted in Alan Sheridan, *Michel Foucault: The Will to Truth*, Tavistock, London, 1980, p.131.

**2** Michel Foucault, *Power/Knowledge*, ed. C. Gordon, Harvester Press, Hassocks, 1980, p.131.

**3** M. Foucault, *Discipline and Punishment*, Allen Lane, Harmondsworth, 1977, p.215.

**4** Ibid., pp.304-5.

**5** Ibid., pp.25-6.

**6** Foucault, *Power/Knowledge*, pp.100-1.

**7** John Tagg, 'Power and Photography', in *Screen Education*, Autumn 1980, no.36, pp.44-5.

**Further Reading**

Since this essay was first published, and since Foucault's death, the number of books and articles on his work has grown enormously. The following is a bibliography is an extended version of that given in 1985 but it represents a small fraction of the current literature. The most complete listing to date of books and articles by and on Foucault is given in James Bernauer and David Rasmussen, eds, *The Final Foucault,* MIT Press, Cambridge, MA, 1988.

**Major texts by Foucault**

*Madness and Civilisation*, Tavistock, London, 1967 (1961).
*The Birth of the Clinic*, Tavistock, London, 1973 (1963).
*The Order of Things*, Tavistock, London, 1970 (1966).
*The Archaeology of Knowledge*, Tavistock, London, 1972 (1969).
*Discipline and Punishment*, Allen Lane, Harmondsworth, 1977 (1975).
*Language, Counter-Memory, Practice: Selected Interviews and Essays*, ed. D.F. Bouchard, Cornell University Press, Ithaca, NY, 1977.
*The History of Sexuality*, Volume 1: An Introduction, Penguin, Harmondsworth, 1978 (1976).
*Power/Knowledge*, ed. C. Gordon, Harvester Press, Hassocks, 1980.
*The Use of Pleasure, The History of Sexuality*, Volume 2, Penguin, Harmondsworth, 1985 (1984).
*The Care of the Self, The History of Sexuality*, Volume 3, Penguin, Harmondsworth, 1986 (1984).
*Politics, Philosophy and Culture: Interviews and Other Writings 1977-1984*, ed. L. Kritzmann, Routledge, London, 1988.

NB: dates given in brackets refer to the publication of the original French edition.

**Works on Foucault**

• David Couzens Hoy, ed., *Foucault: A Critical Reader*, Basil Blackwell, Oxford, 1986.
• Gary Gutting, ed., *The Cambridge Companion to Foucault*, Cambridge University Press, Cambridge, 1994.
• Lois McNay, *Foucault and Feminism*, Northwestern University Press, Evanston, 1993.
• Mark Poster, *Foucault, Marxism and History*, Polity Press, Oxford, 1984.
• Paul Rabinow, *The Foucault Reader*, Penguin, Harmondsworth, 1984.
• Caroline Ramazanoglu, ed., *Up Against Foucault*, Routledge, London, 1993.
• Jana Sawicki, *Disciplining Foucault: Feminism, Power and the Body*, Routledge, London, 1991.
• Alan Sheridan, *Michel Foucault: The Will to Truth*, Tavistock,London,1980.
• Barry Smart, *Foucault, Marxism and Critique*, Routledge & Kegan Paul, 1983.

**Works on Photography with Reference to Foucault**

• Jonathan Crary, *Techniques of the Observer: On Vision and Modernity in the Nineteenth Century*, MIT Press, 1992.

• Jessica Evans, 'The Iron Cage of Visibility', *Ten.8*, no.29, 1988.

• Steve Edwards 'Disastrous Documents', *Ten.8*, no.15, 1984.

• David Green, 'Classified Subjects: Photography and Anthropology', *Ten.8*, no.14, 1984.

• David Green, 'Veins of Resemblance: Francis Galton, Photography and Eugenics', *Oxford Art Journal*, vol.7, no.2, 1984.

• David Green, 'A Map of Depravity', *Ten.8*, no.18, 1984.

• Suren Lalvani, *Photography, Vision, and the Production of Modern Bodies*, SUNY Press, Albany, New York, 1996.

• Roberta McGrath, 'Medical Police', *Ten.8*, no.18, 1984.

• Frank Mort, 'The Domain of the Sexual', *Screen Education*, Autumn 1980, no.36.

• Frank Mort and Nicholas Green, 'Visual Representation and Cultural Politics', *Block*, no.7, 1982.

• Allan Sekula, 'The Body in the Archive', *October*, no.39, 1986.

• John Tagg, *The Burden of Representation*, Macmillan, Basingstoke, 1988.

# 7 Mass Observation: The Intellectual Climate

David Alan Mellor

Introduction by
**David Alan Mellor**

I spent a lot of the 1970s trying to retrieve bits of twentieth century visual culture—especially episodes in photography—which had been obscured in prevalent modernist histories. The historiography of photography had its own peculiar warps at that time. Under the sponsorship of the Arts Council, Ian Jeffrey and I had organised an exhibition in 1974 called *The Real Thing*. This was a survey of British photography between 1850 and 1950 and one of its intentions was to complicate and possibly destabilise the conventional US based account of what constituted a history of British photography. The notion of photography emerging as a sanctioned art form, of a kind of 'coming of age' and a claiming of cultural rights, has always been a perennial trope of the history of photography and the 1970s saw its own version of this delusory narrative. Unquestioned giants were newly framed—Walker Evans, Freidlander—for a heavily Americanised art-photography canon which was largely de-coupled from cultural or social histories. As a countervailing strategy I was interested in moments in European and more specifically British cultural history which were, if you like, a 'dirty history' of commercial pressures, state agencies and anonymous archives where photography had its awkward but distinctive places. I worked with the Imperial War Museum's vast collections of official photography and with fashion magazine files for the preparation of *The Real Thing*, but the most formative source for me, at that time, was the Mass Observation Archive. I should declare here that my first 'real job', in 1973, involved me trying to act as executive director of that archive just after it had arrived at the University of Sussex. I found and interviewed some of the artists and photographers who had been involved in the Mass Observation project of the late 1930s, particularly Julian Trevelyan and Humphrey Spender. It was talking to Spender that impressed upon me the number of contextual elements which went to make up that supposedly unified category of 'documentary' photography. Working with his negatives and then researching the photographs and paintings of Humphrey Jennings set me off thinking and writing other histories of twentieth century visual culture which were interdisciplinary and related to points in German and French modernist practices.

While I was writing this piece for *Camerawork*, in the summer of 1978, I was also editing a volume of criticism and original texts around the topic of *Neue Sachlichkeit* photography in Germany in the late 1920s and early 1930s, which brought me into contact with the remains of a generation of German refugee picture editors and photographers. Their diversity and the plurality of their cultural agendas further influenced me towards a form of writing history which was open, situational and empirically particularised. This empiricism was suspect at the time and I still get hostile reviews for writing a form of 'history as gossip', which is fine with me, since gossip is a very underrated genre of comic historical narration. I admired the totalising force of Don Macpherson's Foucauldian essay on Mass Observation in the same issue of *Camerawork* (reprinted in this volume), but it gave me a sense of over-mastering intellectual terrorism, a rhetoric of suspicion and a blind generality in attributing some myth of nostalgia and 'Britishness' to the process of reading those radically un-English and strange Spender photographs. Looking now at what I wrote I realise that I should, perhaps, have emphasised their remedial alien-ness more than I did when I tried to lay out a constellation of some of the determining factors and thematics that constituted Mass Observation. I think I only partially managed this when I came to write about Bill Brandt in the mid-1980s. By that time Foucault was important to me, but it was his dramatic and energetic style of writing which energised me as much, or more so, than his methodologies.

---

## Mass Observation: The Intellectual Climate

**David Alan Mellor** is Senior Lecturer in Art History at the University of Sussex. He edited the book *Germany: The New Photography 1927-33* (1978) and co-wrote, with Mark Haworth-Booth, *Bill Brandt Behind the Camera* (1985).

How little we know of our next door neighbour and his habits; how little we know of ourselves. Of conditions of life and thought in another class or another district, our ignorance is complete. The anthropology of ourselves is still only a dream. It is left to the intuitions of men of genius to cope with the unknown mass. Such intuitions are to a human science of the future what cookery is to chemistry. The building up of such a science is an urgent problem for mankind.

It was with thoughts like these that that a group of people started Mass Observation, which aims to be a scientific study of human social behaviour, beginning at home. Such a study has already been begun by anthropologists in the case of primitive peoples, and tentatively by psychologists and sociologists in civilised countries. But in the latter case, the field to be covered is so vast and so apparently nebulous that the scientists have little more to offer than generalisations on method.

Mass Observation shares the interest of most people in the actual, in what happens from day to day. Everyday the social consciousness is modified by the news reported in the newspapers and on the wireless. The more exciting the news, the more unified does the social consciousness become in its absorption with a single theme. The abdication of King Edward VIII was a focusing point of this kind. The coronation of King George VI is providing another. At such times, our observers will each be watching the social reactions within their own local environment. They will be the meteorological stations from whose reports a weather map of popular feeling can be compiled. (Mass Observation pamphlet, 1937)

Mass Observation constitutes a substantial but almost entirely forgotten episode in British cultural history at the end of the 1930s, involving photography as well as film and painting. It was an episode that can perhaps be understood as a complex of contemporary forces: populism, statistical social surveys, Surrealism, naïve Realism, anthropology, investigative reportage and Documentary impulses. It cannot be characterised simply as an epiphenomenon of the larger Documentary movement in Britain in the 1930s more likely it was the focus and climax of 1930s Documentary in Britain.

One factor is striking amongst the preconditions of Mass Observation's formation: Victor Gollancz the publisher, seeing the success of Documentary books in Britain, and that Documentary was in the ascendant as a genre, was willing to finance Tom Harrisson—one of Mass Observation's three founders—in Bolton in 1936. Once Harrisson was there he also arranged donations from liberal northern industrialists such as Sir Thomas Barlow KBE and Sir Ernest Simon. In the United States it was industrialists such as these who were putting financial backing behind photo-Documentary books like *Faces We See*,[1] a book which is an exactly parallel project to Spender's photographs—for it too is concerned with celebrating a people working in an area dominated by the cotton industry, but in North Carolina rather than Lancashire: people at work; at home; their habits and customs.

The search for affirmative images of labour and citizenship was a definite populist component of the Documentary genre at the close of the 1930s and on into the 1940s in Britain and the United States. Many of the inner core of Mass Observation, including some of its founders, even if not actually born in the Empire, were either Colonials or associated with it. Tom Harrisson, for example, was the son of General Harrisson who had built the Argentinean railway system, and had spent all his time in Argentina, which was then virtually a British colony. His son was shaped by the Imperial tradition of exploration and administration despite his subsequent rebellion against paternal and authority figures.

Charles Madge, the poet and *Daily Mirror* reporter, was South African, as was Graham Bell, the Social Realist painter. Expatriate detachment gave them a vantage on to British culture from an imagined 'exterior', alien, territory. Indeed Harrisson encouraged Humphrey Spender to figure himself in the role of exploring ethnographer in a foreign country.

Ethnographical and anthropological aims lay behind much German photography in the 20s and 30s (behind August Sander, for example) as well as being at the base of the Documentary movement in film in Britain with Grierson's intention to domesticise Flaherty's ethnographic work. Harrisson had first encountered the Spender family on the 1933 Oxford University expedition to the New Hebrides. During this Harrisson saw Michael Spender (the expedition's photographer) record Oceanic patterns of culture by camera. Only in 1937 did Harrisson seek out Michael's brother, Humphrey Spender, as the photographer to survey cultural patterns in Bolton and Blackpool.

But by then there was a different intellectual climate. During the late 1930s, the high years of Mass Observation, there was a recoil from Europe (Spain especially) and the world on the part of the younger British intelligentsia, and a return home. The high-bohemian idyll of the Mediterranean no longer had any economic underpinning; colonial adventure had subsided. This recoil to home involved, in part, the exploration of the unknown British interior, already made 'foreign' by the ravages of the Depression, distanced by class barriers and thereby populated by 'a race apart'.

It was no coincidence that this was the sort of imaginary scene with which Raymond Mortimer introduced Bill Brandt at the outset of the photobook *The English at Home* (1936):

> One of the pleasures of being English is to return to this country after a longish time...for an hour or two you have caught a surprising vision of your country and your countrymen, you have noticed a hundred details that are peculiar to England; you have, in fact, been able to look through foreign eyes. Mr Bill Brandt is British by birth but has spent his life abroad...shows himself to be not only an artist but an anthropologist. He seems to have wandered about England with the detached curiosity of a man investigating the customs of some remote and unfamiliar tribe.[2]

By the time Harrisson was settled in Bolton in late 1936 and about to join forces with others to found Mass Observation, the model of the privileged expatriate returning home on a redemptive journey into the British interior was established and, significantly, also established within the marketable and expanding genre of Documentary photo-books. Together with the rise of Documentary as a form and a genre there is also the rise of market research (the first extensive Persil survey by Lintas had been in October 1933).

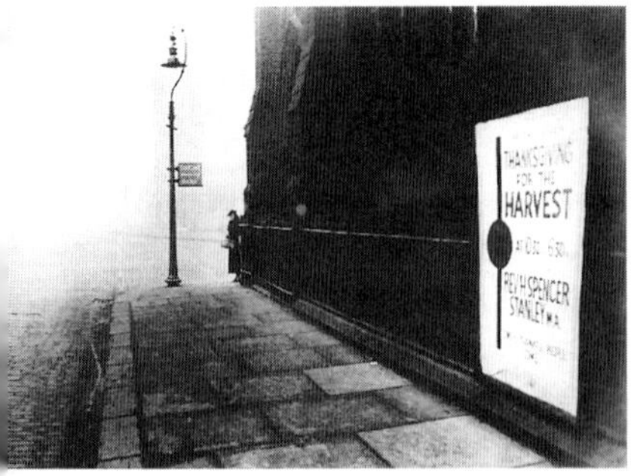


7.1 Wayside pulpit, Bolton, 1937. Humphrey Spender

As a methodology, asking people questions about their habits was novel and appealing: public opinion polls were also very rudimentary but were another source for Mass Observation's drive to collect facts and statistics from individuals. Mass Observation was a hybrid phenomenon composed of disparate factors. It amalgamated not only public opinion polls and market research, but also anthropology into a framework where an 'anthropology of ourselves'[3] seemed to have potential. Endorsement came early for Mass Observation from Professor Bronislaw Malinowski, the leading anthropologist in England; at least part of the conceptual thrust behind Spender's photograph 'The Wayside Pulpit, Bolton' (1937) may be anthropological in origin. At first there is the ironic level—of an uplifting sign for Harvest Thanksgiving in an overwhelmingly gloomy industrialised vista. Beyond this was the anthropological image—the photograph as data, as evidence on the manner in which agrarian rituals like Harvest Thanksgiving are sustained in an industrialised society.

An Observation. 26.4.1938

**Moor Lane Market** There was only Taffy with an audience which comprised of 16 women 22-48 and 9 men 40-55, two children, girls 7, and Observers. Taffy had two men 26, 27, helping Taffy 55.

'Look here Mrs. only 2 d...these...they've never bin offered at this price before—see feel at 'em only 2d...why damn it have your bloody at home or do you want me to give you the damn stuff...?'

'Hello Mrs...haven't seen you for a week or two now, how's your hubby?...Well ladies here we are, look at these lovely undies, fit for the Queen, in fact they're better than the Queen's, only 1/6d. No dammit I'll treat you ladies, 1/3d—who wants one? Yes there's a lady there; thank you lady you've got a bargain'.

Through his advance from Gollancz, Tom Harrisson was living in Bolton in late 1936, making an impressionistic social survey based on his work as a lorry driver and in the cotton mills. At the same time a group of London intellectuals, Jennings, Madge, David Gascoyne, Stuart Legg and Kathleen Raine, the majority of them Surrealists, began the investigation of how contemporary public opinion interacted with widely held phobias and desires. They were interested in events such as the burning of the Crystal Palace which took place at the end of 1936—what might it signify to the British collective imagination and what psychological and political resonances would such an apocalyptic image have? From a Surrealist and Freudian point of view public and political images were seen to have an unconscious psychological dimension. And the London group were concerned with constructing meaning from such mass-circularised images of public events or 'fictions', as Walter Lippmann had called them,[4] that were interiorised from newsreels and headlines. Thus the first Mass Observation publication in June 1937 opened with such a 'fiction'—a facsimile reproduction of the *Daily Mirror's* headline on the abdication of Edward VIII in December 1936.[5]

At the very beginning of 1937 this London group wrote a letter to the *New Statesman*; Harrisson came down from Bolton and they immediately combined. Mass Observation was formed and immediately appealed through the newspapers for volunteers and observers who would report on their daily lives, fantasies, dreams and work. Harrisson returned to Bolton while Madge directed the London group from Blackheath, Jennings remaining with them for the rest of 1937.

Their book on the coronation of George VI in May 1937, *May the Twelfth*, was their first major composite work and it was primarily arranged by Humphrey Jennings. This was the occasion when candid Leica photography was first pressed into service for an Mass Observation survey, when Jennings not only noted down all the overheard remarks in crowds, the music and noise of the day that he heard but he also photographed the coronation crowds and their reactions to the day's events. His technique, the same employed by Spender a few months later on his first visit to Bolton, was one of participant observation. The mass observer became akin to the peeking, spying creature 'Public Busybody No 1' announced by the *Daily Mirror* and personified in a photo of Tom Harrisson himself in a mackintosh with notebook in hand squinting through a keyhole.[6] (figure 7.2)

The point of view was covert: that of the voyeur, the eavesdropper who overheard and oversaw—the point of view from which Spender took the photograph, 'Funeral, Davenport St

Page 14 THE DAILY MIRROR Tuesday, December 6, 1938

*He and his thousand followers are giving their services to the "DAILY MIRROR"*

# Public Busybody No. 1

By TOM HARRISSON

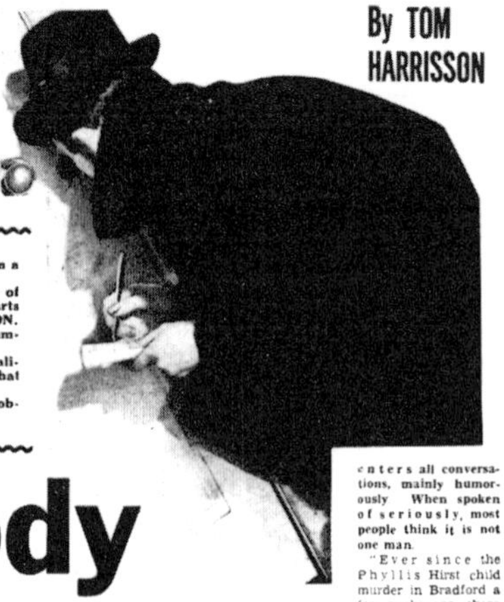

SLASH! . . a shadow in the darkness of an alley . . . the sweep of an arm . . a girl screams.

**The Slasher. .**

**Does he really exist?**

**Is he real?**

**Or is he a fake?**

To try to get at the truth of the whole affair, a Mass Observation unit have been spying in Halifax.

They have been listening to conversations in public-houses and tea shops.

They have even canvassed for opinions from door to door.

This page will tell you what they have found out.

Before we turn to Halifax, let's look at a little "attack" incident at Walworth, London, S.E.

**It actually happened a fortnight before the Halifax ripper broke into the news.**

✦ ✦ ✦

**For two years TOM HARRISSON has been working on a NEW IDEA.**

**This young scientist has gathered round him a corps of men and women in different jobs, living in different parts of England. Their job is called MASS OBSERVATION. They note YOUR BEHAVIOUR in a certain set of circumstances, and make reports on it.**

**During the past weeks Harrisson's men focused on Halifax during the recent outbreak of razor-slashing in that town.**

**Here he tells some of the incredible findings of his observers.**

On November 25 it was reported that young girls in Walworth were being accosted by a man who asked them if they had dropped a comb. He then followed them and attacked just as they were about to enter their homes.

Mass observers went to Walworth, and these were some of the findings.

**Notice them closely, because they have a strong bearing on the slashings which subsequently took place in Halifax.**

There was no scare among residents.

Six out of twenty-five women interviewed in the district neither knew nor cared anything about the attacks.

**Fifteen of the twenty-five had only read about them in newspapers—proof that there was little "scare" talk about the incidents.**

Moreover, observers counted the women who continued to walk through the "attacker" streets alone after the incidents.

**Twenty-six per cent. of the total number of women were unaccompanied. Not much sign of a local scare here.**

In fact, in streets only a few hundred yards from that in which the attacker operated it was found that residents and passers-by actually knew nothing of the incidents.

Now, these facts had been noted during the days immediately before the Halifax slasher struck for the first time.

With the findings of Walworth, mass observers focused their attentions on the Halifax rippings.

First let's find out what the "slasher" looked like according to what people in Halifax told observers.

These are the compiled descriptions of the slasher.

He is made out to be rather like the average thug of detective fiction:—

**"Flat, boxer-like face . . . few teeth. Wearing a dirty-coloured raincoat and a grey trilby . . . Moving in stockinged feet."**

"He has bright buckles on his shoes."

**"Black teeth."**

"Wears no hat."

"Has piercing eyes."

✦ ✦ ✦

Now take the impressions collected by observers in and around Halifax.

**One points out the extraordinary increase in the sale of heavy walking-sticks and knuckle-dusters.**

Read his notes to get a true idea of the terror which stalked abroad in the slasher town at night.

"I was observing people's behaviour in a poorly lit street on the third night of the slashing scare.

"Apparently there was another man who was watching for trouble, too.

"Because about 8 p.m. a girl hurried down the wet cobbled pavement. The sound of her footsteps echoed in the deserted street.

**"Suddenly I heard another set of footsteps coming in the opposite direction. The girl crossed the street. The other walker—I could now see it was a man—crossed diagonally to meet her.**

"When they were about ten yards apart I saw a figure leap from the shadows and make a vicious attack on the man.

"I heard the dull clink as the blow was struck. The man went down. The girl screamed.

"I ran from my position in a doorway—and helped the girl and the man to pick up the half-stunned pedestrian.

"It appeared, however, that the whole thing had been a misunderstanding.

"The man had used a knuckle-duster, misunderstanding the intention of the man he'd hit.

"It turned out that he was a youth well known in the district, who had crossed the road to ask the girl—whom he knew quite well—if he could escort her home through the darkness.

**"What did seem cold-blooded to me was that the man who struck the blow was using—indiscriminately, I maintain—this most murderous looking knuckle-duster.**

"Fortunately it landed on the man's cigarette case, partially winding him.

"Many Halifax men were in possession of these weapons at the time."

Here are excerpts from one:—

**"The slasher is the topic of the day. He enters all conversations, mainly humorously. When spoken of seriously, most people think it is not one man.**

"Ever since the Phyllis Hirst child murder in Bradford a few weeks ago, there have been isolated attacks on young women, and now the slasher.

"There is the certainty here that the person responsible will slip up by being too bold."

Another observer in a textile mill writes:—

**"One man told me that his wife visited a woman who lives on a main street, yet who had the door chained, despite the fact that her husband, heavy and 6ft. tall, was in the house.**

"A carrier from Halifax told me that a man hurrying down a hill to catch a bus had been violently struck by a man on the look-out for a slasher."

There are several good instances here to illustrate the effect the slashings had on local people. For instance:

"A woman was nudged rather heavily when waiting in a bus queue. Something dropped from her inside pocket. It was a hatchet!

"The milkman tells me that he has to shout his identity through his customers' doors before they will unlock them.

**"On the Saturday during the height of the slashings a Halifax fish-and-chip shop took only 5s. in takings, instead of between £4 and £5."**

This observer adds: "Everybody I've spoken to believes in the existence of the slasher. Many people think there are more than one."

## 'HALF-CRAZY CHAP RUNS LOOSE'

And here we come to the report of an observer who raises what is possibly the secret of innumerable other slashings which occurred on the days immediately after the first Halifax incident.

This observer bears in mind the following attacks:

At Brentford (Middlesex), Shepherd's Bush (London), Morton and Irlam (near Manchester), Leeds, Glasgow, Oldham, Bradford, Wakefield, Bolton, Sheffield, Cleethorpes and Sale.

And this is what he says:

**"A half-crazy chap runs loose with a razor in Halifax . . . and all the half-wits in the country want to imitate him."**

But as the days pass we find that at least two of the victims who alleged they had been attacked have since confessed that their injury was self-imposed.

Added to this, we find that in most reports from Halifax and Walworth, the victims were attacked on their own doorsteps or in the immediate vicinity of their homes—**the last place it is thought that the cunning mind of a slasher would choose to do his work.**

✦ ✦ ✦

Is the Halifax slasher a fact or a fantasy?

As the outcry against him dies down, mass observers are continuing their work—and will, in the end, deduce the true answer to that question.

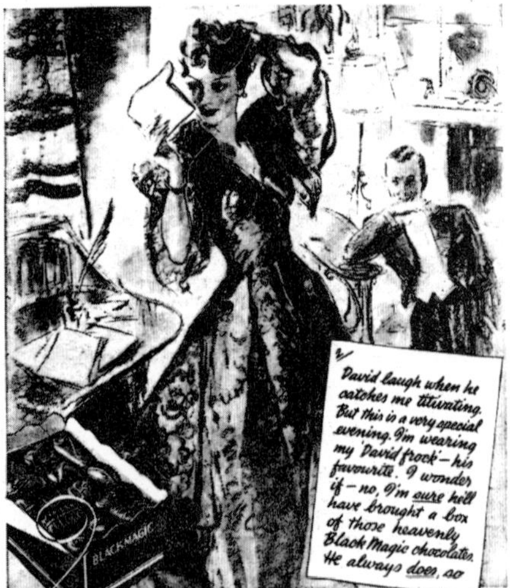




7.2 *Daily Mirror*, 6 December 1938.
'Detective' Tom Harrisson peeping through a keyhole.

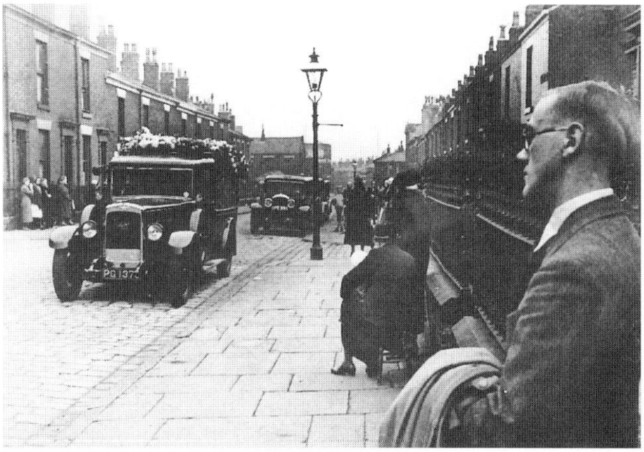

7.3 Funeral, Davenport Street, Bolton, 1937-8. Humphrey Spender

Bolton' (1938), by the shoulder of a mourner. (figure 7.3) The image of 'social detection' began to be important to Mass Observation's reputation (a reputation which was to be fuelled by the scandal of social spies in our midst noting and recording everyday life). But as Harrisson and Madge wrote: 'in the detection we wish to practise there is no criminal...collective habits and social behaviour are our field of enquiry'.[7]

It was to be 'A Nationwide Intelligence Service',[8] which discovered, coordinated and fed back opinions and views in a mass society. To some extent it succeeded; findings, besides being published in Mass Observation books and newsletters, became widely publicised as a best-selling Penguin Special, *Britain*, in *Daily Mirror* and *Picture Post* features and in frequent BBC broadcasts. And Tom Harrisson quickly became a personality on the newly opened BBC television service.

There seems no question that Tom Harrisson was a charismatic person who acted as publicist and magnet. Members of the London arts/politics bohemia were drawn up to Bolton through his intervention, among them Richard Crossman, Tom Driberg, Julian Huxley and the painters Sir William Coldstream and Julian Trevelyan. He also attracted the interest of men like Walter Hood, an unemployed miner who joined the Bolton social survey.

Bolton was chosen by Tom Harrisson for reasons which illuminate the mentality of Mass Observation extremely well.[9] He had spent a long while in Melanesia in the South Pacific and discovered that the only thing the natives knew about Britain was the identity of the Unilever combine which had large chemical interests in their island. Fascinated by this commercial and imperial link, he decided to return to Britain, back to the birthplace of Lord Lever (in Bolton) to the source of that particular imperial network.

The symbolic expression of economic forces obsessed him. He found, for example, Lancashire George Formby's hit record 'Hindoo Man' meaningful as another cultural interconnection between the contracting staple industry of Bolton, cotton, and the Indian subcontinent with its own burgeoning cotton industry.[10]

In the 1930s, during the period of economic depression, a generation of photographers, film-makers and painters were under severe economic pressures. Amongst the generation of mainly middle-class students who left the Slade or the Architectural Association between 1929 and 1935, many failed to find traditional employment. Humphrey Spender was one of them. Coming from an upper-middle-class background he found himself a job as a newspaper photographer (for the *Daily Mirror*) by 1935; he had become declassé and propelled into the mass media along with such distinguished contemporaries as W.H. Auden, Sir William Coldstream, John Armstrong, Anthony Powell and others.

This moment then, around 1935-7, entailed a shift in self-image for some photographers and painters, a change from bohemian models of the artist to one representing the values of corporate responsibility. It was a shift summarised in Myfanwy Piper's remark, 'We are more serious now, not really playboys but agents'.[11] In the guise of 'agents' rather than privileged bohemians a greater mobility to cross class barriers was gained. The metaphor of the artist as agent coalesced with that of the reporter, the 'Public Busybody No.1', who investigated the social landscape in the service of a communalist ideology of *mass observation*.

Something which loomed large in the iconography of arts and letters between the wars was the industrial wasteland, and Bolton appeared to Spender to belong to this iconographic type. It had originated with Eliot in 1922 but Auden refined and systematically developed in his poems the idea of the landscape of Britain as semi-derelict. That iconography of industrial dereliction intrigued Spender because it accorded with much that he saw in actuality on his photo tours for the *Daily Mirror* and later on *Picture Post*. In his photographs, industrial ruin or urban decay was presented diagnostically. Although Bolton was not economically devastated its cotton industry was declining and there was 10 per cent unemployment in the town at the time of the Mass Observation survey.

Making lists or collecting data on everyday mass culture was part of the Mass Observation ethos of 'social detection'. So much so that data collection was seen by Madge, Harrisson and Jennings to be the overriding need in the first year. This was a pronounced drive towards the model of scientific observation of which Harrisson's earlier interest in ornithology was one source, combined with an appeal to impersonal technical equipment—especially

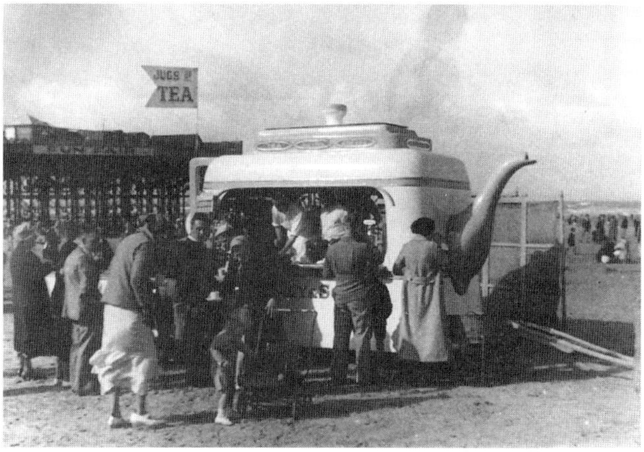


7.4 Blackpool, 1937.
Julian Trevelyan

the camera—to observe and record objectively.

Madge singled out Duchamp as the one Modernist who had succeeded in becoming a scientist,[12] and in this area we should recall Auden's preference, at this time, for 'clinical' writing. Yet 'fact' could be accorded a Surrealist status, too, by the photographers within Mass Observation. Madge and Harrisson had admitted the revelatory value of fact in 1939: 'the drab and sordid features of industrial life will take on new interest'.[13]

The Surrealist aesthetic category of 'the marvellous' could be attained through direct urban photographs, where found social objects uncovered by surveys could be transformed into Surrealist *objets trouvés*; a mobile tea van shaped as a giant tea-pot photographed by Julian Trevelyan in Blackpool in 1937 was one such.

Any discussion of Surrealist determinants on the Mass Observation photography of Spender or Trevelyan returns us to the figure of Humphrey Jennings. He was a most formidable power in British vanguard art in the 1930s; a film-maker, painter, photographer and poet who was admired and had his works collected by leading continental Surrealists: Breton, Aragon and Magritte. Jennings's acute understanding of the effects of photo-mechanical reproduction and the effects of mass circulation photography was made from a standpoint close to that of Walter Benjamin (Jennings actually wrote on the optical unconsciousness along similar lines to Benjamin).

While Mass Observation may have aimed at the production of American-type photo-books like Archibald MacLeish's *Land of the Free*,[14] almost all of Jennings's, Spender's and Trevelyan's photographs taken on surveys went unpublished. They became, especially in Jennings's case, homeless photographs unmarried to the written statistics and opinions that were being recorded on the occasion the photographs were taken. It was only in Jennings's film *Spare Time* and Spender's *Picture Post* city photo-tours with a journalist—both projects of 1939—that Mass Observation fully deployed its methods of domestic anthropology and candid reportage; the war foreclosed further developments.

The kinds of Surrealist photography and poetry that Jennings propounded lie behind other sectors of Mass Observation activities. Volunteers were from early days often directed towards street graphics-chalkings and graffiti in particular. The Surrealist poet David Gascoyne, as well as Jennings, brought an interest in graffiti to Mass Observation; writing of him during his enthusiasm for Mass Observation, Kathleen Raine believed: 'the poet reassumes the ancient role at once of national prophet and reader of the augures, not from entrails but from, literally, the writing on the walls'.[15]

Both Jennings and Spender had been inspired, too, in their photographs by Brassai's portfolio of graffiti photographs that had been published in *Minotaure*, the Surrealist magazine, in 1933.

Mass Observation was permeated by communalist and populist ideology; its formation was precipitated by the failed populist movement surrounding the abdication crisis in December 1936. Independent of one another, Madge and Harrisson, in London and Bolton, recognised the existence of a gap between the actual views of individuals, the 'ordinary' people, and published opinion presented as public opinion in newspapers, radio and newsreel during the crisis. Thereafter Mass Observation repeatedly foregrounded the 'ordinary chap' and 'ordinary people', the undistinguished members of the mass of the population. They, often lower-middle-class in background, found their habits, work routines and leisure activities valued and recorded through interviews or their own self-reports.

The film Documentarists among Mass Observation's founders, especially Grierson's colleague Stuart Legg, stressed the populist idea of 'citizenship' while Arthur Elton and Edgar Anstey had already (in 1934) placed slum dwellers in front of cine-cameras for the film *Housing Problems*, and let them 'tell their own story, virtually make their own film'.[16]

Similarly 'nobodies' found a voice through Mass Observation, just as 'nobodies' had been the chosen photographic subjects in the early 1930s of the humanitarian German photographer admired by Spender, Helmar Lerski.[17] For, apart from one or two German emigrés, arguably no photographer in Britain other than Humphrey Spender had such an intimate knowledge of the modes of German realist photography. Again Spender exactly fitted and reproduced the complex ideology of Mass Observation.

## Reference Notes

1 Mildred Gwin Barwell, *Faces We See*, Southern Combed Yarn Spinners Association, Gastonia, North Carolina, 1939 ('the facts in this book were taken from actual mill records [and] from innumerable conversations').
2 Raymond Mortimer in Bill Brandt, *The English at Home*, Batsford, London, 1936, pp.3-4.
3 Bronislaw Malinowski, 'A Nationwide Intelligence Service', essay in Charles Madge and Tom Harrisson, ed., *First Year's Work in Mass Observation*, Lindsey Drummond, London, 1938.
4 For a discussion of 'fictions' see the influential opening of W. Lippmann, *Public Opinion*, George Allen & Unwin, London, 1929, pp.l4-19.
5 'Confronted with these Headlines, a Nation of 50 Millions Gasped with Astonishment...' *Mass Observation*, Frederick Muller, London, 1937, p.9.
6 *Daily Mirror*, 6 December 1938.
7 *Mass Observation*, 1937, p.30.
8 See note 3.
9 See Harrisson's own account in *Britain Revisited*, Gollancz, London, 1961, pp.25-6.
10 Interview with the Author, July 1973.
11 Myfanwy Evans, *The Painter's Object*, Gerald Howe, 1937, p.3.
12 *Mass Observation*, p.26.
13 *Mass Observation*, p.31.
14 Harrisson was impressed by the *Time* review of *Land of the Free*, 25 April 1938.
15 Kathleen Raine's essay 'David Gascoyne and the Prophetic Role' in *Defending Ancient Springs*, Oxford University Press, Oxford, 1967, p.48.
16 Edgar Anstey in an interview with the Author, July 1978. See also Elizabeth Sussex, *The Rise and Fall of British Documentary: The Story of the Film Movement Founded by John Grierson*, University of California Press, Berkeley, 1976.
17 Lerski's photobook, *Kopfe des Alltags*, Hermann Reckendorf, 1931, was very influential, not only for Spender but for other British photographers including Barbara Ker-Seymor.

## Note

The Mass Observation archive is now kept at the University of Sussex. The most significant publications of Mass Observation up to the Second World War are *Mass Observation*, Frederick Muller, London, 1937; *May the Twelfth*, Lindsay Drummond, London, 1938; *Britain*, Penguin, Harmondsworth, 1939. *The Pub and the People*, Gollancz, 1943, repub. Seven Dials, Welwyn Garden City, 1971, was the only publication to come out of the 'Worktown' research in Lancashire. For a recent anthology of Mass Observation writings see Angus Calder and Dorothy Sheridan, eds, *Speak for Yourself*, Oxford University Press, Oxford, 1985.

## Further Reading

• David Chaney and Michael Pickering, 'Authorship in Documentary: Sociology as an Art form in Mass Observation', in John Corner, ed.,

*Documentary and the Mass Media*, Edward Arnold, London, 1986.
• David Chaney and Michael Pickering, 'Democracy and Communication: Mass Observation 1937-1943', *Journal of Communication* 36, no.1, 1986.
• James Clifford, 'On Ethnographic Allegory', *Representations*, vol.1, no.2, 1983.
• James Clifford, 'On Ethnographic Surrealism', *Comparative Studies in Society and History*, no.23, 1981.
• Stuart Laing, 'Presenting "Things as They Are": John Summerfield's *May Day* and Mass Observation', in Frank Gloversmith, ed., *Class, Culture and Social Change*, Harvester, Brighton, 1980.
• P.C. Ray, *The Surrealist Movement in England*, Cornell University Press, Ithaca, 1971.
• Alan Rosenthal, ed., *New Challenges for Documentary*, University of California Press, Berkeley, 1988.
• Penny Summerfield, 'Mass Observation: Social Research or Social Movement?' *Journal of Contemporary History*, vol.20, no.3, 1985.
• Ken Worpole, 'Oppositional Culture, Yesterday and Today', in *Camerawork*, no.11, Sept. 1978.

# 8 Nation, Mandate, Memory

Don Macpherson

Introduction by
**Don Macpherson and Jessica Evans**

*Don Macpherson*: Nostalgia is infectious. When John Major imagines himself cycling past village greens to drink warm beer to the tune of church bells and the sound of leather on willow, is this really what he experienced as a boy in Brixton? I don't think so. Is he quoting Orwell? Not really. To most of us, it may sound like he's describing some weird Disneyland, untouched by the insecurities of the Thatcher years—as portrayed in the imagery of Martin Parr.

But in reality he's tapping into an unconscious stream of memory images of England that are still in the air despite the post-modern rape and pillage. This ebb and flow of a mythical past is still a fascinating spectator-sport, so earnest debates around these 1930s Mass Observation photos still seem peculiarly timely in the 1990s. Recent books by Raphael Samuel, Patrick Wright and Robert Hewison all point to this ongoing resonance of tradition within end-of-the-millennium Britain. It's difficult to nail down; this brief essay only takes a stab. A whiff of nostalgia already surrounded these elegant Humphrey Spender photos back in the 1970s. I thought it would all be...er, history. Maybe. But after all, what is more contemporary than nostalgia?

*Jessica Evans*: Since Don Macpherson's article, and particularly as a consequence of the important foothold Foucauldian theory gained in photographic history during the 1980s, much has been written of the way in which Spender's photographs, and the *Picture Post* photo-stories, reproduced the structure of a colonial-bourgeois gaze on to the anthropological other. The very presumption of realism in these photographs effaced the position of the knower and thus rendered 'the other' as a savage yet paradoxically impoverished threat.[1] Much stress has been laid on the way in which working-class people are shown self-absorbed in the communal rituals of their immediate locality to the extent that they are unable to attain a state of self-consciousness—a privilege that was only afforded the viewer. It was as if to read a naïve naturalism in Spender's portrayal was to discover a proposal that the people represented are naïve. What Don Macpherson's and the later Foucauldian readings of documentary[2] share is the idea that photographic realism in general, and documentary photography in particular, is a means by which those in power generate a false consensus based on an ideological homology between realist aesthetics and the shared experience of all classes. The question I would like to pose is whether the ethic of 1930s realism can only lead to a false democracy of the image? Is the only contemporary reading of these pictures that they produce a myth of a cohesive Englishness? Can they only ever be sources for nostalgia?

It is easy to forget that when Macpherson and Mellor's articles were published in *Camerawork* the radical Left critique of documentary that we are familiar with today had not yet become hegemonic. It is for this reason that, taken as a whole, the Mass Observation issue of *Camerawork* (no.11, which also contained essays by Ken Worpole and Tom Picton) was ambivalent about precisely what (progressive or conservative) readings could be made of the images produced by Spender et al., and this was no doubt due in no small measure to *Camerawork*'s adherence to the tradition of documentary. It is important to note that Charles Harrisson found that Spender's photographs produced a conundrum; diverse, incoherent when taken as a whole, they were found to be uninterpretable, and lay unused until 'rediscovered' in the 1970s.[3] Part of the reason for this must lie in the fact that the kind of knowledge MO was to gather was positivistic—one which treated human behaviour as if it were a set of solely physical variants. The point here is that the archival skills necessary to impose a logic on the pictures were not available to Harrisson. Whilst it was possible to use (written, spoken) *language* to produce this kind of statistical knowledge—Tom Picton reports on tireless accounts *written* by MO Observers of the amount of matches struck in one night in a pub [4]—the meanings of the photographs that Spender produced were, I suggest, in excess of this narrow definition of knowledge and could not be contained by it. His photographs appeared to arrive at Harrisson's door with their meanings incomplete. We could take this further to suggest that at this time, the idea that the working class had a 'culture' which was more or less intact, more or less expressive of its social and economic position, seemed impossible to those who had the social status to direct knowledge. It was impossible, from within the MO framework, to think of culture as a process of meaning-making, to think of culture as something other than that embedded in the positivistic 'fact' of commodity fetishism.[5] This expression intends to make an explicit connection between MO and the later 'culturalism' of Richard Hoggart and Raymond Williams.

The discipline of 'cultural studies' is now being ossified as a coherent 'tradition' and a particular narrative of the historical evolution of the concept 'culture' is fast becoming standardised.[6] It is a narrative which despite its best intentions remains respectful of, and is contained by, the literary academic ('culture and civilisation') tradition. The story of cultural studies is that, in short, the 'culture and civilisation' way of thinking of culture as discrimination, as represented by Arnold, Elliott and Leavis, irretrievably broke down when, in the late 1950s/early 1960s, Richard Hoggart and Raymond Williams argued for an expanded definition of culture which could take into account the ordinary creative capacities of all citizens.[7] But from what position is this story written? As 'cultural studies' becomes official culture, there is another history of culture which lies 'below' and as such remains thoroughly marginalised. Twenty years before Hoggart, Spender was documenting the culture of the English working class and thus redefining an idea of culture—he showed that culture in the context of modern life is something that is fundamentally urban, publicly shared and conventional—in other words thoroughly socialised yet also an act of creative intentionality. Cultural forms are shown as surplus to, but consistent with, the conditions of people's lives. It is this surplus that is represented in Spender's pictures. If you look carefully at the people in Spender's pictures they are 'getting on with it'—creating and re-creating their lives through social organisation; they may be the subjects of Spender's pictures, but this doesn't mean they are only 'Spender's subjects'.

---

## Nation, Mandate, Memory

**Don Macpherson** edited *Traditions of Independent Cinema in Britain: The Thirties* (1978). Based in the UK, he now works as a Hollywood scriptwriter.

Looking at these images from Mass Observation the question must be asked—what is at stake politically in our fascination with these dead images? It would be merely cynical to leave them as either a spectacle of the past, or another chapter in art history. Now, as then, the images and texts of Mass Observation form vital parts in the construction of a memory-image of the British nation, and together they demand serious questions about the terms which relate photography to a politics of representation.

The following questions can be asked. *Nation*: what relation exists between the image of 'Britain' and its 'national' aesthetic of 'realism'? And therefore what are the political terms in which photography is thought of in Britain? *Mandate*: what is the social status of the photographer and what command provides the link between a photographic practice and its 'public'? *Memory*: if the

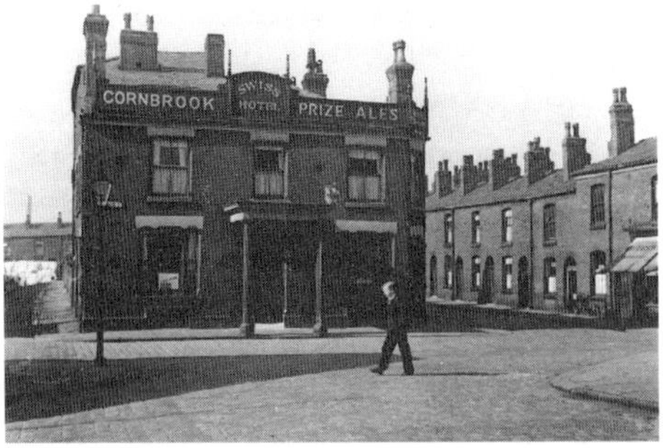


8.1

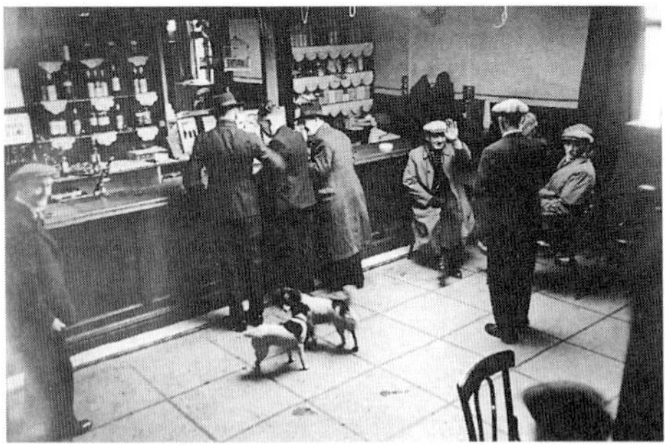

8.2

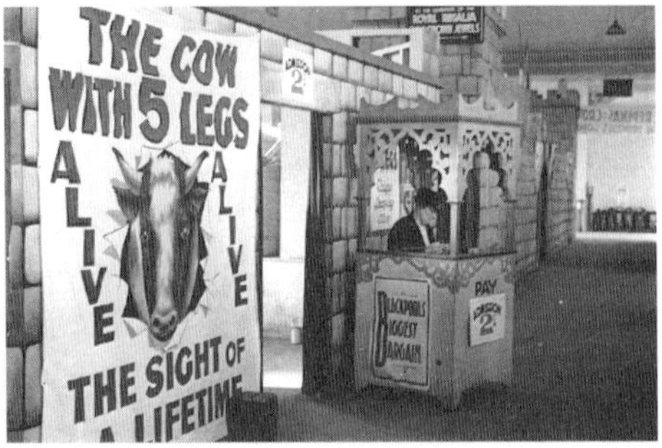


8.3

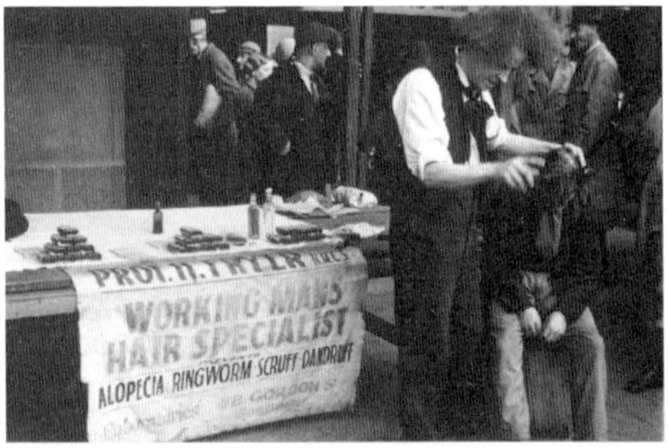


8.4

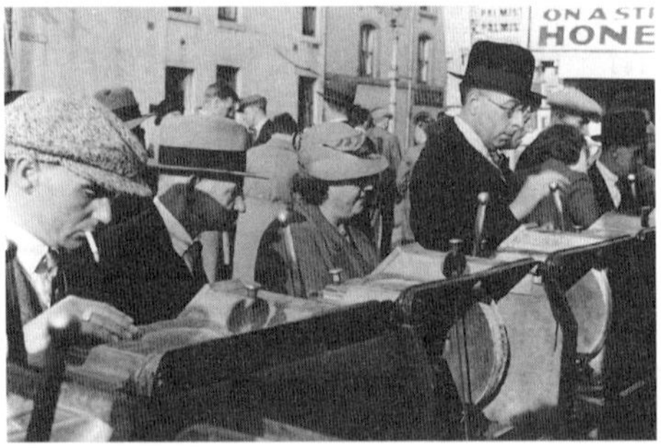

8.5

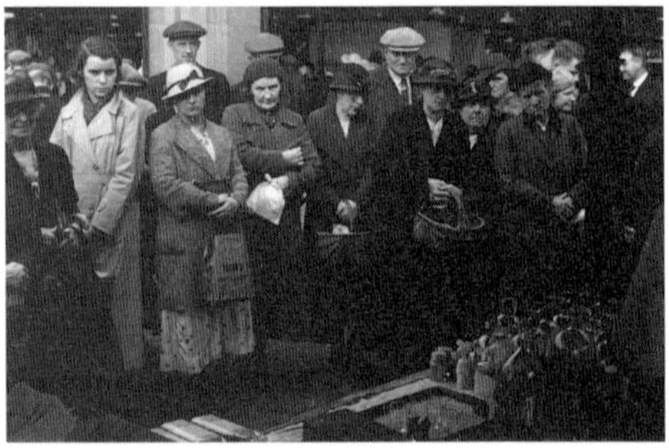

8.6

camera eye is one 'which records in order to forget' (Berger), then what are the terms which govern the entry and disappearance of certain images within our social memory? Can we return to those images and reorder their economy? What are the institutions of social control over the archives of images and texts?

### Nation

In the 1920s and 1930s, during an era of imperial disintegration, economic crisis and political unrest in Britain, the idea of the 'nation' re-emerged as one of the few solid, all embracing social elements. It was reinforced for the first time by the development of the new radio and film technology and by the 'national voice' of BBC radio. As an aesthetic counterpart to political enfranchise-

8.1 Pub exterior, the Swiss Hotel, 1937-8. Humphrey Spender

8.2 The vault, Joiners Hotel, 1937-8. Humphrey Spender

8.3 The cow with five legs, 1937-8. Humphrey Spender

8.4 Quack hair specialist, Happy Homes Exhibition, Bolton 1938. Humphrey Spender

8.5 Blackpool: Olympic Pleasure Beach, playing machines, 1937-8. Humphrey Spender

8.6 Open market: quack medicine stall, 1937-8. Humphrey Spender

ment, the 1930s' style of 'realism' variously developed in Grierson's state-sponsored documentary films, the Mass Observation photos and the photojournalism of *Picture Post*, created a 'democracy of reality'. Reality seen in this way was fundamentally something shared by all classes which minimised the gap between observer and observed in society. This political and aesthetic style of 'social realism' produced a 'reality' which could be looked at from several points of view, but which fundamentally united them to produce the notion of a shared common sense. Only 'extreme points of view' were difficult to understand, but at least they existed essentially *within the same perspective*. The nation validated itself by its seeming tolerance of these very extremes and by maintaining an equilibrium or balance of views. The unity of the nation's body politic repressed 'sectional' discontent in the name of 'the British people'. Ramsay MacDonald, the former Labour leader and then Prime Minister of Britain's National Government similarly reinterpreted socialism in this light: 'Socialists', he said, 'do not speak of "classes", but of "the social".'

This ideology of national unity (consensus politics) and its aesthetic anticipation/validation in realism which arose in the 1930s have decisively influenced both dominant and alternative visual practices in Britain. Indeed the 'social fabric of our nation' has come to be virtually unthinkable without the documentary style of its film-makers, the social realism of its photographers, and the naturalistic aesthetics of its television. But in Humphrey Spender's photographs taken in Bolton in 1937/8 there are perhaps traces of the difficulty of establishing an initial relationship between the exoticism of the Northern working classes (what Spender called 'forbidden fruit') and the all-embracing cosiness of the photographic frame. (figures 8.1-8.6.) On the one hand we are called to observe as strangers the savage rituals of a funeral, religious processions, football match and pub; on the other, we recognise the familiar details of clothing and printed signs, which remind us that we are, after all, in England. Spender's painterly precision of vanishing perspective and composition suffice to give us, like the observer in his picture of a funeral, a point of view from which the social event can both be seen and from which the onlooker can be sheltered. The image freezes that moment, which is no longer troubling since it is now kept at a distance. Spender's photographs define the onlooker's position as that of the anthropologist, whose rational observation of the savage and the exotic only confirms his own existence as 'human', and therefore universal.

### Mandate

In this way Mass Observation offered some of the artists and intelligentsia of the period a social mandate on 'the Left' but firmly within the consensus of this self-styled national democracy. It restored to certain intellectuals the mandate of a mass audience but without their having to reject the traditional values and function of their own class. This stabilising movement was marked by a massive shift from traditional artistic roles to a new importance of professionalism: painters became film-makers (Jennings), poets became journalists (Madge). In this way the hat of the individual artist was traded in for that of the self-appointed servant and prophet of the newly formed entity, 'the public'.

The observers of Mass Observation were ambassadors from one class to another who were to 'provide the points from which can be plotted weather-maps of public feeling in a crisis' (1937). They did not see, or were not said to see their role as destructive, but on the contrary as healers of social and political wounds which had produced what Tom Harrisson was later to call a 'gap between leader and led, between published opinion and public opinion, between Westminster chatter and Lancashire talk [which had] built an invisible barrier dangerous in our democracy'. In this context one might well ask 'dangerous for whom?' If British society were thought to be 'wrong' it was not thought so because its ruling class needed to be replaced, but because of the very danger of extremes or *instability*. It is important to see how a Surrealist concern with the unconscious was reinterpreted with this mandate. A film-maker such as Humphrey Jennings, who was also a member of Mass Observation, drew upon a timeless myth of an essential Britishness, a 'national unconscious' which united the nation seemingly without itself being conscious of it. Certain historical parallels between the age of the 1930s and of the 1970s—mass unemployment and the 'common enemy' of fascism are most often quoted—have led many to talk of a renewal of the mandate offered for artists and intellectuals in the 1930s by the British state. It has to be recognised that such a mandate is no longer possible except under a severely nostalgic attachment to a myth of a past.

**Memory**

The third and most crucial importance of Mass Observation is therefore not so much its existence as a cultural movement in the past, but its contribution to an ongoing process of *remembering*. Mass Observation is not merely a series of representations (texts and photographs) but a process of recording, printing, storing and (now) retrieval of those representations. Analogous to a memory, it has frozen a memory-image of 'Britishness' which has obtained an existence and authority outside history which can be recalled and 'quoted' at will. But it also becomes simultaneously the raw material from which we reconstruct the past in the present.

An urgent task in Britain is to provide the conditions for the reinterpretation of Mass Observation's social mandate and for the possible reconstruction of that memory. But such a call can only be regarded as mere rhetoric unless any guides for action can be given. One might begin with the undoubted attraction of the Spender photographs reprinted in this edition of *Camerawork*. To what extent does their publication merely reproduce those desires for an imaginary past in which 'things were clearer', and 'more visible'? Their presentation might indicate that they 'speak for themselves' without aid of texts in the way that social documentary photography is still held to do by many. They perhaps invite us to recall Spender's mandate of taking photographs which transcended class interests from a perspective which remains universal in its outlook. One alternative would be to use photography agitationally, which at its simplest can mean providing a specific context or political locations for its usage. But a longer-term aim would be one of intervening within the system of representations themselves in the style of Dick Jewell's excellent collection, *Found Photos*, where the anonymous photobooth portraits are literally relics—discarded fragments of personal memory-images now reorganised by their collector. But in looking at these photographs by Spender and reading these texts on Mass Observation there is no simple way of uprooting or erasing them from our memory. The assumptions which formed Mass Observation are ingrained in a whole variety of practices, perhaps most disquietingly in the search for 'British culture' itself. The terms of their construction, the search for knowledge of a national unity, share a common identity. By beginning to question the naturalness of these assumptions we may serve to loosen the knots which bind together those terms of nation, mandate and memory, and so turn their relation into a problem of the present.



---

**Reference Notes**

**1** See for example, Stephen Edwards for a powerful example of this argument: 'Disastrous Documents', in *Ten.8*, no.15, 1984.

**2** I do not hold myself exempt from these arguments—my work on the representation of people with learning difficulties employed precisely these Foucauldian strategies.

**3** See John Taylor, *A Dream of England*, Manchester University Press, Manchester, 1994, p.156; p.162. And see Humphrey Spender's reminiscence of this period in *Worktown People: Photographs from Northern England 1937-38*, Falling Wall Press, Bristol, 1982, p.8.

**4** Tom Picton, 'A Very Public Espionage', in *Camerawork*, no.11, 1978, p.2.

**5** See Don Slater, 'The Object of Photography' in this volume.
**6** See, for example, Graeme Turner, *British Cultural Studies: An Introduction*, Routledge, London, 1990, which apart from this criticism is probably the best survey.
**7** For an account of this see G. Turner's *British Cultural Studies*. For the concept of 'culturalism' see Stuart Hall, 'Cultural Studies: Two Paradigms', in T. Bennett, Graham Martin et al., eds, *Culture, Ideology and Social Process: A Reader*, Oxford University Press, Oxford, 1981.

**Further Reading**


• 'Alternative Photography', *New Society*, 24 August 1978.
• John Berger, 'Ways of Remembering', *Camerawork*, no.10, Summer 1978 (reprinted in this volume).
• Michael Bommes and Patrick Wright, 'Charms of Residence: The Public and the Past', in ed. R. Johnson et al, *Making Histories*, Centre for Contemporary Cultural Studies, Hutchinson, London, 1982.
• David Chaney, '"A Public Imagery": Mass Observation and the Coronation of 1937', unpublished paper for the British Sociological Association Conference, April 1978.
• Franco Fortini, 'The Writers' Mandate and the End of Anti-Fascism', *Screen*, Vol.15, no.1, Spring 1974.
• *Formations of Nation and People*, Routledge & Kegan Paul, London, 1984.
• Michel Foucault, 'Politics and the Study of DIscourse', *Ideology and Consciousness*, no.3, Spring 1978.
• Stuart Hall, 'The Social Eye of Picture Post', *Working Papers in Cultural Studies*, no.2, Spring 1972.
• Robert Hewison, *The Heritage Industry: Britain in a Climate of Decline*, Methuen, London, 1987.
• Dick Jewell, *Found Photos*, London, 1977.
• Annette Kuhn, 'The Camera I: Observations on Documentary', *Screen*, vol.19, no.2, 1978.
• Don Macpherson, ed., *Traditions of Independent Cinema in Britain: The Thirties*, British Film Institute, London, 1978.
• Christopher Shaw and Malcolm Chase, eds, *The Imagined Past: History and Nostalgia*, Manchester University Press, Manchester, 1989.
• Raphael Samuel, *Theatres of Memory Volume 1: Past and Present in Contemporary Culture*, Verso, London, 1994.
• Humphrey Spender, *Worktown People: Photographs from Northern England 1937-38*, Falling Wall Press, Bristol, 1982.
• Patrick Wright, *On Living in an Old Country: The National Past in Contemporary Britain*, Verso, London, 1985.

# 9 Pictured History: The Matchgirls' Strike 1888

Terry Smith

Introduction by
**Terry Smith**

The terms 'Pictured History' in the title signal the politics of method at work in this piece. Against those historians who (still astonishingly, even in the 1970s) clung to logocentric documentary—or if in the context of press, contemporary written records of oral observation—evidence, I wanted to show that pictures could be read for quite exact historical evidence; but only if read with acute awareness of the ways their producers and disseminators were attempting to give their pictures meaning, hence the central stress on an unfolding image analysis, on pursuing the details of their circumstances of generation. And this led immediately to the second main political point, that pictures—these ones, for example—actually *made history*, had quite specific historical effects, influenced the opinions and actions of both the powerful and the powerless, were crucial in the incessant warfare between them. A subsidiary point, hinted at here, is that images increasingly assumed this importance by the 1880s, a pivotal decade in the history of the labour movement.

My piece on the Matchgirls' strike of 1888 was shaped in a conjuncture of events, forces and circumstances which were—like the popularity of the concept 'conjuncture'—typical of the late 1970s. It was one result of a six-month period spent between London and Birmingham. Yet it is marked as much by developments in Australian art, cultural studies and labour movement activism as it is by its overt subject and immediate context.

I had come over from Sydney primarily to work at the Centre for Contemporary Cultural Studies at the University of Birmingham. Stuart Hall was in his last semester there, and was inspirational. Richard Johnson was taking on the director's responsibilities, editing the anthology *Making Histories*, and convening a Popular Memory Group. My job was to research the ways in which newspaper, and particularly photographic, coverage of the 1926 General Strike echoed in the oral history memories of even those who were in the middle of it. All graduate research at the Centre occurred through weekly meetings of people with convergent interests: for all the inevitable tensions, this was a genuine collective practice, and enormously productive.

I had begun the decade with the *Art and Language* group, in its New York manifestation. Back in Melbourne in 1975 I attempted to form a similar grouping, but the sacking of the Labor Government in that year—by a Governor General representing the Queen, widely regarded until then as a harmless anachronism from our colonial past—precipitated a widespread radicalisation of cultural practice. Direct action became an obvious necessity. Artists warred against the reactionary governmental, business, media hegemony. With others I formed the Media Action Group. We projected slide-shows to meetings of workers on how the media misled people, on the wrongs of uranium mining, and, increasingly, on the background to current issues within particular industries. BCCCS Marxist structuralism, Glasgow Media Group analysis, BFI poststructuralism and avant-gardist art design weighed in on the side of the Miscellaneous Workers' Union, the Artworkers' Union and the Public Service Association. MAG soon became Union Media Services and grew to become the leading designer and producer of labour movement journals and election campaigns in the country.

Memory of the working-class struggle had been largely erased by historical amnesia. Labour historians were few and far between. But each May Day parade saw activists, especially the Waterside Workers, transporting atop their cars large banners with cartoon character attacks on local politicians. Soon old banners were unearthed, or repainted, and the new unions, such as the Unemployed Workers, commissioned new ones. Art students were attracted to these tasks, and to the burgeoning mural movement, turning to the lost visual history of the labour movement. Interest became so powerful that the Australia Council, equivalent to the Arts Council in Britain, made Art & Working Life one of its major programmes, funding artists in unions and communities throughout the country.

I came to England in 1979 on sabbatical from Sydney University to do background work for my PhD dissertation on the history of May Day in Australia. The Australian labour movement emerged from local conditions, and is marked by many firsts (such as the 8-hour day and votes for women) but was also profoundly shaped by British experience. On the trail of cartoons by Phil May and the precedents for banner designs I soon turned up at the Museum of Labour History, then spilling out of rooms at Hackney Town Hall.

Curator Terry McCarthy put me on to the Museum's cache of photographs of women working at home assembling matchboxes. I began to contextualise them, relating them particularly to the 1888 strike. I was thrilled to be able to assist in drawing attention to this fabled moment in working-class struggle, and to underline the initiative of women workers and reformists.

Most of what is said in the article still stands, I think, as accurate information and helpful analysis. I no longer believe, however, that the dating of 'early 1890s' for three of the images holds water. It was suggested strongly to me that these were part of a Salvation Army campaign at that time. I was never able to get that absolutely, independently confirmed. It is more likely that they were part of the 1906 *Daily News* exhibition. This does not change the thrust of the article, nor bear greatly on my readings of these images, but it does remove them by fourteen years from the Strike.

Half Moon was itself an interesting collective, and I enjoyed helping to prepare three issues. The mix of structuralist media analysis, new theories of photography, arts activism, political photomontage by Peter Kennard, Conrad Atkinson, the Film and Poster Collective and Leeson & Dunn, historical recovery and hands-on advice to would-be interventionist photographers, was lively, committed and effective.

The Photography Workshop was just as important. Jo Spence and Terry Dennett had the same range of commitments, and more (such as trying to revive a worker photographer movement). Becoming a friend of theirs, and working at Half Moon, was a little delicate, as a split had occurred two years earlier. Yet in the same issue of *Camerawork* as the Matchgirls article my review of Jo and Terry's *Photography/Politics: One* appeared. The editors of *Camerawork* unhesitatingly printed my comments regretting the dispersal of energies and pointed to the fact that *Photography/Politics: One* was independently produced whereas *Camerawork* and the Half Moon Gallery were dependent on Arts Council funding. Thatcher's people were on the warpath then, targeting 'political' arts publications.

I never completed the study of May Day. Others wrote valuable histories of labour movement imagery, and Union Media Services thrived along with many other initiatives, most of which used graphic media and video, rather than the focus on photography that was so vital to political art and theory in London in the late 1970s.

# Pictured History: The Matchgirls' Strike 1888

**Terry Smith** is Power Professor of Contemporary Art and Director of the Power Institute of Fine Arts, University of Sydney. He was a member of the Art and Language Group, a founder of Union Media Services, Sydney, and has written a number of books and articles on Australian, Aboriginal, European and American visual cultures.

The value of photographs to labour history is strikingly illustrated here: the media distorts the conditions which led to the famous strike, the photographs point to the actual conditions. The media misreports the 'girls' as healthy and happy in the factories and fails to point out that half of the work of the industry, the making of matchboxes, was done at home in appalling and dangerous conditions for next to nothing. Photographs made this fact undeniable. Historians who fear photographs are denying themselves a key resource; photographers who ignore the ways history is constructed are limiting the effectiveness of their work.

All of the images on these pages are products of the depression of the 1880s. *Cassell's Saturday Journal* for 10 December 1887 (figure 9.1) illustrates comely girls busily working in open spaces, attractive appendices to the processes of matchmaking. The text is equally distorting; in breathless style it details the growth of Bryant & May's as if it were a natural flowering into modern technology from the primitive rubbing together of two sticks. It lauds the large, scientifically ventilated factory buildings, sets out the simple, almost casual nature of the work, claims that the girls are paid between 12 and 14 shillings a week, and praises them as 'very industrious and remarkably well behaved', adding that 'nearly all the girls look strong and healthy'.

Two years earlier these same girls had struck against the lowering of their wages and the undermining of their health, especially the loss of their teeth from inhaling phosphorus fumes. This led Tom Mann to say of Bryant & May's: 'Their working girls are most miserably paid, getting only some 8s. per week....And that company, during the first six months of its existence, actually paid over £330,000 to shareholders, who had not done a single stroke of work towards producing it.'[1] In July 1888, four girls who had given information on their conditions to social reformer Annie Besant were dismissed. The result was the first step in the 'new unionism'—all the girls walked out.

> 'If a woman can by honest work, earn a little money at home in her spare time (at matchboxes), do you see any objection to it?'
> The Chief General Inspector, Local Government Board, Poplar Union Enquiry, 1906.

CASSELL'S SATURDAY JOURNAL. 249

## HOW IT IS DONE. Dec 10 1887

### XI.—AT BRYANT AND MAY'S MATCH FACTORY.

When it is stated that Messrs. Bryant and May produce a million and a quarter boxes of wooden matches daily, besides vesuvians and wax vestas, some idea may be formed as to the extent of their business. The firm, which is now nearly half a century old, commenced in a very small way. Its founder was Mr. William Bryant, of Plymouth, who devoted his energies with considerable success towards the improvement of the match trade, and whose son, Mr. Wilberforce Bryant, is now the chairman of the limited company which took over the business in 1884.

The great saving of labour caused by the introduction of many ingenious mechanical contrivances enables Messrs. Bryant and May to supply the public with matches at unprecedentedly cheap prices. The firm may now be said to be almost without a rival in England. Match factories in various parts of the country have been bought and amalgamated with Messrs. Bryant and May, and upon their firm the whole of England and many of the colonies have virtually to rely for their supply of matches. In recent years the manufacture of matches has been greatly developed and improved. Even as the primitive method of obtaining fire by rubbing two dry sticks together was superseded by the flint and steel, which, in its turn, about half a century ago, gave place to the sulphur lucifer, so the latter, with its suffocating fumes, is now completely eclipsed by the modern patent safety and paraffin matches. Messrs. Bryant and May's factories in Fairfield Road, Bow, occupy some ten acres of ground. The works comprise three separate establishments, each of which is similarly fitted, and in each of which the process of match making goes on in the same way. This arrangement is made so that in case of the failure of any of the machines or of accident preventing work in any of the buildings, the production of matches may still be continued in the others. The buildings are perfectly fireproof, having stone floors and high roofs, and are scientifically ventilated. To the last-mentioned fact may probably be attributed in a great degree the healthy appearance of the female *employées*.

The packing of the matches into boxes is done by girls, about one hundred and fifty of whom occupy each of the large chambers provided for this purpose. The scene in these rooms is one of great bustle and activity. Boys are hurrying to and fro with trays of matches ready to be packed, and others are removing the filled boxes. The girls are standing in rows at tables, on which are piles of empty boxes and trays of matches, and with nimble fingers are placing the matches in the boxes. Every now and then in different parts of the room are seen a puff of smoke and a flare as a box of matches takes fire in the hands of the packer. This, however, is an unavoidable occurrence. The burning box is thrown into a receptacle provided for the purpose, and nothing is thought of it. When the matches come to the packers they are in double lengths, each end having been dipped into the igniting composition. Each of the girls is provided with a knife, which is attached to a block by a hinge. With this knife they divide the double matches before placing them in the boxes. Force of habit enables them to take up exactly the right quantity of matches to fill two boxes. These are placed all together under the knife and cut through the middle, thus leaving sufficient matches to fill one box in each hand. The knives are, of course, extremely sharp, and so great is the rapidity with which the cutting and packing are done that most of the girls are able to fill over 4,000 boxes a day, or 24,000 a week. They are paid by piecework, and their earnings amount to from twelve to fourteen shillings a week. They work for ten hours a day—namely, from nine in the morning till one p.m., when they have an hour's interval in which to go out for dinner, resuming work from two till seven. There are some twelve hundred "hands" in the employment of Messrs. Bryant and May, about eight hundred being girls, most of whom are under twenty years of age, but none less than fourteen. Some time elapses before they are able to thoroughly learn the work, and while acquiring the expertness necessary for piecework they are paid five shillings a week. The girls are very industrious and remarkably well-behaved. Indeed, seeing that their living depends upon their assiduity, they have but little inducement to frivolity. It is satisfactory to be able to state that nearly all the girls look strong and healthy. It is curious to observe that in nearly every case they wear a fringe of hair cut short over the forehead and smoothed down to the eyebrows. There

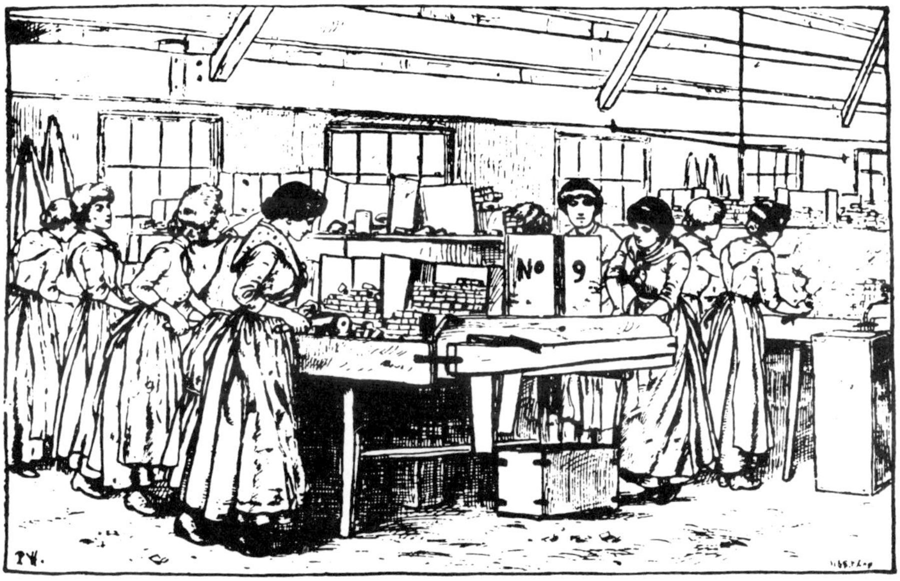


MATCH CUTTING.

9.1 Match-cutting, *Cassell's Saturday Journal*, 10 December 1887.

Public relations puff for Bryant & May's

Why did they see mutual self-defence as worth risking their jobs for? Why did they, ignored by male organisers of predominantly male unions, feel the need to fight for the establishment of their own union? And why at Bryant & May's, recognised by all sides as one of the better employers in the industry?

By rationalising production in specially built factories, Bryant & May's systematically increased its domination of the industry until the depression of the 1880s. Its response was not to lay off workers but the other classic manoeuvre, to reduce pay. When that was resisted, it achieved the same end by stepping up its system of fines. Eleven shillings a week was the theoretically conceivable maximum for a girl working at full speed in optimum conditions. But these conditions rarely obtained, and fines further cut average pay down to a few shillings a week. As well, the work was dangerous: 'phossy jaw' (phosphorus necrosis) became common, spreading pain, inflammation and abscesses from the teeth throughout the jaw and face. Bryant & May's were more concerned to prevent this than the usual small garret factories, but even they responded in the same way when the girls affected could no longer work quickly: they would be sacked. Photographs showing the interiors of match factories do not seem to be available, but medical photographs of 'phossy jaw' are, and they are appalling.

The East End provided capitalists with a huge pool of labour ripe for the sweating, especially that of single girls and mothers with dependants. Bryant & May's drew on this by dividing their production between matchmaking in the factories and matchbox making as 'outwork'. The photographs show the conditions under which thousands of women and their families assembled the parts provided by the factories. Paid at a lesser rate than the factory girls, they worked a sixteen-hour day at a maximum of 3/4d per hour. They had to provide extra materials themselves, and to take the bundles of boxes to the factory to receive the pay. Many were sacked matchmakers, many were the only breadwinners in their family. Their desperate struggle for subsistence was a constant warning to those in factory jobs.

How much of this can be 'read' from these photographs? The information I have just given is based on evidence presented at various enquiries and observations made by various investigators; the analysis is based on the work of those who have researched the subject, especially Reg Beer.[2] Little of it is stated in the photographs, but, in another sense, much more is made clear. The photographs do *not* state that the women pictured worked sixteen hours daily at $^{3}/_{4}$d per hour. They show *something more important: that is,* what it was like to work at that job, for those hours, at that rate. Historians often seem more comfortable with facts *about* experience than with facts *of* experience—for many of them, photographs and other visual material qualify as neither. Rebutting this requires that we go over some old and obvious ground about the nature of photography.

> They left work there and then. The discharged one was taken back but this did not pacify them. A hundred of them marched to Fleet Street yesterday afternoon, and sent a deputation to see Mrs Besant. They expressed their determination to hold out. There is no organisation amongst them, but they seem to stick together well.
> *The Star*, 6 July, 1888.

Photographs are records of what the camera pointed at. They are records of momentary appearances, and relate to reality only to the degree that the recorded surface itself does. The camera records only a limited field of appearance, and thus a photograph is a selection from amongst all possible appearances; its relation to reality is, therefore, only as strong as the selection. Being a selection, a photograph is a *reading* of appearances: we have to ask why the photographer was there at that time, which conventions of photography she was operating, which ideologies were influencing her, what was the context of use of the photograph? As well, appearances can be, and often are, actively constructed—things and people are arranged, posed, juxtapositions faked—just as elements from different times and places can be combined and rephotographed. It is possible to photograph an appearance in a variety of ways, to alter the image drastically in printing it and to change it still further by the addition of other images and texts when it is reproduced or displayed. These are some of the limits within which a photographer arrives at meaning; they are also some of the ways in which meaning is manipulated for the viewer.

How does this bear on the logical status of photographs as evidence? Because photographs record what was before the camera at a particular moment, they are renderings of instances which, strictly speaking, cannot stand for any other instances. In being so easily manipulable, doubt can be raised about the degree to which they stand for even the instance ostensibly 'caught' by the camera. Thus the demand for extra-photographic authentication, by verbal and written documents and statements, implying that they are somehow less subject to partiality and manipulation. For all these reasons, historians tend to use photographs as illustrations rather than evidence, and almost never think visually in their efforts to reconstruct history.

But this caution becomes self-defeating as collections of unofficial, people's memorabilia—such as that at the National Museum of Labour History—continue to grow, making more and more photographs available to researchers, teachers, activist publishers and others. The point is that photographs are not only records of what the camera was pointed at; they are also records of *how* the camera was pointed and how the subsequent print was made. We can, in nearly every case, decipher the technical and ideological operations which went into achieving the image and into reproducing/displaying it. Rules of evidence for photographs will obviously differ from those applicable to written documents, but they are nonetheless rules, with the same logical status. No-one operating such rules takes seriously the claim that photographs are unproblematic representations of reality, truth or whatever. They are partial selections, always for a purpose, always in context. Like written documents, official statements, works of art, that is, like any communicative form. All are constructions, but all can, with proper analysis, be deconstructed.

> The pity is that the match girls have not been suffered to take their own course, but have been egged on to strike by irresponsible advisers. No effort has been spared by these pests of the modern industrial world, the Social Democrats, to bring the quarrel to a head.
> *The Times*, 14 July 1888.

There are, I think, some further reasons why historians tend to distrust photographs. Most writers, especially when looking at early photographs, have attempted to account for the peculiar power of the images by pointing to their ambiguity, their susceptibility to readings beyond those perhaps intended by the photographer. Both Walter Benjamin and John Berger, for example, stress the sense of the subject 'projecting through' the image: the viewer's disturbing awareness that the subject was aware of being photographed, has paused for a moment to be recorded. It is as if the act of photography has disturbed what it aimed to record, changing it from what it was—it has interrupted normal social relationships and communicative exchanges. Yet, at the same time, *both* photographer and subject know that recording 'normality' is the aim of the exercise, so both, in different ways and in different degrees, temporarily contract to achieve it. The subject normally lives this normality; for the occasion of the photograph, she composes herself to 'represent' it. But unless the subject is an actor or a model, the representation is never complete, and often the subject will withhold something from the representation, will refuse to comply, to be 'typical'. Examples abound: August Sander's pictures of workers and peasants are often cited because his project was to record 'objectively' as many social types as possible.[3] Usually, the relationship is described in terms of psychological effect, as if a person-to-person, viewer-to-subject communication were occurring, but one displaced by the fact of the photograph. The undeniable presence of the subject of history as another person (right there, staring at me, knowing I am looking) can be too intrusive for those used to dealing with the abstract character of words as documents—it changes the relationship from eavesdropping to voyeurism. At the same time, the object of history (descriptions of 'reality', of 'what actually happened') becomes elusively absent. It is as if the evidence itself were at once both accepting and rejecting its interpreter. Too much...back to the British Library.



> (At Bryant & May's, Bow) The hour for commencing work is 6.30 in summer and 8 in winter; work concludes at 6 pm. Half an hour is allowed for breakfast and an hour for dinner. This long day of work is performed by young girls, who have to stand the whole of the time. A typical case is that of a girl of 16, a piece-worker; she earns 4s. a week, and lives with her sister, employed by the same firm, who 'earns good money, as much as 8s. or 9s. a week.' Out of the earnings 2s. is paid for the rent of one room; the child lives on only bread-and-butter and tea, alike for breakfast and dinner. The splendid salary of 4s. is subject to deductions in the shape of fines; if the feet are dirty, or the ground under the bench is left untidy, a fine of 3d. is inflicted; for putting 'burns'—matches that have caught fire during the work—on the bench 1s. has been forfeited, and one unhappy girl was once fined 2s. 6d. for some unknown crime. If a girl leaves four or five matches on her bench when she goes for a fresh 'frame' she is fined 3d., and in some departments a fine of 3d. is inflicted for talking.
> Annie Besant, 'White Slavery in London', *The Link*, 23 June 1888.

But the issue is not just formal and psychological, it is also ideological. If we ask what are the key contexts of use for the photograph under capitalism, the answer must be: as advertising, as record (by, for example, the police), as illustration (by, for example, newspapers) and as art...in this order, both quantitatively and in

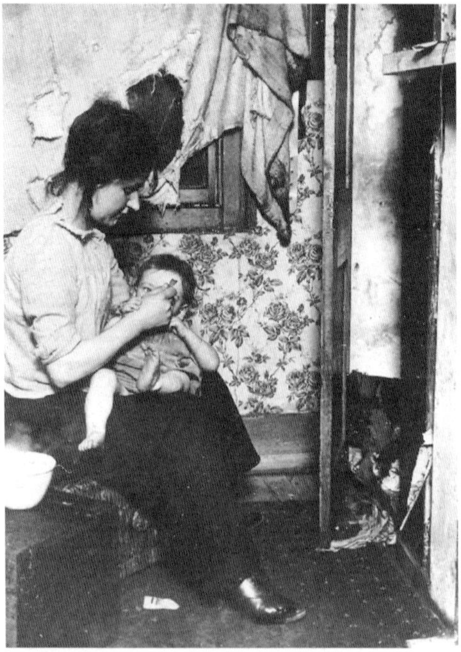
9.2

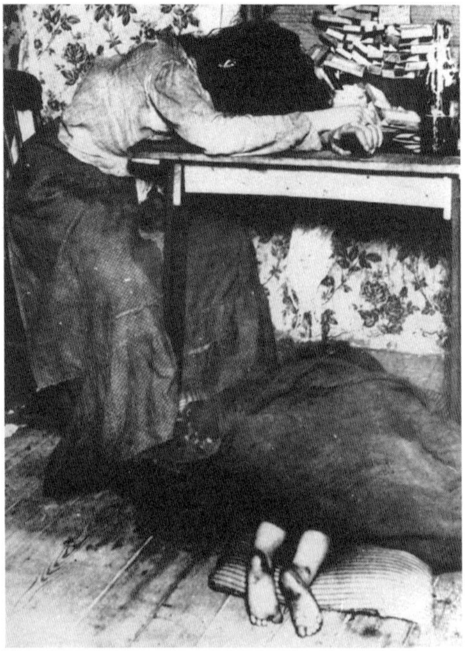
9.3

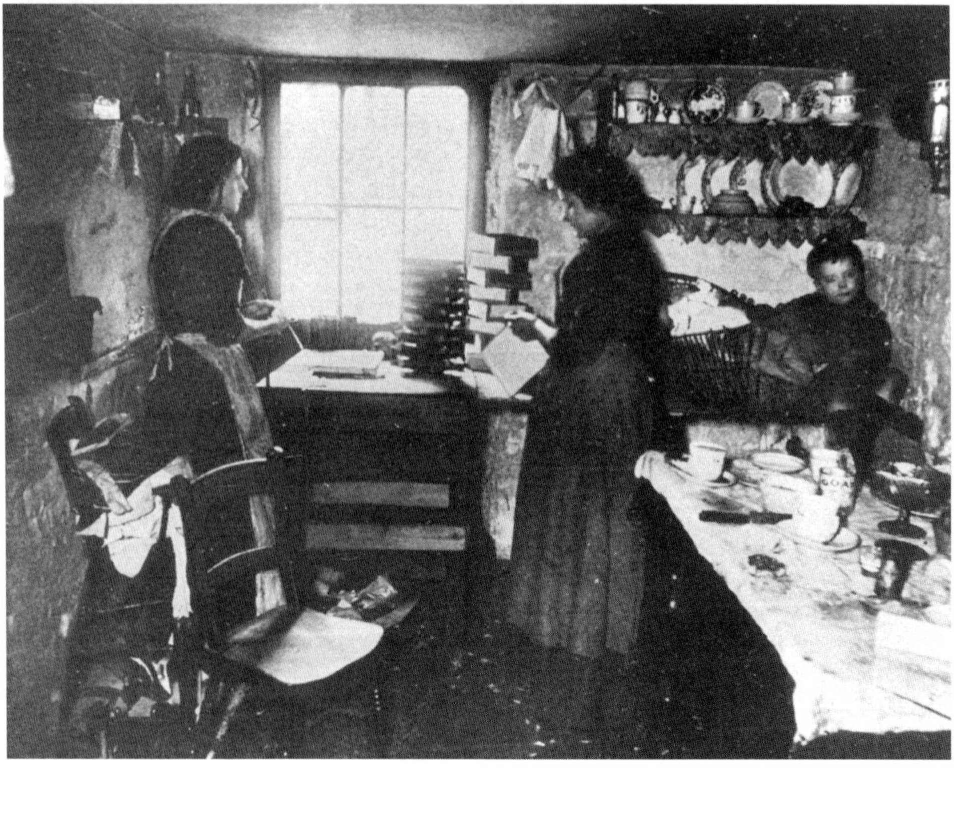
9.4

9.2 Home matchbox maker, East End, London, early 1890s

9.3 Home matchbox maker, East End, London, early 1890s

9.4 Matchgirls at home, East End, London, early 1890s

Top right:
9.5 Cardboard box making, East End, London, from 'Sweated Industries', an exhibition by the *Daily News*, Queen's Hall, London, May 1906

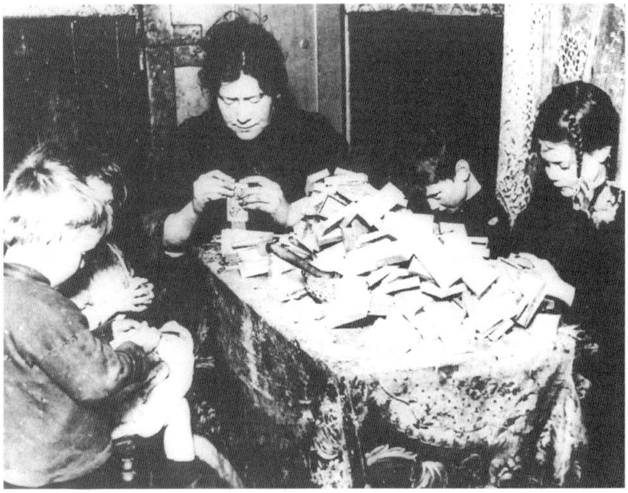

Right:
9.6 Matchbox makers at Bow, *Illustrated London News*, 1871

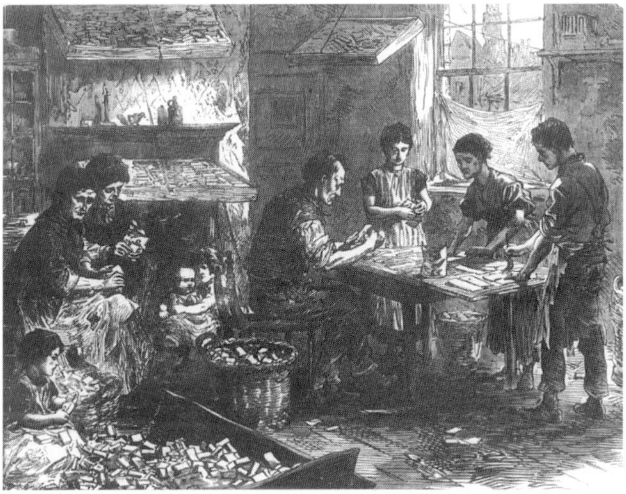

All pictures in this article are from the National Museum of Labour History

The original article was based on Reg Beer's pamphlet *The Matchgirls' Strike 1888*, published by the National Museum of Labour History when it was based in Limehouse Town Hall.

In May 1994 the Museum moved to its new gallery, the Pump House People's History Museum in Manchester. The displays celebrate the lives of ordinary people at work, home and leisure through displays and reconstructions. The Museum tells the story of Hannah Mitchell who campaigned for votes for women; Tressell's 'ragged trousered philanthropists'; sweated labour in a London kitchen in 1889 and the 1984 miner's strike, to name but a few. Also on display are some of the Museum's collection of trade-union banners.

The Labour History Archive and Study Centre is located at 103 Princess Street, Manchester M1 6DD, and it contains the Labour Party and Communist Party Archive among its collections. The Banner Conservation Studio and the Museum's photographic collection are also located at Princess Street. The Museum publishes a twice yearly newsletter. For a copy please send £3 to Newsletter Subscriptions at Pump House People's History Museum, Left bank, Bridge Sreet, Manchester M3 3ER. For further information tel: 0161 839 6061 or 0161 228 7212.

terms of ideological effect. All these are directed mostly against those with little power, and are circulated through communication systems dominated by the bourgeoisie and the state. In contrast, there are at least two other different contexts of use broadly speaking: the amateur snapshot and reformist/oppositional photography. Attempts to control the first by the control of processing mostly succeed in containing it within family settings, recording events, formalised relationships. But there is always the potential, and sometimes the actuality, of critical usage—for example, the Worker Photographers' movement in the 1930s. This shades into reformist/oppositional work, which often has to take on the conventions of dominant contexts of use. For example, 'social documentary' photography often draws on the conventions of record (as 'disclosure'), of the illustration (as 'exposure') and of art ('beauty amid squalor'). Lewis Hine's work for the US National Child Labour Committee is a classic instance. Reformist photography is obliged to operate these conventions, otherwise it cannot be read by those whose exercise of power it is seeking to redirect. The photographs of the matchbox workers are part of this tendency, the most famous contemporary example of which was Jacob Riis's disclosure/exposure of housing conditions in Lower Manhattan, *How the Other Half Lives*.

None of the photographs reproduced on the preceding pages are candid snaps of unaware subjects; all are compositions aimed at producing specific responses. The two single figures (figures 9.2 and 9.3) are unusually expressive, printed in relatively high contrast rather than the diffuse lighting or the spotlighting favoured in the period. They are closeups of the specific effects of matchbox making on a single woman and her child, using the conventions of stage melodrama, the 'police gazette' shock picture. The 'Matchgirls at Home' (figure 9.4) is organised like a Pre-Raphaelite painting of the 'deserving poor': two women silhouetted against the glowing window, 'noble' postures and Sunday-best clothes contrasting sharply with the slavish work. Their poverty is emphasised in the disarray on the right, where the child is an element of the chaos of their thinly stocked kitchen cupboard and table. 'Cardboard box making' (figure 9.5) shows child exploitation, but may well have sought a positive response: the woman is signified as a 'broodhen', the maternal centre of a 'family factory', with a certain warmth of observation which recognises her personal dignity as well as her struggle which is so clearly marked in the disfigured children.

How are we to account for these differences? We have only fragments of information about the specific situations which inform each picture. But each one relates to the concern of the middle-class London reformers to do something about the 'lot' of the East End poor. As images of destitution, the first two photographs depend on a sense of the poor as 'other', nearly sub-human, living in impossible conditions yet breeding like savages, without hope or religion, ignorant of the duties of family life, subject to prostitution—the 'vicious, criminal classes'. The stacked matchboxes serve less as a pointer to the cause of the woman's collapse than as the background to a personal tragedy: the death of her child, whose bruised, cold feet poke out of the rude blanket below the table. Viewers would have been alert to such readings; they are typical of Victorian narrative—on the stage, in song, in stories, illustrated newspapers and in paintings such as Luke Filde's *Applicants for Admission to a Charity Ward*, 1874.

The other two photographers (figures 9.4 and 9.5), with their intimations of the dignity of the women, reflect the reformist efforts of middle-class charity, paralleling crusades such as Mayhew's *London Labour and the London Poor* 1851-62 and institutions such as the Lord Mayor's Fund and the Salvation Army.

> Imagine a time-reversal: that a riot such as Lewisham occurred over a century ago, and the only reporters there were from the *Illustrated London News.* We would still be having academic arguments over it—was it a large or small demonstration, were the police violent or not, were most of the demonstrators black or white? But with a textual argument about why, and a textual and photographic account of what happened, you've got a very good case. Nowadays, you would not study Lewisham or Grunwick, nor present your study, without using photographs. But historians of the later nineteenth century, the turn of this century, don't do this—and there are some superb photographs available.
> Terry McCarthy, Curator, National Museum of Labour History, interview, 1979.

The fourth photograph in fact may well have been taken by or for the latter, which set up a factory in the mid-1880s, mechanising matchbox making and paying a higher rate than Bryant & May's. Its hopes of improving the situation may well be expressed in aspects of this photograph. In practice, however, the reverse occurred—its initiative undercut prices, causing employers to lower rates of pay still further.

None of the photographs refers to the other side of middle-class charity: the fear that these lower classes might be forced into rising up in protest, as they did in the riots of 1886. Nor do they visually declare the parallel fear of the rise of unionism, of organised action on a class basis. The drawings and text in *Cassell's Saturday Journal* (figure 9.5) and similar illustrated weeklies do react to this fear, not overtly, but in their strenuous efforts to depict the girls as healthy and dutiful, model lower middle-class workers for bosses so benevolent that any thoughts of strike action would be foreign and unnatural.

It is not surprising that employers' views were presented in the established print and illustrated media, whereas the reformers turned to photography in their campaigns to alleviate the plight of the matchgirls. But these relationships are not necessarily fixed: a large number of low-priced illustrated newspapers were sold, like the *Illustrated Times*, with more direct drawings; Annie Besant organised publicity for the matchgirls in a variety of ways, from questions in parliament to her $^{1}/_{2}$d paper *Link*; Margaret Harkness's descriptions of life and work in the East End are as detailed, typical and as compelling as any of the photographs.[4] More important than the views of outside observers, however, were the actions of the matchgirls themselves, the effects they sought in the strikes of 1885 and 1888, and in their march on the House of Commons in 1871.

In response to this march the *Illustrated London News* published a sketch and story on matchbox making (figure 9.6). This is an interesting case of reality intruding to such an extent that a contradiction is created. The drawing of the extended family confined in a single room, haggard parents and scrambling children all bound to the job, is a graphic indictment of this kind of life and work. By implication, it explains why a tax on matches would be inhuman: there being no question of the manufacturer absorbing the tax by taking a profit cut, its immediate effect would be on these barely subsisting workers, reducing still further their meagre earnings and throwing many of them into unemployment and starvation. By further implication, it points to why the matchgirls took such an unprecedented step as marching on parliament. The text supports the withdrawal of the proposed tax, but ignores the brutality with which the police treated the marchers and blocks the extension of criticism to the employers responsible for the workers' conditions by attempting to defend these conditions:

> Our illustration, from a sketch taken by our Artist, in the dwelling of a humble family at Bow, represents children busied at this useful task, which they are commonly able to begin at less than five years of age....The only thing painful in their toil is that the sandpaper is apt to make the soft skin of their little fingers sore.

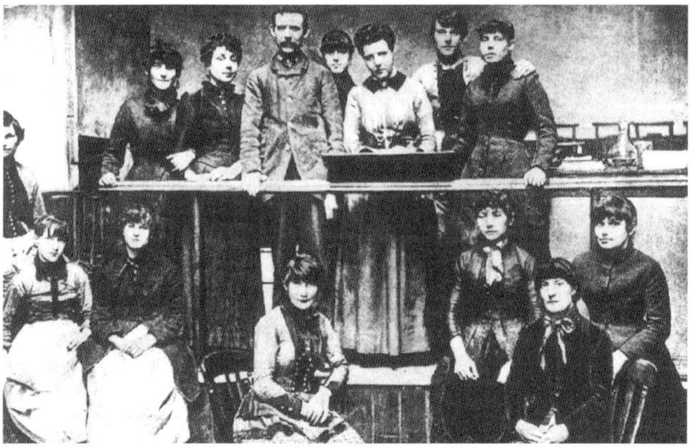

9.7 Strike Committee of the Matchmakers' Union, July 1889, Annie Besant (President) and Herbert Burrows (Treasurer)

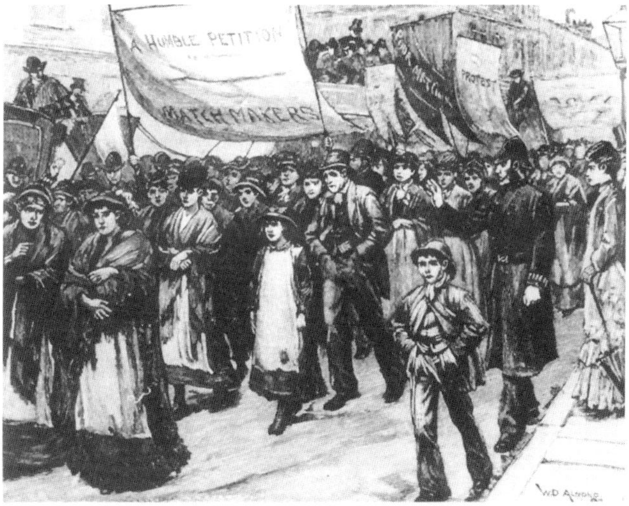


9.8 Matchgirls' demonstration, July 1888

That is, it is doing the same ideological work for the bourgeoisie in the aftermath of the 1871 protest as did the other journals in the period leading up to the 1888 strike.

The 1888 strike is the most famous in which the matchgirls were involved, but it was one of many, part of a growing consciousness on their part. It was triggered, as I have said, by Bryant & May's instant reaction to Annie Besant's investigations: to forbid all talk to outsiders and to sack those who did talk. Their subsequent walk-out was the first by any group of British workers on an issue of solidarity. It pointed to the different style of dispute developed by the 'new' unions—mass, industry-wide combinations of relatively unskilled workers—prefiguring the celebrated 1889 dockers' strike. Importantly, it was a strike initiated, coordinated and negotiated by women workers, as the photograph of the strike committee shows (figure 9.7). This, and other photographs and pictures of girls assembling and demonstrating (figure 9.8), as well as documents such as the strike fund records, indicate a large group of mostly young, illiterate, single women who had created between themselves a network of mutual support strong enough to bring them off work, to coordinate a large strike, to win it and to go on to form one of the first unions of unskilled women workers.

> (At John Baker's, Three Colts Lane, Bethnal Green) The air, especially near where the boys work, feels loaded with phosphorus. It is a very objectionable place. Mary Ann Prancer seems about 14. Does not know how old she is. Lives in master's house and works partly as servant and partly in here box making. Does that that for a living and a shilling a week to clothe herself. Works here and in the house till about 10 o'clock. Never was at school in her life. Does not know a letter. Never went to a church or a chapel. Never heard of 'England' or 'London' or 'the sea' or 'ships'. Never heard of God. Does not know what He does. Does not know whether it is better for her to be good or bad. Note: this girl, though with no outward sign of stupidity, but on the contrary nice looking, seemed, as would be gathered from her answers, sunk in a state of mindless, hopeless ignorance, and to have no ideas whatever beyond her round of work, her 1s. a week and her food and clothing. She has a mother and a home, but some reason which I could not make out, does not even have the chance of going there. It is hard to imagine how anyone, born in possession of reason, can have been kept so utterly out of reach of learning anything beyond what her animal senses might teach.
> Evidence gathered for Children's Employment Commission, First Report 1863.

Other immediate effects included the forcing of an enquiry into sweated labour in London (1889) and the establishment of similar unions (for example, the London Gasworkers' Union by Eleanor Marx-Aveling and Will Thorne in 1889). But 'phossy jaw' continued to ravage factory match girls, and little was done about the core structural exploitation of the industry: homework. This was reduced only by the mechanisation of matchbox production, driving home matchbox makers either into starvation or the plethora of other sweated labour which abounded then in East London—and still does.

## Reference Notes

1 'What a Compulsory 8 Hour Working Day Means to the Workers', 1886, *Reprints in Labour History*, no.2, Pluto Press, London, 1972, pp.25-6.

2 *The Matchgirls' Strike 1888: the Struggle against Sweated Labour in London's East End*, National Museum of Labour History, pamphlet no.2, 1979. Similarly, the inspiration for this article was an interview given by Terry McCarthy, Curator of the Museum, to the editors of *Camerawork* in June 1979. Fatima Rahman, Photo-Librarian of the Museum, has provided valuable assistance.

3 See, for example, Walter Benjamin, 'A Small History of Photography', in his *One-Way Street*, New Left Books, London, 1979; John Berger, *New Society*, March 1979.

4 H.J. Dyos and Michael Wolff, *The City: Images and Realities*, London, 1973, ch.24 in vol.2; John Law (pseudonym of Margaret Harkness), *Out of Work*, 1888, and *In Darkest London*, 1889; and William J. Fishman, *The Streets of East London*, Duckworth, London, 1979.

## Further Reading


• Australian Council of Trade Unions and Community Arts Board, *Art and Working Life*, Australia Council, Sydney, 1983.

• Richard Johnson, Gregor McLennan, Bill Scharz and David Sutton, eds, *Making Histories: Studies in History Writing and Politics*, Hutchinson, Centre for Contemporary Cultural Studies, London, 1982.

• Raphael Samuel, ed., *People's History and Socialist Theory*, Routledge & Kegan Paul, History Workshop Series, London, 1981.

• John Scott, *A Matter of Record: Documentary Sources in Social Research*, Polity Press, Oxford, 1990.

• Allan Sekula, 'Photography Between Capital and Labour', in B. Muchloch and R.D. Wilkie, eds, *Mining Photographs and Other Pictures 1948-1968*, Nova Scotia College of Art and Design, Nova Scotia, BC,1983.

• Terry Smith, *Making the Modern: The Visual Imagery of Modernity, USA 1910-40*, University of Chicago Press, Chicago, 1993.

• Jo Spence and Terry Dennett, *Photography/Politics: One*, Photography Workshop, London, 1979.

• Anne Stephen and S. Reeves, *Badges of Labour, Banners of Pride*, Allen & Unwin, Sydney, 1984.

• John Tagg, *The Burden of Representation*, Macmillan, Basingstoke, 1988.

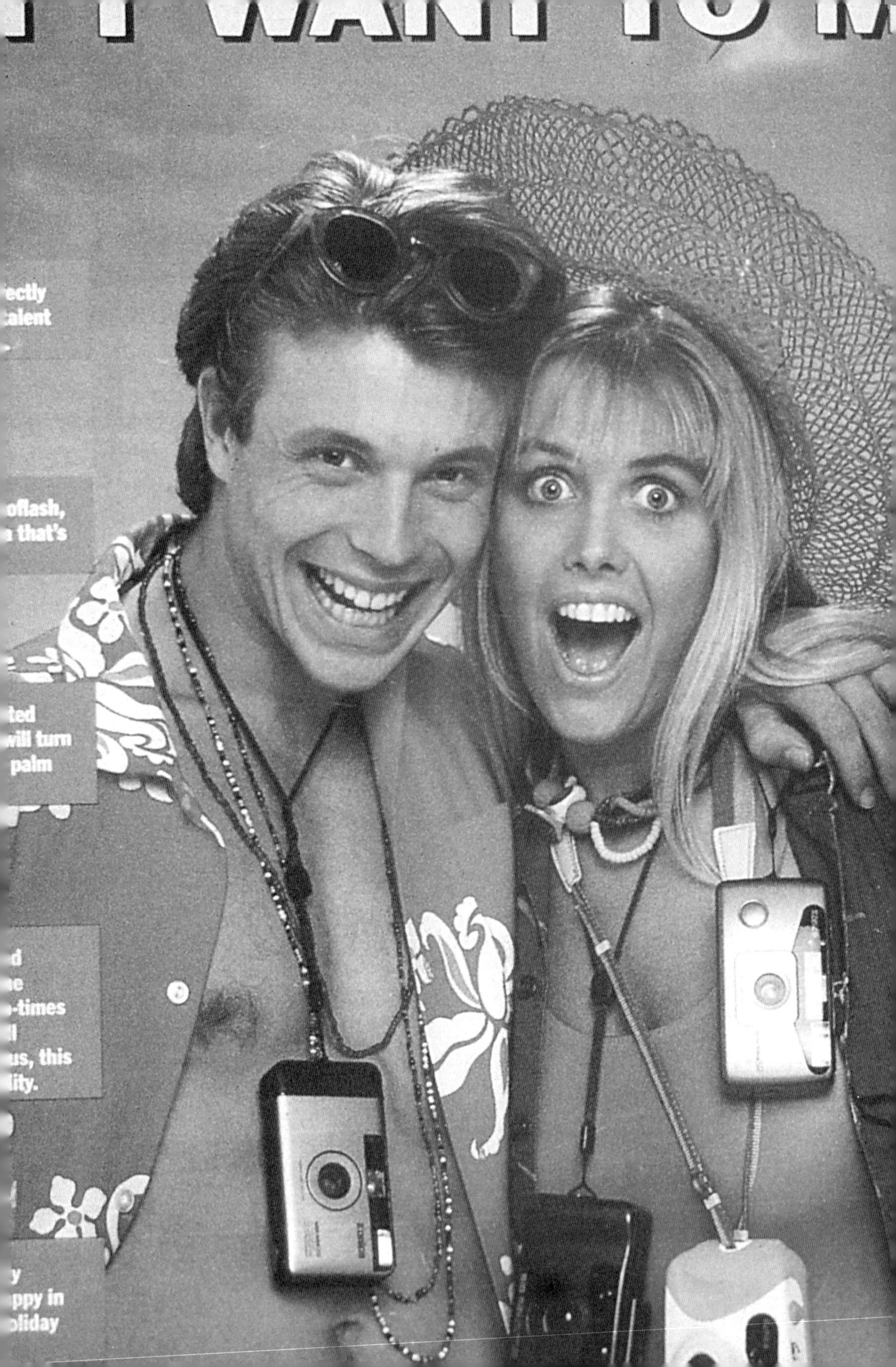

T I WANT TO M

ectly
alent

oflash,
that's

ted
will turn
palm

d
e
-times
l
us, this
lity.

y
ppy in
oliday

# 3

# Institutions and Ideologies in/of Photography

10

# Marketing the Medium: An Anti-Marketing Report

Don Slater

Introduction by
**Don Slater**

Although most of the photographs taken in the real world are snapshots, domestic photography has received little attention. The *popularity* of photography—both its spread and its specialness in people's lives—threatens establishment photography's dominant obsession: to legitimate itself. The idea that some photographers can tell a special truth by producing 'art' or 'documentary' seems to depend on repressing the idea that anyone can take a picture and that most people do. If everybody can do it, it can't be high culture. *Camerawork* was part of a wave of social thought about representation which was more concerned with understanding the power and constraints which structure images in the social world than with achieving aesthetic respectability. The important questions concerned how photographs and practices could constrain or empower people; all aspects of photography in everyday life were therefore matters of urgency.

Mass photography—both amateur and domestic snapshots, though in different ways—was a political rather than aesthetic issue: it was regarded as a reactionary field—all smiling children and happy families, holidays and other private moments. Its content reproduced the banal privacy and patriarchy of the family—'reproduced' in both senses, depicting them and materially sustaining them. It has to be remembered that this period was the peak of Althusserian theories of ideology, semiotics, early post-structuralism: subjectivity was held to be entirely constituted within representation. The systematic banality of domestic photography was therefore politically serious stuff. Moreover, it sinned not only in content but in form: snapshots—we assumed—involved an irremediably 'realist' notion of representation, a conventional and uncritical assumption that the photograph is a transparent window on the world—and this was the greatest sin of all, the most profound barrier to a liberating politics of representation. Until realism was dethroned as the everyday modality through which images were encountered by people—until people stopped believing what they saw and started attending to the way reality was constructed in and through representation—no proper politics was possible at all.

We perceived mass photography as a vast wasteland because it represented the repression of an extraordinary political potential. This intense frustration lay behind the 'Marketing the Medium' article. In a sense, we overvalued representation—images, the media, systems of signification, had total social power. The paradox that so pained my article arose from the almost universal availability of the power to represent—the power to take pictures given us by the likes of Kodak—whose counterpart (indeed whose very condition of possibility, the article argues) was the restriction of the pictures we actually take to banality and to the reproduction of repressive family structures and politics of representation (realism). The very means by which the power to represent was democratised also rendered it impotent.

In many respects, 'Marketing the Medium' was a practical engagement with these issues. Two bits of market research came our way; rather than sneer at this tainted material, I thought to see what picture emerged from them about the kind of photography the industry's commercial interest might lead them to favour. The most interesting thing turned out to be the amount of money bound up with film sales and processing compared to cameras and accessories, as well as the concentration of this revenue in Kodak's hands: the mass of photographic practice was formed—through camera design and advertising—to increase film throughput. This logic seemed to have a remarkable historical continuity—I could trace it back to Kodak's original technical and marketing revolution in the 1880s. However, this logic involved a paradox very close to *Camerawork's* political concerns: the very way in which photography was made into a mass consumer market also involved its limitation within very narrow confines; it involved—for the snapshot market—making the process of taking pictures completely invisible. Realism triumphs as the camera is treated in everyday life as something to look *through* rather than *at*. No technical knowledge should be necessary, but neither should there be any need to consider *what* to photograph (family, holidays, special events). The power of self-representation had been delivered into everyone's hands thanks to Kodak, but only in uncritical, unconsidered, commonsensical and conventionalised form.

All this now sounds rather 'mass cultural' in style: we simply dismissed mass photography as a great wasteland on political rather than aesthetic grounds. Certainly, we were more attuned to analysing the ideological constraints of everyday photography than to thinking through people's everyday engagement with and commitment to photographs. For example, I think it took a while for people to listen properly to Jo Spence's phenomenal *Beyond the*

*Family Album* work: we clearly heard her speaking about ideology, structures of gender difference, exclusions as to what does or doesn't go into the family album. We didn't hear how well she talked about desire and pleasure, about how actively we construct ourselves for the camera not because we are ideological dupes but because we are very active and very needy subjectivities.

As semiotics moved into poststructuralism and then postmodernism, on the other hand, pleasure and desire were virtually all that people talked about. Moreover, whereas earlier work focused heavily on the ideological structuring and constriction of texts, including photographs, work in the 1980s increasingly assumed that all texts *could* be read subversively, against their grain, in liberating directions. More problematically (and with little evidence) it was often assumed that people inevitably *did* read subversively. This trajectory has definitely peaked and seems to be coming back down to earth in the form of ethnographies of media consumption (for example, Morley, Radway, Gray, Silverstone).[1] This work tends to sociology rather than semiotic or cultural studies: the focus is on concrete social structure and relations which organise and constrain people's access to and use of media. After the years of textual anarchy the interest is again in power and social determinants and, if not on the limitations of popular media, then at least on the unequal relations between producers and consumers that are involved. Nonetheless if the 'mass cultural' aspects of the article look old-fashioned now, it is heartening that its sociological concern doesn't.

The details of the article have stood up fairly well, except for one stunningly bad prediction I took over from one of the reports: the death of the 35mm compact camera, which in fact not only revived but wiped out the alternative formats in the snapshooting market. On the other hand, one of its manifestations—the disposable camera (which is all I use now)—represents a return, full-circle, to the origins of Kodak snapshooting as described in the article: the camera is merely an adjunct to the film—you buy it preloaded, send it back to base for processing. Knowledge of photographic process, and therefore consciousness of the medium, is again reduced to zero, and constitutes no impediment to film throughput. At the other end of the photographic spectrum—the ever-increasing amount of electronics built into the camera over the 1980s—lies the major development in our relationship to means of representation in everyday life: whether we are dealing with still cameras, videos, computer graphics or games, the media knowledge we need in everyday life tends not to be about the specific medium at hand, but rather a knowledge about 'programming', about how to choose from preset options built into machines and presented to us via the menus. Complexity and automation now go together (rather than being opposed principles as in the article): in between 'point and press' on the one hand and knowledge of things like depth of field and focus, there is the menu-structured choice between five different preset points of focus. The newest Nikon can now behave either like an old Kodak or an old Leica, not on the basis of its user's knowledge of photography but their ability to input commands.

---

## Marketing the Medium: An Anti-Marketing Report

See Don Slater's 'The Object of Photography' in this volume.

As a worldwide mass practice, amateur photography is a field of enormous economic and ideological significance which needs to be closely analysed by socialist photography. Otherwise any attempts to build an alternative practice will be blind to the prevailing ideas, attitudes and practices against which it has to struggle.

The photographic manufacturing industry sets out to provide as many people as possible with as much film and camera hardware as possible. The immediate purpose is of course to maximise profits— maximum accessibility is sought only when it would not clash with this overall aim. As with any industry, manufacturers balance the benefits of low profit mass sales with those of high profit, more exclusive products. At the same time they seek to aggrandise their share of the market, and also to expand the size of the market. The effect this has on society's access to photography is largely determined by the industry's strategies of marketing on national and international levels. Not only do marketing strategies play a principal determining role in achieving that access—they also largely determine how the medium is used once in the hands of the users.

The pen is the model for media use in the consumer society; it is the cheapest media technology available; every household has or could have one; some sort of literacy is part of compulsory education; 'its' possibilities of expression are limitless (to stretch a point). Yet far from producing a torrent of public discourse, this truly mass medium is mainly reduced to the filling out of official forms, shopping lists and the occasional correspondence: for most of the population it can only be used in passive and privatised ways, while its public use is thoroughly monopolised by a small world of media professionals.

What is true of the pen is equally true of the camera: in contrast to television, film or the record industry, the monopolisation of photography by professional broadcasters has not been based on restricting access to the media technology—it has taken place alongside the high pressured mass marketing of photographic equipment. Almost two-thirds of UK households possess at least one camera (93 per cent in the USA), and each year over 80 million films are sold to 27 million people. Yet this enormous productive power—which should be capable of overwhelming any tiny coterie of media apparatchiks—is effectively contained as a conventionalised, passive, privatised and harmless leisure activity. This is accomplished, for both pen and camera, without visible constraints or enforceable laws.

While the power of public photography—advertisements, news photos, record sleeves, etc.—preoccupies both radical theory and media hacks, the impotence of mass photography (on which that power partly depends) is almost entirely ignored. There has been no attempt at adequate explanation, at a thorough analysis which encompasses the entire complex of relations of economic forces, ideology and power within which is constructed—mass produced—this specific form of photographic practice and practitioner.

This process of construction, and constraint, is composed of many interrelated elements, or more graphically, it is a web of forces—historical and structural—which must be analytically unravelled. The prevalent analytic response, which posits specific discourses within which specific photographic subjects are constructed, is no longer sufficient, though obviously essential, and looks increasingly tautological and purely descriptive. For example, the privatised nature of mass photography (that is to say, practice largely circumscribed by the family, at home or on holiday, by private remembrance and personal vanity) must not only be understood in terms of the construction of subjects for whom activity can only exist within the nexus of leisure-home-hobby or work-money-value; the possibility of transcending privatisation depends also on the objective possibility of 'going public' for which the means do not exist for most people. The means of distribution of photographs have been constructed in a manner appropriate to a monopolised medium: public display space is under the control of advertisers and artified galleries; publishing and the retailing of published material is becoming ever more rationalised and inaccessible. A winning photo in *Amateur Photographer* is now equivalent to getting a letter on to *Any Answers*: the private citizen gets his/her public moment.

My present concern is with one moment of the nexus in which

amateur photography is constructed: the manufacturing and marketing structure of the photographic industry and the structure of photographic consumption, of media use, at which it is aimed. As Marx wrote in the 1859 Introduction to the *Grundrisse*:

> it is not only the object that production creates for consumption. It also gives consumption its precise nature, its character, its finish. Hunger is hunger, but the hunger that is satisfied by cooked meat eaten with knife and fork is a different hunger from that which devours raw meat with hand, nail and tooth. Not only the object of consumption but also the manner of consumption is therefore produced by production, not only objectively but also subjectively. So production creates the consumer.[2]

I am not advocating a form of economism here, any more than Marx was: his statement, that production creates the consumer, is merely one moment of a dialectical argument and therefore isolated from the mediations which complete its meaning.

Similarly, my premise—that the structure of photographic marketing gives us the structure of consumption and media use—does not imply that Kodak's marketing imperatives or the Instamatic itself created the snapshooter of today. However both are imbued with and inseparable from concepts of media use behind which Kodak has put its economic might for almost a century. The story of how the industry's own imperatives have been articulated with other social features—the development of the nuclear family, the structure of work and the postwar ideology of leisure, etc.—is the longer story from which the present one is abstracted. Again, *pace* Marx, production might not create the consumer concretely, without overwhelming mediation, but there is definitely an abstract consumer at which it is aimed, and it is this abstract relationship, of the 'manner' of production to the 'manner' of consumption, whose mechanisms must be explored.

### The Market

Very generously indeed, the capitalist press has come to our aid in this endeavour. Last autumn two major reports on the marketing of photographic equipment in Britain were published. The first was the Economist Intelligence Unit's *Special Report No 70: The UK Market for Amateur Photography* (from which all figures are taken unless otherwise indicated).[3] The second report came from Euromarketing, a service of Mintel. Both reports are designed for interested parties: mainly investors and top management in this sphere (EIU's cover price of £50 is not exactly aimed at the mass market). The information they present is organised in a form conducive to finding opportunities for profitable exploitation, and inextricable from this form of rationality; and thus can reveal much about the aims of the capitalists involved: the structure of the market is represented as it relates to the structure they wish to bring about. On the other hand, the actual information must be re-presented and reorganised in order to make it useful to socialist photographers. This article will attempt to do both.

(It should be pointed out that there are problems with the figures: no regular audits are carried out for the photographic industry, so the sources are varied and more biased than most. EIU claims its figures are based on 'consensus of opinion within the trade'. In most cases this means they reflect at least some wishful thinking on the manufacturer's part. The figures I quote are therefore to be taken as indications of magnitude rather than precise measures.)

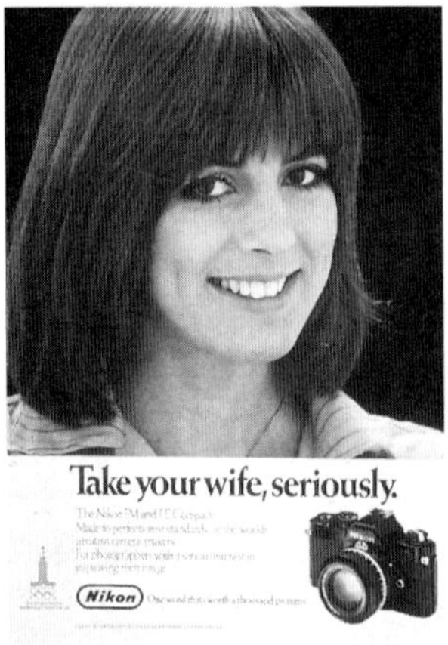


10.1 1980

We can start from a very broad picture of the size and state of the market: two-thirds of British households now have at least one camera; on an individual basis 51.3 per cent of adults own a camera. According to Euromonitor, about 15 million people own a still camera, of whom about 12 million actually use it, a small figure in Western terms. For example, in 1977 average expenditure on photography per household was $37 in the UK, $114 in Germany and $73 in France. Whatever is said about the UK can be simply magnified for other advanced capitalist countries. Photography now accounts for about 0.45 per cent of all consumer expenditure excluding food (a rise of somewhat less than 0.1 per cent over 1972).

EIU's estimate of overall photographic expenditure for 1979 is £400 million. This huge sum represents a 17 per cent increase over the previous year, a growth in real volume of 4–5 per cent. In fact, at the moment photographic expenditure is undergoing a boom, keeping well ahead not only of inflation, but also of the general rise in disposable income which has fuelled Britain's one-year consumer boom (1979). EIU claims that for 1979, 2,515,000 still cameras were sold in the UK. This is a return to the levels of the early 1970s, from which sales slipped in 1974-5.

| Expenditure on: | Percentage of total |
|---|---|
| Equipment £115,000,000 | 29% |
| Film £93,000,000 | 23% |
| Developing & processing £192,000,000 | 48% |

Starting from our overall expenditure figure of £400 million, the most basic and interesting analytical breakdown we can make is as shown in the adjacent table.

These proportions have remained constant throughout the decade: their point is that it would be exceedingly naive to retain the commonsense view that the photographic industry simply exists to sell cameras, and that all the rest of the structure follows straightforwardly from this aim, supporting and supplying it in a subordinate manner. When, at a conservative estimate, 71 per cent of expenditure goes to film and processing, the centre of power cannot be where we expected it. In fact, to push the point further, 'equipment' includes not only accessories—lenses, tripods, etc.—but also cine equipment: still camera sales alone total £84,750,000, only 21 per cent of the total.

In the first place, the 'film' segment of our breakdown is tending to monopoly. In 1978, 90 per cent of all films sold were colour films, the vast majority of which were Kodak, with Agfa a very poor second. It is obvious that monopolistic film manufacturers—as well as the many competing film processing firms—stand to gain from any camera sold. Moreover, Kodak is notable in that on top of selling most of the film, it also participates in much of the revenue from processing through its sale of colour paper and above all chemicals to the trade. The key phrase, then, for film manufacturer and processor alike is 'throughput': the higher the rate film passes through cameras, the more profit all around.

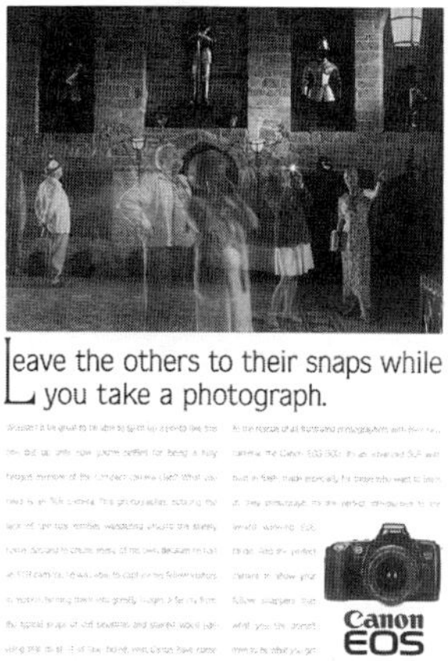


10.2 From *Popular Photography* magazine, December 1994

But there is also a qualitative aspect which characterises the kind of throughput Kodak et al. want. It has become axiomatic in photography (as well as in HiFi and most electronics) that, as EIU put it, 'The more specialised photography becomes, the fewer the number involved.' In terms of sale of film, and therefore of processing, this means that it is the great number of snapshooters who buy only a few films per year which accounts for the vast majority of the trade:

**Heavy film users** (6+ films p.a.)
constitute 11 per cent of film buyers, buying 27 per cent of all films sold.
**Medium users** (3-5 films)
are 39 per cent of film buyers, buying 49 per cent of film.
**Light users** (1-2 films)
are 50 per cent of buyers and buy 24 per cent of all film.

Moreover it is at the margin that the greatest expansion is possible: convincing the light users to buy one or two more films each per year means doubling their consumption and adding 20 per cent to film revenue.

As market leader, Kodak in any case has little to gain from its competitors and need only engage in the occasional defensive operation, as for example with its vastly unprofitable incursion into Polaroid's instant film market. It is the enormous film profits to be made at the margin, through snapshooters, which defines its imperative: to expand the photography market as a whole by selling the idea of photography to non-photographers, thus creating large numbers of new film users. Kodak shows an extraordinary historical continuity in this regard: Eastman began in 1880 as a dry plate manufacturer and processor. His development of roll film after 1885 was his technical innovation: his cameras were a *marketing* revolution. Instead of providing film backs for existing cameras, he began in 1888 to produce the cheapest, simplest cameras imaginable to act as vehicles through which he could sell as much film to as many people as possible. He had sold 100,000 of these by 1896. Originally one bought the camera with the film already loaded; when the 100 frame film was finished, the whole camera was sent back to Kodak for processing and replacement. This end of the operation gave both the continuity and bulk of Eastman's revenues. He rated his cameras as good for 20 film cartridges each.

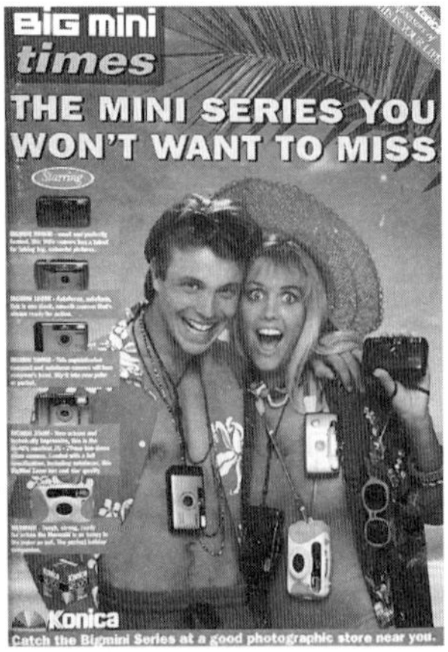


10.3 From *Popular Photography* magazine, December 1994

The development of photographic marketing therefore was and is tied to the expansion of the mass snapshooter market through the sale of cheap vehicles for film. The story of how Kodak constructed mini film monopolies through marketing 126s, 110s and other now forgotten film gauges, is an old one. Monopoly was certainly a powerful motive. However another motive was equally decisive for this development of the media as we know it. The mass marketing of cameras, on which film sales depend, means the selling of photography without the costly creation of 'photographers', which would involve teaching skills, would demand serious interest and would lose that vast part of the population which will not enter the market if the entry fee involves spending time learning and money and frustration in making mistakes. Yet this is precisely the market Kodak and its ilk aim at. Thus Kodak's marketing, from 1888 on, depended on building two features into its technology: simplicity and reliability—'you push the button and we do the rest'. Kodak's solution to this problem—now forming the basis of the whole industry—was as far as possible to divorce the camera operator from the process of photography. By making the process opaque, one makes the practice transparent, if not invisible: it requires no thought to operate, therefore it can be taken for granted, and conventionally—thoughtlessly—inserted into everyday social usages.

The modern instamatic or 110 is merely a refinement of the original Kodak idea: fixed focus and fixed speed, a choice between two (or a few more) apertures marked by pictures of sun and clouds, built-in flash becoming standard. These cameras also incorporate Kodak's greatest twentieth-century innovation, the solution to people's problem with getting film into cameras: the cartridge. Add to this the latitude of modern films and Mr Eastman's dream has come true: utter simplicity and very near total reliability (i.e. the largest number of technically successful pictures). In fact Eastman claimed in the 1890s that the success rate for amateurs with his cameras was 80 per cent.

The camera, which allows practice without process or knowledge, is both liberating and constricting: it put the technology into millions of hands, but in its most restricted form. Reducing process to 'point and press' means designing the technology to operate optimally under certain standard conditions, such as three people out of doors smiling at the lens from over five feet away. Some degree of versatility is possible on an instamatic, but it requires consciously transcending the design bias. But this requires some understanding of process, which is kept hidden, and consciousness of the conventions, which are taken for granted.

Should anyone feel I am overrating the role, power or success of Kodak: first one can add to Kodak's predominance in manufacturing film and processing material, the fact that (according to Euromonitor) 62.2 per cent of *all* the cameras owned in the UK are Kodak. Add to this figure the Polaroid, Agfa and Boots cameras owned (all of which firms are involved in film, processing *and* cameras) we get to 76.5 per cent of all cameras owned. As a comparison, Pentax, Nikon, Olympus and Canon together account for 7.7 per cent of cameras. Second, Kodak, uniquely, is in an overarching position which unites camera equipment, film and processing interests. Its role, as their advertising man (quoted in EIU) puts it, is to 'find its growth by stimulating the market [i.e. photography as a whole] to expand'. (In 1979 Kodak's advertising accounted for 36 per cent of *all* advertising by photographic manufacturers; Kodak, Polaroid and Agfa together made up 59.4 per cent.) Third, on another level, Kodak is simply the exemplar, but also the originator, of a marketing approach which involves the whole industry: it has set the terms in which the others operate.

### Picking up the Crumbs

If Kodak goes for—and gets—photography as a mass (along with Polaroid, Agfa and numerous smaller names, usually tied, like Boots, to a retail outlet), myriad smaller operations are left fighting over the smaller, more specialist crumbs it leaves behind. In the film category, for example, only 6 per cent of films now sold are black and white (following a rapid and steady decline from the mid-1960s when two-thirds of films sold were black and white: presumably the trend will continue given the enormous marketing of colour processing equipment to hobbyists, who are black and white's last domain). Ilford has a 70 per cent share of the black and white film market (Kodak only 20 per cent) and 70 per cent of black and white paper. The point is that to get the required growth in revenue from 'non-mass photography', the specialist market must be clearly differentiated: a kind of rationalisation of the market is enforced on manufacturers.

A striking example of this is EIU's prediction of increasingly hard times for the 35mm compact: its specific market is being eroded by the greater versatility of 110s and the increased simplicity of automated SLRs. So one of the great learning and teaching formats may go to the wall, leaving a yawning price gap between cheap 110s and expensive SLRs, forcing everyone to choose between being a snapshooter and a committed amateur. Needless to say, this would render unto SLR and 110 manufacturers captive and cleanly differentiated markets, simultaneously exploiting, rigidifying and stimulating existing schisms in media use. If formats and special product fields are becoming more differentiated, within these categories the competition is simply bewildering: this is particularly true of the SLR market, the opposite pole to Kodak-style mass marketing. The SLR market is numerically relatively small, but in value terms disproportionately lucrative. Below is EIU's table of estimated 1979 camera sales in the UK, first by volume, then by value.

| Format | Volume (000s) | % of total | Value (3m RSP) | % of total |
|---|---|---|---|---|
| 35mm SLR | 160 | 6.4 | 20 | 23.6 |
| 35mm compact | 160 | 6.4 | 9 | 10.6 |
| 110 | 1000 | 39.8 | 25 | 29.5 |
| 126 | 180 | 7.0 | 2 | 2.6 |
| Instant | 1000 | 39.8 | 25 | 29.5 |
| Roll film | 15 | 0.6 | 4 | 4.4 |

Camera Sales 1979 (EIU estimate)

SLR generates a vast revenue, one quarter of the total, on an insignificant and specialised fraction of market volume—only 6 per cent. Euromonitor puts the disparity even higher, at 36 per cent of value; in their forecast for 1980, they predict that 35mm as a whole will account for 11 per cent of volume and 52 per cent of value, 110 will make up 43 per cent of volume and only 23 per cent of value. In addition these figures only include the camera itself, whereas the biggest real growth area in photography at the moment is in SLR accessories—for example, there are 800 different lenses on the market, and an auto-wind sales push.

The mining of such a market deserves comparison with

Kodak's style. As we all know, the main trend of SLR is to incorporate electronics into cameras which do all the thinking for their human button pushers. On the one hand, this follows the Kodak logic: develop the market as a whole by simplifying operation and guaranteeing 'good results'. On the other hand its main function is quite different. Whatever total growth the SLR market sustains, it still retains its essential character of speciality market, restricted to a relatively narrow population of enthusiasts—more wealthy snapshooters over whom the Big Five (Pentax, Nikon, Olympus, Canon and Minolta), the budget-priced alternatives (Praktica and others) and Zenith battle for a share.

The situation is actually even more restricted by the fact that Zenith alone accounts for 75,000 of the 160,000 SLRs sold in 1979, a full 47 per cent of the market. The others have to compete for what is left. The problem for firms is to achieve a high rate of growth in a restricted market. In Euromonitor's words,

> One need only look at the electronic equipment or electrical appliance market and observe how product development has revitalised sagging sales to realise that any new product begins a complete new cycle as far as consumer acquisition is concerned....With a new product, ownership level drops to nil—nobody has one and everybody wants one.

Here is at least the economic reason why new snapshooter technology ends in an ever more invisible medium, while hobbyist technology is inseparable from the fetishism of technology. In order to grow, SLR must create gaps which did not previously exist by creating products which constitute—and are believed to constitute—totally new categories of desirability.

A tremendous example of this is provided by the case of the Canon A1 which was voted camera of the year by the readers of *Practical Photography* two years running. As EIU comments:

> The staggering thing, however, is that this vote was made by readers who had probably had no opportunity to see or handle the camera because of the delays in delivery. Canon's publicity, which is firmly based on highlighting the innovative features of the A1...has thus made a tremendous impression.

### The Consumer

EIU also presents a broad market profile of the consumer. Not surprisingly, much of it can be logically derived directly from the kind of marketing calculations discussed above. But the form of the profile is revealing. The picture EIU presents is that of a 'consumer ladder' which people enter on the ground floor, generally on a small format camera, and which they are then eased up, purchase by purchase, through hobbyist to, ultimately, semi-professional. Thus various rungs—the types of consumer—are distinguished by the kind of equipment owned and the frequency of its use.

At the bottom of the ladder is the camera owner who is not yet a user: over two-thirds of all cameras sold in the UK cost under £25; the average cost of a 110 or 126 is even lower. No training or understanding of photography is necessary to work them, or to sell them: the camera can therefore take its place at the chemists and supermarket alongside disposable razors and transistor radios, as a relatively unconsidered purchase (no agonising required) as well as a common gift given most often to teenagers and women (EIU). At this end of the market there is a multitude of unused cameras lying in drawers, a reserve army of the unemployed which may enter the market at any time. Thus this rung represents the point of entry into photography (especially as it includes vast numbers of adolescents who will learn to take photography for granted) and a tremendous possibility for commercial expansion.

The second rung is occupied by the beloved snapshooter. S/he owns a 110, 126 or instant camera and, though running through one or two films a year, has no idea what happens inside the black box, often has no idea what kind of camera s/he owns, and simply asks the chemist for 'film', without specifying.

When we come to the advanced snapshooter, the camera is not altogether a mystery, and specifications are beginning to be appreciated: that is to say, a trained consumer is beginning to emerge, a consumer able to read the commodity language of cameras. This is still the realm of the 110 or 126, but the real distinction as far as the manufacturer is concerned is the use of flash: purchase of equipment indicates increased commitment and discernment. At this point the consumer is poised on the brink of becoming a hobbyist, which is primarily defined as the upgrading to a 35mm compact.

The hobbyist marks the beginnings of a major break. EIU estimates that there are over 2 million in this group: they carry a 35mm compact (or a better version of 126) or, in the higher income groups where purchase can be more casual, an SLR; they have an electronic flash without doubt; they buy photographic magazines, but not regularly; he (there is a 65:35 chance of the hobbyist being a male) quite likely uses colour slides (as opposed to prints) at least occasionally and might have a slide projector. 'Socio-economically, hobbyists are usually the newly affluent, adventurous in taste, holidaying abroad, with younger children, and most likely living in London and the South'(EIU).

The line between this level and the advanced hobbyist, by EIU's account, is not simple ownership of SLR or extra lens, or switch from prints to slides, but whether s/he uses a darkroom. EIU estimates that there are 600,000 advanced hobbyists in the UK, two-thirds of whom own or use a darkroom in 'a universe of 3-400,000 darkrooms in use'. This fact, to EIU's eyes, is a material index of the consumer's commitment to photography as his/her main hobby. To fill in this picture of commitment, EIU quotes from an *Amateur Photographer* survey of October 1976. *Amateur Photographer's* readership includes a large number of more casual photographers, but one would assume that more responses would be returned by serious amateurs. Of these: 64 per cent processed and printed their own film; 51 per cent owned an enlarger, and a further 29 per cent were considering buying one; 50 per cent had bought their main camera in the last 2 years; 75 per cent owned electronic flash; 56 per cent owned cameras worth more than £100 (this was four years' worth of inflation ago).

In a rather touching passage, the EIU report notes that 'Advanced hobbyists can become a little sidetracked. Some may like the darkroom work more than the actual picture taking, and their darkrooms, with all their equipment, will seem more like mini-laboratories.' A second group of hobbyists become collectors of 'perfect engineering': Leica freaks, or constant switchers of format and make, who take few actual pictures—they are a joy to the retail trade. A third group, the 'joy of ownership' group, are constantly adding to their system 'more for the having than the using': a lot of these presumably fell for motor winders. Finally a fourth group wear their cameras as jewellery and go for satin chrome finish, motor drive and long lenses.

Finally the semi-professional is differentiated from the advanced hobbyist in putting the equipment to different uses and in often opting for larger formats.

The professional photographer is not included in this ladder, but is said by EIU to account for 15 per cent of all photographic expenditure—£60 million. We are not informed as to its place in capitalist calculation and in mass marketing. For example, it is known that much of Kodak's profit comes from specialist professional films, such as X-ray film and copy film, and it would be interesting to know how this relates to its amateur items.

Euromonitor also offers us some information about ownership of cameras by class, or at least the advertiser's version of class. It bears out what one might expect: ownership decreases in direct proportion to class—76.8 per cent of ABs (middle and upper middle class, 15 per cent of the population) own cameras, descending to 58 per cent of DEs (semi-skilled, unskilled, pensioners, unemployed, 31 per cent of the population). Similarly, of all cameras owned by ABs, 19 per cent are SLRs (well over the norm) and 37 per cent are 110 or 126 (well under). Of DE cameras, 9.7 per cent are SLRs, 48 per cent are 110/126. As to ownership by age, EIU and Euromonitor differ somewhat, but both are agreed that ownership is concentrated on adults with children: EIU gives 25-34 as the main camera-owning age. In terms of sex, there is a male bias: in camera and film purchases, men outnumber women 55:45. But there is a presumption that women are concentrated at the bottom of the consumer ladder and in the younger age groups (young mother). Male hobbyists outnumber female by 65:35, and male readers of *Amateur Photographer* outnumber females 67:33. Overall, 60 per cent of men as against 45 per cent of women own cameras.

This differentiation of consumers by products presented in the ladder model is both by-product and basis of marketing calculation. The divisions marked by the consumer/product types—partly created by the photo industry itself—are its very source of profit, and in exploiting them, the industry accentuates them, creating in the process mystified snapshooters, fetishistic amateurs and the graded escalator running between them.

There are some immediate and obvious extensions to be made from my argument, some of which are actually covered in EIU. For example, the elaboration of the logic I have described into advertising, the retail trade, the relations between manufacturers and retailers, and the photographic press. Also, photographic manufacturers are largely multinational—a point EIU predictably obscures by concentrating on the UK market as a sovereign entity—which certainly has a bearing on their power to intervene in the structure of consumption within any one country. These are all beyond the scope of this article. Beyond these is the more difficult work of contextualising the level of analysis I have offered within a broader framework, of elaborating the way in which the forces I have described are mediated within the totality of the photography nexus.

---

**Reference Notes**

**1** See D. Morley, *Television Audiences and Cultural Studies*, Routledge, London, 1992; R. Silverstone and E. Hirsch (eds), *Consuming Technologies: Media and Information in Domestic Spaces*, Routledge, London, 1992; J. Radway, *Reading the Romance: Women, Patriarchy and Popular Literature*, University of North Carolina Press, Chapel Hill, 1984.

**2** Karl Marx, Introduction to the *Grundrisse* (1857-8), in *The Marx-Engels Reader*, ed. Robert C.Tucker, W.W. Norton & Co., New York, 1978.

3 Economic Intelligence Unit, *Special Report No.70: The UK Market for Amateur Photography*, 1979.

**Further Reading**


• Pierre Bourdieu, L. Boltanski, R. Castell, J.C. Chamboredon, *Photography: A Middle-brow Art*, Polity, Cambridge, 1990 (first published in French in 1965 as *Un Art Moyen*).
• Michael Channon, 'The Kodak Shift: Multinationals, Electronics and Mass Culture', *Wedge*, no.2, 1978.
• Martin Lister, ed., *The Photographic Image in Digital Culture*, op.cit..
• Gaby Porter, 'Trade and Industry', *Ten.8*, no.35, 1989/90.
• Don R. Slater, 'Domestic Photography and Digital Culture', in M. Lister, ed., *The Photographic Image in Digital Culture*, op. cit.
• Jo Spence and Patricia Holland, *Family Snaps: The Meanings of Domestic Photography*, Virago Press, London, 1991.
• Jo Spence and Jo Stanley, *Cultural Sniping*, Routledge, London, 1995.

# 11 Towards a Feminist Erotica

Kathy Myers

Introduction by
**Kathy Myers**

**Towards a Babe Erotica: looking back over two decades of feminist erotica**

'Towards a Feminist Erotica' was written in 1980. A time before Madonna and before the supermodel superbabes had made it on to every satellite station and catwalk. This was a time when feminists worried about the political implications of wearing make-up. When short skirts were only OK when accompanied with punk seditionary bovver boots. When erotic was a dirty word. When 'women's studies', let alone 'cultural studies', hadn't made it on to the syllabus of most universities.

The result of so much innocence was extraordinary optimism.

Everything was going to be OK. Women were going to be in control of their own sexuality and, just as importantly, the representation of that sexuality in art and the media. It was just a question of time, a question of making people with outmoded attitudes—like died-in-the-wool dungareed feminists and Neanderthal men—realise that a lipstick really could be a girl's best friend. 'Towards a Feminist Erotica' tried to argue that images in themselves weren't inherently sexist or reactionary. The pain—and possibly the pleasure comes in how they are used, contextualised and circulated and reappropriated. The bricolage of postmodernism might just save the day.

For much of the 1980s the art work of women like Cindy Sherman and the self-work of recording artists like Madonna seemed living proof that 'Towards a Feminist Erotica' might possibly be worth more than the paper it was written on. In the case of the material girl, here was a role model for millions of tumescent pubescent teenagers who took reactionary stereotypes by the short and curlies and gave them a new spin. Madonna intentionally plundered the undressing up cupboard of the porn model, the femme fatale, the little girl lost, etc. images which she seemed to use and which didn't use her. An ideology readily appropriated by the new breed of Cindy Crawford supermodels who not only wanted the right to play with their images in the best postmodern tradition, but also wanted to be paid a stonking amount of money for the privilege.

In hindsight, the problem with 'Towards a Feminist Erotica' is that it made a strategic mistake. It confused winning the battle with winning the war. It assumed that if women managed to get control of, manipulate and play with the way they were represented then everything would come up rosy. And there have been partial successes from Jane Campion films to a tranche of successful young female artists. Women do have some control over the way they are represented, they do have powerful jobs in the media, they do say *No* when they used to say *Yes*, but that's not really the point.

The problem is that what we consider to be culturally erotic (and in a culture that celebrates pornography, that's always a dangerous word to bandy around unqualified) has shifted. It ain't Charlie's Angels any more. More like Charlie's babies. The erotic has a nasty habit of sliding into areas we would most like to avoid. Take the Calvin Klein commercials of summer 1995.[1] The icon of so-called female power they chose was the anorexic, waif-like adolescent, Kate Moss.

It could have been an accident if the latest Klein offering for jeans hadn't gone one stage further, devising a campaign which appeared to celebrate the worst voyeuristic conventions of child porn: intentionally amateurish photos, gangly sub- pubescent models, splayed leg poses.

There are historical precedents for this shift, i.e. when women achieve a modicum of cultural power they cease to be the focus of so-called 'erotic activity'. Instead the patriarchal gaze strays into the babes' bedroom. We now live in a culture where Thailand's economy is firmly bedrocked on the paedophile proclivities of tourists, where British models are often over the hill at 17, where the most optimistic survey says that a quarter of 12-year-old girls think they have a weight problem. Kiddy porn may not be on the top shelf of the newsagent—yet—but it's already there in cyberspace, glutting the Internet and super-information highway.

Children may have many powers, but control over how they are represented, and by whom, is not one of them. However advanced the Montessori education system, it's still a Playdo and Lego world. Control over the odds and ends of pre-pubescent sexual identity in a postmodern world isn't on the under-fives' syllabus.

The current supermodels from Naomi Campbell to Claudia Schiffer are referred to affectionately as superbabes; it would be funny, if it weren't so poignant. You'd think they'd be old enough to know better.

# Towards a Feminist Erotica

**Kathy Myers** is the author of *Understains: The Sense and Seduction of Advertising* (1986). She was editor of *Camerawork* magazine 1983-4 and the TV editor of the London listings magazine *City Limits*. She now works as a Director with Wall-to-Wall, a TV production company; credits include *The Media Show* (C4) and *Washes Whiter* (BBC2)—a six-part series on the history of advertising.

This paper is a response to the ideas which came out of the Camerawork one-day discussion for women on the subject of pornography. This discussion aimed to set the problematic area of pornography within the wider issue of the politics of sexual representation. It was also hoped that discussion would deal with the controversial subject of a 'feminist erotica': this did not take place, a resistance which speaks of a fundamental dilemma in sexual politics. Many feminist critiques of the representation of women hinge on the assumption that it is the act of representation or objectification itself which degrades women, reducing them to the status of objects to be 'visually' or 'literally' consumed.

I want to argue that this assumption can lead feminism into deep water. On the one hand, it works to deny women the right to represent their own sexuality, and on the other it side-steps the whole issue of female sexual pleasure. I want to suggest that questions of representation and of pleasure cannot be separated, and that a feminist erotica could examine the nature of this relationship. This in turn demands examination of the forces which produce dominant ideas of sexuality and pleasure. Rather than seeing power as a force which 'represses' or 'holds down' our sense of pleasure and sexuality, I want to suggest the opposite: that power actually produces forms of pleasure and sexuality. The forms of sexuality and pleasure produced through pornographic representations are not acceptable for a variety of reasons. However, I want to argue that through a relocation, a respecification of the nature of power, new, potentially progressive images may be produced: the perception of power as a positive force provides the groundwork for a feminist erotica.

Finally, this article holds that images themselves cannot be characterised as either pornographic or erotic. The pornographic/erotic distinction can only be applied by looking at how the image is contextualised through its mode of address and the conditions of its production and consumption.

### The Workshop

Feminists working on the politics of female sexuality have all but ignored the issue of female sexual pleasure: caught on the defensive, most have devoted their energies to a counter offensive against the dead weight of patriarchy, fighting images which are deemed sexist or exploitative. One of the most organised and coherent groups in this sexual defence lobby is WAVAW (Women

Against Violence Against Women). As this group was dominant both in force and number at the Camerawork day event, it would be useful to outline their analysis.

WAVAW's objection to pornography, unlike that of groups on the Right, is not premised on moral or health grounds, but is rooted in their understanding of the role which pornography plays in the antagonism between the sexes. Pornography is objectionable because it 'humiliates', 'denigrates' and 'exploits' women.

Exploitation operates on several levels. First, through the process of representation, women are 'objectified'. Women's gender and social status is reduced to the level of a commodity which may be possessed and exchanged by men. Second, pornography restricts female sexuality by reducing it to specific anatomical characteristics: e.g., the repetitive fetishisation of breasts, legs, vagina, etc. Through this fetishisation, sexuality is fragmented, the part is left to stand for the whole. Third, WAVAW suggest that the proliferation of pornography has actually led to an increase in sex crimes against women. These three processes of objectification, fetishisation and violation are central to the WAVAW critique of pornography.

What is missing from the WAVAW analysis is an understanding of how and why these processes occur: all their analyses are simply traced back to a monolithic notion of patriarchy. All imagery, all practices within the 'dominant ideology' are interpreted as further evidence of 'patriarchal oppression'. This defensive tactic continually reduces women to victim status and leaves very little space within which an alternative female sexual practice may be negotiated. The only alternative which is presented as viable is a total withdrawal from heterosexual relations not as a matter of sexual preference but of political necessity.

WAVAW's concept of power is premised on a fundamental contradiction. On the one hand, power as synonymous with patriarchal oppression works to victimise women. Its force is monolithic and cohesive and, from the point of view of women, politically negative. On the other hand, WAVAW's intentional withdrawal from men, and endorsement of separatism, suggests that women can establish new ways of organising their sexuality, relationships and experiences: that women have the power positively to establish a separate identity. Whilst women may positively organise their 'real' experiences, this sense of positive organisation is not extended to the construction of 'positive' representations of women. The domain of representation is perceived as essentially colonised by patriarchy and leaving little room for manoeuvre.

As an alternative, I want to draw on some of the ideas of Michel Foucault as a way of exploring the power-pleasure-representation nexus, and look at how these relations are produced by, as opposed to held down by, power.

Foucault, in his book *The History of Sexuality*, aims to investigate 'The regime of power-knowledge-pleasure that sustains the discourse on human sexuality'.[2] For Foucault, sexuality has become a means of controlling and administering social relations. The idea that control over sexuality provides a way of controlling a society is not new. What makes Foucault's approach novel is his rejection of the idea that control is exercised through systems of repression. On the contrary, Foucault suggests that the history of sexuality has been characterised by an 'explosion' of 'polymorphous discourses on sexuality'.

One of the characteristics of this 'explosion' is the making verbal, the putting into words, of sexuality. Foucault traces this back to the model of the church confessional. The model of the production of truth through the process of confessing can for example be found in modern practices of psychoanalysis. Our society's obsession with sexuality also permeates many 'unspoken' practices. For example, Foucault argues that the architecture of the eighteenth- and nineteenth-century poorhouses, schools, factories, homes, etc., were all 'saturated' with sexual knowledge. This knowledge informed the layout of bedrooms, toilets, school doors, cloakrooms, etc. In addition, discourses on sexuality spread through the institutions of welfare, jurisprudence, psychiatry, medicine, exercising complex and often contradictory influences on the development of personal and sexual relationships within society.

Foucault refrains from combining these constituent elements into a monolithic theory of the relations between power and sexuality. Power, like sexuality, is perceived as multifaceted, emanating from many institutional 'powerbases'. It is this polymorphous quality of power which gives it its strength and flexibility, but which also denies the possibility of any simple causal or deterministic analysis of power relations.

For Foucault, power works to produce a multiplicity of female sexualities which work insidiously to maintain the social order; for example, the production of the ideology of 'romance', of 'hysteria', the 'nervous woman', 'frigid wife' or insatiable 'nymphomaniac'. Certain forms of female sexuality support the family structure, others are outlawed from it, for example, pornography, prostitution and lesbianism. For Foucault, this public/private dichotomy, far from challenging the social order, works to secure and legitimate the parameters of acceptable and unacceptable behaviour.

This analysis also challenges the idea of an 'essential sexual instinct' waiting to be uncovered, or freed from repression. The concept of power as positive and productive both gives us the tools to analyse the patriarchal order (not as a monolithic system of oppression, but as a specific socio-historic articulation of power relations) and also provides the ammunition for change (a reorganisation of power relations). It shifts feminism from the site of oppositional practice (a defence against the bastions of patriarchal power) to that of a positive practice working to deploy power.

But to say that power produces sexuality and pleasure is itself inadequate: we have to understand how this process specifically occurs. The experience of pleasure is both a social and emotional activity. The two are inextricably linked: we need to ask how the powers of the imagination and fantasy can actually produce and sustain dominant notions of sexual practice. One of the biggest problems with WAVAW's empirical analysis of pornography is its inability to explain this connection.



**The Real and the Representational**

One of the central characteristics of WAVAW's argument is the distinction they make between the material world of 'real' relationships and the imaginary world of representation and fantasy. This separation of the imaginary and the material seems too simplistic an account of the way we live our lives, ignoring the crucial position of systems of representation, whether images or language, in our 'real' relationships.

This separation points to a central contradiction in their argument. On the one hand, they see 'real' relationships and representations as totally separate; on the other hand, they point to the ways in which pornographic imagery not only reinforces but actively instigates the sexual abuse of women. They continually invoke imagination and fantasy as agents of sexual oppression with no possible positive role.

For WAVAW, the sin of pornography is its ability to structure and organise fantasy in ways which are thought to be oppressive. Fantasy, the guilty party, becomes the breeding ground for violent actions. But there is a difference between criticising the social discourses which structure the form and content of the imagination and blaming fantasy and imagination themselves. This is a distinction which WAVAW seem unprepared to make. Yet fantasy, and all the associated mechanisms of daydreaming, the imagination, inspiration and creativity are a fundamental part of experience.

Rather than dismissing the power of the imagination and fantasy as politically undesirable, what is required is a greater understanding of their determination and structure under a phallocentric order. Such an analysis may bring women closer to understanding the nature of their oppression. Of course it also presents the ultimate challenge: how to restructure the systems of language, association and meaning which organise our consciousness.

### Pornography and Sex

As I've already suggested, the sexual isn't already given, but is produced through a variety of social practices which extend across the fabric of daily life. Some of these practices are socially condoned (e.g., heterosexual relations within marriage) and others condemned (e.g., hardcore pornography). Even heterosexual relations within the family are not simply legitimated but governed by social mores about the kind of sex act allowed, the age of participants, etc: there is a complex web of regulation, channelling and development which is not fixed or innate but directly related to the social and historical attitudes of the social formation.

Whilst WAVAW interpret pornography as evidence of the continuing conflict between the sexes, the libertarian tradition, equally starting from the premise of an essential sexuality which is socially repressed, has tended to defend pornography on the grounds that its outlaw status directly challenges the status quo.

The 'sexual radicals' such as Reich and Marcuse played a central role in the development of the libertarian tradition. Following Freud's analysis, they proposed that sexuality was subject to social censorship when it threatened to disrupt the social order. This invested sexual practices with a potentially revolutionary power.[3] However, their idea of a rebel sexuality is continually undermined by the notions of sexuality with which they worked: that is that an 'essential' sex could be uncovered if layers of repression and social oppression were stripped away. Obviously this idea of an essential sex is not a particularly fruitful avenue of enquiry for feminists who wish to challenge dominant notions of the essentially feminine which in the end are found to rest on biologistic or universal criteria.

The heritage of the libertarian tradition has continued to inform many popular notions of sexuality, for example the so called 'permissiveness' of the 1960s as well as many aspects of the male gay liberation front. Libertarianism informs Angela Carter's influential book, *The Sadeian Women.*[4] She suggests that the Marquis de Sade's documentation of nightmarish sexual exploits are fundamentally concerned with the nexus of power, sex and class under bourgeois relations. By caricaturing these relations in their most oppressive and violent forms pornographic literature, Carter argues, is capable of offering a critique of 'accepted' social relations, where oppressive power relations are continually disguised and denied by reference to the natural order, romance, desire, etc.

However, while pornography is apparently invested with the power to subvert accepted gender relations, it may have the opposite effect. Because it lies outside the accepted, it implicitly acknowledges and accepts social privileging of the family, reproduction and heterosexual union. It basks in its role as deviant. Caught in this binary model of acceptability/unacceptability, pornography works to restrict the expression of sexuality.

For example, soft core pornography reduces female sexuality to genital sexuality: a woman's sexuality is defined in terms of her orifices. The sexual no longer refers to the potential of the erotic body as a whole, but to fragmented, fetishised aspects of a woman's anatomy. The sexual is reduced to a series of well-worn scenarios which have their ultimate resolution in the promise of penetration (by the imagined reader, or more explicitly by a male actor). The images are dulled by sameness, a constant repetition of the imagined fuck. The pornographic colludes with what the libertarians purport it to disrupt. The sexual is located in the organs of reproduction. Pornography works to celebrate the union of sexuality and alliance, of pleasure and reproduction; sex is genital sex, and nothing more.

Libertarianism also falsely assumes that everything which is socially unacceptable (and hence subject to censorship) is inherently subversive and liberating. This is because they focus only on pornography's claim to be erotic. It is the eroticism in pornography which is thought to be liberating, symbolising the life-giving forces of love, pleasure, desire, etc.

Thus, libertarianism leaves unexplored the implicit power relations with which pornography is invested. Power is exercised through pornography on many levels which speak of an implicit gender fascism: e.g., that the magazines are produced for the consumption of men, the recurrent portrayal of women as victims, the fact that their sexual pleasure is produced for an imagined male audience, etc.

These power relations within pornography challenge the libertarian claim to its liberating potential. It is this continual overdetermination of the sexual by power relations which renders the pornographic image unacceptable.

Libertarianism also positions freedom as the antithesis of power relations. It is power which keeps freedom down. But to accept this is to see power as repressive, as hindering the development of sexual expression. Foucault's analysis of power, in contradistinction to this, sees power as actually producing sexual discourses. It seems to me that if we are to understand the role of pornography in our society and understand the ways in which our conception of female sexuality is produced, we have to see power as a productive as opposed to a simply oppressive force. Our conception of freedom, of sexual pleasure, needs, on the one hand to negotiate the existing power forces, and on the other move towards the construction of new sexual experiences. What is required is a shift in the location of power, not a denial of its existence. It is through this reworking of power relations that a sense of freedom may be established.

This idea of power-producing pornography cannot be confined to an examination of the image. An analysis of pornography which focuses purely on its content is in danger of falling into a kind of 'reductive essentialism', i.e., the notion that exploitation resides in the representation of female sexuality per se, rather than in its contextualisation: the conditions of its production and consumption; the ways in which meanings are created, etc. Unless we can shift the debate on representation away from the image, there is very little 'positive' work which can be done.

Whilst it is true that we designate certain images as pornographic, pornography also refers to a particular mode of productive relations which market and sell sexuality: e.g., the choice of model/subject matter, the photographer–model relationship and the conditions under which they work, the choice of medium and distribution, all affect our reception and interpretation of what constitutes pornography. This economy of pornography works to structure not only to whom the material is made available, but also the kinds of pleasures and responses which are elicited.

The false claim of libertarianism is to suggest that eroticism lies outside the nexus of existing power relations. But this is not the same as saying that the erotic is powerless, and that work cannot be done to explore its full potential. This is the ultimate meaning of a feminist erotica; to reappraise the ways in which versions of female sexuality have been produced, and to use thus as a springboard to develop new dimensions and meanings for female sexuality. We have to understand the ways in which images work to construct our own experience of our sexuality. Rather than running away from the powers of the imagination and fantasy, we have to reappraise the role of representations in structuring our needs and desires as a step towards constructing new meanings for the experience and representation of our sexuality.

I want to illustrate this point with one image taken from a soft core porn magazine and one from a woman's journal. By comparing them, I want to suggest that woman's sexuality is deployed in a variety of ways. This deployment is dependent upon the context in which the image appears, its mode of production as well as consumption.

On first impression, the two images seem remarkably similar: the model's pose and attitude, the seaside setting, etc. The main difference appears to be that the Slix model sports a bikini whilst

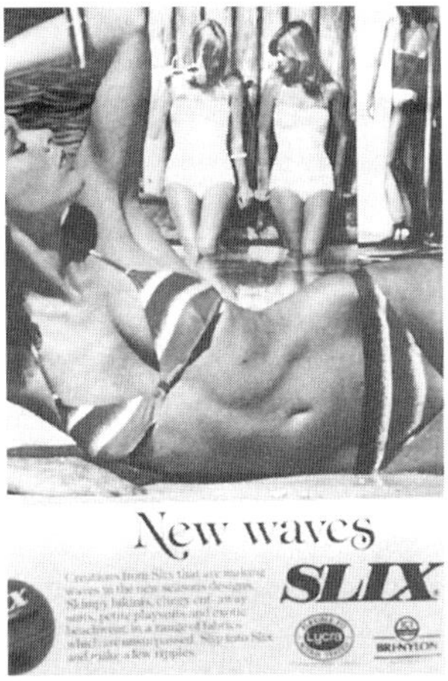


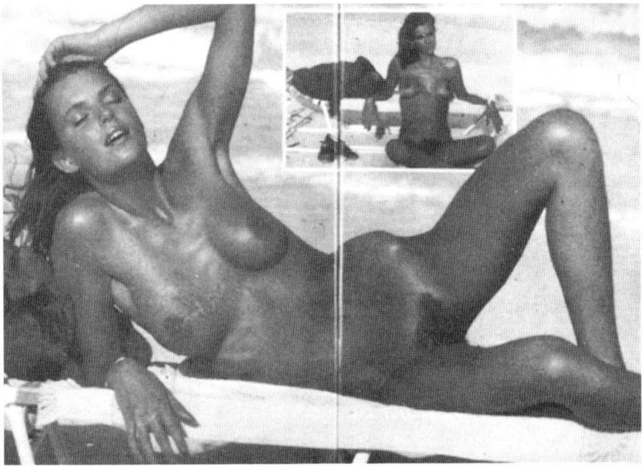

Above: 11.1 Slix advertisement, 1982

Right: 11.2 Dutch pornography, original unidentified, 1982

the porn model is naked. It could be argued that women's exploitation is only a matter of degree along a scantily clad continuum. However, the surface similarities belie fundamental differences in the representation of female sexuality and in the kinds of pleasures offered to audiences.

Many of these differences are hidden from the viewer. For example, the production of pornography differs in most respects from the production of a fashion advert. This affects their economic foundation, the choice of studio, photographer, model, etc. They are specialist discourses which retain their autonomy. For example, the 'photographic life' of models is extremely limited. Few nude models ever make the transition to become fashion models, partly because of the stigma which certain forms of nude modelling carry, and partly due to the fact that different selection criterion operate. Fashion models have become increasingly slender, younger and taller. Most nude models are considered too 'curvy' for fashion work: different 'aesthetics' operate. In turn this visual aesthetic cannot be divorced from the respective audiences for fashion and pornographic imagery. To put it simply, there is an overall tendency to market 'fleshier' women to men and thinner, sometimes sexually androgynous, images of women to female audiences. This micropolitics of body style speaks of the aesthetic and pleasurable segregation of sexuality across a range of visual discourses, which cannot be simply explained away in terms of 'taste' nor patriarchal oppression but require further examination.

Selling female sexuality to a woman is not the same as selling it to a man. The anticipated gender of the audience is crucial in structuring the image. For example, look at the angle of the women's heads in the two images. The pornographic model's face is angled towards the viewer. Her mouth is open, a classic signifier of sexual receptiveness and anticipation. In the small inset photo the same model faces and acknowledges the camera. Behind the camera, we, the audience are located.

By comparison the Slix model, sweeping back her hair, looks across the scope of the camera rather than facing us. She does not face us, her mouth is closed. Not so much a sulky pout as an expression of relaxed languor. Like the pornographic image, she is aware of being on display. But the tenor of her demeanour is proud and inaccessible. She sweeps back her hair from the heat of the sun, not from passion.

By comparison, her legs are together. The Slix model's mouth and legs offer no point of entrance. The body of the Slix model is a matt sandy tone, she is relaxed. The skin of the nude model is oiled to give the effect of a sheen of perspiration which can signify sexual activity and tension.

The girls in the background of the Slix image look at each other not at the camera. Self-absorbed, they reiterate the confident, self-engrossed narcissism of the foregrounded model. She takes pleasure in her sunbathing, not in the presence of her audience. Only the small inset model in the beach jacket to the right of the image pays the camera a cursory glance.

What differentiates the pornographic image from the fashion shot is the mode of address. The Slix mode of address is characterised by the tension which it establishes between the model's desirability in conventional terms, and her inaccessibility. The advert works to secure a distancing effect between image and audience.

By comparison, the nude model's sexuality is posed as invitational. The pleasure of looking at her merges with the pleasure of being with her. Her sexuality stretches out to embrace the viewer. The nude model 'asks' the audience to possess her. It is a form of sexual consumption which implicitly genders the audience as male. The model's apparent expression of pleasure is not for herself. She is not autonomous, her pleasure is always for the consumption of another, and herein lies one of the fundamental alienations of pornographic imagery.

By comparison, the Slix advertisement positions the audience as spectator, to keep a safe distance and to observe, not to touch. Sexual inaccessibility is conveyed through the structure of the image. For example, the self-absorbed pose of the model, the cropping, editing, and retouching of the photograph work together to reinforce the displayedness of the model, and in doing so, distance the audience.

The impact of the Slix advert is based on the strength of the photograph. Its scale and use of full colour works to dominate the page. The seaside location, the pattern on the bikini, the sense of displayed style are all anchored in the copy line 'New Waves'. These associations are cemented by reference to the brand name of Slix which is in bold type. Image and copy line work together. 'New Waves' links the image to the body of the text.

Whilst the image celebrates the tension between desirability and inaccessibility, the body of the text suggests sexual provocation. Unlike the provocative pose of the pornographic image, the Slix advert suggests sexual power as opposed to sexual availability and perhaps vulnerability. The wearer of the Slix bikini is promised power over others, the power of sexual display: 'Slip into Slix and make a few ripples'.

The target audience for this advert is women. The advert is designed to appeal to women. One of the pleasures which the advertising system offers women is the promise of a kind of power and self-determination. Images of women marketed to women rarely present female sexuality purely in terms of vulnerability, accessibility or availability. But the power which the advertising of beauty and personal products offers women is always of a limited kind, located in terms of sexual display, appearance and attractiveness. What the advert may offer for consumption is an ideal version of self. It also plays on women's pleasure in looking at attractive women. This kind of visual pleasure is inscribed in the image.

We may find many images of women unacceptable, glamourised, exploitative or whatever; but we cannot simply interpret women's pleasure in reading them as evidence for the extent to which the female consciousness has been colonised by patriarchy. We have to account for women's pleasure in looking at images of women.

The advertising image and the pornographic image offer different kinds of pleasure to their respective audiences. If audiences did not find them in some way pleasurable they wouldn't work; magazines and products wouldn't sell. It is their pleasurable associations which perpetuate them. But pleasure as a concept cannot be tackled in isolation, we need to understand how pleasure is produced through the structuring of power and sexuality.

### Towards a Feminist Erotica

One of the central objections put forward by feminists in their critique of pornography and other modes of representation is that it 'objectifies' women. Objectification has become a much abused term. There is a sense in which the process of sight and perception necessarily entail objectification in order to conceptualise and give meaning to the object of our gaze. Within feminism, objectification has quite a specific meaning: through the process of representation, women are reduced to the status of objects. This is partly derived from a commonsense use of the Marxist idea of commodity fetishism: images of women have become commodities from which women are alienated. Their status as commodity works to deny their individuality and humanity. The second sense of objectification which has informed its current usage is derived from Freud's concept of sexual fetishism: the idea that objects or parts of the anatomy are used as symbols for and replacements of the socially valued phallus. Hence, the argument goes, men have difficulty in coping with women's sexuality: because of its castrating potential, and because of its lack of a phallus. In order to cope with this anxiety, men fetishise aspects of female sexuality—for example, the legs or breasts—as symbols of acceptable sexual power.

The use of the term 'objectification' is coupled with a tendency to interpret all forms of sexual symbolisation as evidence of sexual fetishisation. In the analysis of female imagery two processes of symbolisation are brought under closer scrutiny: that of sexual fragmentation and sexual substitution. Frequently these processes of metonym (where the part stands for the whole) and metaphor (where one object or aspect of the anatomy stands for another) operate together. For example, the depiction of female sexuality through the representation of a stiletto-shod foot isolates and fragments the sexual by focusing on a part of the anatomy and fetishises the foot by over-valuing it as a phallic symbol. Psychoanalytic interpretations of this kind of imagery have suggested that the stiletto as phallic symbol serves to give the woman her missing phallus, thus circumnavigating the castration threat which she poses for male sexuality and rendering her safe.

Whilst this kind of analysis may provide an adequate interpretation of the dominant associations of stilettos in our culture, can we say that all forms of sexualised imagery can be interpreted in terms of phallic substitution? There exists a repertoire of conventionalised symbols which have become imbued with fetishistic associations of which the stiletto is only one example; but symbolisation is not a closed system of limited or fixed meaning. Symbolism is polysemic (has no one, fixed meaning), there always exists the possibility of powerful symbolism which works to activate forms of sexual expression which are not recognised by phallocentric interpretation.

Because fetishisation usually employs a fragmented image there is a danger of assuming that all fragmentary images are necessarily fetishistic. The process of sexual fetishisation (specific phallic associations) is always complicated by that of commodity fetishisation, whereby the image of a woman's legs for example becomes isolated and estranged. They become a commodity, an object of display to be visually consumed by an audience.

What is at issue is not so much the perceptual processes of objectification and fragmentation which are a necessary part of rendering a complex world meaningful but rather the specific forms of objectification entailed in commodity and sexual fetishism. It therefore seems important to create a working distinction between the process of fragmentation, which implies a breaking up or disabling of the physical form, and what could be termed 'a pleasure in the part'—the pleasure derived from looking at a picture which depicts the curve of an arm or the sweep of the neckline. Such images could be interpreted not as a butchering of the female form but as a celebration of its constituent elements, giving a sense of the scope and complexity of sensual pleasure which breaks with specific genital sexual associations and with the necessity of overdetermining phallic substitution in the representation of the female form.

It seems that we have to clarify whether it is the process of necessary objectification entailed in perception which we object to (used for example whenever we look at the world, at art, at a book, etc.) or the meanings which it carries for women under specific patriarchal formations. These are two separate issues which tend to be collapsed into each other when feminists talk about the representation of women in art, photography, etc. To refuse to differentiate between the two modes of objectification is to endorse a kind of perceptual essentialism—that objectification is inherently exploitative and demeaning.

To see objectification in essentialist terms is to deny the possibility of any alternative practice within the representation of women. Feminists would be denied the possibility of visual communication and new forms of perception.

What is crucial is that existing theories of male power based on phallocentrism cannot provide a basis for the development of a progressive female sexual politics. One of the oppressions of patriarchy is to constrain female sexuality through a system of binary oppositions: e.g., masculine as opposed to feminine, passive versus active, emotional and sexual, sexual receptiveness as opposed to sexual drive, etc. This binary system works to perpetuate unacceptable ideologies about the nature of sexual relations. This means that feminist sexual practice cannot simply position itself in opposition to the dominant ideology. The kind of questions which it must ask have implications not only for what is meant by a representational system (and the part which it plays in structuring fantasy and the imagination) but also what is meant by power, sexuality and pleasure.

It is in terms of the pleasure derived from representational systems that we need to reintroduce a notion of the erotic. Within sexual politics we have to find a way of accounting for women's sexual attraction to each other; the visual pleasure of leafing through a glossy women's magazine; the appeal of the heroine star systems, etc. Such pleasure cannot be simply dismissed as more evidence of patriarchal oppression, that women are continually gulled into a search for the ideal type simply to appeal to 'their man'. We cannot dismiss sexual attraction as further evidence of patriarchal mystification.

What we need to do is explore the ways in which female sexuality is marketed and represented. As I've tried to show with the help of two images, this representation is far from homogeneous. Nor can we assume a fixed meaning for an image with which we are familiar. Meaning is produced through the process of representation, the context in which an image appears, its mode of production and consumption.

I haven't attempted to problematise definitions of the pornographic and erotic which are historically and socially defined. At any one moment there will exist competing definitions: for example, those which exist within the feminist movement, as opposed to the liberal Williams lobby or the Whitehouse brigade. Rather than looking for any simple causal analysis we need to further our understanding of how the exercising of power produces forms of sexuality which work to structure the process of pleasure, fantasy and the imagination. Ultimately the distinction between pornography and other modes of sexual representation cannot rest on the characteristics of the image. The differences between pornographic vaginal imagery and medical vaginal imagery are learned through contextualisation: they are not innate.

In the reappraisal of our sexuality, there may appear to be an overlap between the kind of images designated as pornographic as opposed to erotic. This means that the exploration of female sexual pleasure through imagery will remain politically controversial.

**Some suggestions for the kind of questions which need to be asked when producing or appraising potentially progressive images of women**

How is the image produced?

Whose fantasy is being recorded?

What power relationship exists in the photographer–model relationship?

How are models selected? What is their relationship to the overall production process?

| | |
|---|---|
| How will the image be distributed and where will it be circulated? | The politics of distribution cannot be separated from those of production, nor of consumption. Where an image is distributed will affect who will see it, in what context, etc. It is obviously important to sort out whether an image is for private or public consumption, whether it will be seen in a gallery or a magazine, etc. It needs to be asked whether an image's validity or 'usefulness' depends on how an audience will use or interpret an image. For example, does the risk of appropriation by men invalidate producing erotic imagery for women? This risk could be counted by showing these images in, for example, *Camerawork*. |
| Visual conventions of the image | How do we classify an image as erotic? What conventions and genres of representation does an image trade on?<br>To what extent does an oppositional system need to re-use and question familiar styles in order to go forward and create new meaning?<br>What are the signifiers of sexuality?<br>How do we recognise the gender of the subject?<br>In fact how important is the thwarting of easy gender assignment important for erotic pleasure? |
| The audience and pleasure | What kind of pleasures does an image offer its audience?<br>How is the sexuality and subject position of the audience constructed—are they sexed as male or female?<br>What kind of emotional responses does the image demand?<br>Does it demand any kind of audience interaction to interpret the meaning of the image? To what extent does the image challenge assumptions already held? |



**Reference Notes**

**1** See the *Guardian*, 29 August 1995.
**2** Michel Foucault, *The History of Sexuality, Volume 1: An Introduction*, Penguin, Harmondsworth, 1978.
**3** See W. Reich, *The Sexual Revolution*, Vision Press, London, 1957; H. Marcuse, *One-Dimensional Man*, Sphere, London, 1968 and *Eros and Civilisation: A Philosophical Inquiry into Freud*, Sphere, London, 1969.
**4** Angela Carter, *The Sadeian Women*, Virago, London, 1979.

**Further Reading**


- Jean Baudrillard, *America*, Verso, London, 1988.
- Beverley Brown, 'A Feminist Interest in Pornography', *m/f*, no.4 & 5, 1981.
- Jane Caputi, *The Age of Sex Crime*, The Women's Press, London, 1987.
- Rosalind Coward, 'Sexual Violence and Sexuality', *Feminist Review*, no.11, Summer 1982.
- Rosalind Coward, *Female Desire*, Paladin, London, 1984.

• Rosalind Coward, 'Liberty, Perversity and Freedom for All', *Guardian*, 16 October 1995, p.13.
• Michel Foucault, *The History of Sexuality*, Pelican, London, 1978.
• Sarah Holdsworth and Joan Crosslet, *Innocence and Experience: Images of Children in British Art from 1600 to the Present Day*, Manchester City Art Galleries, Manchester, 1992.
• Lynne Segal and Mary McIntosh, *Sex Exposed: Sexuality and the Pornography Debate*, Virago, London, 1992.
• Simon Watney, *Policing Desire: Pornography, AIDS and the Media*, Comedia, London, 1987.
• Jeffrey Weeks, *Sex, Politics and Society*, Longman, Harlow, 1981.
• Jeffrey Weeks, *Sexuality*, Ellis Horwood, London, 1986.
• Carole S. Vance, ed., *Pleasure and Danger: Exploring Female Sexuality*, Routledge & Kegan Paul, London, 1984.

# 12 Fashion: Double-Page Spread

## Rosetta Brooks

Introduction by
**Rosetta Brooks**

There was a moment at the end of the 1970s and the beginning of the 1980s when some of us believed that the arenas of fine art and popular culture were beginning to merge, to develop an interaction that lay beyond the formalism of modernism, and the crass fundamentalism of consumer capitalism: the belief that the best in fine art might co-opt the best in popular art and vice versa. It was an exhilarating moment.

Artists in both America and in Britain began to adopt images from consumer culture in an attempt to move art into the field of culture rather than operating only within the restricted lineage of art history. Simultaneously, media images were aspiring to new levels of aesthetic consumerism.

The tendency was particularly visible in fashion photography, the bodily centre of advertising. It was here that the relationship between product-image and product (i.e. form and content) changed dramatically in the mid-1970s. I still experience a sense of shock when I encounter the photographs of Guy Bourdin or Helmut Newton from that time because their images proved that advertising need not be an invitation to a cosy other-world of the imagination: it can be a challenge. If the promises of advertising are clearly fake, their photos seemed to suggest, then why not emphasise the falsity of the image and challenge the threshold of our imaginary world? Clothes to be raped in, shoes to be found dead in, a scarf to be strangled by: the promises of these photographs are of violence, bestiality and death.

For these fashion photographers the product was less important than the product image. Newton in fact seemed almost indifferent to the fashions he was shooting. It was the image he was after. Meeting the client's needs (the magazine) was clearly secondary. Of greater significance to him was the degree of control the photographer could wield to dictate the terms and context within which fashions are created and consumed. He brought to the viewer's attention the fetishism, the power relations and the sexual violence which are implicit in all fashion photography

In art too, artists like Jack Goldstein, Robert Longo, Cindy Sherman and Barbara Kruger shared a common attitude of familiarity towards popular culture and its products. Their mix of love and hate for the ever-present images of capitalist consumerism resulted in art that could hold its ground on both fronts and correspondingly impact upon and influence activity in both worlds.

Sadly though, the excitement and exhilaration experienced back then has given way to gloom and disillusionment. A passing glance in the fashion magazines or a brief visit to any art gallery reveals a re-entrenchment, a movement back into the conservative worlds of fashion photography in the service of titillating illusion where the body is again the centre for male appropriation, and the elitist formulae of formalism in the art galleries.

One can only speculate why this happened. Perhaps the worldwide recession in the 1990s resulted in consumer culture reticence to take risks or revel in adventurous new arenas. With rare exceptions like Benetton, most companies have resorted to an attitude of better the devil you know than the devil you don't and results have been more Albert Watson look-alike fashion photographs and a corresponding dearth of images that challenge old ways of image-making for popular consumption.

Correspondingly in the art world, the 1990s have reacted against the commodity status of art that reared its ugly head in the Reagan era. The art business in the 1980s was like a runaway truck without an off-ramp: new artists, new galleries, new collectors, new critics and new money all conspired to create an atmosphere of breakneck speed, excitement and fast-lane fun. Time was of the essence in the endgame called art. Throughout the decade, art seemed something like a coprophagean—an animal feeding off its own excrement. The avant-garde transgressions of one month quickly became the historical trash of the next, and the art world took a fastidious and greedy pleasure in discovering artists seemingly at random, consolidating a market around them, and creating new Old Masters in lightening succession.

The downside to all of this, though, was that art became a specialist area with a specialised audience. In order to 'get it' you had to be an insider. More and more, art appeared to be talking to itself. In the process, a good deal of contemporary art lost its audience and lost its hard-won connection to the world. The last nail in the coffin appears to be artists such as Jeff Koons who has successfully manipulated his way into magazines, television and movies, pirating pornography and calling it art.

Future prospects are looking bleak. Albert Watson's photographs that highlight sex in the service of straightforward, male-centred erotic imagery? Or Jeff Koons's prototypes for keeping ahead of the game, his cons-called-art rendered only in the service of publicity? Some choice.

# Fashion: Double-Page Spread

**Rosetta Brooks** is a writer living in the desert of Southern California (Pioneertown). She writes a bi-weekly art column for *LA Village View* and is the Graduate Advisor at the Art Center College of Design in Pasadena. She also writes for *Artforum* and *Frieze* magazines and is LA correspondent for *World Art Magazine*, and contributing editor for *Art Issues* magazine.

## Fashion Photography as Anonymous History

Fashion photography is traditionally regarded as the lightweight end of photographic practice. Its close relationship to the economic imperatives of turnover makes the fashion photograph the transitory image par excellence. For historians and critics concerned with isolating unique photographic images and according them enduring significance, the commercial sphere of photography—the domain of the everyday image—represents the debasement of the convention of such 'great' photographs. For most people, however, the commercial image represents the essence of their experience of photography.

Cultural analysis of the commercial photograph has habitually treated it as a departure from the naturalist and realist historic tradition, in which the 'unique' image is identified by excluding those characteristics most closely identified with the commercial world. Economic forces are seen as altering and negating the 'reality' of the photographic image. Market forces introduce the caption which can determine and distort what is seen in the picture. 'Silence' is converted into the 'speech' of the advertising caption or newspaper headline. Whenever photographic conventions hit the streets, they are encountered as 'diluted'. Commercial images, so the argument goes, are produced under constraint, compromised or distorted by their proximity to the technological division of labour and responsibility.

This view of the culture industry sees the destruction of the individuality of the images and the uniqueness of their production. We see the typical instead of the unique moment or event. We see stereotype and cliché where we want to seek the creative representation of human expression and emotion. The texture of mechanical reproduction seems alien and deadening; the image in currency is reduced to the commonplace of urban experience.

Given this prevalent critical and historical attitude, photographers are inclined to regard the economic and technological processes as a 'threat' to their domain—the taking of the photograph. This, the 'decisive moment', is seen as the most powerful point in the process, the point at which the 'real' world reproduces itself; it is more creative than the mass production processes which deplete and assimilate the image, stamping it with the uniformity and monotony of a commodity. Photographers produce images and see them as fuel for the sequence of formulae and stereotypes within the turnover of trends and fashions, and within the machinery of production.

Critical and historical tradition have thus made us see the creativity of the photographer and mass production as opposed to each other. This has prevented investigation of those features of photography produced by the combination of these processes. Although photography has its origins in the reproduction of nature by machine, fashion and advertising photography must be studied as a process of mechanical reproduction of the mechanical image.

The 'other' side of photography is the ability to reproduce a number of copies from a single moment. The picture is one of many on the streets, in magazines, television and film. Media technology is structured for the repetition and proliferation of images as commodities appearing and disappearing in and out of mass circulation. Images are seen in relation to one another, as stereotypes going in and out of currency, rather than as unique peepholes into reality. Not only does the camera enable us to look at the world, it also establishes the conditions for the world to look on us. Image is not simply something seen; it is also something we 'wear'. The mass circulation of photographic images emphasises our awareness of self-image, and establishes a relationship between the particular and the typical.

Historians of photography have yet to do justice to this 'other' side of photography, possibly because it is too familiar. Perhaps what is needed is what Siegfried Gideon calls 'anonymous history': an account of the effects of technology on personal experience.

But how does one look at photographic history and do justice to the processes which make the imagery typical and transitory, without selecting certain great images in their uniqueness? The answer might be found by looking at the sphere of photography most tied to the machinery of the media: advertising photography. Changes in the nature of recent advertising and fashion photography also necessitate such an analysis, as well as a re-appraisal of the caricatures of commercial photography.

The availability of photographs in the galleries of many major cities has enabled photographers to develop further areas of sponsorship in the 1970s, and has created a market for the Masters and for an established historical tradition, and yet the recent malaise of the realist/naturalist tradition has been accompanied by a greater inflexibility of its norms in the establishment of academic and economic sponsorship which has grown up around these genres.

Incessant reiteration of the 'zero-point' of the photographic document has transformed it into a rhetoric of its own. The contemporary politically-committed social document produced for gallery exhibition tends to speak more of rhetorical nostalgia for its 1930s' precursors, and for the innocence of style, than of its subject. This deathly quality of nostalgia, the event's pastness rather than its currency in our political perceptions pervades so many self-conscious servants of tradition.

However whilst the realist/naturalist genres are at a standstill, or are even regressing, there have been dramatic changes in the photography encountered in the streets—and particularly in the intimacy of the double-page spread.



### Helmut Newton: Manipulating Stereotypes

Many see the new representation of women in advertisements and especially in fashion photographs as a sort of masculine counter-offensive against the new feminist consciousness of sexual stereotyping. That some of the significant individual contributions to this recent change happen to be from women in no way contradicts the claim that we are seeing the development of the most perniciously sexist imagery yet encountered in the very core of sexual stereotyping, fashion photography.

Fashion photography in the 1970s has in one sense produced nothing particularly new, no recognisable ideal like Jean Shrimpton or Twiggy in the 1960s. No particular look or appearance seems to dominate. Models seem to be straight off an assembly line, representing a well-established physical norm. Most conspicuous is the repression of the model's distinctive individuality. She is treated in her identity with her type, not as a particular kind of woman, but as a model.

Stereotyping appears to occur through suppression of the awareness of stereotype and by identification with the unique. The dynamics of fashion are embodied in the dualism of the world itself: fashion is what is general and typical, and yet it is also restricted and individual. The fashion photograph is on a threshold between two worlds: the consumer public, and a mythic elite created in the utopia of the photograph as well as in the reality of a social group maintained by the fashion industry. Recent fashion photography seems to convert the utopias into dystopias.

The Helmut Newton model is one of a type, presented with the cold distance of a fleshy automaton, an extension of the technology which manipulates her and converts her into an object. Her veneer, which is at one with the gloss of the image, is to be flicked past and consumed in a moment. When the models strike up stereotyped poses, it is their deadness and frozenness which is foregrounded. The suggestion that they are frozen from a narrative continuum emphasises their strangeness and their discontinuous, fragmented nature, like film stills isolated from the cinematic flow.

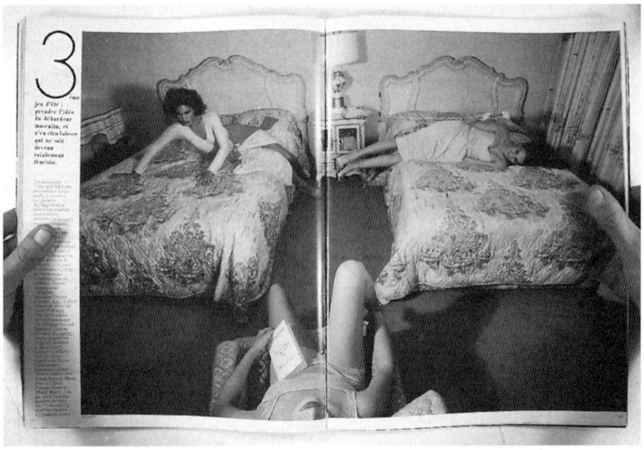

12.1 Guy Bourdin, *Vogue* (France), May 1978
To turn the page is not only to open and close the spectacle of the fashion spread but to cut up the figure with which we are spatially identified—to open and close her legs.

Some have interpreted the strange, unusual settings in the work of Guy Bourdin and Helmut Newton—accidents and suicides—as the intrusion of a 'real world' into fashion photography. I think quite the reverse is the case: it is because scenes of rape and death are commonplace in film and television that they can be treated with such distance in fashion photography. The aura of a particular kind of image, not the aura of the streets, is utilised. The artificiality of the image, its gloss and not its reality, is emphasised. It is the deathly aura of mediation which encases everything in gloss. Newton's harsh colours, particularly his use of red and blue, make an association with poor quality reproduction and thus invoke the limitations of the medium.

This emphasis upon the alien and artificial qualities of the picture makes a straightforward accusation of sexism problematic. All fashion photography, as the dominant currency of female images, could be seen as inherently sexist, manipulating exchanges between self and self-image. Yet this is conventionally suppressed in the image of the moment, as it binds us to a model of femininity beyond existing norms, converting them into stereotypes. To recognise an image as a constraint, as a violation or repression of femininity, is to glimpse the demise of a stereotype going out of circulation, its descent hastened by its mass circulation. Each ascendant, newer image promises to escape those constraints. Accordingly, fashion photography seeks to suppress any sense of the strangeness of sexual typification, the conversion of femininity into a static type or commodity. The sense of stereotype must be reserved for hindsight in the succession of female images.

Newton manipulates existing stereotypes; their alienness is accentuated, and yet they are almost eternal archetypes in their sexual dramas. The passive reclining woman offers no threat: she

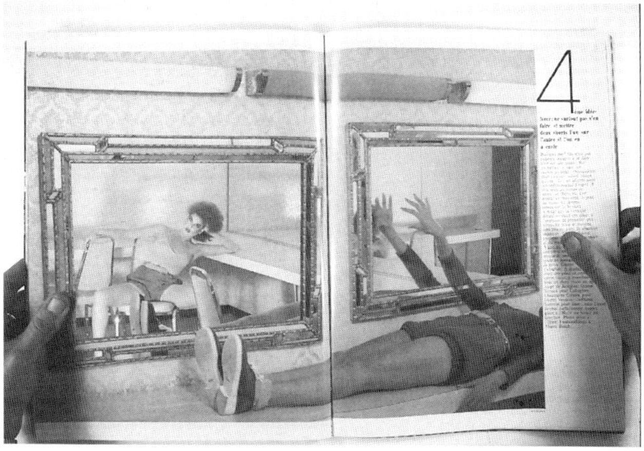

12.2 Guy Bourdin, *Vogue* (France), May 1978
The alternation of deep and shallow spaces to juxtapose façade and depth...we are re-directed from (the product) to the spatial ambiguities of its setting.

is completely malleable, a dummy made of flesh. The object of gratuitous sexual violence and violation, she offers no resistance, but because of this she becomes unreal, like de Sade's libertines. As the threat of personality diminishes, her image-like quality transports her beyond eroticism of the living to fetishism of the inanimate object. She fits into dominant stereotypes so completely that she ceases to connote a reality apart from the images which constitute her life. By mixing dummies with live models in the French *Vogue* of June 1977, Newton makes an unambiguous erotic response (from either sex) impossible. (figure 12.4) Instead, the picture sequence directs voyeuristic attention to the conversion point between object and flesh, and to their deathly reciprocity in the photographic act. While the photographs are undeniably erotic, the eroticism is attached to the process of mediation itself. Many of his more successful photographs hold a distanced engagement with the manipulative devices of fashion photography and with the process of mediation. Those alien features present in suppressed form in fashion photography and current images of women are exposed and foregrounded. The image is presented as alien: a threat rather than an invitation. Stereotypes are presented as falsity.

**Guy Bourdin: 'A Trap for the Gaze'**

In the postwar period the growth of mass production and reproduction was greeted in some circles as a threat to individuality and to the uniqueness of human activity. The horrific spectre of the totality of industrial culture was the familiar expression of a fear of what seemed inevitable as a result of consumer culture: the false universalisation and homogenisation of human experience. Theodor Adorno saw the stamp of the machine everywhere,

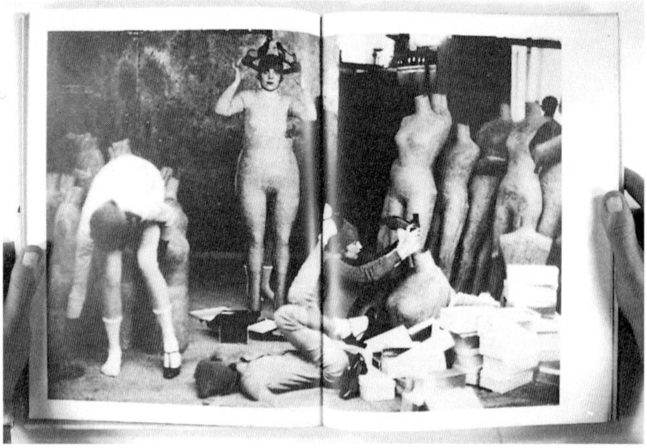

12.3 Deborah Turbeville, from her book *Wallflower*, 1978
Her photographs are presented scratched, violated, and montaged together.

reducing everything to a 'sameness', reflecting and reinforcing a sense of alienation in all aspects of private life and experience. As mass-entertainment and advertising become more dominant, they increasingly level experience down to 'the lowest common denominator'. The threat of the culture industry is the production and reproduction of sameness in all spheres of cultural life. Adorno saw the media as part of a great machine serving to encompass, assimilate and absorb all opposition and all individual variation by acceding to the sameness of machine production.[1]

Current cultural trends could be interpreted as posing quite the opposite threat—the loss of common cultural experience. The decentralisation of fringe cultures and the increase of minority opinions cannot be accounted for in the view which foresees the media industry triumphing in an identity and uniformity of cultural experience. For Marcuse, avant-garde art as oppositional culture is depleted by absorption and assimilation into mainstream 'affirmative culture'.[2] While this may seem prophetic in view of the current state of art, indifference to oppositional art is the result not of a depletion or assimilation of its meanings, but of its isolation. It appears as one cultural ghetto amongst many, with its own diminishing media stake. It is not that the values of a minority culture are distorted and absorbed into the mainstream. They pose no threat at all.

The principle of negation itself, which avant-garde culture once represented, is now built in to all spheres of cultural activity. Even disco music, ostensibly the alignment of human-expression-dance with the rhythm of the machine, has its negation in groups like *Kraftwerk* for whom the machine pulse which 'animates' disco-dance is the object of morbid contemplation. It is not merely a 'progressive' extension of popular culture. What is incorporated is negation. This now guarantees a sort of all-round authenticity. I can enjoy it for itself, or for its parody of itself. Irony mediates these days—it is no escape.

Tolerance of mechanised cultural products has ascended to a higher level: an acceptance of the limitations of the medium in an engagement with the process of mediation. As Adorno and Horkheimer said: 'The triumph of advertising in the culture industry is that consumers feel compelled to buy and use its products though they see through them'.[3]

They could not, however, have predicted the peculiar route to this triumph. From the vantage point of the 1940s and 1950s it was difficult to imagine a fashion photographer complaining about censorship by the machinery which Adorno predicted would subsume cultural producers like Helmut Newton. The latter's complaints about English *Vogue* are echoed by fashion photographers beginning to talk about being 'given free rein' by magazines. When Guy Bourdin claims to be an artist, he is laying claim to a specific type of formal problem encountered with a particular kind of image in circulation. It is not so much that 'the double page is his canvas', but that the double page is not canvas is the basis of the claim.

His material is what canvas stands in antithesis to: the texture of mechanical reproduction. In Bourdin's work, the double-page is not the vehicle for communicating the image, it is a structure characteristic of a particular kind of encounter. He organises his images around the form of mechanical reproduction, around the divide of the double-page and the turn of the page. In the May 1978 French *Vogue* the female voyeur/spectator figure is divided by the centrefold as she watches the almost symmetrical division of her reclining self-images.(See figure 12.1) To turn the page is not only to open and close the spectacle of the fashion spread, but to cut up the figure with which we are spatially identified—to open and close her legs. The model is completely engulfed in the vertical divide as though by a mistake in binding, leaving the two legs isolated on facing pages.

At other times the double-page becomes its own mirror. In a March 1976 French *Vogue* spread, a colour reproduction faces a black-and-white reproduction of almost the identical scene, as though frozen from successive moments. The process of reproduction itself is being reproduced. Within these more dramatic formal devices, spatial relationships are set up within the pictures which rebound upon the strangeness of our ordinary encounter with the double-page, the photograph and with the advertisement itself. We are re-directed from the object (the product) to the spatial ambiguities of its setting, which jar with the expectations built into encounters with photographs and advertisements. Bourdin enhances the spatial strangeness of the conventional spread, to accentuate the alienness of what is unfolded in that horizontal continuum and around the vertical division in the process of unfolding. This spread best exemplifies the division and alternation of shallow and deep spaces, which is used to juxtapose façade and depth, the frontality of the image with the three-dimensionality of setting. Bourdin plays upon a hesitation in the spatial and temporal expectations of the double-page, emphasising the alienness of the setting of both the product and the advertisement. Brechtian distanciation and the formalist 'exposure of the device' have become mainstream rhetorical manoeuvres.

Bourdin's shoe advertisements provide a case in point. Without the manufacturer's name as caption, some would be unrecognisable either as advertisements or as having shoes as their subject. In a passing encounter with the image that the fashion magazine produces, it is profitable to exert the negative principle as a subversion of the neutrality of 'flicking through'. An arrest of vision is required at all costs—even at the expense of accentuating the alienness of clothing itself. Our sense of puzzlement seeks double confirmation which is provided by the product name.

A 'trap for the gaze' [4] may be the solution to the immediate pressures of the market, but the implications of an increasing dependence upon an enlarging and increasingly autonomous advertising industry are less easy to estimate. The new autonomy and independence from the product achieved by the product image seems to promise a fulfilment of the totalitarian ideal of propaganda for its own sake. In 'The Work of Art in the Age of Mechanical Reproduction' Walter Benjamin saw fascism as the political 'consummation of *l'Art pour l'Art*', in an elevation of propaganda to a new level of aesthetic self-justification.[5] The emancipation of the image from its caption, and of the product-image from the product, means that the advertising image has become the pure imperative, not divisible into form and content, the pure veneer, the absolute facade for and of itself.

**Deborah Turbeville: Nostalgia, Wallpaper, etc.**

This new autonomy of the product-image has created another market sector. The collecting of ephemera, the practice of surrounding oneself with old and sometimes not-so-old advertisements, is now almost a middle-class stereotype. A large business has established itself selling not so much old as 'fixed' brand images. Mass production exploits the borderline between consuming and collecting, between the connoisseurial attention to qualities and the sheer neutrality of the product-image in the context of the cash exchange. Obsolete product-images have been revived as nostalgia for the mythical past of the product itself. There is an obsession with the conversion point between the currency and redundancy of the image.

In the same way, recent fashion trends have been exclusively nostalgic. Even current sci-fi and high-tech fashions come over as a nostalgia for older stereotypes of 'futurism', as a taming of images of technology which were once threatening. But recent forms of revivalism are not a specific attachment to a bygone age—they are more like 1960s nostalgias romanticising the peasantry, or other kinds of primitivism. This nostalgic undercurrent has come to dominate and has almost caught up with itself.

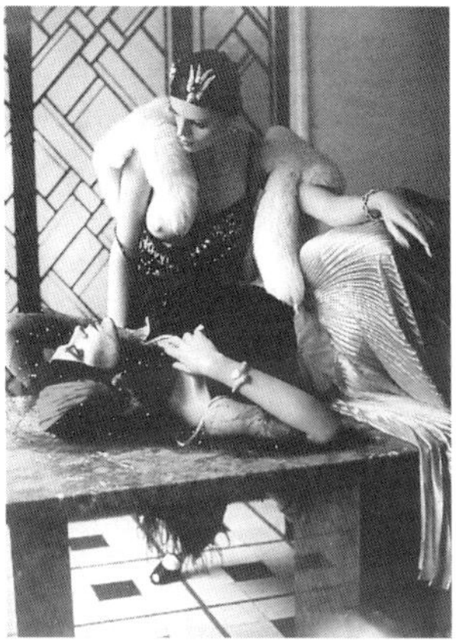

12.4 Helmut Newton, *Vogue* (France), June 1977
The cold distance of a fleshy automaton, an extension of the technology which manipulates the model and converts her into an object.

Nostalgic attachment to the immediate past becomes an attachment to the process of turnover, a narcissistic identification with the alien qualities of one's own past. That point of self-awareness at the juncture of the up-to-the minute and the out-of-date becomes an identification with the very process of mediation that fashion represents.

The photography of Helmut Newton and Guy Bourdin reflects a self-awareness of fashion photography and of its falsities. They convey the sense of an impenetrable veneer, resistant to the very movement of stereotypes. In the work of one of the best woman fashion-photographers, Deborah Turbeville, a different sense of the alienness of the image is represented as a sort of hesitation between self-images. In many ways her photographs are at variance with characteristics of her male counterparts. For example, her models are not chosen for their identity with a fairly neutral type, but usually for their divergence from the type or image which they appear to represent. At best her work involves this hesitation between the image presented by the model and the image presented by the picture, although finally this sense is always communicated by the latter. Conveying this uncomfortable relationship with the model's self-presented image pushes her towards portraiture, or her models towards acting. However, she is clearly not satisfied with communicating the strangeness of the female image through the illustrative neutrality of the photograph. In her book *Wallflower*, her recent photographs are presented scratched, violated and montaged together. (figure 12.3)

In the foreword to this book she describes her photographs as:

> Like the women you see in them. A little out of balance with their surroundings, waiting anxiously for the right person to find them, and thinking perhaps that they are out of their time. They move forward clutching their past about them, as if the ground of the present may fall away.[6]

Perhaps they accede a little too easily to an automatic overlay of nostalgia resulting from the association of limited colour range with the faded photograph or with the technical qualities of early photography. At the moment her work seems unresolved, as she herself says: 'My pictures walk a tight-rope....I am not a fashion photographer, I am not a photojournalist, I am not a portraitist.'

Whatever one's opinion of the 'success' of her pictures, it is interesting that a photographer preoccupied with the kinds of of self-image mass circulation produces should find the fashion spread the most accommodating site for her exploration, however provisional she may feel this to be.

Whether the alienness of the recent fashion image is an extreme expression of the autonomy of fashion photography, whether this implies a distancing from the form of coercion which the fashion spread represents, whether it constitutes the elevation of the advertisement to a higher power and greater autonomy, or whether it is the beginning of a break-up of that structure of representation: these questions have implications far beyond fashion alone.

---

**Acknowledgement**

I would like to acknowledge the writings of John Stezaker, especially his ideas on stereotyping. I refer to 'Archetype and Stereotype', a paper delivered to the Photography Convention organised by the Psychology Department of Southampton University, and to *Fragments* published by the Photographers' Gallery.

**Reference Notes**

**1** Max Horkheimer and Theodor Adorno, 'The Culture Industry: Enlightenment as Mass Deception', in *The Dialectic of Enlightenment*, trans. John Cumming, Verso, London 1979 (first published 1944).
**2** H. Marcuse, *One-Dimensional Man*, Sphere, London, 1968.
**3** M. Horkheimer and T. Adorno, 'The Culture Industry: Enlightenment as Mass Deception', p.167.
**4** Lacan characterises all pictures as 'traps for the gaze', but the phrase is used in the context of a discussion of the use of distorted images to 'catch' the eye and maintain the engagement of the gaze.
**5** W. Benjamin, 'The Work of Art in the Age of Mechanical Reproduction' in Hannah Arendt, ed., *Illuminations*, Schocken, New York, 1968, p.242.
**6** Deborah Turbeville, *Wallflower*, Quartet, London, 1978.

**Further Reading**

• Juliet Ash and Elizabeth Wilson, eds, *Chic Thrills: Fashion History, Fashion Theory and the Fashion Industry*, Pandora, London, 1992.
• Jean Baudrillard, 'Mass Media Culture' in his *Revenge of the Crystal: Selected Essays*, Pluto, London, 1990.
• Rosemary Betterton, *Looking On: Images of Femininity in the Visual Arts and Media*, Pandora Press, London, 1987.

• Rosalind Coward, *Female Desire*, Paladin, London, 1984.
• Jennifer Craik, *The Face of Fashion—Cultural Studies in Fashion*, Routledge, London, 1993.
• Caroline Evans and Minna Thornton, *Women and Fashion, A New Look*, Quartet, London, 1989.
• Caroline Evans and Minna Thornton, 'Fashion, Representation, Femininity', *Feminist Review*, no.38, Summer 1991.
• Stuart and Elizabeth Ewen, *Channels of Desire: Mass Images and the Shaping of American Consciousness*, McGraw-Hill, New York, 1982. See Part Four, 'Fashion and Democracy'.
• Arthur Kroker, ed., *Body Invaders: Panic Sex in America*, New World Perspectives: CultureText Series, 1987. See Section Two: 'Fashion and the Politics of Style'.
• Abigail Solomon-Godeau, 'The Armed Vision Disarmed: Radical Formalism from Weapon to Style', in *The Contest of Meaning*, ed. Richard Bolton, MIT Press, London, 1989.
• Elizabeth Wilson, 'All the Rage', *New Socialist*, no.14, Nov/Dec. 1983, pp.22-6.

# 13 Left in Sight

## Stuart Hall

Introduction by
**Jessica Evans and Stuart Hall**

*Jessica Evans*: Throughout the 1980s Stuart Hall offered a coherent analysis and critique of Thatcher's Conservative administration. His aim was to consider the 'lessons' which a continually wrong-footed Labour Party could learn from 'Thatcherism', and he drew upon the irony implicit in this in order to rethink the sacred cows of Left political culture.

As he argued in the interview 'Left in Sight', Labour and the Left must find a language which expresses the traditional socialist preoccupation with those oppressed by capitalism whilst also acknowledging and building upon the new conditions, expectations and 'freedoms' created, for the majority of the population, by an advanced welfare-state capitalist economy. (For commentators such as Anthony Giddens, the latter has also to be seen as part of a larger process—that of capitalist modernity, which has far-reaching and near-universal consequences in its undermining of traditional patterns of living and relating.)[1]

Well over a decade later, we are faced with pressing questions in our current political culture. Is Tony Blair's 'New Labour' Party able to represent these paradoxical demands, outlined above, in the service of a radical democratic politics and in a way which does justice to their extreme complexity? Or do we interpret the present situation as one in which the Labour Party has adopted 'Tory values' as its own, as is evidenced in their increasing predilection for economic neo-liberalism and moral puritanism—what Hall called, referring to Thatcherism, 'authoritarian populism'.[2]

If the latter proves to be so, to what extent is Tony Blair's rapid triumph symptomatic of a Labour Party which has internalised Thatcherite values precisely in order to avoid their subjection to a discriminating socialist 'superego'? I earlier used the metaphor of 'adoption' to suggest the incorporation of foreign 'stuff' that does not organically belong and which is thus uncomfortable to assimilate. Who, indeed, is it uncomfortable for? Stuart Hall's—and Kathy Myers's—pieces in *Camerawork* 1983 were partly concerned with the problem of Labour's 'image'—an image based on a fear of the language and visual seduction of consumerism and embedded in a pious conception of politics articulated through 'social realist' imagery that could only speak of working-class victims and their saviours, 'the state'. Hall and Myers, in the context of the Labour failure of 1983, were careful to talk about Labour's 'image' in its relationship with the wider political 'content' of Labour policy and the question of to and on behalf of whom it needed to speak. However, over recent years the Labour Party itself has responded to social changes and pressures by internally splitting issues of 'form' from those of 'content'. It appears that the former becomes the 'property' of the so-called modernisers and the latter that of the traditionalists. The traditionalists believe it is necessary and possible to have politics without paying attention to its rhetorical form, to the ways in which political parties construct and regulate people's wants and aspirations; they also ignore the existent desires of the 'electorate' in a world of rapid change. The modernisers appear to believe in sacrificing socialist policy commitments to image manipulation and pandering to what they actually believe are the 'gut' instincts of an entity called 'middle England'. This predicament, combined with an acceptance throughout much of the Party that certain social policy ideas have been irretrievably colonised by the Right, has driven the Labour leadership into creating taboos around certain words, such as 'taxation', 'public ownership', 'drugs'. The very capacity even to think about these in the public arena, let alone hammering them out into creative pathbreaking policies, is at risk.

From a wider perspective, the discomfort of assimilating 'Tory values' arises through the difficulty of also trying to maintain a separate identity—to what extent should the Labour Party be different, in policy and ideology, from the Conservative Party? And this question has to be posed in a deeply altered political and economic landscape, one in which the practices and mentalities of deregulation and market forces have left their mark on every institution in society. The difficulties facing a socialist politics that wants to do more than compete with the Tories on the technical management of the economy cannot be underestimated. If Labour has had to learn lessons from its failure over the past 15 years then how can this very learning lead it to a different place than its political enemies—a path that will make a real difference?

*Stuart Hall:* We know what the Tory 'revolution' would be, if only they could bring it off. But what is the 'Blair' revolution? What shift or current of feeling among the great majority of the population is he 'instinctively speaking and feeling in harmony with'? The first question is much easier to answer than the second. The 'Blair revolution' has been pre-eminently focused on transforming and reshaping the Labour Party, making it electable and at the same time the effective engine of his political ambitions and aspirations. No one should underestimate the achievements here. There were always two aspects to any Labour revival: the first had to do, broadly speaking, with *modernisation*. The second was to do with a political strategy and programme for the country that addressed major social and economic problems in a novel and distinctive way, clearly contrasting its approach with that which had governed the previous regime, and which captured the popular imagination, crystallising the disparate and sometimes contradictory elements of dissatisfaction into a new kind of politics. It is no secret that Blair's modernisation of the Labour Party—the test-bed of the first aspect—has been far more successful than the second strand, where the 'seizing of moments' is less in evidence.

Political traditions are absolutely necessary for any political party, but there is all the difference in the world between confronting the radical novelty and contingency of the future from within a deeply grounded 'sense of history' as a resource, and being imprisoned—frozen by the past. The view which was expressed at the time of the revision of Clause Four—that Labour needed this clause, not because anyone believed in it or intended to implement it, but because, like Everest, 'it was there'—is the remnant of a totemistic form of thought. The opinion, which some serious figures on the left expressed at the time—that Labour could no more send its troops into electoral battle without Clause Four than Britain could send its troops to war without the Union Jack—was so unnerving, so revealing in its unconscious implications, so eloquent of a political culture riveted to empty symbols and vacuous rhetoric, as to be seriously embarrassing to contemplate.

As for Blair himself, he is someone who seemed to be born and to have grown up through the same historical experiences as younger voters. He actually knew the 1960s had participated in the social movements, was married and bringing up kids in Thatcher's Britain, may even have known an unmarried mother or even had a friend who was HIV-positive. He was, in generation at least, a post-feminist man. We could expect him, not to become the mouthpiece for these 'new times' but to know on his political impulses what it was all about. But in leadership the impression he creates is almost the diametrical opposite. Blair is a sort of 'new' or modern man, but a deeply conservative version of the species. On crime, on family values, on one-parent families, on questions of sexuality, on the particular variant of communitarianism that he espouses, one can find no echo at all of the underlying sociological analysis that one would expect of a so-called 'moderniser'. The idea that, at the end of the twentieth century it would be possible to advance the 'modernisation' of British society by an ideological commitment to the nuclear family as the only credible family form, gives 'modernity' such a deeply conservative inflection that it hardly deserves the name. If there is a post-Thatcherist mood in the country, this surely is what it is—there must be a better way of doing things. What other reason would there be for voting Labour for the vast majority of non-genetically programmed potential Labour voters?[3]

---

## Left in Sight

**Stuart Hall**, Professor of Sociology at the Open University, was Director of the Centre for Contemporary Cultural Studies at Birmingham University from 1972 to 1979. He has co-edited many volumes and written numerous articles on contemporary social and cultural theory and on British politics. He wrote *The Hard Road to Renewal: Thatcherism and the Crisis of the Left* (1988) and has recently co-authored the *Understanding Modern Societies* series of books for the Open University.

*Camerawork:* In terms of imagery and the politics behind images, the Left appears out of touch with its constituency. Most people are used to a sophisticated diet of adverts and TV, yet this media professionalism is often dismissed by the Left as bourgeois. Would you agree?

*Stuart Hall:* The Left has to look around and see the language that consumer capitalism speaks to people in. It's very up-to-date with a high stress on technology. People know that's going to define the future, and images of technology are much more widespread than the technology itself. The Left has to be professional. Just look at the slickness of adverts designed to appeal to the mass consumer.

*Camerawork:* You talk of the importance of engaging with the language of advertising, yet the Labour Left continually reworks socialist realist photography and Heartfield-style montage. Socialist realism carries with it a certain kind of Dickensian philanthropy as if photographing the poor, the needy, the homeless were enough to rouse political action. As a style of photography it appears curiously dated, more appropriate to the 1930s dole queues than today. Yet despite the cultural and political changes it is the dominant form of Left photography. It also subscribes to the idea of photography as a transparent medium which can capture or document the reality of the event depicted. Why do you think this is so?

*Stuart Hall:* I guess socialist realist imagery is the one which the Left is most stuck with. I don't share the view that ideology is inscribed in the form alone. I think what has happened is that the

Left has got stuck in a certain period, which is why the realist imagery seems appropriate, of 'the State' doing good. The photographs never have a sense of agency in the images or people themselves. They're always depicted as clients, or objects at the bottom of a pile. Very inert images.

*Camerawork:* Montage is an old fashioned technique, but do you think it has more potential than social realist photography?

*Stuart Hall:* Montage is different. I don't think it was properly absorbed into the imagery of the Left until the 1960s. Heartfield's montages were turned down by *Picture Post*, though they eventually used some. The German political movement at that time was much more typographically advanced. Also, montage is the language of advertising and even Heartfield took it from that tradition. It has a lot of potential, although it is sometimes over-used, and has come to stand for 'the alternative'. It has a lot of potential, which is more than can be said for social realism, which has serious problems. It looks outdated using 1930s stylistic techniques to depict poverty in the 1980s. Working-class culture is still depicted like a Jarrow March, which it isn't. That is not the reality of unemployment today. Social realism is not realist in the way it pretends to be. It's a regressive language.

At least montage through juxtaposition can engage with contradictory images and realities, but it's important to go beyond that to achieve positive, more integrated visual languages.

*Camerawork:* But 'the Left' isn't a unified group. Although the Labour Left may be locked in the past, other constituents of the Left have been concerned with developing new images.

*Stuart Hall:* When you're talking about images of the left in the general sense it's important to look at the constituent elements. Because I would say that feminism is far closer than the Labour Left to finding that positive language, that image of the future. Through transformation of images, fiction, fantasy, poetry, etc., they've gone beyond that montage idea of reality as the product of a simple juxtaposition—itself a very limited visual language which always seems to need to mobilise the rhetoric of capital or labour to make its point.

I think the 1960s was really important as a root for those ideas. It was a time when an advanced modern aesthetic was capable of engaging with interests on the Left: take a look at magazines like *Oz*, etc. But it was also the time of the split. The radical avant garde moving on through *Time Out* and things like *City Limits*, and

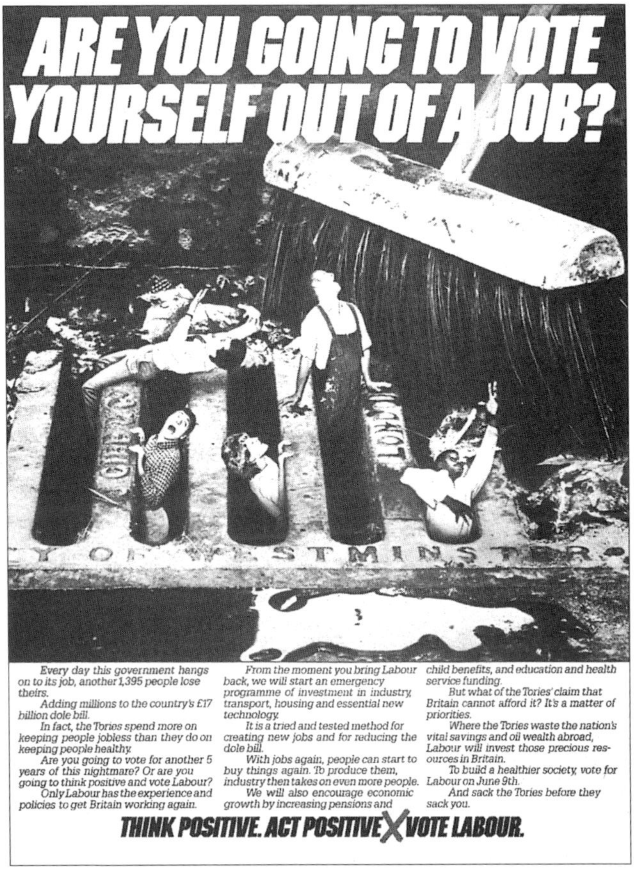


13.1 Labour Party election poster, Wright Agency, 1983



the traditional labour movement falling behind. I mean if the TUC ever got a magazine together can you imagine what it would look like? Straight out of the 1890s probably, with small type and no pictures. It's unthinkable. Of course this kind of argument about the politics of imagery has been going on for a long time. William Morris in the 1890s was a committed socialist and at the same time produced amazing designs and visual ideas which seem to have been lost today. We've witnessed an explosion in communication and cultural language and the Left seems unaware of that.

*Camerawork:* There is a sense in which the English Labour Left is guilty of a kind of visual illiteracy. A lot of the Third World political design is much more exciting, less locked into the rhetoric of its own past. How do you account for that difference?

*Stuart Hall:* Take Latin America where the political imagery is so striking visually. That's a real cultural conquest, very dynamic. Take

Cuba where in the early 1960s you had extraordinary primitive socio-economic and material circumstances, you had ideas addressed to a twentieth-century consciousness. The political posters of the period are very 1960s, bright and colourful, influenced by the American consumer culture and very definitely addressed to a modern audience as well as backward peasants coming to Havana for the first time. Maybe that modernism is a product of the strong influence of American culture on Latin America, a dominant and oppressive culture, but nevertheless a modern language. So they're not so inhibited about trying to develop new realities and say new things. Plus of course you're up against mass illiteracy which means that the visual image is very important. We have this slowly evolving culture, with a slowly evolving political language.

Looking at South America, it's politically exciting. The fractures and ruptures have produced new languages, new ways of thinking. Which is why I suppose I like photomontage, because stylistically it uses those fractures and ruptures, even if it's in too clumsy and obvious a way. On the one hand, fragments, ruptures can be politically alarming, things appearing to fall apart, but on the other, they can be quite productive. I don't take any pleasure in the fragmentation and pessimism of the Left.

I think it's important not to lose a sense of the public space. Which is why I warm to the GLC posters even if I don't like the way they look. I think it's necessary to remind us that somebody cleans our streets, that the river is a public asset to be used or whatever. I just wish they'd remind us in a more recognisably twentieth-century language.

The elements are around in the fragments waiting to be used. People have a lot of skills and want to use them. Those skills need to be harnessed. It's less important where they come from, as how they can be used. I mean you just have to walk into the Labour Party headquarters and you instantly know what's wrong, they're just not tuned in. People with the necessary skills are available and do work for socialism. You see it in film, in journalism, in community arts, all over the place. But they're divorced from the traditional labour movement. And the movement is hostile to these forces. The trouble is they just don't see the point. They think that updating means of communication is just a frill. Maybe we'll think about it in better days, but now we have to get down to the nitty gritty problem, which is—guess what—how to reach the people, so the ideological question about Left rhetoric is not marginal at all. It's central.

*Camerawork:* Yet looking at the Labour Party campaign produced by the Wright Agency for the last election, the combination of realism and montage reinforces a desperate, pessimistic vision of reality. Clearly these things need to be said, but there's also a case for arguing that people cannot bear too much reality. Like with the Oxfam posters, you get to a point beyond which people switch off. Do you think that pointing out the horrors of capitalism is the best way of mobilising the popular vote?

*Stuart Hall:* You mean if you can see yourself being pushed by the broom down the hole in the road will you pop up in the Labour booth? OK there's three million people to whom that applies, but how do you persuade the twenty million still employed not to vote for the other side? You have also to speak to them. You can't get votes purely on the strength of defensive measures: protecting the old, the weak, the young, etc. First they will always be a minority, and second, they don't always feel positive about seeing themselves in that way, as victims.



*Camerawork:* In your *New Socialist* article 'Whistling in the Void' you said: 'Labour shows less and less capacity to connect with popular feelings and sentiments, let alone transform them or articulate them to the left. It gives the distinct impression of a political party living on the capital of past connections and successes, but increasingly out of touch with what is going on in every day life around it.' You add that Labour has mistaken 'the moment of 1983 for 1972 or 1974', and that 'Labour currently possesses no image of the future. It provides no picture of life under Socialism'.[4] To what extent do you think that Labour's nostalgia for its own past makes it appear old-fashioned and out of touch?

*Stuart Hall:* I don't think that the future of the Left can be fought solely with reference to the political landmarks of the past. Things have to be thought afresh. You can't just invoke the past, which I think Foot was trying to do with his references to the 1940s. I think that is political nostalgia. On the other hand I don't agree with the view that one has nothing to learn from the past. There's an enormous amount to learn from 1945 because it was when socialist ideas and Marxist ideas which were generating during the 1930s really touched a lot of people. Ideas which had been developing in pockets of the Left really touched a popular core. A lot of that is still relevant now, so there's something to feel and understand about periods when socialist ideas have become popular. So you have to use the past, draw on memory, fiction, utopia, all those languages which are important to reach and move people.

*Camerawork:* You talk about Utopia and the future, yet the images of the Labour Party with which we are familiar appear almost archaic. What has happened to the Left's vision of Utopia?

*Stuart Hall:* Those languages of Utopia have to be recaptured, and in terms of providing socialism with an image of the future which people can really connect with. I'm suspicious of a language of Utopia which only talks about the future and doesn't make the right uses of the past. Nostalgic use is inhibiting. The image of the working class as it was presented in the 1930s and is still represented is clearly out of date. It's comprised of women, blacks, university-educated people. Unless the Left can see that, it has no way of addressing people about the future. That kind of flat-cap nostalgia is dangerous.

Utopias have always combined something of the past with something of the future. Utopian language isn't just a projection into the future. I want to make a distinction between proper and improper uses of history.

*Camerawork:* But I think there's been a fetishistic as opposed to dialectical use of the past. For example there's nothing dialectical about Foot's nostalgia for Labour's golden moment in the 1930s and 1940s when socialism was strong. On the other hand Thatcher seems to successfully rework ideological myths about the nineteenth century and Victorian values.

*Stuart Hall:* Thatcher invokes the past, Victorian values, in a different way from Foot's interest in the 1940s. She invokes that aspect of competitive individualism which is in people today, whereas Foot refers to the 1940s because it was a time when ordinary people felt things had to change. Now they're terrified of change. So Thatcher addresses the present fear of freedom, of change, inserting things like the family, the grammar school. Foot isn't talking about recreating the feeling of the 1940s in the 1980s. He's saying nostalgically, oh don't you remember the welfare state? But he forgets that he is talking to people who have had the welfare state up to their heads in terms of bureaucratic institutions. Which again gives Thatcher an edge because she's re-using that old, almost eighteenth-century idea of privatising those big companies and institutions.

So when you talk about Utopia, I think it's a real socialist struggle over language of the past. I think it's absolutely crucial that we have positive images of the future which meet people's rising expectations, and I think that there's a lot about labourist thinking on the Left which is going to have to change. You know, that notion that you're only a Labour voter if you live in the most run-down council and are the most oppressed.

*Camerawork:* How do you see a vision of the future linking up with Labour's commitment to document the 'realism' of life under capitalism?

*Stuart Hall:* I don't think that the Labour Party or the Left understands how to find a language that encompasses both of those realities, and so it is very stuck in the minorities, the oppressed, war, the poor, etc. But I don't think it could avoid that. Because it's not just a question of developing the right image to show people. It's a question of developing the right politics.

The thing is so contradictory, and finding a politics, let alone an image which can speak for the Left as if it were a unified thing, is very difficult to do. I'll give you a concrete example. Take Scargill. I think he's right about the miners. But I think he's idiotic about Solidarity which is clearly a socialist movement against state oppression. At the same time he talks to the men as if they all turned out tomorrow and stood in front of the Coal Board everything would change, which is a very masculine trade union thing to do, and at the same time he's never heard of women. Analysis, internationalism, trade union practice and personal politics are four different sites of politics, four different constituencies, and you have to find a way of addressing them all. It can't be one language.

What we've got at the moment is a language which has become deformed by being attached to the circus appearance of the past—the cloth cap, a working class which looks like an Engels lithograph and which doesn't exist.



---

Stuart Hall was interviewed by Kathy Myers, on behalf of *Camerawork*.

**Reference Notes**

**1** See A. Giddens, *The Consequences of Modernity*, Polity Press, Oxford, 1990; Stuart Hall, David Hall and Anthony McGrew, eds, *Modernity and its Futures*, Polity Press/OU, Oxford, 1992 (Book 4 of OU Course D213, 'Understanding Modern Societies').

**2** See Stuart Hall, *The Hard Road to Renewal: Thatcherism and the Crisis of the Left*, Verso, London, 1988.

**3** This is an adapted extract from Stuart Hall's article 'Son of Margaret?' in *New Statesman & Society*, 6 October 1995.

**4** In *New Socialist*, May 1983.

**Further Reading**

• Beatrix Campbell, *Wigan Pier Revisited: Poverty and Politics in the 80s*, Virago, London, 1984.

- Stuart Hall and Martin Jacques, eds, *The Politics of Thatcherism*, Lawrence and Wishart/*Marxism Today*, London, 1983.
- Stuart Hall, *The Hard Road to Renewal: Thatcherism and the Crisis of the Left*, Verso, London, 1988.
- David Morley and Kuan-Hsing Chen, eds, *Stuart Hall: Critical Dialogues in Cultural Studies*, Routledge, London, 1996.
- Christopher Norris, 'Old Themes for New Times: Postmodernism, Theory and Cultural Politics', in Judith Squires, ed., *Principled Positions*, Lawrence and Wishart, London, 1993.
- Gareth Steadman-Jones, *Languages of Class: Studies in English Working-Class History 1832-1982*, Cambridge University Press, Cambridge, 1983.
- Alan O'Shea, 'Trusting the People: How does Thatcherism Work?' in *Formations of Nation and People*, Routledge & Kegan Paul, London, 1984.

# 14 Loves Labour Lost

## Kathy Myers

Introduction by
**Kathy Myers**

Nothing, not even light, moves faster than Labour party policy. It is hard to believe—but true—that in the early 1980s when 'Loves Labour Lost' was written, the Labour Party was still grappling with the ideological implications of using advertising (the handmaiden of capitalism) to sell its message. The soap box and ballot box, not the TV box, were still their primary means of communication. Labour, unbelievably, was nervous about pitching its politicians into the media frenzy of satellite, cable and Jeremy Paxman's ball-breaking interview techniques.

When it did use advertising its prognoses on the world were dowdy, depressing and reminiscent of the worst kind of 1930s photographic realism. It still relied on the depiction of inequality and injustice to rouse votes. The iconography of despair is of course familiar. Since Dickens we've been flooded with images of dole queues, shoeless children, rotting wallpaper, litter-strewn streets, ill health and hopelessness. Nor was this mere tear-jerking because for a lot of people these were—and remain—the real conditions of existence.

The problem for the Labour Party by the early 1980s was that this style of political and social representation had stopped working. It wasn't that people didn't care. It was simply that those already fighting a hand-to-mouth existence could no longer rally around such a bleak representation of tomorrow. They wanted something better, shinier, more optimistic.

When I wrote the *Camerawork* article we felt the Labour Party had reached a cultural hiatus. That the representation of the road to the dole queue—was a road to nowhere. Of course what we didn't know was what the solution was—or how the Labour Party should represent a more optimistic self that didn't coincide with the Thatcherite obsession with shiny happy people. I think at the time we hoped that the 1980s would spawn a new radical era in left-wing iconography. If the 1930s had commandeered geniuses of photomontage such as Heartfield, what would the *fin de siècle* produce?

The Labour Party may now be working in tandem with top advertising and marketing agencies—it may have harnessed capitalism to its cause, but the imagery it has chosen is not cutting edge; it is derived from the soft-focus Fairy Liquid end of the spectrum. The images they use to sell themselves are bizarrely conservative. Endless party political promos saturated with soft music, soft-filtered lenses, slow-motion caring politicians and families that a 1950s Persil commercial director would have been proud of.

None of this has come cheap. Top commercials directors have been behind their party political broadcasts—names like Hugh Hudson were busy reinventing the image of Neil Kinnock long before Tony Blair came along. Their in-house media wiz-kid Peter Mandelson, once a lonely voice down a Walworth road corridor, pushing Labour uphill into the spotlight of a wired world, has himself been elevated from spindoctor to politician. The message is simple—new Labour loves the media, it loves advertising and anything that sells it to the people. But nothing too different, too radical, too innovative; Labour wants to be seen as 'fit to govern'. No loony Lefties here. Nothing 'weird'.

This is, of course, the ultimate irony. Late twentieth-century capitalism has found out that 'staying safe' doesn't sell. Adverts designed to appeal to the masses to push the dull products of industry are increasingly avant-garde: flaming fields of corn to sell cars, rubber S&M to sell Dunlop tyres, savage blood-spattered Steadman-esque cartoons to sell Oddbins booze, strange morphed orange maniacs to sell Tango, surreal flights of Dada-esque fantasy to sell Guiness.

These are images that challenge—even if the sole aim is to shift another washing powder. How sad, that with all this talent around, Labour should be lost politically and aesthetically in an uninspired soft-focus world of Bambi-featured politicians and cotton wool policies. In the 1990s it is Labour who have become the 'New Conservatives'; how Thatcher must have laughed.

---

## Loves Labour Lost

For author details, see Kathy Myers's 'Towards a Feminist Erotica' in this volume.

The year 1983 was an important moment in labour history. The Labour Party lost the election, and it was the first time it had used an orthodox advertising agency, Wright and Partners, to promote its image to the public. Of course the agency can't be blamed for the electoral failure but, as Garnet Edwards, creative director of the campaign, put it, 'I expect we will be scapegoated!'

If anything, the evidence points in the opposite direction. MORI research suggests that the public responded well to the campaign and were moved by the credibility and conviction of the tightly budgeted press and poster campaign. Whatever the result, the use of an advertising agency has been an important, if controversial step for the Labour Party. Some have argued that it was a sign of the times, the Labour Left selling out and deploying the evils of capitalist PR machinery to promote its flayed image. Others have argued that politics, ideas and social commitment don't market themselves. What's the good of a manifesto if the bulk of the population is ignorant of its content?

As Simon Hoggart commented in his article on the public profile of Michael Foot: 'Many politicians tend to think TV doesn't really matter. Even if a thousand people a day see Foot speak in person during the campaign, they will total no more than 0.05 per cent of the population, a tiny fragment of those who will watch him on TV.'[1]

Foot's media aversion is no accident. Like many members of the Labour Party he has a preference for grass-roots contact and public speeches. While this is an essential part of political credibility, it is myopic to leave that most powerful of media, television, to the opposition. In the wake of Wilson's 'white heat' technological revolution, Foot has pitched for a nostalgic vision of the party.

A colleague of Hoggart is quoted as saying:

> The problem is that Michael's golden age was the 1940s when we all worked for the good of the country. Now Thatcher has somehow contrived with her talk of Victorian values to make 1885 sound like 1985. But there's no way Michael is ever going to make 1940 sound like a vision of the future.

Whereas Thatcher reworks the ideology of privatisation, nationalism and individualism to make it appear contemporary, Foot has substituted history for nostalgia. Serving up a 'don't you remember when?' tune of socialist strength in the 1940s. A time of heavy industry and patriarchal union solidarity. A time which cannot be returned to, and which has no meaning for the modern working class. Foot's aversion to the technological, technocratic media is part of this nostalgia. This opposition to media exposure meant that Thatcher repeatedly received more than her fair share of TV time. As one producer commented at the 1983 Edinburgh Television Festival: 'Michael Foot's men just didn't lay on such good pictures'. Criticism that TV was biased against the Left was countered by one angry presenter:

> We can't be expected to compensate for the inefficiencies of the Labour Party campaign. The Tory Party at least knew where Thatcher would be,

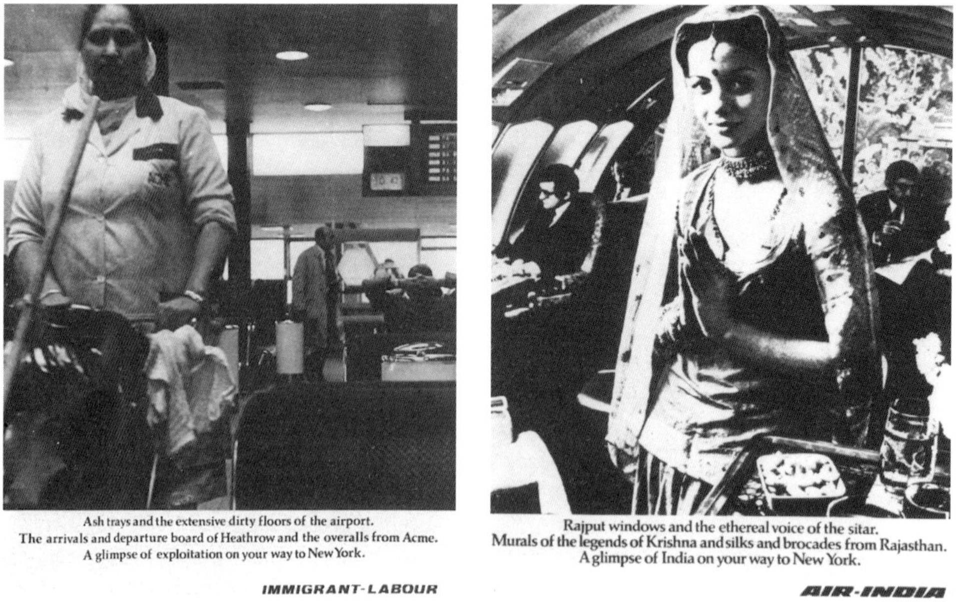


14.1 *Air India*, 1975. Paul Wombell

Images of Correction:
During the mid-1970s many political artists were concerned with the ideological method of advertising. This 'misleading' information was commented upon through the devices of montage, simulation and juxtaposition. In different ways the work of the Hackney Flashers, Yve Lomax and Paul Wombell sought to correct the world represented in the advert. The cleaning staff of Air India and the drudgery of housework refer to an aspect of women's sexual identity and labour which is absent in the advertisement. In this sense these images of correction referred to a reality which was thought to exist outside the image.

and had an understanding of TV's needs. This was not the case with the Labour Party. It is not up to broadcasters to compensate for such inept inefficiency.

What was at issue in the Edinburgh debate was whether marketing and advertising were an acceptable part of contemporary political procedure. As Michael Cockrell, the producer of *Panorama*'s *The Marketing of Margaret*, pointed out:

> Thatcher's campaign, complete with songs, banners and tightly choreographed appearances, is the nearest thing we've ever seen to an American presidential election. Behind her was Saatchi and Saatchi, USA adviser Gordon Reece, and her marketing manager Billy Grayham. With coaching, Margaret has emerged as the most skilled prime minister we've ever had.[2]

It would be wrong to suggest that Labour lost simply because their marketing machine was badly organised. Rather, the campaign represented and re-created many of the political policy confusions already endemic within the party. The Labour Party had decided to sell itself to the constituency on the strength of its caring properties. It would be the young, the old, the sick and the needy who would benefit. Defence was the message. The copy lines which the Wright Agency created were appropriate to this. Pictures of children on a scrap heap, or the broken chair of a classroom, were accompanied by captions which read: 'Are you going to vote your-

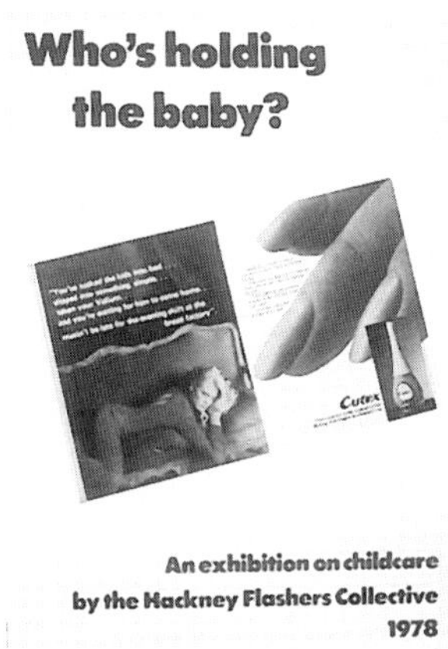


14.2 From *Who's Holding the Baby?* series, Hackney Flashers Collective, 1978

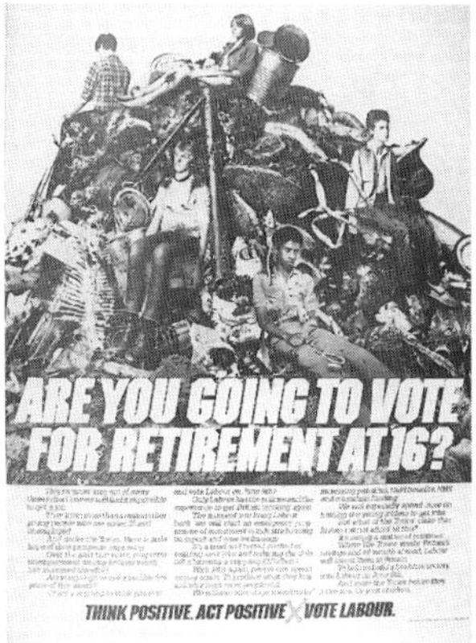


14.3 Labour Party election poster, Wright Agency 1983

Below:
14.4 Night Boys in Sleeping Quarters, 1890. Jacob Riis

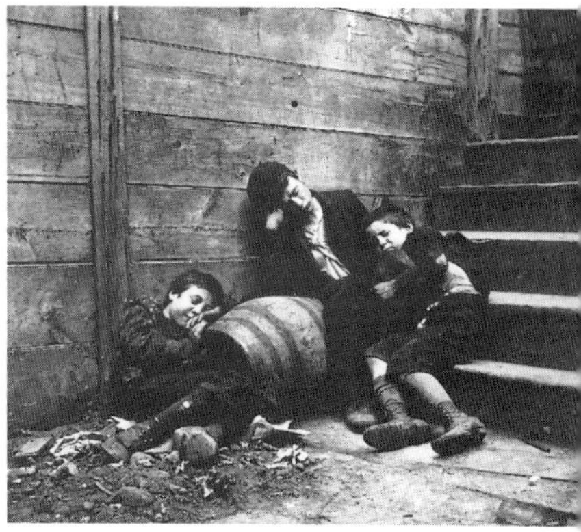

Unlike montage, which is the progeny of early advertising, photographic social realism stems from nineteenth-century philanthropy and Liberalism. Examples are the work of Lewis Hine, Jacob Riis or the Worker Photographer movement which document the oppressive 'reality' of people's lived experiences, the grime, the poverty, the hopelessness. 'Are you going to vote for retirement at 16?' is peculiarly reminiscent of 'Night Boys in Sleeping Quarters'. Social documentary work like the anthropological Mass Observation of the 1930s, has more recently been supplemented by community photography, which seeks to put the photographic means of production in the hands of the workers. Ownership and production may have changed, but the style of photography and the belief in documentary realism has not.

self out of a job?' 'Are you going to vote for the death of the health service', or 'Vote your children out of a future?' (figures 14.1 and 14.3)

Ironically this was a campaign strategy which colluded with the needs of the opposition and Saatchi and Saatchi, who wanted to put Labour on the defensive. Following a campaign by Saatchi which compared the Labour manifesto with that of the Communist Party, they were quoted in *Campaign* magazine as saying: 'The Tory party determined at the outset to make the campaign into a blistering attack on Labour and the SDP so that the opponents would be forced on to the defensive.'

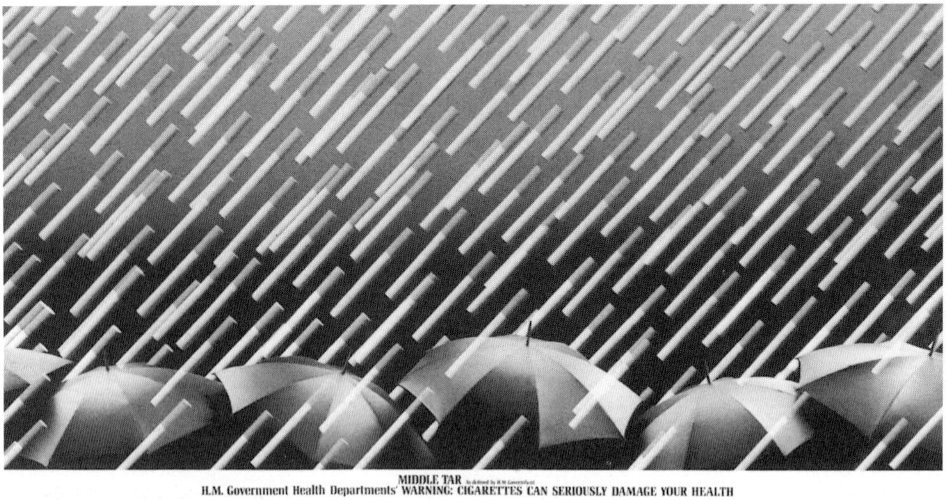


14.5 John Hammond (Photographer) and Neil Godfrey (Art Director), 1983
In the rare moments when the visual means of communication are given some attention we encounter a reliance upon old visual techniques, especially socialist realist and photomontage methods of the 1920s and 1930s, and advertising styles of the 1950s. This implies a cultural conservatism which is out of step with progressive political views.

Finally, the Wright campaign images devised for Labour recreated the nostalgia which Foot was busy promoting. The montages and social realist black and white poverty sketches were reminiscent of 1930s design. They appear to be 'legitimate' propaganda techniques because they have spearheaded Left political rhetoric and revolution in the past. But they are dated, and image-hungry modern audiences know this.

The Labour Party is caught in a contradictory position. On the one hand it has been forced to recognise the importance of using the media effectively as part of a political campaign. On the other it is hindered by a scepticism and wariness of the medium. Accusations of bias against the Left were well documented in research projects such as the *Bad News* report conducted by the Glasgow Media Group.[3] But even when Labour gains access to technology and modern marketing techniques, it backs off. Advertising is cast as the handmaiden of the bourgeoisie. Slick glossy productions are earmarked as brainwashing or media 'seduction'. TV is identified as a placebo to avert popular rebellion.

But the most important techniques which can be learned from advertising are the invisible skills of marketing, not the 'visible' techniques of airbrushing. Marketing is not a euphemism for 'conning'. Involving a twofold process of 'branding' and 'target marketing' it refers to 'demand management', that process by which audiences or constituencies are identified, and messages tailored to maximise their reception and impact.

Branding means giving a product—or a political party—an image with which a constituency can identify. Labour's need to promote a unified front after the internal strife was in conflict with

*In order to communicate an idea which is by and large not consciously understood by working class people, yet an explanation of their lives, we must rely upon a visual vocabulary and style which is recognisable, knowable and entertaining. We are therefore immediately reliant to a degree on the methods of advertising if we are to attract people's eyes away from the seduction of the snappy competition we face. Our work must be as good or better than the competition at selling cigarettes.*
From Robert Golden, *Photography/Politics: One*, eds. Spence, et al., Photography Workshop.

its desire to champion the causes of many 'minority' groups. Party rifts were confused with the different needs and identities of the constituencies which Labour sought to represent.The response to this contradiction was to fall back on an outmoded vision of the Labour Left. Patriarchal 'flat cap' Northern man reappeared throughout the party political speeches on TV and on the posters. An image which had little appeal for young people, women or ethnic minorities for example. The product on offer appeared out of date. The Labour brand of politics was in no position to compete with Tory glitter and domestic homilies.

Labour's lack of sensitivity to its audience and potential voters manifested itself in clumsy target marketing. There seemed to be a belief that if an idea was good enough it would sell itself. Rather than opting for a campaign with a stable of images each designed to appeal to specific audiences they opted for 'something for everybody'. This search for a common denominator produced a plethora of emotive imagery offering up the poor and the sick. However worthy, all the needy cases don't add up to a majority vote. Kinnock in his short time as party leader has already set out to mobilise the 'trendy' vote, which must include those in business, employment and good health.

If Labour wants to be a viable party of the future it has to change its political vision of the media and how to use it. It has to be able to construct patterns of demand and offer the pleasure of consumption. It has to be aware of the needs of an increasingly privatised culture in which TV, cable and the computer promise to be the arteries of the future.

But it's not just a question of appropriating the skills of bourgeois culture and glossy advertising. Over the past thirty years, elements of the political Left, including feminism, have reassessed the role which the media can play. This concern erupted out of an interest in the concept of ideology as central, not marginal, to any political theory of change. Feminism, for example, had long asserted that material change is no guarantee of social change for women. Rather a change of consciousness was needed to accompany material transformations, and that meant a shift within ideology.

Writers such as Barthes, Althusser, Lacan, Kristeva and Derrida were central to this recalculation of ideology, and by extension the mass communication system of the media. Advertising, the 'art form of capitalism' became crucial for a number of reasons. As mass communication it linked commodity production with commodity consumption. It appeared as transparent ideology in action, mobilising false fantasies and unlivable lifestyles. It promoted bourgeois culture as the only culture and reproduced archaic sexual identities and social roles. One approach to the ideology of advertising was 'correction'. The art work of John Stezaker or Victor Burgin, *Decoding Advertisements* by Judith Williamson, or the numerous feminist art exhibitions, sought to reveal the lies and falsehoods of advertising. This was achieved visually by juxtaposing an advertising image with a contradictory (correct) text.

But as recent exhibitions at the ICA or the Riverside's *Beyond the Purloined Image*[4] demonstrates, things are beginning to change. The emphasis on correction or demystification has been replaced by construction and redefinition. Moving from a position of defence, political artists have started to combine the visual sophistication of advertising with the social insight needed to provide new visions and fantasies for the future.

---

**Reference Notes**

**1** *Observer*, 24 April 1983.

**2.** See Michael Cockerell, *Live from Number 10: The Inside Story of Prime Ministers and Television*, Faber and Faber, London, 1988.

**3** Glasgow Media Group, ed., *Bad News*, Routledge & Kegan Paul, London, 1976.

**4** Exhibition and Catalogue of the work of O. Richon, S. Trangmar, K. Knorr, Y. Lomax, Riverside Studios, London, 1983.

**Further Reading**


• Nigel Fountain, *Underground: The London Alternative Press*, 1966-74, Comedia, London, 1988.

• Bob Franklin, *Packaging Politics*, Edward Arnold, London, 1994.

• John Gorman, *Images of Labour*, Scorpion Publishing, 1985.

• Sylvia Harvey, 'Who Wants to Know What and Why?' *Ten.8*, no.23, 1986.

• David J. Kingsley, 'Photography and the Election', *Creative Camera*, nos 223 and 224, July/August 1983, pp.1056-9.

• Stuart Laing, *Representations of Working-Class Life 1957-1964*, Macmillan, Basingstoke, 1986.

• Kathy Myers, *Understains: The Sense and Seduction of Advertising*, Comedia, London, 1986.

• John Taylor, 'The General Theory of Icebergs (or what you can't see in political advertisements)', *Ten.8*, no.26, 1987.

• Andrew Wernick, *Promotional Culture*, Sage, London, 1991.

# 15 An Affront to Taste? The Disturbances of Jo Spence

Jessica Evans

Jo Spence's work, since the late 1970s, was an extraordinary narrative of loss and control, powerlessness and assertion. Photography itself could expose their points of intersection. As she said,

> I now think about photography whilst I am undergoing anything at the hand of others, particularly when I consider myself to be powerless. At the same time as I am trying to work out how to take photographs of what is happening to me, I also know that whatever I am about to photograph isn't actually what is happening. That it is only the tip of the iceberg because of censorship and self-censorship, and because you can't show the structures which produce that situation.[1]

Spence's work in its eclectic excessiveness and 'messy' experimentalism is a challenge to the innocence of much documentary realism. But it also presents a philosophical alternative to the hermetic, stage-managed studio practices of deconstructionist photography, predominant in the 1980s in the academy and the art photography sector. Both of these, in different ways, can be understood as authoritarian structures in their repression of the capacity for human agency and their reduction of subjectivity to the social processes of subjection. There is a space in Spence's work for an embodied praxis, rooted in the self-reflexive politics of feelings, which allows for a conception of the human subject as more than just a container of social relations. How can one act without repeating the past but also without denying its hold over the present? It is the dynamic inherent in this question which, I will argue, is central to Jo Spence's life and work.

In this chapter I want to present some thoughts in response to her work and explore what implications her work has for the development of cultural and photographic theory. I am assuming some familiarity with Spence's work and I refer readers to her posthumous book *Cultural Sniping* which provides an excellent overview of the trajectory of her concerns through 20 years of work.[2] I believe that Spence's work—in its changing tasks and interests, its traversing of traditional genre distinctions and diversity of subject-matters and forms—is necessarily discontinuous and resists an easy coherence from those who now seek to interpret it. One reason for this is that her 'work' cannot be reified as a mere professional product, the result of a purposeful and incrementalist 'career' path on and up through a particular institution, such as the academy or the art world. Spence did not have a 'job' that could contain some implicit idea of progress; she lived largely outside both the security and the discourses of the professionalised world. Nonetheless, the latter, in part, constituted her public, but they were also, especially in the case of the medical profession, the objects of a sustained critical analysis.

Spence took seriously the proposition that in photography lies the potential for a more democratic and accessible means of representation, one which could be embedded in the unremarkable moments of the 'everyday'—and one which didn't have to rely at all on being trained as a particular 'type' of photographer, within the prescribed codes of a narrowly conceived professional practice. Refusing the definition 'photographer' for these reasons, she preferred the broader, more inclusive definition of educator, cultural producer, facilitator and, towards the end of her life, 'cultural sniper'. Rather like Berger's 'radial' method of photographic practice (see his 'Ways of Remembering' in this volume) the use of photography that she advocated was one that was only valuable in so far as it could be embedded in both non-specialised, non-professional photographic constituencies and non-photographic communities, such as adult education classes, women's health groups, medical student groups.

This may be countered with the important Bourdieuian point, made by John Tagg, that any innovation and dissent at the level of amateur photography cannot carry the weight of cultural significance because by definition its field is not culturally privileged.[3] Those who, like Jo Spence, have sought to challenge the codes of representation within the paradigm of amateur photography cannot do so within that space—'what it involves, if it is to be visible at all, is a change of level, moving upwards in the hierarchy'—and so the gravitational pull is upwards to those spaces of professional or more usually Art photography.[4] Nonetheless, the art gallery was in fact only a small element of the means of distribution of Spence's work—much of it took place in publications, talks and group activities, and television. Moreover, it is important to place Jo Spence, and her long-term collaborator Terry Dennett, in a much wider context. Their work was founded upon a long tradition of working-class 'self-help' and education movements, which were orientated in the 1970s to community activism, local working-class history and oral life-story projects, adult worker education and children's rights; it was from this sense of 'history from below' that *Camerawork* magazine was born. This is a culture of necessary 'amateurism' (and I do not mean this in its contemporary sense—the mocking of a culture of aspiration), of bricolage and 'making do' from an experience derived from the particular, the concrete, and most importantly, the unofficial. I notice that this holds for her writings too; lying outside the academic field they do not attempt abstract objectivism nor methods of systematic argumentation and specialised language, to demonstrate the 'lineage' for sources and the logics of thesis building—the careful weighing up of counterfactual arguments and the deferral of resolutions.[5] Spence's writing, like her photography, bows to the dictates of 'the practical sense': the motivation is, can it support a line of cultural–political commitment? Furthermore, there could be no separation between her sense of self and the voice of the text for the purpose of creating some universalising impartial knowledge. Part of the explanation for this lies in a longstanding attempt, exacerbated by the onset of cancer in the early 1980s, to find a way of mediating between the separated realms of expert cultures and the everyday system of understanding amongst individuals.[6] Increasingly the crisis traversing her own body coincided with her perception of the violence—symbolic and actual—of the dominant paradigm in health, that of scientific and technological intervention. Self-representation was the only way of linking the two, from inside (the body) outwards, as it were. There is another aspect to Spence's work, exemplified by the project she made with Terry Dennett, *Remodelling Photo History*, and her later photo-therapy practice, and that is her use of the drama-therapy of Augusto Boal whose 'spect-actor' techniques are appropriate for both therapy and political action.[7] At the onset of her health crisis this was tempered by her involvement in the therapeutic values of the 'New Age Psychotechnologies' with their faith in the body's self-healing faculties and their holistic spirit of looking after oneself in one's own environment.[8]

Photography for Spence, as she said many times, is a weapon to be used tactically. Although she rejected the military metaphor popular in orthodox cancer treatments it was integral to her strategy for 'fighting-back'. Much of the time this projectile was not the end product, the photograph, but the process of gaining entry to the enemy camp and exercising a 'right' to appropriate a piece of it with a camera. Clearly this has long been a trope of photojournalism and documentary practices—the fetishisation of gaining access to places previously unseen has often gone hand in hand with a positivism that assumes an omniscient autonomy of the knower and his/her radical separation from the known (object of investigation); often those photographed are reduced to 'docile bodies' in the service of a liberal 'social concern'.[9] But for Spence the very act of photographing is a way of creating a sense of agency and these problems of documentary are overcome by this new reflexivity between herself as photographer and her self as photographed object. I want to explore more precisely in what way she was able to do this.

She could, for example, use a camera in order to wage a struggle over the ownership of property and the ownership of bodies in the specific environment of the hospital:

> The point is that generally people (whether in power or not) are frightened of the camera. In a naïve sort of way, at a subjective level, I feel they are going to give me better attention (this is a complete double-bind I now realise) if they think I am photographing what is going on. And the truth of the matter is (for all the problems around the naturalism of the photograph) that this is so. The medical profession is totally paranoid about being seen to make 'mistakes'. On several occasions I had to evolve strategies for getting permission to take pictures....Each time I had to think up a different strategy to be allowed to take photographs. In that respect it is exactly the same as when I was in the Hackney Flashers Collective when we had a project to document women's invisible labour, needing to get into factories and various state institutions, when nobody really wanted us to be there....That is also a question of negotiation because usually you have very little rights in the matter if you are going onto private property. It's not part of so-called patient's rights, that you can take photographs in hospital.[10]

Her 1985-6 project *The Picture of Health?* makes visible in Foucauldian fashion those 'micro-capillary' forms of power which in touching the body are made corporeal. Foucault's critique of the modernist narrative of European progress, a narrative which claims that modern rationality has brought us out of a barbaric past, is made dramatically real. In *The Birth of the Clinic* Foucault shows how the body subtly replaces the subject in the discourses and institutions of medicine and psychiatry. The question 'What's the matter with you?', with which the seventeenth-century doctor would open the exchange with the patient was replaced by our modern one: 'where does it hurt?'.[11] Thus was inaugurated a splitting process, between the doctor as mind/subject and the patient as body/object. Further 'incompatibilities' are typical here such as that of reason with emotion which, as medicine became increasingly gender-stratified, became associated with masculine (doctor) and feminine (nurse) capacities respectively.[12] But Foucault is mainly concerned with spatial transformations—in modern scientific medicine, disease can be pinned down to its localisation in a specific place, a point of origin; the symptom is the disease in its entirety. Therefore the hospital, considered in the seventeenth and early eighteenth centuries as a most unnatural domain that hindered correct treatment, was by the late eighteenth century established as the place where disease could be compared and classified from body to body in order to invent a system of symptomatology. Before the late eighteenth century, diseases were thought of as nomadic, roaming the body, with diverse paths of determination, linking them up to the patients' environment and the patients' story.

Here it is useful to make a distinction, adapted from de Certeau's *The Practices of Everyday Life,* between 'place', its objective system-orientated state (thinking of it as if it worked independently of the particular individuals occupying roles and operating a culture), and 'space', one's own use of it.[13] Space for de Certeau is a practised place and what is interesting is how Spence appropriates the place of the hospital in order to tell the story of the patient. In her 'self-documentary' pictures, made as a patient when in hospital diagnosed with breast cancer, Spence challenges not just the infantilisation of being a subject-patient but also puts the subject back into the body of the patient. Taking pictures is to enter into immediate performed relationships with a particular setting, to stage an interaction with an environment which alters during the process. The hospital system is no longer depersonalised and reified as an abstract system, comparing and classifying bodies, it has been brought into consciousness as material, having effects on this person, now. Moreover, Spence de-idealises authority figures such as doctors, to whom we often give up total responsibility for our health. Spence referred to 'infantalisation' frequently, as a state which is introjected by individuals when in the grip of a medical system which robs them of a certain maturity of mind. We can think of this as creating a state of dependency.

In the twentieth century, psychoanalysts, writing on the relationship between the group and its leader, have added considerably to our understanding of how situations of extreme anxiety can encourage avoidance of personal responsibility, such as are manifested in guilt. We put part of ourselves into our leaders in a process described as projective identification.[14] In the medical context, which for Spence represents a condition of permanent war, investment in the medical profession ensures that illness is experienced as a split-off external object. This way of thinking is prevalent in everyday talk about illness; it is felt to be an unpredictable 'attack' on a helpless body, and obituary columns are filled with references to those who 'lost a battle' with a disease. In the popular imagery doctor and disease fight a battle over and on the body of the patient.

From the patient's point of view doctors (absent, distant) and nurses (emotionally close) can readily be the objects of transference experience—they may become surrogate mothers and fathers and the patient may experience intense infantilisation.[15] Freud's studies of culture and society, the British object relations and the Kleinian school of psychoanalysis indicate that the source of this powerful dynamic of transference is the early helplessness of the infant. As Jessica Benjamin has pointed out, 'the child who is beginning to confront his own helplessness can comfort himself with the belief in parental omnipotence'.[16] Patients are particularly vulnerable to infantilisation, precisely because the terror of illness and its cultural associations of dependency and death is diminished by the projection of infallibility on to the medical and nursing profession. In hospitals, the idea that doctors do not know everything, cannot necessarily provide a magical cure and may even make mistakes is hard to take in and quite literally to believe.

When a doctor walked up to Spence on the hospital ward and marked her breast with a cross saying 'this is the one that is coming off', she was branded as if she were an animal being led to a slaughterhouse (see figure 15.1).[17] That she was able to put this into representational form at all was in itself an act of retaliation, trying to make a sense out of barbarism. The capacity to think while under fire was nurtured with a camera. She became an embodied social witness.

## The Feeling Body

Jo Spence's method of working in her *A Picture of Health?* project provides one answer to the question John Berger asked in 'Ways of Remembering' (see this volume). Referring to Daumier's famous engraving of Nadar photographing from a balloon over Paris, Berger asks, 'How is it possible to use photography so that it doesn't function like the eye of a totally estranged God?' he was grappling with the tyranny of objectivism identified by Simmel and Marx.[18]

Spence tried to reconnect parts of ourselves that have become subjected to the process of splitting and hierarchisation: the mind and the body; reason and feelings. For example, how is it that on the one hand doctors are widely seen as objective authoritative and scientific in the context of the health institutions, yet at the same time they are the objects of intense sexual interest and fantasy in the popular romance novels? How do we manage to negotiate this complexity as patients and as readers? Spence's approach can be aligned with those contemporary feminist theo-

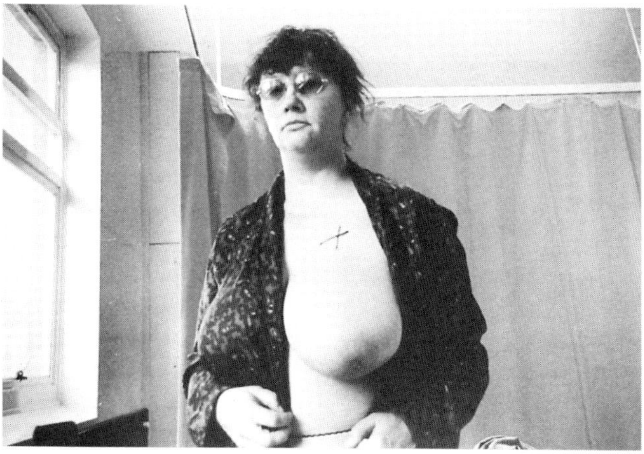

15.1 Marked up for amputation, from *The Cancer Project*. Jo Spence/Terry Dennett, 1982

ries that have branded rationalisation as a profoundly gendered discourse. They have argued that the instrumental orientation and rationalist impersonality that governs modern social organisation and thought should be understood as masculine.

Rationalisation, as Max Weber conceived it, defines the process in which abstract, calculable and depersonalised modes of interaction replace those founded on personal relationships and traditional authority and beliefs. Male domination, like class domination, is no longer a function of personal power relationships, though these do exist, but something objectified in the social and cultural structures, independent of what individual men and women will. As Jessica Benjamin has argued,

> The public institutions and the relations of production display an apparent genderlessness, so impersonal do they seem. Yet it is precisely this objective character, with its indifference to personal need, that is recognised as a hallmark of masculine power. It is precisely the pervasive depersonalisation, the banishment of nurturance to the private sphere, that reveal the logic of male dominance, of female denigration and exclusion.[19]

The medical view of the body as mind-less, and therefore emotionless, is thus symptomatic of the process of masculine rationalisation. But this view reaches far beyond the confines of medical practice. It goes to the heart of Cartesian epistemology, with its implication that the observer is outside of the world he looks upon. With the words 'I think therefore I am' Descartes, the rationalist philosopher, defined the essence of the self as the self that thinks. One way of putting this is to say that 'a thinking thing' or mind is what I am, whereas my body is simply something I have. Whilst the body, an impermanent entity, is governed by mechanical laws, the mind or soul was free and immortal. In the *Meditations* he says: 'I am a being whose whole essence or nature is to think, and whose being requires no place and depends on no material being.' His image of the self as immanently created and maintained by thought, and as not dependent upon any material thing, replicates a typically masculine fear of regression to an infantile state in its loss of autonomy and independence. Like Nadar in his balloon, the disembodied and 'high' eye looks down upon the material, 'low' world.

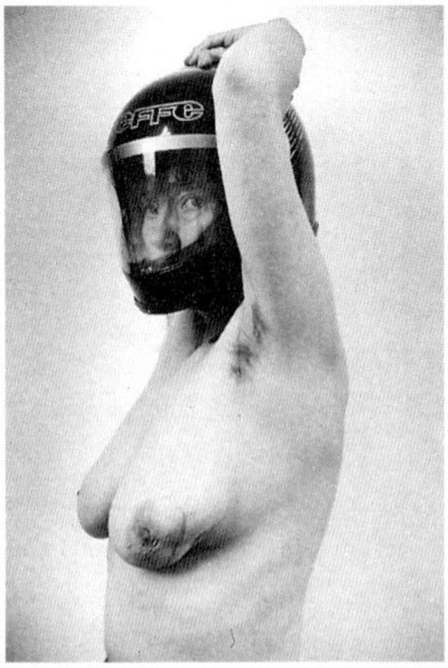

15.2 Jo Spence/Terry Dennett, from *The Picture of Health?* project and touring show, 1982-5. *The analogy between the war on cancer and the war in Vietnam is more than metaphorical. Since the rise of the cellular hypothesis—that cancer is a mysterious, tumorous condition of localised origin—the medical establishment has sanctioned only three methods of treatment: surgery, radiation and chemotherapy. On a larger scale these are precisely the three major weapons (search and destroy, bombardment and chemical warfare) utilised by the military against social problems (i.e., political and economic insurrections in Vietnam and other parts of the Third World).* Alex Jack, *Cancer Control Journal*, vol.5, no.3/4

A photograph of Spence taken for the exhibition *A Picture of Health?*, shows her naked to the waist, wearing a motorbike helmet (figure 15.2). The helmet is a protective shield against those who seek to wound her. The image oscillates between a mixture of defiance and damage. There is a contrast between a shielded 'hard' head and a damaged 'soft' body. Imagine, for a moment, if this picture would be so strange were it of a man. It tells us something about the power of the female body to represent the origin, in infantile fantasy and in reality, of the experience of being nurtured, the succour for life. But this power is at a price, particularly given a culture where women are relegated to the caring services and exploited for their mothering capacities. Spence shows that the material reality of the body—its essentially female or male characteristics—are fundamental to what we feel to be the differential power of women and men.[20]

### The 'Catharsis of Revelation': the Excess of Jo Spence

One day, in the drawing class of the academy of Antwerp, they gave the students a cast of the *Venus de Milo* to copy. Van Gogh, who evidently was struck by one of the essential characteristics of the model, strongly accentuated the breadth of the hips, and made Venus the victim of the same disfigurements he introduced into other pictures he was to copy in the course of his career. The beautiful Greek Goddess had become a robust Flemish matron. When honest Mr. Sieber saw this, he tore Van Gogh's drawing sheet with the furious strokes of his crayon, reminding his disciple of the inviolable canons of his art. Then the young Dutchman...flew into a violent passion and roared at his professor, who was scared out of his wits: 'So you don't know what a young woman is like, God damn you! A woman must have hips and buttocks and a pelvis in which she can hold a child!'...This was the last lesson Van Gogh took—or gave—at the Antwerp academy.[21]

A persistent theme of Jo Spence's work is the routing out of idealised form at all ievels, but especially in terms of the body image, and this has its antecedents in the paintings of Van Gogh and Courbet. The notorious attacks that these painters made on the canons of taste and decorum in the nineteenth century were achieved through a refiguring of the body and understood as such by outraged critics. But Spence's later work on the body, undertaken within the aegis of photo-therapy, can perhaps be interpreted as undermining aesthetics for the purpose of attacking the very idea of a body that is self-contained. She shows just how far our ideas of taste are tied up with feelings about our bodies, its processes, surfaces and protuberances.

Throughout the 1980s, Jo Spence's work was increasingly underpinned by a basic assumption that I term, for want of a better phrase, the 'catharsis of revelation'. The idea of revelation traverses Spence's work, which is full of Freudian–Marxist metaphors of 'exposing', 'hiding', 'repressing', 'uncovering', 'unmasking', 'demystifying'. I suggest that her work, particularly the later studio photo-therapy, offers a kind of naturalism of the body. This is premised upon the popular expression/repression model of Freudian psychoanalysis. In particular, Marcuse's idea of social liberation as consequential upon instinctual liberation has been a contributory factor to Spence's thinking. However, it is important to point out here that the mainstream of psychoanalysis has long moved away from the rituals of cathartic release towards associative methods in which the transference and countertransference relations between analyst and patient are central. It seems clear that the visual demands of photo-therapy cannot incorporate the latter as the 'object' of therapy. In brief, the concerns I have with Spence's photo-therapy, which I have not the space to develop here, are along the lines of its status as psychodynamic psychotherapy. It seems to me that the necessary public/private division is often blurred in a way which is not conducive to good psychodynamic practice. Spence purposefully transgresses this boundary by placing into the public sphere the results of private therapy sessions (with her 'client's' full agreement I hasten to add). But of most concern is the broader philosophical and analytic framework of her photo-therapy practice, in terms of the themes it deals with, and its aims. The 'personal is political' has become a platitude which forgets that in a truly totalitarian society, the personal and the private is the first thing to be sacrificed. We therefore need to be sensitive to that psychoanalytic teaching which seeks to respect a boundary between outer and inner worlds in order that it may attend to the complex inner life of the interior, but which in doing so does not reproduce the ideology that there is no relationship between the outer and inner worlds—that false cult of authenticity which distances ourselves from our relations (of dependency and need) with others. My feeling is that in general Spence treats her 'clients' as if they were simply representatatives of social issues.[22]

For Spence, to reveal and to show is a cathartic act, providing some release from the distress of repression but also from the tyranny of a world which cannot connect up the truth of appearances with their underlying processes. What both psychoanalysis and realism share as 'depth-models' of analysis is a conception of a distinction between underlying structures and appearance and a theory of the relations between them—the former understood to be the (generating) conditions for the latter. Psychoanalysis and Marxism both explain observable phenomena by conceptualising unobservable processes such as mode of production, surplus value, or defence mechanisms and the unconscious.

It can be argued that Spence was trying to integrate an idea of the body as a product of social discourse with a more phenomenological nature of the lived body. Freud's dictum 'the ego is first and foremost a body ego' holds that the 'body' is a perceiving subject and simultaneously or dialectically a perceived object. It is psyche-soma not mere soma. When this dialectical wholeness breaks down, the terror of shame ensues. One is hunted back to a place of no self-protection, which Spence is able to witness in her photo-therapy—the sheer exposure of the body. When Gramsci said that 'The starting point of critical elaboration is the consciousness of what one really is, and is "knowing thyself" as a product of the historical process to date, which has deposited in you an infinity of traces, without leaving an inventory',[23] he was both acknowledging the materiality of the lived subject and arguing that the search for a sense of self is a narrative referring to history, class and politics. Jo Spence's work is about nothing if not about these traces and the oscillation between identifying with herself as mind and as body. An incredible mixture of discourses intersect in Spence's self-identity work: the baseline of Freudian Marxism is modified by the 'new age' or postmodern rationalities of the newer therapies of 'self-reliance' but these are held in check by the agit-prop drama-therapy of the activist Augusto Boal. Consequently Spence's use of terminologies and philosophies is so eclectic as to defy attempts to forge a coherence from them. There are two main strands though—first, that changing the self is dependent upon changing existing social relations, and second, though this is something of a contradiction, that the political can only be understood as refracted through the personal.

The theme of class shame pervades Jo Spence's own phototherapy work. It is a feeling that she describes as a 'form of internalised self-oppression which blinds us and prohibits us'.[24] Shame is a consequence either of feeling that 'one cannot live up to' social ideals or it is a matter of identifying with those defined as 'others' by a hierarchical society which needs 'inferiority' in order to flourish. Sometimes this means, in therapy, 'revisiting the childhood scenarios of the "family romance"—the fantasy that we did not belong to our actual families in the first place but come from a better background.'[25] The shame attached to 'not-having' or being deprived is often too painful to acknowledge and the idealisation of another class arises as a defence against these feelings of self-hatred. Shame has strong links with Spence's practice of revelation since a sense of the culturally policed boundaries for the protection of privacy is integral to its meaning. Spence often complained of being accused of 'hanging out her dirty washing in public'—but this is more revealing of her detractors. Her intention was precisely *'épater les bourgeois'*, to get under the skin of the normalising bourgeois conscience that wants to repress the disturbing and the dirty.

For the philosopher Hannah Arendt the distinction between the public and the private is the distinction between 'things that should be hidden and things that should be known'.[26] For her the traditional notion of the private sphere is that it is etymologically linked to deprivation; the private is what should be hidden from view, or what cannot be brought into view. It is associated with shame and incompleteness and implies excluding bodily and personally affective aspects of human life from the public. The association, in the aforementioned folk-phrase, of dirty washing with the public sphere points to the tabooed nature of bodily exudations such as excrement. Transgressing public/private social divisions is not necessarily what is at issue here as, from an anthropological and psychodynamic view, it is also a question of boundaries between self and other. For Freud, for example, the anal stage is where the child develops autonomous muscular control for the first time and toilet training becomes a battle between child and parent where shitting in the right place and the right time can be the sign of compliance with or attack on the parents.[27] Infants are extremely sensitive to the surface of their body, for the edges between their body and the body of the (m)other is how the difference between self and other, me and not me is discovered and negotiated. The psychoanalyst Donald Melzer, following Edith Bick's influential paper of 1968, 'The experience of the skin in early object relations', has argued that in fact even in its most primitive form the parts of the personality are felt by the young baby to have no binding force amongst themselves and must therefore be held together and contained in a way that is experienced passively by the skin functioning as a boundary.[28]

How this may relate to shame is that shame is a product of a feeling of relatedness—shame protects our integrity and tells us if we have been invaded and exploited. If conformity to parental

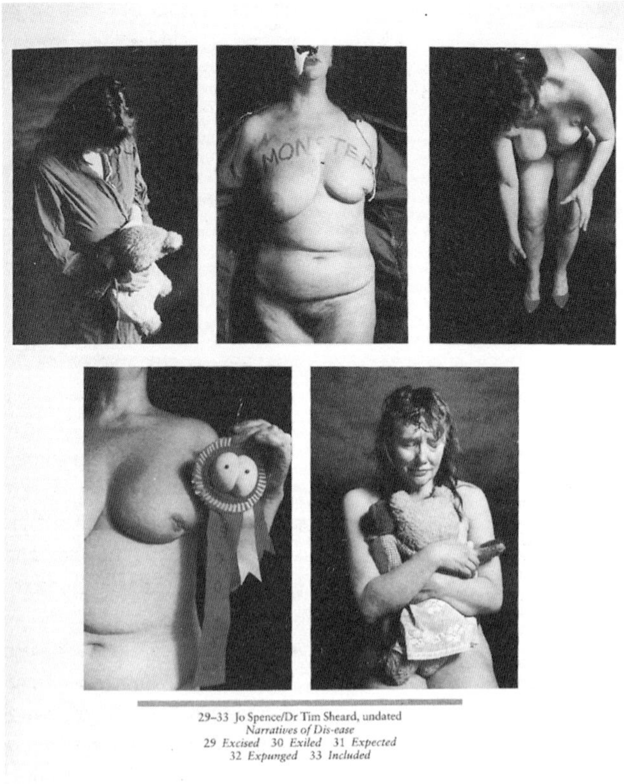


15.3 Jo Spence/Dr Tim Sheard, 'Narratives of Dis-ease', undated. Clockwise, from top left: Excised, Exiled, Expected, Expunged, Included

expectations is sanctioned rather than autonomy from them, we have been invaded or taken over by our parent's desires. Shame is 'the effect of un-desire, one that comes through the painful realisation that I, and you, feel rejected, unwanted, repulsive, ugly, deformed' and poor'.[29] I no longer feel the object of my own desire—this is the rock bottom of shame which Jo Spence frequently spoke about as she worked through her feelings about the idealisations and coverings up of her working-class parents, their overwork and their illnesses and their attempts to maintain respectability.[30]

The Indo-European root of our English word 'shame' is from skem which is a word for cover. Originating from this root are also words for structures that cover and protect us, for *chambre* (room) and *camera*. The photo studio for Spence is a protected space—she talks of the therapeutic process as permission-giving—from which it is safe to expose her self. Shame also has protective and concealing aspects; when we are subjected to harsh scrutiny we are over-exposed and the chamber of our mind has failed to protect us. As Malcolm Pines has put it in his recent study of shame, '[we want to] sink into the ground, the mother earth with whom we may be reunited thereby losing our painful self-consciousness'.[31] With guilt you can say 'I am guilty' but do not feel guilty but shame directly corrodes a sense of integrity in self. The pain of shame is unbearable for we experience a sense of 'inner abandonment'. Shame is to do with mourning the loss of the idealised parts of ourselves, which are linked with parental or cultural ideals. Pines points out that the inner personal experience of shame has roots in bodily experiences—after all, Adam and Eve's shame was their nakedness. In much religious and philosophical thought the idea of a clean soul divorced from the body's filth is prevalent.

Spence uses her own body either as a metaphor (in *Remodelling Photo History*) or as the actual subject of her pictures from the early 1980s onwards. What is notable about Spence's later photo-therapy projects is that they show a concern with the surface of her body, which is shown as a site where others have made their mark and often as a site where she can 'write back' (figure 15.3). Spence's photo-therapy appropriates its visual tropes and props from the mode of the carnivalesque. Peter Stallybrass and Allon White, following Bakhtin, have described the European rituals of the carnival from the seventeenth century onwards as a moment of licensed transgression where hierarchical rank and prohibitions are suspended. Involving vulgar folk-humour and jokes, comic verbal compositions and profanities and open air amusements with costumes and masks, its speech patterns were excluded from official discourse, which could be used for parody and subversive humour.[32]

In *Rabelais and his World*, Bakhtin made a distinction between the classical body and the grotesque body.[33] The classical body is the iconography of the high languages, elevated to the plinth or pedestal, preaching transcendent individualism and an ideology of self-containment; whereas the grotesque is a teeming, multiple subject of pleasure, so much so that the body surface cannot function as a container. Its norms are dirt, mixed categories, symbolic filth and matter out of place. Spence allows herself to be carnal—her images are of the pleasures, pains, and problems of controlling that which is taken in and then expelled: food and sex. Viewers of Spence's work are made to feel both repelled *and* fascinated. Her Bakhtinian use of 'grotesque' realism is an exploration of the body felt to be bulging, protuberant, incomplete, multiple. There is something excessive about Spence's photo-therapy—a sense of a world without limits where anything can be said.[34] Perhaps the obsessive manipulation of the surface of the body is a manifestation of deeper anxiety about the loss of self-containment. It is possible that, as in horror films, Spence re-enacts the disintegration of the body into flesh, thus undermining the category of the individual. Marike Finlay de Monchy has indicated how horror reduces the self to its body so that 'the body' is no longer a feeling/perceiving subject.[35] She also notes that in many cultures the rites of passage are commonly marked by inscriptions—scars, tattoos and circumcisions—on the body of the individual. But while modern European-cum-American cultures have attempted and at times succeeded in eradicating its ritual performance, tattooing survives as a practice in the marginal areas of Western society: convicts, sailors, gangs and *social deviants*. Spence writes on the body with words, and uses placards in order to 'speak out' inner feelings that are not easy to photograph. Is it that words provide a measure of control, representing the speaking subject, in battle with a marked body? Is it that she returns to words as signs which can lift her out of the 'state' of her body? It is the ambivalence of this act of graffiti on the body—and you are made aware of the texture and physicality of these as signifiers—which lends these images their power. The sadistic connotation of branding and wounding is paradoxically offset by the controlled and artificial environment of the studio in which we watch Spence 'assaulting' her own body, as if part of an initiation ritual. Thus the ambivalence to which I referred is based in an unconscious process of oscillation—between an identification with the perpetrator/abuser and the victim/abused.

**The Subject and its Environment**

Raymond Williams made some interesting and much overlooked points about naturalism and its development as a way of 'thinking' the social world, which are pertinent to Spence's work. As he pointed out in *Keywords*, the original sense of the term was the idea of the study of material, physical nature in contrast to the 'supernaturalism' of systems of thought based in the metaphysics of religion. Hence the idea of a close and detailed observation of nature in which 'a new importance was given to the *environment* of characters and action'. Williams emphasises the special meaning of environment as 'a primary sense of the conditions, including the physical conditions, within which someone or something lives and develops'.[36] Character and action were seen as framed by an environment, which especially in a social and social-physical sense had then to be accurately described as an essential element of any account of a life. The idea of determination was strengthened by its specialised Darwinist sense emphasising the struggle and conflict in natural and human relationships. It is important to be sensitive to the nuances of Williams's discussion of the concept of 'determination'. Its root sense is that of setting bounds or limits, but this has to be balanced by its other sense derived from the verb 'to determine', meaning to do something as an act of will and purpose. So naturalism is concerned with the process by which social and historical conditions establish the limits within which cultural products and social activity can be formed—and Williams is clear that he is not referring to a mechanistic 'cause and effect' model but more to a sense of the shaping of possibilities for action.[37] However, as Williams so rightly points out, the meaning of the term naturalism has become narrowed during this century to that of representing the external world in an accurate manner. What was once its broader sense, the study of the processes and effects which are not necessarily available to direct visual observation, now comes under the term 'realism' in specifically Marxian social theory. In contemporary cultural theory, naturalism has become almost wholly associated with the ideology of empiricism, which has been the subject of devastating critiques in both cultural theory and in the philosophy of the social sciences (see for example 'The Object of Photography' by Don Slater in this volume).

In one sense the evolution of Jo Spence's work can be interpreted as a series of ethical-political critiques of naturalism (in Williams's contemporary sense) and an embracing of a more complex realist strategy. The critique begins with the community projects of the Hackney Flashers, which early on began to experiment with non-naturalist forms, using montage, manipulating the ideological contents and forms of mass media images by breaking them up with text and juxtaposing them with their own documentary images. There was at this stage a residual belief in the evidential efficacy of the black and white documentary image but at the same time a concern that documentary could not address the sheer complexity of social relations.[38] Don Slater points to the problems of this moment:

> the [predominant] notions of photographic empowerment still involved distancing ourselves from domestic photography. Although *Camerawork* never descended to assuming (as some then did) that the only proper political photograph is of a good demo or bad fascist, it laid a heavy stress on ordinary people learning to 'document' their lives and conditions and using photographs for agit-prop. We said that the personal was political, but that never quite included the family snap. (private conversation)

However, the 1979 Hayward Gallery show, *Beyond the Family Album*, began a critique of Spence's own family album, all the photographs in which were paradoxically of 'her' own past but

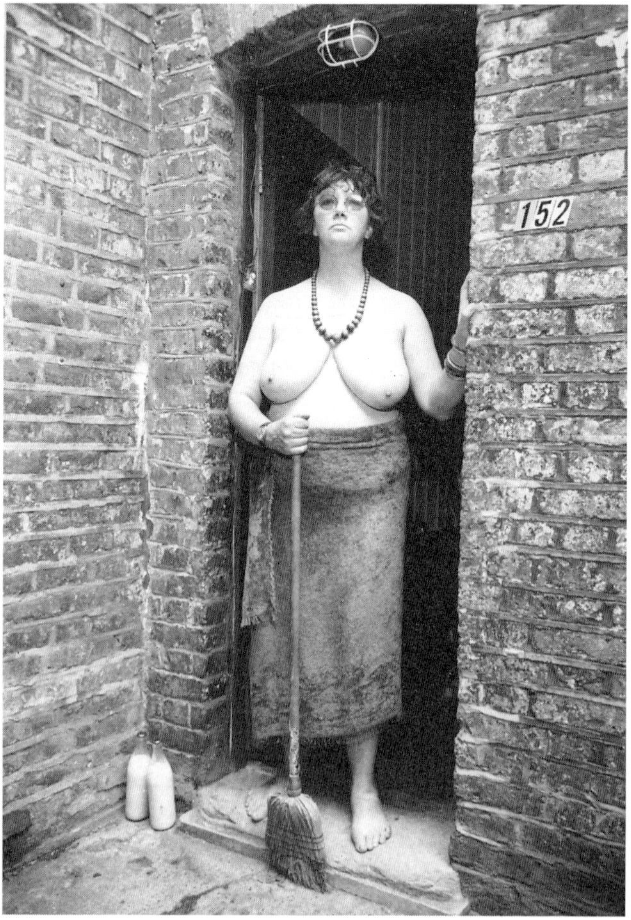


15.4 Jo Spence/Terry Dennett, 'Colonisation', from *Remodelling Photo-History*, 1981-2

none had been taken by her. As she said,

> There is no way I could have understood fully the political implications of trying to represent other people (however well intentioned) if I had not first of all begun to explore how I had built a view of myself through other people's representations of me.[39]

At this stage the critique of the family album had not extended into photographing phenomena the family album customarily screened out, but indicated the stultifyingly narrow repertoire of its iconography and showed that the construction of one's image is a structuring operation on memory. The important project *Remodelling Photo History*, made by Spence and Terry Dennett, constituted the final break with naturalist practice. They took several photographic genres—landscape, documentary, for example—and used the method of Boal's 'disruption' to upset the assumption of a natural synthesis between the signifiers of a genre and its classed and gendered signifieds. In *Colonisation*, which refers to the genre of anthropological documentary, Spence as a social actor is pictured standing, breasts exposed and broom in hand on the doorstep of a working-class home (figure 15.4). There are enough significant signs in this image to allow us to recognise it as a representation of class that is old and familiar. The power of this image lies in its disturbance of the ease with which the anthropological gaze naturalises 'the species in their habitat'. Here, the inevitable 'fit' between the physical/social environment of a particular class and the passivity and unselfconsciousness of its oft-photographed subjects—is upset. We, the viewers, are in the spotlight, caught in a moment of self-consciousness. Something else has been revealed that doesn't fit the genre; moreover, what has been revealed completely undermines a stereotype of the middle-aged working-class woman. To use Boal's phrase, from his book *Theatre of the Oppressed*, within a poetics of the oppressed 'one must keep in mind the main objective to change people from "spectators", passive beings in the theatrical tradition—into subject, actors, transformers of the dramatic action'.[40]

From Spence's health crisis onwards, her photography rejects a representation of the 'external' world and turns in on herself, to questions of social identity, fantasy, re-enacting parental relations, etc. Photo-therapy takes place in a studio 'play space' where techniques of co-counselling, Gestalt, visualisation and psychodramatic re-presentations are used. The photo-therapist, as the advocate of the child's 'inner child' (Alice Miller), helps 'sitters' to witness, through memory and fantasy, their own dissonant history. The early forms of photo-therapy incorporated aspects of the family album into the space of the therapy—Spence saw the family album as a visual index of the unconscious desires of parents, whose persecutory voices continue at an unconscious level to repress the child's voice of protest.

Debates in photographic theory throughout the 1980s were dominated by the ethical and political problem of the relationship between observing subject—the photographer-producer and by proxy the spectator—and the observed object. One response has been to beat a retreat from the problem, or perhaps to displace it, by excising the 'other' altogether. For example, in her paper delivered to the Arts Council's 1987 National Conference of Photography, Jo Spence says,

> if a documentary practice involves only the exposure or revelation of one party, then it is an unfair transaction. I am not suggesting that all photogra-

phy be done on a reciprocal basis, but that we mark out this territory as problematic.[41]

Don Slater in his introduction to 'Marketing the Medium' in this volume, makes the point that during his time at *Camerawork* in 1979 there was a paradoxical 'crisis' in which representation was 'overvalued'—'images, the media, systems of signification, had total social power'. At the same time 'the almost universal availability of the power to represent—the power to take pictures given us by the likes of Kodak' restricted the pictures actually taken to banality. He puts it succinctly: 'The very means by which the power to represent was democratised also rendered it impotent'. Don Slater has made the following comment to me about this critical moment:

> It is hard to recapture the intensity of this feeling but one image stands out for me: it was around this time [1980-2] that quite a few of the most politically and theoretically 'advanced' photographers stopped taking pictures altogether. The act of photographing someone had been so analysed as a relation of power that it came to be experienced as politically impossible. Jo Spence and colleagues would only photograph dolls. Any photography other than self-representation was oppressive. It sometimes felt like a return to the 'primitive' notion that in photographing someone you steal their soul: you remove them from their own life and place their image in your own narrative and ideological structures, in different social relations of distribution and consumption, and thus remove it further and further from their control. This was merely an extreme and more theoreticist aspect of wider ways of thinking of self-representation as 'empowerment': community photography, worker photography, as well as feminist and socialist photography were all banners for projects of both returning the power to represent back to 'the people', and liberating it as a tool for political struggles to improve the people's life, both subjective and material. (Private conversation)

The explosion of work throughout the 1980s in the 'independent' art sector and the higher educational institutions in Britain, dealing with identity-formation and adhering to the slogan 'the personal is political', could be interpreted in the way I have suggested as a response to the epistemological and ethical crisis in representing politics. It is work which concerns itself with an expansion of what can be deemed to be political and this has characteristically centred on the 'politics of representation'—involving appropriations and manipulations of media images, montage techniques, studio stagings of models and props. The task of this work has been to exorcise the spell of the so-called dominant ideology by demonstrating its forms and mechanisms. Without Spence, a shift of this kind in the structure of feeling of photography's relation to politics probably would not have occurred. This is so despite her own feeling that her experiments and practices were at best ignored, at worst denigrated as 'popular'—as not academically pure enough—within the academic photography field.

How can we interpret this move to the studio, established by the mid-1980s as the safest, most anti-ideological of places in which to make images? Steven Edwards has recently followed the proposition of the Bakhtin school of Russian linguistics that we should make a fundamental distinction between the natural and the human sciences. The elements of this argument are that natural science presupposes the contemplative mode; since only the subject does the contemplating and investigating, there is no comeback from one's objects (hence its monologic form). But as the human sciences are constituted by a relation between subjects they are fundamentally interpretive. Here the subject of study cannot be treated as voiceless as he/she would cease to be a subject at all. Edwards's argument is really twofold; first, he wants to allow for dialogic interpretations of apparently monologic 'studio' images. Second, and more radically, he implies that those who use the studio inevitably enforce a monologic form of speech, a rationale in which the photographer can assert mastery over her/his objects, and repress the uncontrollable, the accidental and the contradictory. There is, he argues, a process of reification in which the subjects in the studio are turned into objects and as such cannot be conceived as having the capacity to answer back.[42]

Edwards's equation of realism with the study of 'real life' and dialogic forms, and his equation of a studio 'constructed images' practice with monologism assumes that visual and formal strategies have essential meanings. I suspect it relies upon a residual romanticism concerning non-studio practice. The point of production is fetishised and the studio as environment determines the photograph's meaning. Edwards assumes that other (more naturalistic?) photographic practices may be more sensitive to the potential resistances of photographed subjects.[43] Consequently there is an underplaying of those discursive contexts for the placing and viewing of photographs, contexts which create a 'significance' for images. It seems to me that how the photograph is contextualised across a diversity of fields, institutions and practices is a better index of whether an image can be interpreted as monologic or dialogic. But, my criticisms notwithstanding, Edwards's call both for dialogic readings of photographs in the cultural theory and history of photography and for a radical dialogic practice is important. Spence and Dennett achieved something of this in *Remodelling Photo History*.

We need to bring to bear on our analysis of the production and reception of photographs a psychodynamic theory which is rooted in the everyday, so that those moments of 'contradiction and uncontrollability' can become theorised as belonging to the conflicted domain of the inner world. It can be argued that Jo Spence's photo-therapy studio work and her earlier critique of documentary do show a concern with the relationships between environment, embodiment and a close observation of the body that were a part of what Williams identified as the original meaning of the word naturalism. Is it possible to wrest the definition of naturalism from its narrow definition operative today, one solely concerned with its technique and formal conventions, and recover a more substantive definition? What interests me about the earlier meaning of the term is that it involves a substantive claim about the nature of the world, about the character of relationships, not just a claim about how best to represent it. Although, as I have indicated, I am critical of the status of Spence's work as psychotherapy, I think that she has found a way of visualising the unacceptable thought and the shameful feeling; moreover, this has been achieved through attention to the complex relationships between thought and feeling, themselves contextualised by the pressing political matter of the relationships between subjectivity, remembering, action and environment.

Spence's work may offer a solution to the challenge thrown to cultural theory recently by Angela McRobbie. Criticising the theories and methods now established in cultural studies as betraying a concern only with textual or discursive identities, she called for an 'identity ethnography' which departs from the model of carrying out interactive research on groups and individuals who are conceptualised as no more than audiences for texts. 'The site of identity formation in cultural studies', she argued, 'remains implicitly in and through cultural commodities and texts rather than in and through the cultural practices of everyday life'.[44] She wants to move away from the discursive crutches of cultural studies, its dependency on the binary oppositions of media and reality, text and lived experience. In the context of photographic theory her argument would need to be modified somewhat since there has been almost a complete silence on the issue of undertaking any kind of ethnographic approach to the social uses and reception of photographs (although plenty has been said on documentary production *as* ethnography).

McRobbie's comments relate to my critique of the representation–reality model outlined above that dominates photographic theory and history, and although I do not think this can be replaced I do think it needs to be enriched. Dialogics is not concerned so much with 'representation'—which implies a distance from the social world—but rather emphasises the specific moments of conflicted interaction. For Volisinov, language is a way of establishing social relations between human beings in a society.'[45] For Spence, following Volisinov, the sign is a site of struggle: 'the camera is not a window on the world, nor are meanings of pictures fixed, but...visual signs (in this case photographs) are in themselves sites of struggle.'[46]

In Spence's work, the feature of spoken language that would come to the fore would be the everyday re-negotiations, the hierarchies of classed language and 'evaluative accents' that are practically engaged responses to the material situations in which people find themselves. In her complete disregard for the distanced ethos of *aesthetic* contemplation and in her use of the visual anarchy of the carnivalesque, Spence was able to show how certain states of mind are consequent upon class and gender identities, themselves refracted through the dynamics of family life. In Spence's photographs we see a staging of the internalised 'other' in a dialogue with her adult self. But there is a further, more compelling dialogue with us the viewers, who are conjured into the dramatic space. Many of her photo-therapy photographs employ a direct address to camera as if in an appeal to a witness, perhaps as if the camera is a mirror, offering her an unjudgmental listener. But therefore of course we too are her witnesses, subjected to the unfolding events of Spence's life drama yet also having the capacity to think about the dialectic between witnessing and acting.

The psychoanalyst and organisational consultant Gordon Lawrence has recently argued that 'a future cannot be recovered, or brought into being, until we experience and call to mind the significance and meaning of tragedy in our private and public lives at this time in history.'[47] He has argued that, under conditions of late modernity, tragedy, ranging from disappointment through loss to death, is construed by people as an intrusion in their lives, an impertinence of fate. We have come to believe that tragedy is not supposed to happen and is to be wished away. Certain cultural pressures encourage a sense of omnipotence which prevents us from integrating tragedy into our personal lives—it has become split off into characters in films or something that happens to the weak and the 'underclasses'. He argues that 'until we accept tragedy as a private trouble we cannot comprehend it as a public issue' nor will we be able to protest against the tragedy which is inflicted on others by the social system.[48]

A recently published posthumous volume of Spence's writings and photographs ends with a 'tragic' picture of her dying: a deeply troubling picture, not least because it comes at the end of a book which is shot through with a dynamic sense of a vibrant life and, I might add, with the proffering of her life as an entirely publicly knowable project. This image is perhaps Spence's last act of shocking imagery and her attempt to make her mark on imminent death, on the event that is most uncontrollable of all. She seems to make death meaningful and thus restore to it a sense of its being part of a life. But in making this image was she really finding meaning from the void of death, the place where you cannot be? Or was she pointing to the inadequacy in the end of metaphors of 'control' which are based on a fantasy prevalent in much of our culture—that death can be made good, that we can get something positive out of it, and so avoid the terror, anger and confusion that death evokes?[49] Whatever her intention, about which we can only speculate, this image seems to make real the complexity of the question of power and loss that is a hallmark of her life's work.

---

I would like to thank the following for helping me to think through various ideas in this essay: Paul Antick, Janina Struk, Michael Evans.

**Reference Notes**

**1** In 'Body Talk? A Dialogue between Ros Coward and Jo Spence', in Patricia Holland, Jo Spence and Simon Watney, eds, *Photography/Politics: Two*, Photography Workshop/Comedia, London, 1986.
**2** Jo Spence and Jo Stanley, eds, *Cultural Sniping*, Routledge, London, 1995.
**3** John Tagg, *The Burden of Representation*, Macmillan, Basingstoke, 1988, pp.17–19. For a different interpretation of the significance of intervention into amateur practice see Don Slater, 'Domestic Photography and Digital Culture', in Martin Lister, ed., *The Photographic Image in Digital Culture,* Routledge, London, 1995.
**4** Tagg, *The Burden of Representation*, p.18. See also John Walker, 'Context as a Determinant of Photographic Meaning' in this volume for some thoughts on Spence's foray into the art gallery.
**5** See Pierre Bourdieu, 'The Sociologist in Question' in his *Sociology in Question*, Sage, London, 1993 for a defence of the specialised forms of academic language.
**6** See Jean Lave, *Cognition in Practice*, Cambridge University Press, Cambridge, 1988, for an argument against teaching mathematic calculation as a universal, non-contextualised practice.
**7** See Mady Schutzman, 'Brechtian Shamanism: The Political Therapy of Augusto Boal', in M. Schutzman and J. Cohen-Cruz, eds., *Playing Boal: Theatre, Therapy, Activism*, Routledge, London, 1994.
**8** For a sympathetic analysis of these, see Andrew Ross, 'New Age Technoculture' in L. Grossberg, C. Nelson and P. Treichler, eds, *Cultural Studies*, Routledge, London, 1992. For a sharp critique of the metaphors

and practices of the holistic health movement see Ros Coward, *The Whole Truth: The Myth of Alternative Health*, Faber & Faber, London, 1989.

**9** See Jessica Evans, 'The Imagined Referent', *Block*, Winter 1986/7, and 'The Iron Cage of Visibility', *Ten.8*, no.29, 1988 for an argument along these lines. See also Jo Spence, 'Questioning Documentary Practice? The Sign as a Site of Struggle' and 'Cultural Sniper: Passing/Out Thoughts on Split Class Subjectivity (Jo Spence in conversation with John Taylor)' in Spence and Stanley, *Cultural Sniping*. See also Sylvia Harvey, 'Who Wants to Know What and Why?' in *Ten.8*, no.23, 1986.

**10** In 'Body Talk? A Dialogue between Ros Coward and Jo Spence', *Photography/Politics: Two*, p.25.

**11** M. Foucault, *The Birth of the Clinic*, Tavistock, London, 1983, p.xviii.

**12** See Jessica Evans, 'A Feminist Interest in the Mind/Body Problem', in *Silent Health: Women, Health and Representation*, Camerawork/Arts Council, London, 1990.

**13** De Certeau, *The Practices of Everyday Life*, University of California Press, Berkeley, 1984.

**14** See Sigmund Freud, 'Group Psychology and the Analysis of the Ego', in J. Strachey, ed., *Standard Edition of Freud*, vol.18, Penguin, Harmondsworth.

**15** See Jo Spence, 'The Picture of Health?' in J. Spence, *Putting Myself in the Picture*, Camden Press, London, 1986. For some further thoughts on this, using feminist object relations theory, see Jessica Evans, 'A Feminist Interest in the Mind/Body Problem', op.cit.

**16** J. Benjamin, *The Bonds of Love*, Virago, London, 1990, p.107.

**17** See J. Spence, *Putting Myself in the Picture*, p. 151.

**18** See J. Berger, 'Ways of Remembering' in this volume.

**19** J. Benjamin, *The Bonds of Love*, p.187.

**20** In the picture *Regulation*, part of the *Remodelling Photographic History* series, Spence is shown suckling Terry Dennett in a reworking of Madonna and Child iconography—see Spence, *Putting Myself in the Picture*, p.131.

**21** Van Gogh, *Letters Revealing his Life as a Painter*, selected by W.H. Auden, Thames and Hudson, London, 1981, p.277.

**22** This will be the subject of further reflection in a forthcoming article on Jo Spence in *The Oxford Art Journal.*

**23** Gramsci, *The Prison Notebooks*, Lawrence and Wishart, London, 1971, p.324.

**24** Spence and Stanley, *Cultural Sniping*, p.177

**25** Ibid., p.180.

**26** H. Arendt, *The Human Condition*, University of Chicago Press, Chicago, 1958, p.72.

**27** From Ian Craib, *Psychoanalysis and Social Theory*, Harvester Wheatsheaf, Brighton, 1989, p.40.

**28** D. Melzer et al., *Explorations in Autism*, Clunie, Perth, 1975, p.241. See also E. Bick, 'The Experience of the Skin in Early Object Relations',

*International Journal of Psycho-Analysis*, no.49, 1968.

**29** Malcolm Pines, 'The Universality of Shame: A Psychoanalytic Approach', *British Journal of Psychotherapy*, vol.11, no.3, Spring, 1995, p.351.

**30** See Spence and Stanley, *Cultural Sniping*, pp.158-9.

**31** M. Pines, 'The University of Shame', op.cit., p.348.

**32** See Peter Stallybrass and Allon White, *The Politics and Poetics of Transgression*, Cornell University Press, Ithaca, 1986.

**33** Ibid., p.21.

**34** See Nancy Chodorow, *Feminism and Psychoanalytic Theory*, Yale University Press, New Haven, 1989, p.275, and Ian Craib, *Psychoanalysis and Social Theory*, op.cit., pp.32-3.

**35** Marike Finlay de Monchy, 'The Horrified Position: An Ethics Grounded in the Affective Interest in the Unitary Body as Psyche/Soma', in *Body and Society*, Sage, vol.1, no.2, 1995.

**36** R. Williams, 'Naturalism' in *Keywords*, Fontana, London, 1988, pp.216-19.

**37** See his chapter 'Determination' in R. Williams, *Marxism and Literature*, Oxford University Press, Oxford, 1977 for this discussion.

**38** See Liz Heron's account of the Hackney Flashers in Spence, *Putting Myself in the Picture*, pp.66-74.

**39** Spence, *Putting Myself in the Picture*, p.83.

**40** A. Boal, *Theatre of the Oppressed*, Pluto, London, 1974.

**41** Spence and Stanley, *Cultural Sniping*, p.105.

**42** Steven Edwards, 'The Machine's Dialogue', in *The Oxford Art Journal*, vol.13, no.1, 1990.

**43** I owe the formulation of these points to a conversation with Paul Antick.

**44** A. McRobbie, 'Post-Marxism and Cultural Studies: A Post-script', in L. Grossberg et al., eds, *Cultural Studies*, Routledge, London, 1992, p.730.

**45** M. Barker, 'A Dialogical Approach to Ideology' in John Storey, ed., *Cultural Theory and Popular Culture: A Reader*, Harvester Wheatsheaf, Brighton, 1994, p.256.

**46** Spence, *Putting Myself In The Picture*, p.119.

**47** W. Gordon Lawrence, 'Tragedy: Private Trouble or Public Issue?', paper delivered to the Annual Conference *Psychoanalysis and the Public Sphere*, 18 November 1995, University of East London, p.1.

For some stimulating thoughts along these lines see Ian Craib, *The Importance of Disappointment*, Routledge, London, 1994; C. Lasch, *The Culture of Narcissism*, W.W. Norton, New York, 1979; Walter Benjamin, 'Some Motifs in Baudelaire', in H. Arendt, ed., *Illuminations*, Schocken, New York, 1968.

**49** For this idea I am indebted to Ian Craib's work on the social processes affecting attitudes to mourning and death: see his *The Importance of Disappointment*, op.cit.

## Further Reading


- Augusto Boal, *Theatre of the Oppressed*, Pluto, London, 1974.
- Ian Craib, *The Importance of Disappointment*, Routledge, London, 1994.
- Terry Dennett, David Evans, Sylvia Gohl, Jo Spence, eds, *Photography/Politics: One*, Photography Workshop, 1979.
- Terry Dennett and Jo Spence, 'Remodelling Photo-History: An Afterword on a Recent Exhibition', *Screen*, vol.23, no.1, 1983.
- Terry Dennett and Jo Spence, 'Ten Years of Photography Workshop', in *Photographic Practices: Towards a Different Image*, Comedia, London, 1986.
- Steven Edwards, 'The Machine's Dialogue', *The Oxford Art Journal*, vol.13, no.1, 1990.
- Jessica Evans, 'A Feminist Interest in the Mind/Body Problem', in *Silent Health: Women, Health and Representation*, Camerawork/Arts Council, London, 1990.
- John Roberts, 'Jo Spence: Photography, Empowerment and the Everyday', in his *The Art of Interruption: Realism, Photography and the Everyday*, Manchester University Press, Manchester, 1996.
- Andrew Ross, 'New Age Technoculture' in L. Grossberg, C. Nelson and P. Treichler, eds, *Cultural Studies*, Routledge, London, 1992.
- M. Schutzman and J. Cohen-Cruz, eds, *Playing Boal: Theatre, Therapy, Activism*, Routledge, London, 1994.
- Don Slater, 'Domestic Photography and Digital Culture', in Martin Lister, ed., *The Photographic Image in Digital Culture*, Routledge, London, 1995.
- 'Body Talk? A Dialogue between Ros Coward and Jo Spence' in Patricia Holland, Jo Spence and Simon Watney, eds, *Photography/Politics: Two*, Photography Workshop/Comedia, London, 1986.
- Jo Spence, *Putting Myself in the Picture*, Camden Press, London, 1986.
- Jo Spence and Jo Stanley, eds, *Cultural Sniping*, Routledge, London, 1995. This includes a comprehensive bibliography of Spence's publications and exhibitions.
- Peter Stallybrass and Allon White, *The Politics and Poetics of Transgression*, Cornell University Press, Ithaca, 1986.

# Index